LEADERS

Also by Richard Nixon

Six Crises
RN: The Memoirs of Richard Nixon
The Real War

RICHARD NIXON

LEADERS

WARNER BOOKS

A Warner Communications Company

The title LEADERS is used by permission of Leaders Magazine, Inc.

Every effort has been made to ensure that permission for all material was obtained. Those sources not formally acknowledged will be included in all future editions of this book issued subsequent to notification by such sources.

Warner Books, Inc., 75 Rockefeller Plaza, New York, N.Y. 10019.

A Warner Communications Company

Printed in the United States of America

First Printing: October 1982
10   9   8   7   6   5   4   3   2   1

Book Design: Judy Allan

Library of Congress Cataloging in Publication Data
Nixon, Richard M. (Richard Milhous), 1913–
   Leaders.

   Includes index.
   1. World politics—20th century.   2. Statesmen—
Biography.   3. Nixon, Richard M. (Richard Milhous),
1913–   .   I. Title.
D445.N58   909.82′092′2 [B]   82-4820
ISBN 0-446-51249-4   AACR2

To the leaders of the future

CONTENTS

1. THEY MADE A DIFFERENCE   *1*
   Leaders Who Changed the World

2. WINSTON CHURCHILL   *7*
   The Largest Human Being of Our Time

3. CHARLES de GAULLE   *40*
   The Leadership Mystique

4. DOUGLAS MacARTHUR AND SHIGERU YOSHIDA   *81*
   East Meets West

5. KONRAD ADENAUER   *133*
   The West's Iron Curtain

6. NIKITA KHRUSHCHEV   *169*
   The Brutal Will to Power

7. ZHOU ENLAI   *217*
   The Mandarin Revolutionary

8. A NEW WORLD   *249*
   New Leaders in a Time of Change

9. IN THE ARENA   *320*
   Reflections on Leadership

   AUTHOR'S NOTE   *346*
   INDEX   *349*

LEADERS

THEY MADE A DIFFERENCE

Leaders Who Changed the World

IN THE FOOTSTEPS of great leaders, we hear the rolling thunder of history. Throughout the centuries—from the ancient Greeks, through Shakespeare, to the present day—few subjects have proved more perennially fascinating to dramatists and historians alike than the character of great leaders. What sets them apart? What accounts for that particular, indefinable electricity that exists between the leader and the led?

What makes the role of these leaders so compellingly interesting is not just its drama, but its importance—its impact. When the final curtain goes down on a play, the members of the audience file out of the theater and go home to resume their normal lives. When the curtain comes down on a leader's career, the very lives of the audience have been changed, and the course of history may have been profoundly altered.

For the last thirty-five years I have had an exceptional opportunity, during an extraordinary period of history, to study the world's leaders firsthand. Of the major leaders of the post–World War II period, I knew all except Stalin. I have visited more than eighty countries and have not only dealt with their leaders but also seen the conditions in which they operated. I have watched some leaders succeed and others fail, and have had a chance to analyze the reasons from the perspective of my own experience. Having known both the peaks and the valleys of public life, I have learned that you cannot really appreciate the heights unless you have also experienced the depths. Nor can you fully understand what drives a leader if you have only sat on the sidelines, watching.

One of the questions I have most often been asked during my years in public life has been "Who is the greatest leader you have known?" There is no single answer. Each leader belongs to a particular combination of time, place, and circumstances; leaders and countries are not interchangeable. Great as Winston Churchill was, it would be difficult to imagine him playing so successfully the role that Konrad Adenauer did in postwar Germany. But neither could Adenauer have rallied Britain in its hour of greatest peril as Churchill did.

The surefire formula for placing a leader among the greats has three elements: a great man, a great country, and a great issue. Churchill once commented of Britain's nineteenth-century Prime Minister Lord Rosebery that he had the misfortune of living at a time of "great men and small events." We commonly rank wartime leaders more highly than peacetime leaders. This is partly because of the inherent drama of war and partly because histories dwell so largely on wars. But it is also because we can fully measure a leader's greatness only when he is challenged to the limits of his ability. When awarding the Medal of Honor, I often used to reflect on how many of those who won it must have appeared to be quite ordinary people until they had risen with supreme valor to an extraordinary challenge. Without the challenge they would not have shown their courage. In leaders the challenge of war brings forth qualities we can readily measure. The challenges of peace may be as great, but the leader's triumph over them is neither as dramatic nor as clearly visible.

The small man leading a great nation in a great crisis clearly fails the test of greatness. The large man in a small country may demonstrate all the qualities of greatness but never win the recognition. Others, though big men in big countries, live in the shadow of giants: Zhou Enlai, for example, who discreetly let the limelight shine on Mao.

One distinction must be kept clear: Those commonly acclaimed as "great" leaders are not necessarily good men. Russia's Peter the Great was a cruel despot. Julius Caesar, Alexander the Great, and Napoleon are remembered not for their statesmanship but for their conquests. When we speak of the great leaders of history, only occasionally do we refer to those who raised statecraft to a higher moral plane. Rather, we are talking about those who so effectively wielded power on such a grand scale that they significantly changed the course of history for their nations and for the world. Churchill and Stalin were both, in their different ways, great leaders. But without Churchill, Western Europe might have been enslaved; without Stalin, Eastern Europe might have been free.

In writing about leadership, it was tempting to include some of the outstanding leaders I have known from fields outside of government. I have watched leaders of giant corporations and labor unions fight their way to the top as doggedly as any politician and then wield power with a diplomatic skill to rival that of a foreign minister. The intrigues of the academic world are fully as Byzantine as those of a party convention. I have known leaders in the news media—Henry R. Luce, for example— who have had a larger impact on the world than the leaders of many nations.

But this book is very specifically about the kind of leadership I know best and which to me matters most: It is about those who lead nations, with not only the power such a position carries, but also the responsibility.

Each person treated here had a goal, a vision, a cause, that to him was supremely important. Some have names that are certain to echo through the centuries. Others may be little remembered outside their own countries. Each has something important to tell us about the nature of leadership and about the conflicts that have swept the world during these decades.

There are many leaders I have known whom I would like to have included but did not: outstanding Latin American leaders, for example, such as Mexico's Adolfo Ruiz Cortines, Arturo Frondizi of Argentina, Colombia's Alberto Lleras Camargo, and the visionary Brazilian President who opened his country's interior, Juscelino Kubitschek. Or Canada's Lester Pearson and John Diefenbaker, very different from one another in personality and political orientation, but each with a sense of Canada's destiny and a clear view of the world. Gulam Mohammed, the Governor-general of Pakistan, and Pakistan's President Mohammed Ayub Khan. Yugoslavia's Marshal Tito. Francisco Franco of Spain, a man so different in private from his public impression. Popes Pius XII and Paul VI, each of whom, in his own way, played a profoundly significant role not only spiritually but on the world political stage. Pioneering leaders of the postwar international community, such as Belgium's Paul-Henri Spaak, Italy's Manlio Brosio, and Robert Schuman and Jean Monnet of France. To consider even these few of the many others who might have been included is to remember how broad and varied the world's array of leadership talent has been in recent decades.

Of those whom I do treat in the chapters that follow, I have chosen some because of their transcendent stature or sweeping impact on the course of history, some because of their inherent interest as people, some as examples of forces that were sweeping the world during this tumultuous period of history. I have not included American leaders, except for Douglas MacArthur, whose most lasting contribution was his role in the shaping of modern Japan.

Most histories are about events and only incidentally about the men who played a role. This book is about the leaders and how they shaped the events. It is about how they made a difference and how they differed, about the characteristics that enabled them to have an impact and how they did it.

Great leadership is a unique form of art, requiring both force and vision to an extraordinary degree. There has long been a widespread belief in the United States that what the country really needs is a top-flight businessman to run the government, someone who has proven that he can manage a large-scale enterprise efficiently and effectively. This misses the mark. Management is one thing. Leadership is another. As Warren G. Bennis of the University of Southern California's business school puts it, "Managers have as their goal to do things right. Leaders have as their goal to do the right thing."

Leadership is more than technique, though techniques are necessary. In a sense, management is prose; leadership is poetry. The leader necessarily deals to a large extent in symbols, in images, and in the sort of galvanizing idea that becomes a force of history. People are persuaded by reason, but moved by emotion; he must both persuade them and move them. The manager thinks of today and tomorrow. The leader must think of the day after tomorrow. A manager represents a process.

The leader represents a direction of history. Thus a manager with nothing to manage becomes nothing, but even out of power a leader still commands followers.

Great leadership requires a great vision, one that inspires the leader and enables him to inspire the nation. People both love the great leader and hate him; they are seldom indifferent toward him.

It is not enough for a leader to *know* the right thing. He must also be able to *do* the right thing. The would-be leader without the judgment or perception to make the right decisions fails for lack of vision. The one who knows the right thing but cannot achieve it fails because he is ineffectual. The great leader needs both the vision and the capacity to achieve what is right. He hires managers to help him do so, but only he can set the direction and provide the motive force.

The great cause that grips a leader may be one of creating something new or of preserving something old—and often strong leaders on opposite sides of a conflict have causes that collide. A strong leader with a weak cause may prevail over a weak leader with a strong cause, or a bad cause may prevail over a good one. There is no simple set of immutable rules by which to predict history, or for that matter by which to judge it. Often causes, like leaders themselves, look different in retrospect. Sometimes the judgment depends on who wins. Historians tend to be kinder to winners than to losers, among causes no less than among leaders.

All of the really strong leaders I have known have been highly intelligent, highly disciplined, hard workers, supremely self-confident, driven by a dream, driving others. All have looked beyond the horizon. Some have seen more clearly than others.

The years since World War II have been a time of greater and more rapid change than any comparable period of world history. We have seen a clash of titans as the superpowers have risen to confront one another, a series of cataclysmic upheavals as old empires have given way to scores of new nations, a time of mounting peril as weapons developments have stretched even the science fiction–altered imagination. Great events bring forth great leaders. Tumultuous times bring out both the best and the worst. Khrushchev was a powerful leader but a dangerous force. Mao moved mountains; he also crushed out millions of lives.

The years ahead will require leadership of the highest order. It has been said that those who fail to study history are condemned to repeat it and, conversely, that if the leaders of one age see further into the future than did their predecessors, it is because they stand on the shoulders of those who have gone before. This book is written about leaders of the past, but for leaders of the future. Each of the leaders in this book studied the past and learned from it. To the extent that we in turn can learn from them, the world may have a better chance of moving forward in the years to come.

WINSTON CHURCHILL

The Largest Human Being of Our Time

WHEN WINSTON CHURCHILL was a young man, he talked to a friend about the meaning of life. His thoughts were suitably philosophical and typically candid. "We are all worms," he said. Then he added, "But I do think that I am a glowworm."

Throughout his life Churchill was driven by an unshakeable sense of his own destiny. It infuriated some. It inspired many. When he was after something that he was determined to get, he did not know the meaning of the word *no*, no matter how often he heard it. Once he was engaged in a military battle or a political campaign, he purged the word *defeat* from his vocabulary.

I first met Churchill in June 1954, when I headed the welcoming party that greeted him on his arrival in Washington for his official visit as

Prime Minister. I still remember the eager anticipation, even the excitement, that I felt that day as I waited for his plane to come into view. I had already traveled extensively abroad. I had met many national and international leaders and many famous celebrities. But none matched Churchill as a larger-than-life legend. In the Pacific during World War II, I had been moved by his speeches even more than by those of President Roosevelt. Since moving into the political arena, I had come to appreciate more than ever what his leadership of Britain had meant to the world during that supreme test of courage and endurance. Superlatives hardly did him justice. He was one of the titanic leaders of the twentieth century.

It was my good fortune that, under the protocol followed at that time, the President went to the airport to greet visiting heads of state, but heads of government first met him at the White House; thus Eisenhower would have greeted the Queen, but it fell to me to greet the Prime Minister.

The night before, I spent over an hour preparing a ninety-second set of welcoming remarks, and I quickly reviewed it in my mind as his plane came into view.

The four-engined Stratocruiser touched down, taxied from the runway, and finally came to a halt in front of us. The door was opened. After a moment Churchill appeared alone at the top of the ramp, wearing a pearl-gray homburg. I was rather surprised that he looked so short. Perhaps it was because his shoulders slumped and his large head seemed to rest on his body as if he had no neck at all. In fact he was five feet eight inches tall, and you would never have thought to call him a "little" man, any more than you would have thought to do so with the five-foot-eight-inch Theodore Roosevelt.

His aides were hovering around to assist him down the steps. After quickly surveying the scene and seeing the welcoming party and the cameras down below, he rejected any assistance. Using a gold-headed walking stick, he started slowly down the ramp. He had suffered a stroke the year before, and he was very hesitant and obviously unsure of himself as he took each step. About halfway down, he noticed four Air Force men saluting him and paused momentarily to return the gesture.

We shook hands and he said he was very happy to meet me for the first time. Like so many Englishmen, his handshake was more of a pressureless touch than a firm grasp. After greeting Secretary of State Dulles, he headed straight for the cameras and microphones. Without waiting for me to make my welcoming remarks, he proceeded to make his arrival statement. He said that he was glad to be coming from his fatherland to his mother's land. (He was referring, of course, to the fact that his mother had been an American.) Amidst the warm applause when he concluded, he flashed his famous V for victory sign and then strode toward the black Lincoln convertible that we would use for the ride to the White House. The remarks I had so painstakingly prepared were never delivered, but neither did they seem to be missed.

As I reread the diary notes that I dictated that day, I am amazed to find that this seventy-nine-year-old man, who had recently suffered a stroke and who had just crossed the Atlantic on an overnight prop-plane ride, could have covered so many subjects so well in the thirty minutes it took us to reach the White House. And all the time he talked, he continually turned to wave to the crowds that lined the route.

He began by telling me that he had followed with interest the trip I had taken to Southeast Asia a few months before. He especially appreciated the fact that during my stop in Malaysia I had gone out into the countryside to visit the British troops who were combating the Communist insurgency there. I told him that I had been very impressed by General Gerald Templer and the other officials who were easing the transition of British colonies to independence. He quickly responded, "I only hope we didn't give them their independence before they were ready to assume the responsibilities of government." When I saw him for the last time four years later in London, he again expressed his concern on this same point.

He then commented on Indochina, which I had also visited on my Asian trip. He said that at the end of World War II the French should have made up their minds whether they were actually going in to save Indochina or whether they were only going to make a halfhearted effort to do so. With his arm still waving to the crowd, he looked over at me and said, "Instead they made the decision to go in, but not to go all out. This was a fatal mistake."

After a few moments of smiling at the crowd, he looked back at me and said, "The world, Mr. Vice President, is in a very dangerous condition. It is essential for our two peoples to work together. We have our differences. That is normal. That is inevitable. But they are, after all, relatively small. And the press always make them seem larger than they really are."

This seemingly innocuous exchange in fact had considerable significance. It was clear that he was signaling to me, and through me to the administration, that he wanted to smooth some waters he had troubled two months earlier when Admiral Arthur Radford, the Chairman of the

Joint Chiefs of Staff, had visited London. Radford had had a disturbing meeting with Churchill on the subject of Indochina, and the press had subsequently published rumors about it that had strained Anglo-American relations.

Churchill had apparently been annoyed when Radford urged him to help France in its effort to keep its colonies in Indochina. Churchill churlishly asked why the British should fight so France could keep Indochina if they would not even fight to keep India for themselves. Radford, not the most diplomatic of men, observed that Congress might not be particularly happy with the British if they refused to go along with our efforts to repel Communist aggression in Asia.

Churchill's reply to this was blunt: "I'll be glad when we are no longer dependent on U.S. aid."

Churchill was reluctant to move against the Communist Vietminh in Indochina because he feared the Communist Chinese might intervene. This, he thought, might lead to war between China and the United States, which would drag in the Soviet Union and make Europe a battle-field and Britain a target. But when Radford reported on this meeting to Eisenhower, the President was obviously surprised and shocked that Churchill, the symbol of resistance despite all odds in World War II, seemed almost resigned to defeat in Southeast Asia.

As he continued to wave to the crowds, Churchill expressed his grave concern about the atomic bomb. He said that it was all right for us to talk about retaliating with this "terrible weapon," but that the theory of "saturation" in connection with nuclear weapons concerned him.

When I told him that I had just finished reading *The Hinge of Fate*, the fourth volume of his World War II memoirs, he commented that for a period of four months before Roosevelt's death there was very little communication or understanding between Churchill and the American government. He was surprisingly direct when he added, "President Roosevelt was not himself. And President Truman did not know what he was doing when he suddenly entered upon his great office." His face became completely serious and once again he ignored the crowds and looked at me. "That was a grave mistake," he said. "A commander must always keep his second in command informed when he knows that he is ill and that he will not be on the scene for very much longer."

By now we were nearing the White House. I said that after reading his memoirs I often wondered what would have happened if the Allies had accepted his recommendation to launch an offensive against the "soft underbelly" of Southern Europe rather than concentrating on making the D-Day invasion in Normandy. As we turned into the Northwest

Gate, he lightly remarked, "Well, it would have been handy to have Vienna."

The private diaries of Lord Moran, Churchill's doctor, give a revealing account of the British Prime Minister's condition during this visit to Washington. Churchill at times suffered a great deal of pain but once he was on stage, no one who saw him would have known of his disability. Somehow he was always able to get "up" for big events.

Despite the heavy schedule of official talks during this visit, Churchill seemed to enjoy thoroughly the long and, I thought, at times boring dinners held in his honor. He was one of those rare great leaders who seemed to enjoy small talk as much as the heavy discussions of world-shaking issues. Thanks to his customary afternoon naps, which he had taken even during the war years, he was at his best in the evening.

During the state dinner at the White House, Mrs. Eisenhower, without making a big to-do about it, helped Churchill cut his meat when he seemed to have difficulty with it. She thoughtfully pointed out that the White House knives were not very sharp. When John Foster Dulles was served his usual highball instead of wine during dinner, Mrs. Nixon asked Churchill if he would also prefer one. He said no and added that he usually had his first drink of whiskey at 8:30 in the morning and that he enjoyed a glass of champagne in the evening.

During dinner Churchill dominated the conversation by retelling stories from his past. Though he did not try to involve others in the discourse, he never appeared to be rude. Like MacArthur's, Churchill's monologues were so fascinating that no one resented it when he took the stage and did not yield it to anyone else. Mrs. Nixon later told me that Churchill was one of the most interesting dinner partners she had ever had. He had held Mrs. Eisenhower and her spellbound as he recounted his dramatic adventures during the Boer War.

The best chance that I had to observe our formidable guest was at the stag dinner at the British embassy on the last night of his visit. Once again protocol kept Eisenhower away, so I was the senior American guest.

Churchill joined us about fifteen minutes late. He greeted all the guests and stood talking for a while, but as Secretary of Defense Charles Wilson embarked upon what was obviously going to be a rather long story, he moved deliberately over to one of the chairs and sat down. I had walked with him, and he looked up at me, grinned, and said, "I feel a little better when I'm sitting down than when I'm standing."

During dinner I asked him how the heavy schedule of the three-day conference had affected him. He said that except for a few "blackouts" he had felt better during this conference than he had for some time. He added, in his characteristically orotund way, "I always seem to get inspiration and renewed vitality by contact with this novel land of yours which sticks up out of the Atlantic."

The conversation later turned to a discussion of vacation plans. He said that he was going to travel by sea to Morocco for a holiday. I responded that I always traveled by air because I tended to get seasick. He fixed me with a rather stern but amused gaze and said, "Young man, don't worry. As you get older, you'll outgrow it." I was forty-one years old at the time.

Churchill was remarkable not only as a maker of history but also as a writer of it. Having read almost all of his prolific writing, I have found him to be a much better writer when describing events in which he was not directly involved. His history of World War I was far better than that of World War II because in the latter Churchill's reflections and observations often get in the way of the story. The best volumes of his account of World War I were *The Aftermath,* in which he recounted the Versailles Peace Conference, and *The Eastern Front,* which he wrote two years after he had completed the other five volumes. In neither of these books was Churchill a major participant. In both his multivolume histories, however, Churchill very effectively practiced his famous maxim "The best way to make history is to write it."

As a historian, Churchill's interest in the American Civil War was always renewed when he visited Washington. This trip was no exception. At the stag dinner he observed that in his opinion Robert E. Lee was one of the greatest men in American history and one of the greatest generals of all time. He said that somebody ought to "catch up in a tapestry or a painting the memorable scene of Lee riding back across the Potomac after he had turned down the command of the Union armies in order to stay with the Southern side."

He said that one of the war's greatest moments came at the end, at Appomattox. Lee pointed out to General Ulysses Grant that his officers owned their horses as personal property and asked that they be allowed to keep them. Grant said, "Have all of them take their horses, the enlisted men and the officers as well; they will need them to plow their fields." Churchill's eyes glistened as he looked around the spellbound group and said, "In the squalor of life and war, what a magnificent act!"

I inquired about his views regarding talks with the Soviet leaders who had succeeded Stalin. He said that the West must have a policy of strength and must never deal with the Communists on a basis of weakness. He told me that he was looking forward to visiting Russia, but that he had no intention of making any commitments that would bind the United States.

He mentioned that except for the wartime alliance he had opposed "the Bolsheviks" all his life and remarked that he was "sure that the people of the United States would trust me as one who knew the Communists and was a fighter against them." He concluded by saying, "I think I have done as much *against* the Communists as McCarthy has done *for* them." Before I could say anything, he grinned, leaned toward me, and added, "Of course, that is a private statement. I never believe in interfering in the domestic politics of another country!"

Churchill complained bitterly to me about the vicious rhetoric of the radical firebrand Aneurin Bevan. In 1947, as Minister of Health in the Labor government, Bevan had embarrassed even some of his colleagues by remarking that the Tories were "lower than vermin." I could not help but think that although Bevan's remark lacked any elegance or cleverness, Churchill himself had few peers when it came to the use of cutting invective.

Accusing James Ramsay MacDonald of lacking political fortitude, Churchill spun out the following tale:

> I remember, when I was a child, being taken to the celebrated Barnum's Circus, which contained an exhibition of freaks and monstrosities, but the exhibit on the program which I most desired to see was the one described as the "The Boneless Wonder." My parents judged that spectacle would be too revolting and demoralizing for my youthful eyes, and I have waited fifty years to see the Boneless Wonder sitting on the Treasury Bench.

He described John Foster Dulles as "the only bull I know who carries his china closet with him."

Lady Astor, who was the first woman to hold a seat in Parliament, once told him, "If I were your wife, I'd put poison in your coffee." Churchill retorted, "If I were your husband, I'd drink it."

After a speech in Parliament by Laborite Clement Attlee, Churchill remarked, "He is a modest man with much to be modest about."

When George Bernard Shaw sent him two theater tickets and a note reading, "Come to my play and bring a friend, if you have a friend," Churchill sent a reply that read, "I am busy for the opening, but I will come the second night, if there is a second night."

And of Aneurin Bevan, Churchill once said, "There is, however, a poetic justice in the fact that the most mischievous mouth in wartime has also become in peace the most remarkable administrative failure."

Churchill certainly gave as well as he received when it came to hard-hitting rhetoric.

Churchill made a revealing comment at the stag dinner about his life-style. Speaking of Lord Plowden, the British atomic specialist, he said, "No man has given so much to the world and taken so little out. He did not eat meat; he did not smoke; he was not married." Churchill himself loved the good life. I think he would have admitted that, while he gave a lot to the world, he also took a lot out.

He had a certain flair for life that led one biographer to call him the "Peter Pan of politics." In his later years, after he gave up polo, his favorite relaxation was painting. His bold strokes and bright colors seemed to release his pent-up energy. As he once said, "If it weren't for painting, I couldn't live; I couldn't bear the strain of things."

During his visit to Washington, we compared our writing habits. I told him that I generally found that I worked best by using a dictating machine. He flashed a delightfully impish grin and said, "I much prefer to dictate to a pretty secretary than into a cold, impersonal machine." He added that he had two "very good-looking" secretaries.

Many years later I recounted this incident to Brezhnev during the Soviet-American summit in Moscow in 1972. The Soviet leader said he agreed with Churchill's preference of a secretary to a machine. He then added with a wink and a broad grin, "Besides, a secretary is particularly useful when you wake up at night and want to make a note."

Churchill hated to do without the comforts of civilization. During World War I he always brought a tin bathtub along on visits to the front. And during an American lecture tour in the days of Prohibition, his contract stipulated that he must receive a bottle of champagne before each appearance.

Shortly after my inauguration in 1969, one of the older White House butlers told me of another incident. President Roosevelt invited Churchill to stay at the White House during his visits and quartered him in what is called the Queen's Bedroom, which is elegantly decorated and has a very comfortable bed. On one of Churchill's visits, Roosevelt insisted that his guest stay in the Lincoln Bedroom so that he could say he had slept in Lincoln's bed. The Lincoln Bedroom is decorated in the stark, rather austere style of mid-nineteenth-century America and has without question the most uncomfortable bed in the White House.

About a half hour after Churchill retired for the night, the butler said that he saw Churchill wearing an old-fashioned nightshirt and carrying his suitcase as he walked tiptoe from the Lincoln Bedroom to the Queen's Bedroom across the hall. Churchill was not about to spend a night in an uncomfortable bed no matter what its historical significance. After hearing this story, I remembered that in 1954 when Mrs. Eisenhower offered Churchill a choice of the Queen's Bedroom or the Lincoln Bedroom, he promptly chose the former, leaving the Lincoln Bedroom to his Foreign Secretary, Anthony Eden.

Churchill was also a connoisseur of fine wines. Recently I visited Château Lafite Rothschild, which produces what many consider France's finest wine. My host told me that Churchill had once visited the château, and in his honor they had opened a bottle of 1870 Lafite Rothschild, which was the greatest vintage of the nineteenth century. After dinner Churchill wrote in the guest book, "1870—Not a good year for French arms but a great year for French wines."

As I observed Churchill during those three days in Washington, I often thought back to the time when I had first become aware of him. It was in 1936, after I came east to law school. He had become highly visible and controversial, partly because of his support of King Edward and Mrs. Simpson in the abdication crisis but mainly because of his insistence that Britain must rearm and the democracies must unite to resist Hitler.

America in those days was isolated as well as isolationist. Today I know people who get impatient if the Concorde takes off twenty minutes late. But in the 1930s the fastest way to get to Europe was several days on an ocean liner. None of the people I knew in California or North Carolina liked Hitler, but few were willing to go to war to get rid of him. I suppose his comic appearance and his outrageous bombast led people not to take him seriously enough. And we knew that even in England, Churchill was widely considered to be sort of a bellicose gadfly. His rhetoric seemed overblown and exaggerated, and most of us sympathized with what we knew of Neville Chamberlain's determination to avoid war and admired the patience and dignity with which he absorbed Hitler's abuse. I can remember the relief everyone felt when Chamberlain returned from the Munich Conference and announced that he had brought back "peace for our time."

It was only in 1939, when Hitler finally made it clear that he would never be satisfied with anything short of conquering Europe, that we began to realize how wise and how prophetic Churchill had been all along. Amidst the shocking suddenness of Europe's collapse, Churchill's colorful personality and dramatic oratory became the stuff of instant legends. Churchill perfectly captured his role when he said, "It was the nation and the race dwelling round the globe that had the lion's heart. I had the luck to be called upon to give the roar."

From the very beginning of the war he paid special attention to the United States. He knew that as the "arsenal of democracy," only our support—and preferably our intervention—would enable Britain to survive. He was especially well suited temperamentally to this role because his mother had been born an American: Jennie Jerome of Brooklyn. He even claimed with pride—and some melodrama—that the Jeromes had Iroquois Indian branches on their family tree.

Born in Blenheim Palace in 1874, he was the eldest son of Lord and Lady Randolph Churchill. His parents had an intense impact on his early years. He loved and worshiped them. But the sad fact was that neither of them had much time or much use for him.

Lord Randolph was a brilliant but highly volatile politician who gambled his whole career on one roll of the dice and lost: He resigned from his cabinet office in protest against a government policy, believing that the Prime Minister would refuse his resignation. Instead, it was accepted, and Lord Randolph never again held cabinet office. Coincidentally his health began to decline as the result of a venereal disease he had contracted some years earlier. Wrapped up in his own problems, Lord Randolph had little interest in his son, who was mainly a nuisance because he did poorly in school and because he added expenses to their already strapped household.

Politics fascinated Winston more than his schoolroom subjects did. He longed to be able to talk to his father about the political events and personalities of the day. But Lord Randolph rebuffed his every attempt. Winston later wrote, "If ever I began to show the slightest idea of comradeship, he was immediately offended; and when once I suggested that I might help his private secretary to write some of his letters, he froze me into stone." Lord Randolph's early death at the age of forty-six ended any chances of a close association between them.

Winston wrote that his mother "shone for me like the Evening Star. I loved her dearly—but at a distance." In fact Lady Randolph was essentially a frivolous beauty for whom marriage had little effect on her fondness for the flattery and company of men. Her liaisons were well known despite the well-bred discretion of the time. Not least among them was the Prince of Wales, the future King Edward VII.

I happen to think that most of the so-called new "science" of psychobiography is pure baloney. For example, in a book he coauthored with former Ambassador William Bullitt, Sigmund Freud suggested that Woodrow Wilson, who worshiped his father, subconsciously hated him and that this hatred contributed to his arbitrary rigidity in dealing with those who disagreed with him on foreign policy. This strikes me as so outlandish as to be downright silly.

I would agree, however, that if one wants some insight into how an individual thinks and feels as an adult, it makes common sense that his family background and early years will often provide a clue.

In Churchill's case it does not appear that the emotional deprivation of his early life had any serious effect on him. He was enormously proud of his father and defended his memory and many of the causes for which he had fought. Lady Randolph lived long enough to see her son become a famous soldier, author, and politician. Like MacArthur's mother, she used her extensive social connections with powerful men to further her son's career. In her later years she became genuinely fond of Winston and quite dependent on him.

It is well known that Churchill, like Einstein, was a mediocre student in his early years. One of his tutors observed, "That lad couldn't have gone *through* Harrow, he must have gone *under* it." In China or the Soviet Union he would not have been selected as one of the elite who are sent on for higher education and given an important position in government or industry. On one of my trips to Peking a Chinese educator told me with pride that all children in China are guaranteed a free elementary education. When they finish grammar school, he went on, they are given a comprehensive examination, and only those who pass are allowed to go on to the higher grades. Those who fail are sent to work in the factories or on the farms. He then added, somewhat wistfully, "Under our system we provide better education for the masses, but we lose our Churchills."

A perceptive scholar would have detected in Churchill a unique ability that a mass examination would not. He was a genius in English. He hated Latin and the natural sciences, and his poor marks in those subjects pulled his overall average down below the norm. His grades placed him in Harrow's lowest class, where the curriculum emphasized learning to write English. "Thus," he later wrote, "I got into my bones the essential structure of the ordinary British sentence—which is a noble thing." He soon fell in love with the English language, and that love affair enriched his life and that of the English-speaking peoples for generations.

Because the normal route to a political career via Oxford or Cambridge did not seem right for Churchill, it was decided that he would become a cavalry cadet at Sandhurst, Britain's West Point. He enjoyed his military training, and his grades showed it: He was graduated near the top of his class.

Young Churchill now surveyed the world scene, searching for any place that offered adventure. He went to Cuba as a newspaper correspondent to report on the guerrilla war between island rebels and the Spanish colonial administration. He later wrote that he felt "delicious yet tremulous sensations" when he espied the outline of Cuba on the horizon. "Here was a place where real things were going on. Here was a scene of vital action. Here was a place where anything might happen. Here was a place where something certainly would happen. Here I might leave my bones."

He soon returned to Britain to prepare for his first military assignment: an eight- or nine-year stint in India. He viewed this prospect with dread, writing to his mother that "you cannot think how I would like to sail in a few days to scenes of adventure and excitement . . . rather than to the tedious land of India—where I shall be equally out of the pleasures of peace and the chances of war."

At his post in Bangalore, Churchill had long periods of free time and resolved to put them to good use. He practiced polo for hours and became an excellent player. He also started to give himself the education he had never acquired at school. His approach was typically broad and methodical. He asked his mother to send him a complete set of *Annual Register*s. These were yearly almanacs of politics from Britain and news from around the world. He read them carefully, took notes, and gradually mastered the wealth of facts and information they contained. Before reading summaries of the major parliamentary debates, he would carefully outline his personal view on the particular issue and then compare his own opinion and analysis with those of the actual participants.

He also asked his mother to send him the writings of some of the great prose stylists of the English language, particularly the historians Macaulay and Gibbon. While his comrades napped through the blistering Indian afternoons, Churchill absorbed the words and the rhythms of these books.

Before long he began sending back war reports to a London newspaper. This was a very unconventional practice for a young officer, and many of his colleagues and most of his superiors did not approve of it. When his reports on the fighting in the North-West Frontier Province were published as a book, it was sarcastically suggested that it be titled *A Subaltern's Hints to the Generals*. This kind of attitude pursued him throughout his life—and he could not have cared less about it.

Churchill never believed in observing conventions that would curb his individuality. He had no use for people who preserve their positions by stifling the creativity of others. He was driven crazy by the pettifogging bureaucratic mentality that reduced life to its lowest common denominator, drew a line there, and forbade anyone to cross over it. He despised the psychology of what Kipling called the "Little Folk"—petty officials "too little to love or to hate" who would "drag down the State!" When Churchill ran up against examples of the "Little Folk," he would often go so far as to recite Kipling's poem aloud.

In America over the recent decades, we have added a new twist to this old problem. While many of the Little Folk in our own bloated bureaucracy are institutionally lethargic and are concerned solely with protecting their jobs, there are also many who are politically active for liberal causes. Thus, while it is always difficult to get the bureaucracy to move on anything, it is now almost impossible for a conservative cabinet secretary, agency director, or even President to get it to move on anything with which it disagrees politically.

Churchill ruffled many feathers by going right to the top for something he wanted rather than wasting time on people lower down who would be fearful of making decisions outside ordinary channels. After World War I there was a story told in London about Clemenceau, Lloyd George, and Churchill. The three died and one by one arrived outside the pearly gates. Clemenceau got there first and knocked to be let in. Saint Peter came and asked Clemenceau to identify himself so that he could consult the records and determine what eternal reward would be his. The same thing happened with Lloyd George. Then Churchill arrived. He also knocked. Saint Peter answered and asked Churchill to identify himself so that he could consult the records and let him know his eternal reward. Churchill replied, "Who the hell are *you*? Get God."

While still on duty in India, Churchill marshaled all the influence his and his mother's contacts could muster to convince Lord Kitchener to allow him to accompany British forces going after the dervishes in the Sudan. Thus it was as a war correspondent that he took part in what turned out to be one of the last cavalry charges in history at the battle of Omdurman.

In 1899 Churchill left the army and ran for Parliament from the Oldham district of Manchester—the same one his father had represented. He was defeated. The loss was a blow. After this first political defeat he wrote that he felt "those feelings of deflation which a bottle of champagne or even soda water represents when it has been half emptied and left uncorked for a night." But he was young, and a new adventure soon beckoned.

He went to southern Africa as a war correspondent to cover the Boer War. Only two weeks after his arrival, while heroically defending a train from a Boer attack, he was captured and became a prisoner of war. He escaped from his Boer captors and they offered a twenty-five-pound reward for him—dead or alive. Years later he kept a framed copy of the wanted poster in his study and would remark to visitors, "Is that all I'm worth? Twenty-five pounds?"

While he was still in Africa, a romantic adventure novel he had written was published in New York and London; three months later his book on the Boer War and his exploits in it was published to good reviews and brisk sales.

When he returned to England two months later, he was a national hero. Eleven constituencies asked if he would do them the honor of running to represent them in Parliament. But he chose to run again for Oldham, and this time he was elected.

Winston Churchill loved the House of Commons the way few men love anything in this world. From the first time he took his seat there in 1901, it was his spiritual home in the deepest sense. Through his father's family and with his own romantic sense of history, he felt himself a living part of the House and its traditions. It is fascinating to read his speeches about his determination to rebuild the House exactly as it had been before German bombs destroyed it during World War II. These are not the words of a man talking about a building. This is a man talking about a deeply passionate personal relationship with history.

He was well received by his new colleagues. Many of them had served with his father, and there was almost a protective feeling for the young Churchill. He wrote and polished and practiced his maiden speech until, as he later wrote, he could have started it anywhere and picked it up without a hitch.

A superb public speaker, he could hold thousands spellbound in a hall, or millions with a broadcast microphone. He combined a brilliant mastery of the English language with a sure instinct for showmanship. But even more important, he was inspiring because he himself was inspired by the ideals for which he fought. As Australia's former Prime Minister Sir Robert Menzies once observed, Churchill's wartime speeches were as stirring as they were because he had "learned the great truth that to move other people, the speaker, the leader, must first move himself; all must be vivid in his mind."

But public speaking did not come easily to him. At the beginning of his career he wrote and memorized every speech, working on the gestures in front of a mirror and even trying different ways of using his lisp for greater effect.

At the Republican convention in 1952, I met Churchill's son Randolph for the first time and I told him how impressed I was by his father's brilliant extemporaneous speeches. He laughed and said, "Well, they ought to have been good. He spent the best years of his life writing and memorizing them." As I talked with Randolph, I sensed how difficult it is to be the son of a great man. I found him to be highly intelligent, interesting, and witty, but anyone would have suffered by comparison with Winston Churchill. This was doubly true for someone who happened to be his son.

As a brilliant and well-connected young member of Parliament, Churchill was on top of the world with seemingly unlimited possibilities spread out before him.

Then he suddenly began attacking some of the positions taken by the leaders of his party. A major crisis arose when he advocated a policy of free trade in direct contravention of the official Conservative party stand, which favored the imposition of tariffs to protect British goods. Such breaking of ranks by junior members was totally unacceptable, especially if they had ambitions of advancing to the cabinet.

In 1904 Churchill took the bold step. He "crossed the floor" of the House of Commons. He changed his party from Conservative to Liberal. There are times in politics when you have to take a big risk. The stakes are as high as they can possibly be, and the results will be remorselessly clear: success or failure. People outside the political arena, or newcomers to politics, frequently do not understand the unique qualities of political risk taking. In business risk taking can be nerve-racking, but at least there are scientific tools to predict the parameters of the possible results. But in politics, risk taking means riding on pure guts, intuition, and the ability to be decisive at the right time.

Today the whole protectionism debate seems remote and lifeless. One has to wonder whether Churchill did not make a mistake by risking so much for such a cause. But Churchill saw the issue of free trade in its broadest terms, including its direct relation to domestic employment and the British standard of living. At a time when many Britons lived uncomplainingly in conditions that would not have been out of place in one of Dickens's bleaker novels, Churchill understood that the quality of life of the average British citizen was going to be the major issue facing the British government in this century.

He was appalled, not just by the economic unfairness of British society, but also by the spiritual toll it inevitably took. One day as he was walking through the streets of his Manchester constituency, he said to his assistant, "Fancy living in one of those streets—never seeing anything beautiful—never eating anything savory—*never saying anything clever!*"

I am often asked by young people to name the qualities an individual must have to succeed as a candidate for office. Intelligence, instinct, character, and belief in a great cause all come to mind. But many have these qualities; very few have the indispensable quality for political success—the willingness to risk all to gain all. You must not be afraid to lose. This does not mean you should be rash. But above all you must be bold. If a potential candidate tells me that he will run only if he has the guaranteed financial and political support of the party organization and if polls show he is sure to win, I say to him flat out, "Don't do it. You will be a lousy candidate." Throughout his career, Churchill was always bold, and he was sometimes rash. But he was never afraid to lose.

The shock waves from Churchill's change of party were tremendous. Many of his friends publicly accused him of being an ingrate opportunist who had used people to advance his career and then turned on them by joining a party that sought to subvert the entire class structure of British society. He pushed for electoral reforms that went far beyond what they saw as the prudent and slight expansion of the number of people eligible to participate in the process of governing. Churchill had joined the forces that were going to open the floodgates of popular democracy and let the rabble in.

Feelings ran strong and bitter. He indulged in British understatement when he later wrote, "I did not exactly, either by my movement or my manner, invite any great continuing affection." Churchill became a pariah in many of the circles in which he had recently been touted as a young man with brilliant potential and an unbounded future. He was labeled "the Blenheim rat" and suddenly found he was no longer welcomed at many of the most fashionable houses in London. Nor were the resentments born in this early period soon forgotten. Eleven years later the Conservatives tried to make it a condition of their participation in a wartime coalition government that Churchill not be given a cabinet post.

It was not so much that the animosities eventually died as that the people who held them did. There is a saying that runs, "Living well is the best revenge." In politics it might be paraphrased to say, "Living longer than anyone else is the ultimate revenge!"

The social ostracism Churchill was subjected to would have crushed many politicians. Many people enter politics because tbey enjoy receiving public acclaim. It takes a different temperament—not necessarily a *better* one—to be willing to put up with the unpopularity, the bitterness, and the sheer hassle of becoming a controversial political figure.

In my thirty-six years of public life I have seen many able young men and women give up their political careers and return to private life because they did not want for themselves—or for their families—the kind of pressure and isolation that go with public controversy. The difference between politics before and after Watergate is striking in this regard. Today the chances of receiving much approval or esteem for accomplishments in public life are slim. The risks of glaring invasions of privacy are much greater, and the kinds of sacrifices and disclosures required for entering politics in the first place have simply become prohibitive for many. This is bound to affect detrimentally both the quality and the number of men and women who are willing to present themselves for public office.

By 1906 Churchill received a cabinet post in the first Liberal government at the age of thirty-two. Over the next several years he held half a dozen cabinet offices. To each of them he brought his voracious curiosity and his enormous energy. As President of the Board of Trade, Churchill provided the legislative leadership for initiatives that laid the foundations of modern Britain. Among many other things and as head of the Home Office, his innovations gave coal miners an eight-hour day and required that safety equipment be installed in the mines; he stopped underground employment of boys under fourteen, made rest breaks mandatory for shop workers, established a minimum wage, set up labor exchanges throughout the country to help reduce unemployment, and instituted major prison reforms.

These achievements were, in fact, the beginning of today's British welfare state. But even as he enacted these reforms, Churchill drew a sharp line between socialism and liberalism. In a speech that Churchill considered to be one of his best, he said, "Socialism seeks to pull down wealth; Liberalism seeks to raise up poverty. Socialism would kill enterprise; Liberalism would rescue enterprise from the trammels of privilege and preference. . . . Socialism exalts the rule; Liberalism exalts the man. Socialism attacks capital; Liberalism attacks monopoly."

His legislative record was substantial. He was creative, cajoling, and controversial, but on first impression he often seemed rude and tactless. He made many enemies where he needed friends. In some cases if people got to know him better, the damage could be repaired. But frequently the first impression was the one that stuck. As one of his closest friends said, "The first time you see Winston you see all his faults, and the rest of your life you spend in discovering his virtues."

People with high-strung tempers and temperaments like Churchill used to be fairly common in politics. When I first came to the House of Representatives in 1947, it was filled with powerfully prickly personalities and some marvelous eccentrics. But since then the growth of television has led to a homogenization of political personalities. In homogenized milk the cream does not come to the top. The same is true of homogenized politics.

In times past we tended to admire the political leader who had the courage to be different—not only in ideas but also in style. But today, in order not to pale from overexposure or to seem excessive or unbalanced, most politicians either have or pretend to have an essentially bland and inoffensive manner. "Don't make waves" seems to be the guideline of most of the new breed.

I am not suggesting we need kooks or crazies in government. But we could do with a few more original thinkers and risk takers. Our young generation of political leaders needs to learn that if you want to succeed, there is only one thing worse than being wrong, and that is being dull. I sometimes wonder whether the great originals like Churchill or de Gaulle would be able to survive the constant barrage of trivial coverage our political leaders are subjected to today.

Churchill paid a heavy price for his high-handedness. He had few close friends and many enemies. According to C. P. Snow, even Lloyd George, who had great personal affection for Churchill, thought that he was "a bit of an ass." While he was successful, everything was fine. But the botched execution of his bold—and, I believe, brilliant—plan to shorten World War I by landing an attack force at Gallipoli in the Dardanelles gave his critics the weapon they needed to cut him down to size. He was put out to pasture in an honorary position.

He could not stand it—not because he minded the controversy or because his ego was bruised. And certainly not because he doubted that the Dardanelles expedition would have succeeded if it had been carried out according to his plan. It was losing the ability to shape events that really got him. As his assistant put it, "The worse things go, the braver and serener he gets—it was the feeling of being condemned to inactivity that was so terribly depressing to him."

It was at this time that Churchill first began to suffer from what he called "Black Dog"—periodic debilitating bouts of depression that could immobilize him for weeks at a time. It probably gave him no comfort that another master of British prose, Samuel Johnson, the author of the first English dictionary, had suffered from the same affliction. As painful as these periods must have been for him, they were probably the way his otherwise optimistic and energetic soul recharged itself to prepare for future battles.

One constant source of peace and satisfaction was his marriage. In 1908 he married Clementine Hozier, and as he later wrote, they "lived happily ever afterwards." Because the marriage was happy does not mean that it was always uncomplicated. Mrs. Churchill was her husband's strongest supporter and fiercest partisan, but she never liked politics as a profession. Nor could she tolerate many of his political friends and cronies. Since he could not give up his political career, they had to reach some accommodations. They spent much time apart, he on official business and she on holidays in France or at their house in the country outside London. Churchill never indicated any interest in other women, and they wrote to each other often and at length. Those letters are a perfect reflection of the depth of their love and trust.

By the beginning of the 1920s, events seemed to have passed Churchill by. He was only forty-seven years old, but many of the new generation of politicians were already thinking of him as an old man. He had had a distinguished, if checkered, career, and it seemed unlikely that he would ever rise higher. Some of the residual distrust over his switch of parties still pursued him, and he could not shake the bitter recriminations from the Dardanelles expedition.

He hit the lowest of a number of low periods in 1922 when an emergency appendectomy prevented him from campaigning for reelection. Without being able to apply his exceptional powers of personal persuasion, he was defeated. It was the first time in twenty-two years that he was not a member of the House of Commons. As he lightly quipped, "In the twinkling of an eye I found myself without an office, without a seat, without a party, and even without an appendix." But his spirits were very far from high. One of Lloyd George's former assistants who saw Churchill at this time reported that "Winston was so down in the dumps he could scarcely speak the whole evening. He thought his world had come to an end—at least his political world."

Talleyrand once said, "In war one dies only once, in politics one dies only to rise again." Churchill's career certainly bears out the truth of this observation. But an adage is precious little comfort for the man who has just lost an election. Having lost a couple of them, I know how it feels. Friends tell you, "Won't it be great to have no responsibility and to be able to travel, go fishing, and play golf anytime you want?" My answer is "Yes—for about one week." Then you have a totally empty feeling that only one who has been through it can understand.

The immediate aftermath is not so bad because you are still numbed by the exhaustion of the campaign, and you also are still operating with a high level of adrenaline. Weeks or months later the realization hits you that you have lost and that there is nothing you can take back or do differently to change the outcome. Unless you are wealthy, there is also the necessity of beginning another career in order to pay the bills that keep coming in every week regardless of how you feel.

This was certainly the case with Churchill. He resumed writing newspaper articles to bring in an income. He tried twice to get back into Parliament but failed. He showed the world a brave and resilient face, but I am sure that each defeat was a bitterly frustrating and humiliating disappointment. But defeat is not fatal in politics unless you give up and call it quits. And Churchill did not know the meaning of the word *quit*.

By the mid-1920s the Labor party had almost completely eclipsed the Liberal party. The few remaining Liberals were joining with the Conservatives. Running as a born-again Conservative, Churchill was finally returned to Parliament in 1924.

One month later Churchill had a bit of good fortune that turned out to be a stroke of bad luck. Through a fluke he suddenly found himself appointed Chancellor of the Exchequer, the second highest member of the cabinet after the Prime Minister himself. Ironically Neville Chamberlain was responsible for this unexpected event.

Prime Minister Stanley Baldwin was planning to make Chamberlain Chancellor of the Exchequer and appoint Churchill Minister of Health. But at the last minute Chamberlain unexpectedly said that *he* wanted to be Minister of Health. All the other positions had been allotted, and Churchill was waiting in the anteroom. Baldwin just reversed plays and bowled Churchill over by asking him if he would like to be Chancellor. Churchill jumped at the chance.

Churchill's four years as Chancellor have always been controversial. It was an impossible job in many ways. Britain was still economically weak as a result of World War I. All the prominent economists urged further tightening of the fiscal belt in order to put the economy on a sound basis for real recovery. The military called for enormous new expenditures in all the services to recover from the devastation of the war and to reassert Britain's military supremacy.

There were few voices raised on behalf of the expensive social welfare programs—such as a national pension plan and insurance for widows and children—that Churchill was determined to enact. He introduced a bold scheme for contributory pensions and used several novel changes in the tax codes to ease the burden on middle-class taxpayers and to increase employment by stimulating productivity and investments.

I think Churchill's reputation as Chancellor may have suffered from the same problem that blackened the image of Herbert Hoover. Both had the misfortune to be in power when worldwide depression struck in 1929. Who else could be held responsible for this catastrophe if not the men in power? Unlike Churchill, Hoover did not have the appealing, warm personality that would have enabled him to let the people know how deeply he cared about their plight. When I came to know Hoover decades later, I found that beneath his rather stiff, cold exterior was a shy, sensitive, and warmhearted man. During his presidency, only his closest friends and the members of his family saw him when tears welled up in his eyes as he spoke of the suffering of the unemployed.

A stroke of unexpected luck had raised Churchill very high; now forces beyond his control had cast him down. Another long, lonely, and frustrating period in the political wilderness began. The Black Dog of depression was frequently unleashed. Churchill wrote despondently, "Here I am discarded, cast away, marooned, rejected, and disliked."

During this period he wrote several books, including his six-volume *Marlborough* and *Great Contemporaries*, and numerous magazine articles. Many literary critics today scoff at Churchill's style as being too florid and even bombastic. But I believe that his books are second only to his wartime leadership as his greatest legacy.

He did not help himself by taking a number of stands that added to his reputation for maverick undependability. He strongly opposed the government's plan to make India independent. He resigned from Stanley Baldwin's shadow cabinet over this issue, thus putting an almost unbridgeable distance between himself and any possible return to power. He broke party ranks again by siding with King Edward VIII in his attempt to find an arrangement by which he could retain the crown while marrying the twice-divorced Mrs. Simpson. And he also began his campaign to alert Parliament to the danger of Germany's rapid rearmament.

Whatever the merits of his stands on India and the abdication, his warnings about Germany made him the prophet of truth in a landscape of dangerous self-deception. Churchill was able to play the role of Cassandra as effectively as he did because he regularly received inside information from civil servants in the military departments who were worried about the blindness of their superiors. In a very real sense this handful of men, whose identities have only recently become known, made Churchill's role possible. Without their facts and figures, he would have been dismissed out of hand as a bellicose blowhard.

Until human nature itself changes, people will leak information in order to accomplish their ends. In most cases those ends are individual self-advancement. In some cases, however, people are concerned about the dangers of a policy they consider to be wrong. Some would argue that it is inconsistent for me to honor the men who leaked information about German rearmament in the 1930s while condemning those who leaked documents about the Vietnam War to the press in the 1960s and 1970s. But the two cases are totally different. In the latter we were at war. When *The New York Times* began publishing the Pentagon Papers, over forty-five thousand Americans had already died in Vietnam, and scores were being killed every week. We were engaged in highly sensitive negotiations to try to end the war. The torrent of leaks—including many others besides the Pentagon Papers—jeopardized our negotiations and, rather than shortening the war, prolonged it. I am certain that this was not the intention of the people who leaked the documents, but nonetheless it was the consequence of their actions.

The leaks to Churchill were made selectively and enabled him to phrase telling questions about government policy in parliamentary debate. Churchill's sources would never have dreamed of giving their raw information to a reporter for publication. I am certain that Churchill would have considered the leaking of the Pentagon Papers during wartime to be treasonable.

Churchill's warnings were proven right with tragic suddenness when the Nazi juggernaut rolled over Poland in the summer of 1939. Chamberlain immediately called Churchill back as First Lord of Admiralty— the same job he had held twenty-five years before. The famous signal was sent from London to the entire British fleet: *"Winston is back."*

It was clear that the discredited Chamberlain could not stay long as Prime Minister. But neither he nor the King wanted Churchill to replace him. They preferred Lord Halifax. On May 10, 1940, only after it had been reluctantly decided that there could not be a Prime Minister from the House of Lords, was Winston Churchill, at the age of sixty-five, finally offered the position. He wrote that, "as I went to bed at about 3

A.M., I was conscious of a profound sense of relief. At last I had the authority to give directions over the whole scene. I felt as if I were walking with Destiny, and that all my past life had been but a preparation for this hour and for this trial."

I suppose one can find a kind of parlor-game fascination in speculating about what might have happened if Churchill had been passed over for Prime Minister and left at the Admiralty to run the war at sea. But I do not know of any leader who spends much time thinking this way. You can become totally immobilized by thinking about the "what ifs" of life.

In America, what would have happened if Robert Taft rather than Eisenhower had been elected President in 1952? Taft died of cancer ten months after the election. What if Churchill had died in 1939? He would have been considered one of a number of picturesque failures in British history. His epitaph would have been "Like father, like son." But what happened happened. And once again Churchill's luck, persistence, ability, and longevity paid off.

In his first speech to the House of Commons as Prime Minister, Churchill said, "I have nothing to offer but blood, toil, tears, and sweat." He could well have added *leadership* to the list. Had it not been for his leadership, Britain might not have survived, Western Europe might not be free, the United States might now be an embattled island in a hostile world. To paraphrase one of his most memorable wartime statements, "Never has one man done so much for so many."

Churchill treated Neville Chamberlain with great generosity when their positions were suddenly reversed. Churchill insisted that Chamberlain stay in the government and continued to include him in all meetings. Churchill did not publicly criticize Chamberlain; rather, he spoke kindly about the nobility of his predecessor's intentions. This kind of magnanimity is typical of the best of politics in any country. Franklin Roosevelt showed no such generosity as President. Never once during the thirteen years of his presidency did he invite the Hoovers to the White House for any occasion. It brought tears to Hoover's eyes when one of the first things Harry Truman did as President was invite him to a meeting in the Oval Office.

The Second World War gave Churchill a backdrop commensurate with his larger-than-life abilities and personality. It seems a sad fact of life that great leadership seems most evident only under the terrible conditions of war.

One of the greatest British Prime Ministers was Sir Robert Peel, who made the tough decision to repeal the Corn Laws. But he is not as widely remembered as Disraeli or the other Prime Ministers who lived in 10 Downing Street during wartime. In the United States the same could be said of James Polk, who probably ranks among our top four or five Presidents in ability and accomplishments. Eisenhower is another example. He ended a war and kept the peace for eight years. But many consider him not to have been as strong or decisive as President Truman, who by an accident of history gave the order to drop the atomic bomb in August 1945. It seems that waging wars, rather than ending or avoiding them, is still the measure of greatness in the minds of most historians.

Despite the total defeat of Germany, Italy, and Japan, the outcome of World War II was hardly victorious as far as Churchill was concerned.

It was C. P. Snow who observed that Churchill's famous statement "I have not become the King's First Minister in order to preside over the dissolution of the British Empire" was wonderfully dramatic but at least a little disingenuous, for that is clearly what anyone who became Prime Minister in 1940 was going to have to oversee. Even without FDR's determination to free all colonial peoples after the war, the momentum toward independence was already growing irresistibly from within the British Empire itself. For Churchill to try to resist it would have been like King Canute ordering the tide not to come in as it lapped higher around his legs.

Even the defeat of Germany involved ironic consequences for the British. Churchill knew that Germany would have to be rebuilt if there was to be any counterbalance to the Soviet monolith and any stability on the Continent. He also knew that rebuilding from the total devastation from which Germany had to recover was ironically preferable to Britain's partial crippling. When Germany was rebuilt, a modern industrial plant replaced the one that had been bombed to smithereens. Britain, though victorious, had to make do with what had been a largely obsolete industrial infrastructure even before the war. As a result, the defeated nation became richer and stronger than the victor.

The British people also had to live with the continued privations of rationing and with the nagging realization that, despite all their efforts, pain, and sacrifice, Britain would never again play the leading part in world affairs to which it had been accustomed.

Anglo-American unity had been one of Churchill's principal interests long before the war began. In the postwar years it became a demanding obsession. In the 1930s he sought it as a means of increasing the prosperity of both nations; in the 1940s it was the prerequisite for Britain's survival; by the late 1950s he saw it as the only way to hold the ring against the expansion of Soviet communism in Europe and around the world; and by the 1960s I suspect he perceived it as the only way for Britain to retain influence in world affairs.

Churchill had to swallow many bitter pills to preserve Anglo-American unity in the postwar years. The British had held the line against Hitler at a very dear price for two hard years before we entered the war after Pearl Harbor. Great as our casualties were, theirs were far greater in both World War I and World War II. They were deeply grateful for our efforts because without us they would not have survived. But they had to feel that without them *we* might not have survived against a Europe totally controlled by Hitler. Now they found it necessary to defer to American attitudes and opinions.

The torch of leadership had passed to us, not because we had a greater ability to lead, but because we had greater power. I do not mean to imply that Churchill was openly envious or resentful. But deep down, the British must have had the nagging thought: "With all of our centuries of experience in foreign policy and the great affairs of the world, don't we really know better how to lead than these Americans?" In my meetings and conversations in 1954 I could sense that the British officials, including Churchill, seemed to have a rather resigned, almost hopeless attitude.

Although the United States has many able foreign service people, I have found in my travels to countries in which the British were influential that their diplomats have often been far more knowledgeable and better qualified than ours. I believe that American policymakers today can profit from actively seeking the advice of their European counterparts before making major decisions, rather than just "consulting" and informing them afterward. We must keep in mind that those who have the most power do not necessarily have the most experience, the best brains, the keenest insights, or the surest instincts.

Even though Churchill felt that U.S. policy toward the Soviet Union immediately after the war was dangerously naive, he did not push things to a breaking point. Instead he continued to flatter us while he tried to educate us. Many people forget that the central point of his famous Iron Curtain speech was to urge Anglo-American unity as the best means to resist Soviet expansionism. This prophetic speech was highly controversial at the time. Eleanor Roosevelt said she thought it was dangerous. One hundred members of Parliament denounced it as trash.

When Churchill warned the world about the threat from Nazi Germany in the 1930s, many refused to face up to it. With the launching of the United Nations at the end of the war, many hoped and prayed that a new era of peace and goodwill among nations and peoples had arrived. When they heard Churchill's warning about the dangers of Soviet expansionism in the late 1940s, again many refused to believe him. But once more he was right. Once again he was ahead of his time, leading public opinion rather than following it.

During the war Churchill had been prepared to accept any help necessary for defeating Hitler. When the Nazis invaded the Soviet Union, Churchill welcomed Stalin into the anti-Hitler camp. Many critics chided him about the 180-degree turnaround in his attitude toward Stalin. He replied, "If Hitler invaded Hell, I think I would find a kind word to say about the Devil in the House of Commons."

Churchill got along well with Roosevelt, his other principal ally. The American President once wrote to Churchill, "It is fun to be in the same decade with you." And Churchill once said of Roosevelt, "Meeting him was like opening your first bottle of champagne."

But the two often strongly disagreed on policy. Churchill considered FDR's insistence on unconditional surrender by Germany to be disastrous and thought the Morgenthau Plan for turning postwar Germany into an agricultural nation was ludicrous. Most importantly, they disagreed on what their policy toward the Soviet Union should be. At least from the time of the Katyn massacre in 1940—when it was learned that ten thousand anti-Communist Polish officers had been murdered by the Soviets—Churchill realized that Stalin might be as rapaciously unappeasable after the war as Hitler had been before it. Meanwhile Roosevelt seemed to be more suspicious of the imperialism of Britain than of Russia. "Winston," he once said, "this is something you just are not able to see, that a country might not want to acquire land somewhere even if they can get it."

As Henry Grunwald wrote in 1965:

> Churchill found himself increasingly isolated from Roosevelt, who did not want America and Britain to gang up on "Uncle Joe" and instead tried to play the moderator between Churchill and Stalin. Thus began a series of disastrous agreements which, among other things, resulted in the loss of Poland to the Communists and brought Russian participation in the war against Japan . . . by giving the Russians territorial and economic concessions in Asia, concessions which played their part in China's fall to the Reds.

Events would have turned out much differently if Churchill had been able to prevail over Roosevelt.

He was worried by FDR's increasing willingness to trust Stalin, and attributed it to the President's failing health. After Roosevelt's death, he feared that Truman, who had been kept poorly informed by FDR, was being influenced by a naively pro-Russian State Department.

Churchill was convinced that it was important to prevent the Soviets from occupying all of Eastern Europe because he was afraid they would never give it up. He wrote to Eisenhower at the beginning of April 1945 to urge him to send American troops into Berlin, Vienna, and Prague. "I deem it highly important," he stated, "that we should shake hands with the Russians as far to the east as possible." But Eisenhower held his troops in their positions as the Russians rolled westward.

Two months later Churchill sounded another warning in a message to Truman, pressing him to hold the Potsdam Conference as early as possible. It was in this message that he first used the phrase that would become emblematic of the coming Cold War: "I view with profound misgivings the retreat of the American Army to our line of occupation in the central sector, thus bringing Soviet power into the heart of Western Europe and the descent of an iron curtain between us and everything to the eastward."

Churchill considered Eisenhower largely responsible for letting the Soviets overrun Eastern Europe. Eisenhower was not Churchill's kind of general. The Allied commander's firm but, in Churchill's view, unimaginative style of command and his easygoing personality may have accounted for the remarkable amity that characterized the collaboration within the Allied command. That alone was an indispensable contribution to winning the war. But Churchill later speculated that if MacArthur had been the Supreme Commander in Europe, America would not have sat back and watched Eastern Europe succumb to Soviet domination.

Eisenhower considered Churchill to be a great leader. Shortly after Churchill's death he wrote, "Through my wartime association with him, the whole globe seemed to be an exercise ground for a mind that could, almost in the same instant, wrestle with an immediate problem in the deployment of air and land and sea forces and probe into the far-off future, examining the coming peacetime role of the embattled nations, shaping for his listener the destiny of the world."

While this statement is evidence of his great respect for Churchill, Eisenhower had his differences with Churchill and seldom spoke about him in our meetings at the White House. On one of the rare occasions when he did, he told me that Churchill was one of the most difficult people he had to deal with because he became so emotionally involved in whatever he was doing. "You know, Dick, he would even cry while arguing his case," he said. I can just picture Eisenhower sitting there uncomfortably while Churchill's eyes overflowed with tears!

This is not an unusual trait among leaders. Khrushchev and Brezhnev, for example, sometimes were on the verge of tears as they tried to make a point to me. With them, however, I wondered how much of it was really felt and how much was an act for my benefit.

I do not doubt that Churchill was capable of manufacturing a few tears at the right moment or of getting carried away by his own oratory. But he was a genuinely emotional man. Lord Moran's diary records that Churchill was moved to the verge of tears when he learned that after his stroke he might not be able to continue in leadership. And his secretary reported that he was sobbing like a child when he dictated the peroration of one of his most famous speeches in the dark days of World War II: " We shall not flag or fail. We shall go on to the end. We shall fight in France, we shall fight on the seas and oceans, we shall fight with growing confidence and growing strength in the air. We shall defend our island, whatever the cost may be. We shall fight on the beaches. We shall fight on the landing grounds. We shall fight in the fields and in the streets. We shall fight in the hills. We shall never surrender."

The growing realization that the end of the war would bring major new problems for Britain must have been tremendously painful for Churchill. But the biggest blow was yet to come.

On July 25, 1945, Churchill left Stalin and Truman at the Potsdam Conference and flew back to London for the counting of the votes in the first postwar general election. He woke up that night with a stabbing pain in the stomach, a portent of the impending news. The results struck Churchill—and the rest of the world—like a bolt from the blue. Labor won in an overwhelming landslide. The Conservatives were thrown out of office. Clement Attlee was Britain's new Prime Minister.

It is not unusual for successful wartime leaders to be rejected once the peace has been secured. This happened to de Gaulle as well. One reason is that the qualities that make a man a great leader in war are not necessarily those that the people want in peace. The successful soldier-statesman—Wellington, Washington, and Eisenhower—is the exception, not the rule.

How could this be? Churchill must have asked himself as, numbed, he sat taking in the results. Was this the thanks he should receive for the victory he had not only promised but delivered? As usual he had a quip to hide the pain. When his wife told him, "It may well be a blessing in disguise," he replied, "At the moment it seems quite effectively disguised." Ironically it was Churchill himself who had noted just ten years earlier in his *Great Contemporaries*, "It is the brightest hours that fade away the fastest."

The humiliation of the general election, the realization that the British Empire was not going to survive intact, the knowledge that the United States had supplanted the United Kingdom as the world's greatest power, and the difficulties in maintaining Anglo-American unity in the onset of the Cold War must have made Churchill very unhappy during this period. Some thought that he might take this opportunity to retire and rest on the laurels of his wartime accomplishments. When I went to England in 1947 as a freshman congressman, no one I spoke with expected Churchill to return to power. After all, he was seventy-two years old and had recently suffered a stroke.

But no one who really understood Churchill thought that he would bow out under ignominious circumstances. Instead he persevered in the House of Commons as the leader of the opposition for six years until, in October 1951, the Conservatives were returned to power and he was once again Prime Minister. Even in a Hollywood movie such a return to power would have seemed like make-believe. But what would have been make-believe for others was real life for Winston Churchill.

As the seventy-six-year-old Churchill again took on the responsibilities of Prime Minister, it was widely assumed that he would delegate power more broadly than he had before. It was also assumed that after consummating his triumphal return he would turn over the reins to his chosen successor, Anthony Eden. But for most it is very hard to give up power. For an old man, it can be the same as giving up life itself.

I talked to President Tito's wife about this when I was in Belgrade in 1970. She told me about her husband's last meeting with Churchill. As Tito entered the room, Churchill comically growled at him, "You know, I didn't like you during the war, but now that you have taken the position you have vis-à-vis the Russians, I find that I like you better." In fact the two old World War II veterans apparently hit it off quite well.

Churchill, who was in his eighties and had finally retired from politics, was being strictly rationed on his cigars and his alcohol. The still-vigorous Tito puffed away on a big Churchillian cigar and drank his quota of scotch and Churchill's quota as well. Churchill looked at Tito rather wistfully and said, "How do you keep so young?" As anyone who met him could see, Tito looked so young partly because he dyed his hair. Without waiting for Tito to answer, Churchill said, "I know what it is. It's power. It's power that keeps a man young."

If an older political leader does not suffer from any serious ailments, he will usually make up in wisdom and judgment for what he may lack in stamina, vigor, and mental quickness. When I saw Zhou Enlai in 1972 he was seventy-three; de Gaulle in 1969 was seventy-eight; Adenauer in 1959 was eighty-three. They were still in power because they were stronger and abler than the younger men in their governments.

Churchill simply could not bring himself to give up power voluntarily. He kept putting back the date of his retirement. First he said he would stay until Queen Elizabeth's coronation; then it was to be until she returned from a trip in Australia; then it was to be until Eden fully recovered from a major intestinal operation; then until after the upcoming Geneva conference. Years passed and Churchill was still firmly planted at 10 Downing Street. Finally he could not ignore his own infirmities or his colleagues' importunings. He quipped, "I must retire soon. Anthony won't live forever." He resigned on April 5, 1955.

, Even at the age of eighty, retirement was not a happy time for this man of action. When Eisenhower returned from the Geneva summit in 1955, he told me of a letter he had received from Churchill. The retired British leader wrote that while he was in some ways relieved not to have responsibility, he felt a sense of "nakedness" when an important diplomatic conference went ahead without him.

I saw Churchill for the last time in 1958 when I went to London for the dedication of the memorial to the American dead in World War II at St. Paul's Cathedral. I hesitated to ask for an appointment with Churchill because I knew he had not been well. But his aide felt that it would be good for him to talk to someone about problems other than his own physical condition. I had learned long before never to ask a sick man how he feels, because he may tell you. But many, and this is especially true of leaders, *want* to talk about the world rather than about themselves. When I called on John Foster Dulles in his last months when he was dying of cancer at Walter Reed Hospital, I always asked him for his opinions on current foreign policy problems rather than dwelling on how he was feeling. Mrs. Dulles, his nurse, and his secretary all told me that my visits gave him an enormous boost because they lifted him out of his own desperate troubles.

At the arranged time I went to Churchill's house at Hyde Park Gate. When I was ushered into his room, I was shocked to see how his physical condition had deteriorated. He was in a reclining chair with his eyes half-closed. He looked almost like a zombie. His greeting was barely audible. He weakly held out his hand. He asked his aide for a glass of brandy and, when it arrived, drank it in one swallow. Then he almost miraculously came to life. The light came back into his eyes, his speech was clear, and he became interested in what was going on around him.

I had read in the morning newspapers a report from Africa that Ghana was considering annexing Guinea. I mentioned it to Churchill and asked what he thought about it. "Well, I think Ghana has enough to digest without gobbling up Guinea," he growled. With surprising forcefulness he went on to remark that Roosevelt had forced Britain and the other imperial powers to give their colonies independence too soon. These countries, he said, took on the responsibilities of government before they were ready to do so and were worse off than before. In this he echoed a point he had made as we were driving to the White House at our first meeting four years earlier.

I asked for his analysis of East-West relations. He still held firmly to the view that only if free men are strong can they preserve peace and expand liberty throughout the world. He emphasized that there could be no détente without deterrence.

After about sixty minutes I could see that he was tiring. I knew that I would not see him again so I tried—somewhat ineptly, I fear—to tell him that millions in America and throughout the world would be forever in his debt. I just could not find the right words to express my feelings.

As I rose to leave, he insisted on escorting me to the door. He had to be helped out of his chair and he could only shuffle along the corridor with an aide supporting him at each side.

When the front door was opened, we were blinded by a glare of television lights. The effect on him was electric. He straightened up, pushed the aides aside, and stood alone. I can see him now: his chin thrust forward, his eyes flashing, his hand raised in the famous V for victory sign. The cameras whirred and the bulbs popped. A moment later the door was closed. Right to the end his star shone most brightly when the cameras were trained on him. Old age could conquer his body but never his spirit.

What would Churchill's message to the free world be today?

Though he was a superb leader in war, Churchill was profoundly committed to peace. He prepared for war in order to avoid it. He waged war with only one goal in mind: to build a world in which a just peace could prevail. He was for peace but not at any price.

On the one hand, he would insist that the only way to keep the peace is to maintain strength. He would continue to warn the West about the dangers of Soviet expansionism and, unlike some present European leaders, would consider Soviet thrusts toward the sources of the industrial world's mineral and oil resources to be as great a threat as tanks rumbling across the central plains of Germany.

He would applaud Prime Minister Margaret Thatcher's concern about Soviet adventurism in the developing world. And while he would not follow every American foreign policy initiative, he would denounce with withering rhetoric the tendency in Europe to consider the United States and the Soviet Union as equal threats to peace.

On the other hand, Churchill would give life to the rather tired and trite cliché "Never negotiate out of fear, but never fear to negotiate." He would urge the free world to negotiate with its adversaries in order to reduce conflict where possible and to make the ultimate conflict of war less probable. He expressed his attitude about negotiating with the Soviets in the House of Commons in May 1953: "It would, I think, be a mistake to assume that nothing can be settled with Soviet Russia unless or until everything is settled."

Despite his awareness of the dire perils we face, Churchill was at heart optimistic—about himself and about the world in which he lived. I believe that his message to today's world would also reflect the buoyant hopefulness of the last great foreign policy speech he made in the House of Commons, on November 3, 1953. After expressing his concern about the destructive power of nuclear weapons, he said, "I have sometimes the odd thought that the annihilating character of these agencies may bring an utterly unforeseeable security to mankind. . . . There is no doubt that if the human race are to have their dearest wish and to be free from the dread of mass destruction, they could have, as an alternative . . . the swiftest expansion of material well-being that has ever been within their reach, or ever within their dreams. . . . We, and all nations, stand, at this hour in human history, before the portals of supreme catastrophe and of measureless reward. My faith is that in God's mercy we shall choose aright."

Shakespeare wrote that "some are born great, some achieve greatness, and some have greatness thrust upon them." During his long life and career Winston Churchill provided examples of all three. Unlike leaders who seek power for its own sake or who find self-definition in possessing it, Churchill sought power because he honestly felt he could exercise it better than others. He believed that he was the only man who had the ability, the character, and the courage to handle some of the great crises of his time. And he was right.

He had the good judgment to be right on most of the things he fought for, and he had the luck to live long enough to be on the scene when his country finally needed the experience and leadership that only he could provide in 1940.

Of the scores of excellent books on Churchill's life and times, a passage in the last paragraph of a tiny thirty-nine-page volume by Isaiah Berlin describes him best: "a man larger than life, composed of bigger and simpler elements than ordinary men, a gigantic historical figure during his own lifetime, superhumanly bold, strong, and imaginative, one of the two greatest men of action his nation has produced, an orator of prodigious powers, the savior of his country, a mythical hero who belongs to legend as much as to reality, the largest human being of our time."

CHARLES de GAULLE

The Leadership Mystique

ON NOVEMBER 12, 1970, more of the world's leaders converged on Paris than had ever before done so, even when the city was the center of an empire that spanned the globe. Three days earlier, less than two weeks before his eightieth birthday, Charles André Joseph Marie de Gaulle had suddenly died. Now, sixty-three current or former heads of state and heads of government who had assembled to pay honor to de Gaulle's memory walked solemnly down the 260-foot main aisle of the Cathedral of Notre-Dame. As the President of the United States, I was among them. But I was also there as a friend.

We came not to bury de Gaulle, but to honor him. Years earlier he had left his own strict instructions for his funeral: no pomp, no panoply, no dignitaries, only an austere, private ceremony in the little churchyard in the village of Colombey-les-Deux-Églises. In accordance with his wish, he was buried in a plain seventy-two-dollar oak coffin, borne to his grave by his fellow villagers—a butcher's assistant, a cheesemaker, a farmhand—and laid to rest beside the body of his beloved daughter Anne, who had been born retarded and died twenty-two years earlier at the age of nineteen. His tombstone, as he wished, read simply, "Charles de Gaulle, 1890–1970."

The huge memorial service at Notre-Dame was not part of de Gaulle's plan. It was an accommodation by the government to those throughout France and the world who wanted to pay tribute to de Gaulle.

Ask someone what he most remembers about Charles de Gaulle, and he may say "tall." Or "austere," or "difficult," or "strong-willed." Or he may associate de Gaulle with French "grandeur." Or, if he is older, he may remember de Gaulle as the man who led the Fighting French under the banner of the double-barred Cross of Lorraine during World War II, or perhaps recall the comment attributed to Churchill afterward that "of all the crosses I have had to bear, the heaviest was the Cross of Lorraine."

When I think of de Gaulle, I think of all these things, but I also remember him as a man who was exceptionally kind, gracious, and thoughtful, no less in my years out of office than when I was in office. He was also one whose counsel I valued immensely, even when I disagreed with him.

What is there about de Gaulle that so impresses him on our consciousness? Why does he so tower over the twentieth century, so much more so than many leaders of nations more powerful than France?

We remember leaders for what they did, but also for what they were: for their contributions, but also for their character. Others made greater contributions than de Gaulle, but few had his strength of character. He was stubborn, willful, supremely self-confident, a man of enormous ego and yet at the same time enormous selflessness: He was demanding not for himself but for France. He lived simply but dreamed grandly. He acted a part, playing a role he himself created in a way that fit only one actor. Even more, he fashioned *himself* so that he could play it. He created de Gaulle, the public person, to play the role of de Gaulle, personification of France.

Charles de Gaulle could be an enigma—he worked at being an enigma. But he also was a genuine hero, one of the towering figures of the twentieth century and, for France, one of the towering figures of all its centuries. Like a fine French wine, he was complex, powerful, and subtle all at once, and like such a wine, his character has stood the test of time.

I first met de Gaulle when he made a state visit to Washington in 1960, two years after his return to power. For years I had held many of the usual stereotypical ideas about him. He had long been a favorite object of that special form of brittle, sardonic derision that passes for wisdom in so many Washington circles. De Gaulle's manner lent itself to verbal caricature, just as his features lent themselves to cartoon caricature. Those who like to puff themselves up by putting others down found an easy target in de Gaulle.

Before I met de Gaulle, I had a clear impression of him as being cold, petty, haughty, insufferably egotistical, and almost impossible to deal with. Churchill's Cross of Lorraine comment had contributed greatly to that impression—an illustration of the extent to which a single phrase can have a devastating effect on the way a public person is perceived, creating an impression so difficult to erase that it becomes almost indelible. Alice Roosevelt Longworth's characterization of Thomas E. Dewey as the "bridegroom on the wedding cake" had a similar effect; some even argue that the false impression created by the description cost him the election in 1948. If Dewey's opponents had described him with such adjectives as *small, pompous, somewhat plastic,* and *artificial,* they would not have had nearly the impact they did with that one phrase.

When I visited France as a congressman in 1947, virtually all the French and American officials I met reinforced the negative image I had of de Gaulle. They brushed him off as an arrogant extremist who would never return to power.

My thinking was also influenced by the almost open contempt that our foreign service officers had for de Gaulle. Even Charles Bohlen, who was one of America's ablest career diplomats and who served as Ambassador to France under Presidents Kennedy and Johnson, made little effort to hide his dislike for the French President. William Bullitt, President Roosevelt's Ambassador to France, told me that Bohlen would often delight his embassy dinner guests by making devastatingly witty remarks about de Gaulle and by mimicking his mannerisms in a brilliant but undiplomatic way. De Gaulle caught wind of Bohlen's dislike for him and reciprocated. I have often felt that this personal hostility explained to an extent what many assumed was an anti-American prejudice on de Gaulle's part.

Shortly before my first meeting with de Gaulle in 1960, I took what in effect was a quick cram course on his background. The more I learned about him, the more I found the old stereotypes fading. I learned that, like MacArthur, he had shown exceptional courage in war and that he had been ahead of his time in warning his country of its dangers. I was also impressed by the fact that, like Churchill, de Gaulle had written both extensively and brilliantly before coming into a top position of leadership; and, like Churchill, he had been "in the wilderness"—rejected, out of power—and had used those years to do some of his finest writing.

Like MacArthur, Churchill, and Eisenhower, de Gaulle had been one of those world figures who seemed both larger than life and exceptionally remote to me during World War II. As a young junior Navy officer sitting on a Pacific island and reading sketchy news reports about the obstreperous leader of the Fighting French, I never imagined that sixteen years later I would be greeting him in Washington—much less that a quarter of a century later he and I would sit down together in Paris as the Presidents of France and the United States.

When I first met de Gaulle in 1960, I was struck at once by his appearance. I knew he was tall—at six feet four inches he had been the tallest general in the French army—but his soldier's posture made his height even more imposing. Only later did I notice that he was slightly stooped.

During his visit, I noted that, for a man of his size, his movements had an extraordinary grace. He never seemed awkward or clumsy, whether gesturing or walking or handling silverware at the dinner table. He had about him a quiet, impressive dignity that was complemented by a certain old-world courtliness in his manners.

The de Gaulle I met in 1960 was very different from the arrogant, abrasive character portrayed by reporters and foreign service personnel. I found him to be a very kind man with a somewhat shy quality that is hard to describe. He was not warm, but neither was he harsh. I would say he was almost gentle. But, as with most leaders, gentleness of manner was one thing; policy was another thing.

Most leaders I have known had a gentle side to their natures, but it would be a mistake to call them gentle people. Those who are in fact gentle are seldom good at wielding power. A leader has to be brutally tough at times in order to do his job. If he frets too much about the toughness of his task, if he lets himself be deterred too much by sentimentality, he will not do what he has to do right, or even do it at all.

As I got to know de Gaulle better over the years, I developed enormous respect for him both as a leader and a man, and the feeling seemed to be mutual. In 1967 my friend Vernon Walters arrived in Paris to take up duties as U.S. Military Attaché. He had known de Gaulle since 1942. After giving a farewell luncheon for Ambassador Bohlen, de Gaulle sent for Walters and asked whether he had seen me recently. Walters replied that he had. De Gaulle declared emphatically that he believed that I would be elected President, adding that he and I had "both had to 'cross the desert' "—a term he used to describe his own years out of power. He then made a remark that Walters later found strangely prophetic: "Mr. Nixon, like me, will have been an exile in his own country."

De Gaulle was a creature of the twentieth century, but also of the nineteenth. He pulled France in both directions, forward and back. Throughout his life and career he was imbued by a sense of the continuity of French history and by the presence of the past. His name itself—Charles de Gaulle—reverberated with echoes of Charlemagne and Gaul. Grandeur, glory, greatness—the French word *grandeur,* when written or spoken by de Gaulle, is sometimes translated as each of these—were, in de Gaulle's view, essential to a nation and particularly to France.

If de Gaulle can be said to belong to history, that is no accident. De Gaulle willed it that way. He directed his life toward shaping history in the pattern of his own vision. As one commentator wrote, "For de Gaulle politics is not primarily the art of the possible; it is the art of the willed." To de Gaulle will was the central moving force of nations, and he was supremely confident of his own ability to mold history by the exercise of his own will.

He also felt a need to make France will itself toward greatness. He consistently summoned his people to the "heights"; though these heights were sometimes only dimly seen or ill-defined, the important thing to de Gaulle was that the people feel themselves engaged in the climb. Only this way could the nation be great. He once said, "France is never her true self except when she is engaged in a great enterprise." He saw himself as the embodiment of France, and his role as one of exalting the spirit of France.

De Gaulle is fascinating as a person, not only for his historical importance, but also for the exceptional insights he has given us into the requirements and techniques of leadership. Few have analyzed those so cogently as he, or written of them so perceptively. Few have left such a clear chart of their own methods—and yet, few have remained cloaked in such shrouds of mystery, shrouds that he carefully drew about himself even as he explained how he was doing so. He was a master of illusion. And, like a skilled illusionist, he was a magician of sorts. By appearing to do the impossible, he often achieved the improbable.

To a degree rare among great leaders, the key to penetrating the mysteries of de Gaulle can be found in his own writings—not only his exceptionally literate and thoughtful memoirs, but also some of his earlier analytical works.

Long before he first came to prominence and then to power, he wrote what in effect was a manual for leadership—*The Edge of the Sword,* a short book written originally as a series of lectures at the French War College and then published in 1932. It was not until after de Gaulle's death that I discovered this book. But when I read it, I found that it was almost uncanny in the extent to which it described the characteristics and techniques that would later be exhibited by the de Gaulle I knew. It was clear that when the time eventually came for him to craft so meticulously the half-mythical "General de Gaulle" who would rally the nation and lead it, he followed the prescription he had laid down in this book, published when he was a forty-one-year-old army officer little known outside of a few military circles.

The Edge of the Sword thus provides more than a handy device for examining de Gaulle. It also provides an indispensable framework for understanding him.

In *The Edge of the Sword,* de Gaulle defined three crucial qualities that a leader must have: To chart the right path, he needs both intelligence and instinct; and in order to persuade people to follow that path, he needs authority.

Because they live in an academic world, political scientists understandably stress the intellectual component of leadership. But de Gaulle noted that leaders themselves have always understood the crucial importance of instinct. Alexander called it his "hope," Caesar his "luck," and Napoleon his "star." When we speak of a leader as having "vision" or a "sense of reality," we really are saying that he instinctively understands how things work. Instinct, de Gaulle wrote, enables the leader to "strike deeply into the order of things."

As he put it, "Our intelligence can furnish us with the theoretic, general abstract knowledge of what is, but only instinct can give the practical, particular, and concrete *feel* of it." It cuts through the complexity of the situation and seizes upon the essentials. Intellect then elaborates, shapes, and refines what he called the "raw material" of the intuitive insight.

Only when a leader achieves the right balance between intellect and instinct, he argued, will his decisions be marked by prescience.

Prescience—knowing which way to lead—lies at the heart of great leadership. The very word *leader* implies the ability to act as the guide, to see beyond the present in charting a course into the future. When I visited France in 1969, de Gaulle commented to me, "I make policies for the newspapers of the day after tomorrow." Too many political leaders get caught up with the headlines of the day and the pressures of the moment, losing sight of the longer perspective as a result. De Gaulle, however, did not live for the moment: He used the moment.

Long before he became famous, de Gaulle showed a talent for seeing over the heads of his contemporaries. He stood virtually alone in arguing against the strategy of the Maginot Line, in defying the decision to capitulate to Hitler, and in opposing the jerry-built political system of the Fourth Republic. But in each of these cases events were to prove him right.

In 1934 de Gaulle outlined his theory on the nature of modern warfare in a book entitled *The Army of the Future.* He argued that strategies for set-piece battles had been made obsolete by a revolution in technology: the invention of the internal combustion engine. He wrote that "the machine controls our destiny." Machines had transformed every sphere of life, and war could be no exception.

He proposed the formation of a 100,000-man force of elite troops that would operate six fully mechanized divisions. Mobility and offensive striking power, he continually stressed, would carry the day in the next war, just as numerical superiority and preponderant defensive firepower had in the previous one.

De Gaulle's ideas were unwelcome in France. Marshal Henri Philippe Pétain dismissed the book as "witticisms." General Maxime Weygand branded it "an evil criticism."

The Army of the Future sold fewer than 1,500 copies. But two hundred of these went to Germany, where it was read closely. In 1934 French journalist Philippe Barres met with Adolf Hitler and General Adolf Huenhlin, the commander of the German motorized forces. In an exchange about mechanized warfare, Huenhlin asked Barres, "And what is my great French colleague doing to develop these techniques?" Barres, who had never heard of de Gaulle, looked perplexed. The Ger-

man general then prompted, "I mean your great specialist on motoriza-
tion, your Colonel de Gaulle."

The Germans were impressed by his advice. The French were not. In
a memorandum he wrote four months before the German invasion, de
Gaulle proclaimed that no matter how well the government reinforced
the Maginot Line, the enemy could destroy or circumvent it. If
breached, he warned, the entire Maginot system would collapse, with
Paris only six hours away by automobile. And as he had said in *The
Army of the Future*, "Each time Paris was taken during the last century,
French resistance crumbled within an hour." On June 14, 1940, that
hour came, and de Gaulle's tragic prophecy came true.

While France was collapsing before the Germans, de Gaulle saw, as
few other Frenchmen did, that the war was not over but had really just
begun. He flew to Britain, determined to continue the resistance even if
his government would not. "France has lost a battle," he insisted, "but
France has not lost the war."

In his first radio appeal from London, de Gaulle declared that France
was not alone, for the battle of France had ignited another world war.
He said that the French could prevail in the end by continuing the war
from their empire, supported by British domination of the seas and by
the vast potential of American war production. That bit of prescience
immortalized de Gaulle in the hearts of Frenchmen, enabling him, in
that darkest hour, to become the keeper of the eternal flame of France's
soul.

After the war, de Gaulle's hopes for France were smashed on the
rocks of politics-as-usual. Though they had hailed de Gaulle as their
savior, the French people turned their backs on his proposed constitutional reforms, enabling the politicians and parties of the prewar period
to elbow him into retirement.

De Gaulle opposed the return of the parliamentary system of the
Third Republic because he blamed it for the unsound military policies
that had led to defeat in 1940. There had been so many political parties
that none could command a majority and devise a rational policy. The
fractious assembly had come to resemble the Hobbesian state of nature:
a war of all against all. De Gaulle warned that, if restored, parliamentary
government could only result in a series of fragile, impotent coalition
cabinets that would tumble at the slightest political tremor. As he said
many years later, "Members of parliament can paralyze action; they
cannot initiate it."

De Gaulle understood that France was at heart a Latin country.

Speaking of his own Latin heritage, Luis Muñoz Marin, a one-time governor of Puerto Rico, once told me, "I am proud of my Latin heritage. Our devotion to family and to the Church and our contributions in philosophy, music, and art are admirable. But we Latins are just not good at government. We find it difficult to strike the balance between order and freedom. We go to extremes—too much order and too little freedom or too much freedom and too little order." De Gaulle's genius was his ability to strike that delicate balance in France.

Because de Gaulle opposed the return of the "regime of parties" after World War II, many journalists and politicians on the left accused him of seeking to establish a dictatorship. They misjudged him. During and immediately after the liberation of France, a "sort of monarchy," as de Gaulle called it, was necessary. But he moved without delay to allow the people to choose their government when conditions permitted. He never challenged the principle that sovereignty resides with the people. But he believed that consensus leadership was no leadership and that a President or Prime Minister must *lead* a parliament, not follow it.

By late 1945 de Gaulle realized that he had lost this argument. The constitution of the Fourth Republic created an all-powerful legislature that controlled a weak executive. He became convinced that he should resign from government and "withdraw from events before they withdrew from me." He called a meeting of his cabinet, announced his decision to abandon his office, and strode abruptly out of the room and into retirement. He firmly believed that the time would come when France would call on him to lead, but on his own terms. Again de Gaulle was ahead of his time, but his time eventually came.

He had a sense of destiny and did not want to be the President of France simply for the sake of being President. He wanted to be President only when he felt that he was the only man who could give France the leadership the nation needed. What separates the men from the boys in politics is that the boys want high office in order to be somebody; the men want high office in order to do something. De Gaulle wanted power, not for what it could do for him, but for what he could do with it.

Less than a year and a half after giving up power, de Gaulle launched a vigorous drive to recapture it. He had tailored his personality to be the master of great events; now he contemptuously watched others fumble with small ones. Unable to wait any longer for France to call him back, he launched a political movement, the Rally of the French People (RPF), to bring him back.

In 1947 the thunderheads of the Cold War were forming on the horizon, and the French people suffered from acute shortages, low wages, and high prices. De Gaulle did not address their mundane concerns, saying that he had not liberated France "to worry about the macaroni ration." Instead he spoke to the questions of global power and proclaimed the greatness of France.

In those troubled times the political stock of de Gaulle, whom the French people often called the "man of the storm," rose dramatically. By 1951 the RPF had won more seats in Parliament than any other party. From the outset de Gaulle forbade his delegates to support any government, an order that had the strange effect of putting the RPF into a de facto alliance with the Communist party.

With unyielding opposition from the left and the right, centrist governments fell in quick succession. But almost despite themselves, they succeeded in improving domestic and international conditions by the early 1950s. In effect the politicians of the Fourth Republic had succeeded in stealing the thunder of the "man of the storm." De Gaulle seemed to agree, for he despairingly told visitors, "The Republic governs France badly but defends itself well."

By 1952 it was apparent that the RPF could not bring down the Fourth Republic. After de Gaulle ordered his delegates to reject an offer to try to form a government, party discipline broke down. Defections reduced the RPF to the status of a parliamentary splinter group by 1953. After a dismal showing in the next municipal elections, de Gaulle disassociated himself from the movement.

The long episode of the RPF proved that a leader can be wise without always being right. De Gaulle took the long view of the future, but sometimes the present fooled him. At times he seemed to have an awesome, instinctive feel for his people; at other times their temper escaped him. The failure of his political party was a case in point. His criticism of the parliamentary regime would prove prophetic. But the times were not yet right. As a result his efforts to bring about his prophecy were disastrous.

The crisis that returned de Gaulle to power had its origins in late 1954. Segments of the Algerian Muslim population formed the Front de Liberation Nationale and began to wage a guerrilla war against the French colonial administration. The war dragged on for years, the brutality of the French army growing with its frustration. The politicians of the Fourth Republic showed themselves incapable of ending the war one way or the other.

In 1958 the inability of the regime to come to grips with its problems in Algeria became a crisis in itself. The army, particularly after suffering the humiliation of defeat in Indochina in 1954, was determined to keep French Algeria French at all costs. The Gaullists, the right-wing politicians, and the French colonists in Algeria joined the army in a loose alliance against the French government. And they were ready to act, while the government was incapable of doing so.

The Fourth Republic was in its twenty-fourth cabinet crisis since de Gaulle's resignation in 1946 and had been without a sitting government for almost a month when the problems in Algeria came to a head. A mob attacked the government building in Algiers as security forces calmly looked on. Under the pretext of reestablishing order, the generals overthrew the French government in Algeria. Less than two weeks later, troops on Corsica joined the rebel generals. The Algerian generals planned to go on within days to conquer metropolitan France, and the government was powerless to stop them.

Throughout the whole affair, de Gaulle showed remarkable political shrewdness. He refused either to condemn or to endorse the military coup publicly, although some of those involved were his supporters. His silence ensured that all were listening when he finally announced that he was "ready to take over the powers of the Republic." He had watched the politicians of the Fourth Republic exhaust all their options, and when they finally turned to him, he was ready to dictate the terms of his cooperation.

Though he dictated his terms to the government, these did not include making him dictator. Nevertheless many Frenchmen continued to view him with suspicion. Biographer Brian Crozier wrote that after hearing de Gaulle's conditions for returning to power, the chairman of the National Assembly, André le Trocquer, exclaimed to him, "All this is unconstitutional. I have known you pretty well since Algiers. You have the soul of a dictator. You're too fond of personal power!" De Gaulle replied sternly, "It was I who restored the Republic, Monsieur Le Trocquer."

By the time de Gaulle took over, the authority of the Fourth Republic had crumbled into so pitiable a state that it would be wrong to say that he came to power in a coup d'etat. He simply delivered the coup de grace to a fading regime.

De Gaulle demanded that the Fourth Republic grant him the power to propose constitutional reforms directly to the people in referenda, and by these means he enacted the constitution of the Fifth Republic. Its centerpiece is the presidency. The President is given the authority to create and execute policy without undue interference from the National Assembly, thus preventing the drift and paralysis that had brought the Fourth Republic to the verge of political, economic, and social collapse.

Some have criticized de Gaulle for giving the President so much power. But with the clarity of hindsight I believe that the political stability that the constitution gave France was de Gaulle's greatest legacy, just as the Napoleonic Code was Napoleon's.

During my vice presidency I always greeted visiting Prime Ministers at the airport, because, under the protocol of the time, President Eisenhower did so only for visiting heads of state. In the years before de Gaulle's return to power, it seemed that on alternate months I would meet a new French Prime Minister and a new Italian Prime Minister. Italy still has not conquered the problem of instability; de Gaulle conquered it in France. Any astute student of constitutional law might have devised a similar governmental framework. But only de Gaulle had both the prescience to see the need for it and the authority to get it enacted.

In Greek mythology, Apollo gave Cassandra the gift of prophecy. But he then turned the gift into a curse by causing all who heard her warnings to disbelieve them. De Gaulle knew that prescience is not enough. A leader must not only decide correctly what should be done, but also persuade others and get them to do it. Every occupant of the White House has felt at one time or another the curse of Cassandra, confronted with the aggravating problem of seeing a correct course but being unable to move the bureaucracy, the Congress, or the public to go in that direction. In *The Edge of the Sword*, de Gaulle wrote that a leader "must be able to create a spirit of confidence in those under him. He must be able to assert his authority."

Authority, de Gaulle argued, derives from prestige, and prestige "is largely a matter of feeling, suggestion, and impression, and it depends primarily on the possession of an elementary gift, a natural aptitude which defies analysis." This gift is a rare one. He wrote that "certain men have, one might almost say from birth, the quality of exuding authority, as though it were a liquid, though it is impossible to say precisely of what it consists."

This has lately gone by the fashionable term *charisma*. It remains a quality none can explain but all can recognize.

To this ineffable quality, de Gaulle wrote, a leader must add three concrete ones: mystery, character, and grandeur. "First and foremost," he declared, "there can be no prestige without mystery, for familiarity breeds contempt. All religions have their tabernacles, and no man is a hero to his valet." In his plans and demeanor a leader must always have something "which others cannot altogether fathom, which puzzles them, stirs them, and rivets their attention."

I vividly recall de Gaulle's striking presence when he came to Washington for President Kennedy's funeral in November 1963. Mrs. Nixon and I watched the funeral procession from a window of our suite in the Mayflower Hotel. The great and the near-great from all over the world were walking behind the casket. De Gaulle was a big man physically, but he seemed to tower over the rest in dignity, stature, and charisma as well as in height.

Whenever I met with de Gaulle, whether publicly or privately, he displayed an enormous, even stately dignity. His resolute bearing gave him a certain air of aloofness. Some interpreted this as stuffiness, but in de Gaulle's case it was not. The essence of stuffiness is being unnatural. In de Gaulle's case aloofness was natural. He had a certain ease of manner when dealing with another head of state, whom he considered an equal, but he was never informal, even with his close friends.

In this respect, de Gaulle was similar to all of the American Presidents I had known before taking office in 1969, with the exception of Lyndon Johnson. Herbert Hoover, Dwight Eisenhower, John Kennedy, and even Harry Truman all had a very deep sense of privacy and did not like to be treated in too familiar a manner.

Even in his youth de Gaulle maintained his distance from his peers. His family quipped that his personality was so cold that he must have been trapped in an icebox as an infant. An instructor at the French War College wrote that de Gaulle had the "attitude of a King-in-exile."

I cannot imagine him slapping someone on the back, grabbing someone by the arm to emphasize a point, or engaging in buddy-buddy familiarity with his constituents or colleagues. He did not object to others doing so, but he felt that it would be out of character for him. But at the same time his personal manner had none of the condescending arrogance that is a common characteristic of small men in big jobs.

As a national figure, de Gaulle attracted a fiercely loyal cadre of supporters, but he remained aloof from them, reflecting his own dictum that a leader can have "no authority without prestige, nor prestige unless he keeps his distance." In his office in the Élysée Palace, de Gaulle had two phones on a table near his desk. But they never rang. He considered the telephone as an intolerable nuisance of the modern world, and not even his closest advisers dared to call him directly.

Like MacArthur, de Gaulle had little patience for small talk. Whenever I met with him, it was clear that he wanted to turn immediately to serious issues. He was also like MacArthur in the precision of his language, whether in a press conference, in an extemporaneous speech, in answering questions, or even in informal conversation. Both men spoke with polished sentences that captured precisely their nuances of meaning. If either had been in the U.S. Congress, he would not have had to revise his remarks before they were printed in the *Congressional Record*.

De Gaulle did not tolerate ineptitude. At the official dinner that I gave in his honor in 1960, he used as his interpreter the French consul general from a major American city. As he translated de Gaulle's toast, the interpreter's hands were shaking, and he fumbled considerably. I could see that de Gaulle was very irritated. I learned later that he had dismissed the consul general and gotten a substitute for the balance of the trip.

De Gaulle never participated in bull sessions. In cabinet meetings he would listen closely to his ministers and courteously take notes on what they said. If he wanted to exchange views with a minister, he usually arranged for a private meeting.

The decisions on the big issues were de Gaulle's alone. He did not believe he had the knowledge of a Solomon, but he did believe he had the judgment of one. He would first call for "all the papers" about a particular issue and, using his immense capacity for the mastery of detail, would learn everything there was to know about it. He would then withdraw from his advisers to study and contemplate his decision in solitude. He understood how vitally important having time to think can be for a leader, and at his insistence his staff reserved several hours a day for undisturbed thought.

I tried to follow a similar pattern as President, but found that one of the hardest things for a leader is to enforce this discipline against the demands of administration officials, legislative leaders, and others for a portion of his time. They typically assume, when they see an opening in his schedule, that he therefore has time for them; they are intent on making their priorities his priorities. But usually their priorities are not—and must not be—his priorities. His responsibilities transcend their responsibilities.

Very few of my major decisions as President were made in the Oval Office. When I had a major decision to make, I always tried to get away for a few hours in the Lincoln sitting room or the small libraries at

Camp David, Key Biscayne, or San Clemente. I found I could do the best thinking and make the best decisions in places that provided solitude away from the babel of voices in Washington.

In addition to aloofness, de Gaulle wrote, mystery requires an economy of words and gestures and a studied manner in bearing and movement. "Nothing more enhances authority than silence," he continued. But silence, "the crowning virtue of the strong," produces its effect only if it appears to conceal strength of mind and determination. "It is precisely from the contrast between inner power and outward control that ascendancy is gained, just as style in a gambler consists in his ability to show greater coolness than usual when he has raised his stake, and an actor's most notable effects depend upon his skill in producing the appearance of emotion when he is keeping strong control of himself."

De Gaulle knew that politics is theater—in its practice if not in its substance—and it was in part through his mastery of the theatrical that he imposed his political will.

Like Caesar and MacArthur, de Gaulle often referred to himself in the third person in his writings. He would, for example, write of "a growing impulse toward an appeal to de Gaulle," of the necessity of "answering 'yes' to de Gaulle," and of how "there could be no alternative to General de Gaulle." A journalist once asked him to explain the reasons for this habit. He replied that, while he occasionally used the third person for stylistic purposes, "the more important reason was my discovery that there was a person named de Gaulle who existed in other people's minds and was really a separate personality from myself."

He first encountered the power of his public persona in a wartime visit to the city of Douala in French Equatorial Africa. Thousands of people lined the streets and chanted, "De Gaulle! de Gaulle! de Gaulle!" As he moved through the throng, he realized that General de Gaulle had become a living legend, a larger-than-life figure who dwarfed Charles de Gaulle. "From that day on," he later said, "I knew I would have to reckon with this man, this General de Gaulle. I became almost his prisoner. Before I made a speech or reached a major decision I had to ask myself, 'Will de Gaulle approve of this? Is this the way people expect de Gaulle to act? Is this right for de Gaulle and the role he plays?' " He added wistfully, "There are many things I would have liked to do but could not, for they would not have been fitting for General de Gaulle."

Charles de Gaulle made certain that he always acted in character with General de Gaulle, whether in minute detail or in grand gesture. In his later years cataracts badly impaired his vision. Unless he was wearing his thick-lensed glasses, he sometimes could not recognize the person with whom he was shaking hands. Georges Pompidou told me of an instance when he was riding in a motorcade with de Gaulle: The French President leaned over and asked his Prime Minister if there were any people to wave to along the parade route. Throngs lined the streets, but de Gaulle simply could not see them. The image of General de Gaulle would not permit him to wear his glasses in public. Because of his vanity and his remarkable ability to memorize his speeches, he never used a teleprompter.

Like MacArthur, de Gaulle was unfazed by personal danger and was acutely aware of the powerful effect this courage could have. In their book *Target de Gaulle*, Pierre Démaret and Christian Plume describe thirty-one attempts on the life of the French President. In 1962 a barrage of machine-gun fire strafed his car as he rode through a Paris suburb, with one bullet missing his head by only two inches. As he got out of his car at the airport, he brushed away the slivers of glass and said, "I was lucky. This time it was close. Those gentlemen are poor shots."

De Gaulle expertly staged all his public appearances. His twice-a-year meetings with the press were more like audiences than conferences. Held in the Élysée Palace's Hall of Festivals, with its grand pendant crystal chandeliers and its gilded and painted ceiling, they were events in themselves and attracted about a thousand journalists.

During one of my visits to Paris in the mid-1960s, I watched a de Gaulle press conference on television in Ambassador Bohlen's office. On cue two men in white ties and tails parted the red velvet curtains behind the stage, and everyone stood for de Gaulle's entrance. He took his place behind the microphone, flanked by all his ministers, and motioned for everyone to sit down. He spoke for about twenty minutes on the single subject he had chosen. He then answered no more than three questions and adjourned the session.

We knew he had written the script for the encounter all the way down to the questions, which his press officer had planted beforehand with certain reporters and for which he had memorized answers. But even though we knew it was staged, it had an almost hypnotic effect. As de Gaulle concluded, Bohlen, who usually spoke disparagingly of the French President, just shook his head and exclaimed, "What a stunning performance."

He took no less care with other public functions. During the state dinner de Gaulle gave for our visiting delegation in 1969, he delivered an eloquent toast that seemed to be improvised, because he had no text before him. After the affair had concluded, one of my aides complimented de Gaulle on his ability to speak at length without notes. De Gaulle replied, "I write it down, commit it to memory, then throw the paper away. Churchill used to do the same thing, but he never admitted it."

Though he was a master of histrionics, de Gaulle never used this talent when presenting his case in meetings with me. I never knew him to raise his voice. He never tried to get his points across by bluff or bravado. If he disagreed, he would ignore the point rather than pretend to agree. When he felt something rather deeply, he would gesture somewhat emphatically but gracefully. He thought with pristine clarity, and his speech in public and in private reflected this. He never talked or thought sloppily. He might not arrive at the correct conclusions, but he had the rare ability to think things all the way through and then to express his views with a very compelling, persuasive logic.

In this age of blow-drier–and–hair-spray media politicians, it is useful to recall that de Gaulle was the first consummate media figure. Charles de Gaulle created General de Gaulle on the radio. Many leaders have expertly used the electronic media, but it is de Gaulle's distinction to have been a pioneer, the airwaves his only forum as he rallied the people of France to his cause. It was by radio from London that de Gaulle, in the dark days of World War II, became a part of the legend of France.

Returning to power in the late 1950s, de Gaulle entered just as television was becoming the preeminent medium. He recognized the dazzling possibilities it offered. As he later put it, "Here, suddenly, was an unprecedented means of being present everywhere." He knew that he would have to adapt his style to succeed on television. He had always read his radio addresses from a script. "But now the televiewers could see de Gaulle on the screen while listening to him over the air," he wrote. "In order to remain faithful to my image, I would have to address them as though we were face to face, without paper and without spectacles. . . . This septuagenarian, sitting alone behind a table under relentless lights, had to appear animated and spontaneous enough to seize and hold attention, without compromising himself by excessive gestures and misplaced grimaces."

His delivery was masterly. The combination of his deep, serene voice and his calm, self-assured manner gave him a distinctly paternal appearance. He used the French language with the same grandeur and eloquence with which Churchill used English. It was a classical, almost archaic French. Yet he spoke so articulately and with such precision that his message seemed to resonate apart from his words. I think someone who had not even studied the language could get the sense of what he was saying.

In an instance of theatrical brilliance, he donned his general's uniform for his televised address to the nation when the colonists and the generals in Algeria were challenging his authority. Many American critics scoffed at the gesture and dismissed it as a bit of corny melodrama. They could not understand that, by presenting himself in his general's uniform, de Gaulle touched a deep, emotional chord in all Frenchmen and forged a unity among them that exists only in the worst of times in the hope for better times.

But it was not just through symbolism or oratory or dramatics that Charles de Gaulle created the personage of General de Gaulle. It was the whole occasion of his public appearance—the buildup, the setting, the elaborate staging, the precision with which he crafted his often deliberate ambiguities, winning support from disparate groups with statements that could be read in different ways by those with different interests. General de Gaulle was a facade, but not a false one. Behind it was a man of incandescent intellect and phenomenal discipline. The facade was like the ornamentation on a great cathedral, rather than the flimsy pretense of a Hollywood prop with nothing behind it.

Mystery can intrigue, but it cannot attract. For this a leader needs what de Gaulle called character. Most people think of character as moral strength and fortitude. But de Gaulle defined character in a leader as the fervent desire and inner power to exert one's will. As he put it, "The setting up of one man over his fellows can be justified only if he can bring to the common task the drive and certainty which comes of character."

De Gaulle wrote that, when confronted by the challenge of events, the leader with character turns inward and relies only on himself. The leader with this "passion for self-reliance" finds an "especial attractiveness in difficulty" because only by coming to grips with difficulty can he test and expand his limits. He does not cower at the moment of decision, but takes the initiative with a daring to meet the moment.

The leader with character brings order to the collective effort, he wrote. The "stuffed dummies of the hierarchy"—soldiers and ministers obsessed with safeguarding their ranks and portfolios—can never command the confidence and enthusiasm of others, for "they are parasites who take everything and give nothing in return, weak-kneed creatures forever trembling in their shoes, jumping jacks who will turn their coats without scruple at the first opportunity."

Only leaders who prove their worth in action, who confront and overcome difficulty, and who "stake their all upon the throw" can win the crowd, he went on. "Characters of this temper radiate a sort of magnetic force. For those who follow them they are the symbol of the end to be achieved, and the very incarnation of hope."

The man of character does not seek above all to please his superiors, but rather aims to be true to himself. The abrasiveness of his personality and the brazenness of his actions make him unpopular with superiors who do not realize that they need men with strong wills underneath them. He may have been subconsciously describing himself when he wrote, "The best servants of the State, whether soldiers or politicians, are seldom the most pliable of men. Masters must have the minds and nerves of masters, and it is the worst of policies to exclude men of strong character from office for no better reason than that they are difficult. Easy relationships are all very well when things are going smoothly, but in times of crisis they may well lead to disaster."

De Gaulle often counseled other leaders on the need for strength, self-reliance, and, above all, independence. To the Shah of Iran, who had great respect for de Gaulle, he said, "I have only one suggestion to offer you, but it is important: Put all your energy into remaining independent." In 1961 he advised President Kennedy to adopt the principle that had always guided his own conduct: "Listen only to yourself!" As we rode into Paris from the airport in 1969, he turned to me, put his hand on mine, and said, "You look young and vigorous and in command. This is very important. Stay that way."

De Gaulle's wartime leadership epitomized his idea of character. He displayed extraordinary zeal when the difficult tasks of World War II were before him. In this regard, de Gaulle was similar to Mao. Both seemed to take on new life when faced with great trials. The difference, however, was that Mao upset order to bring about struggle and de Gaulle struggled to bring about order.

As Zhou and I were driving to the Peking airport, Zhou spoke of a poem Mao had written upon returning to his hometown after thirty-two years. He said it illustrated the fact that adversity is a great teacher. I agreed and pointed out that an election loss was really more painful than a wound in war. The latter wounds the body; the former wounds the spirit. But the election loss helps to develop the strength and character that are essential for future battles. I mentioned that the twelve years de Gaulle spent out of power helped to build his character. Zhou concurred and added that men who travel on a smooth road all their lives do not develop strength. A great leader develops strength by swimming against the tide, not with it.

Some political leaders never encounter adversity; others never overcome it. A few build upon it. De Gaulle was one of those few. He was no stranger to adversity. In World War I he was injured so severely that he was left for dead on the battlefield, only to be captured and imprisoned for most of the war. In World War II he fought to restore the honor of France against the longest odds and was discarded by the nation soon after its victory. Yet twelve years later he came back into power.

When de Gaulle retired from politics, he went "into the wilderness." Most politicians, having once tasted power, cannot bear to be away from it. Many senators and congressmen are reluctant to return to their home states after defeat or retirement. They prefer to stay in Washington, on the fringes of power. De Gaulle never forgot the land from which he came; he always returned to it and drew his strength from it.

The town of Colombey-les-Deux-Églises was de Gaulle's sanctuary— "the wilderness," both figuratively and literally. Situated on the edge of the Plateau de Langes in the Champagne region of France, Colombey is 120 miles southeast of Paris. With its population of 350, it did not appear on most road maps. De Gaulle's fourteen-room house, La Boisserie, a white stone building with a brown tile roof and a hexagonal tower at one end, was obscured by trees and shrubbery from the view of passersby. Isolated in this country manor in this tiny village, de Gaulle could have chosen no better setting to enhance his mystery.

In Colombey, de Gaulle found that, if it could be lonely at the top, it could be even lonelier elsewhere. But there was no remorse. "In the tumult of men and events," he wrote, "solitude was my temptation; now it is my friend. What other satisfaction can be sought once you have confronted history?"

Both Churchill and de Gaulle fell from leadership after World War II, despite their brilliant wartime contributions. They tried to recapture power in very different ways, however. The defeat of the RPF had taught de Gaulle that in politics the shortest distance between two points is rarely a straight line. After he announced his retirement from politics at a press conference in 1955, he took a detached, magisterial course, making almost no effort to keep himself in the public eye. He was a great actor and, like most great actors, knew when to get off the stage.

He was also a master politician. His intuition told him that high office must be courted like a woman. He followed the prescription of the French proverb "Pursue the woman and she will flee; retreat and she will follow." Like Eisenhower, he intuitively knew that sometimes the best way to get power is to appear not to seek it. But waiting on the sidelines was not in Churchill's nature. Churchill continued to lead the loyal opposition in Parliament, and there was never a moment when he was not openly working every possible angle to recapture power. Both men succeeded in returning to office, though by different means.

In American politics I always advise those aspiring to high office that ambition in the heart is one thing, but ambition on the sleeve is another. The first is a necessary and proper characteristic for a leader; the second is an unattractive and repelling one.

De Gaulle left the provincial simplicity of Colombey once a week for appointments at his Paris office on the rue de Solferino. While the men of the Fourth Republic rejected de Gaulle as a leader, many eagerly came to solicit his political advice. But often they left believing that he had learned more from their talks than they had. Through these meetings de Gaulle became perhaps the most knowledgeable man in France on the workings and failures of the Fourth Republic.

He also kept in touch with his fiercely dedicated supporters, who were even more loyal in defeat than they were in victory. They were a vitally important political asset for de Gaulle, providing him with a core of support that enabled him to seize the opportunity to return to power the moment it presented itself. When he was in office, they also gave him the strong, reliable support that is indispensable to a leader in periods of crisis.

Many of his followers were attracted more to the man than to his ideas. André Malraux, who was further left than de Gaulle politically, was so fascinated by de Gaulle's character that he became an almost abject supporter. As I escorted Malraux to his car after a White House dinner in his honor shortly before my first trip to China, he spoke worshipfully of de Gaulle. "I am not de Gaulle—no one is de Gaulle," he said. "But if de Gaulle were here, I know what he would say: 'All men who understand what you are embarking upon salute you!'"

Cults of personality usually die with the man. It is a tribute to de Gaulle that Gaullism did not. Even now Gaullists play an important, if diminishingly powerful, role in French political life. During his years in Colombey de Gaulle often met with these disciples and nurtured the flame of their loyalty.

Most importantly, de Gaulle grew in wisdom during his time in political exile. Adenauer told a reporter that those years in Colombey "had done him immense good and now he is the ablest statesman in the West." Great leaders almost always learn more from their mistakes than they do from their successes. De Gaulle critically reexamined his actions when he wrote his three-volume *Mémoires de Guerre*. In discussing his actions, he often reappraised them by examining alternative courses he might have taken. The detached perspective that such reevaluation and self-criticism requires is rare among political leaders, but is imperative for one trying to wage a comeback.

"Writing the memoirs made him a political tactician," noted one of de Gaulle's associates. This was most evident shortly after he became Premier in 1958. He requested that the assembly grant him special powers to handle the country's crises. The old de Gaulle would have demanded that the assembly grant him these powers and threatened to resign if it balked. The new de Gaulle understood the value of stroking. The political mechanic in him realized that the machine would run more smoothly if he oiled it.

He showered the parliamentarians with pleasantries when he came to the chamber. He courted his adversaries by chatting amiably with them during recesses. He reassured them by saying that all of his actions would be calculated "to make the republic stronger, healthier, more effective, indestructible." And he charmed them by saying, "I want you all to know how much I feel the honor and the pleasure of this occasion to be here among you tonight." On hearing this, the parliamentarians who had tried so hard to prevent his return looked agape, burst into applause—and granted de Gaulle the powers he requested.

De Gaulle could also perceptively analyze American politics. During his visit in 1960, de Gaulle showed great interest in the approaching presidential campaign. He was careful not to appear to take sides, but he did offer some shrewd advice. He told me that he knew that as Vice President I would and should run on the record of the Eisenhower administration, but that this would make it difficult for me to take the position that he felt the times demanded. He said very emphatically, "You must campaign for a 'New America.'" Of course, I could not do this because I would have appeared to be criticizing the administration of which I was a part. But the advice was sound. Kennedy did run on the "New America" theme, and he won.

After my defeat in the election for governor of California in 1962, my family and I took a trip to Europe and stopped in Paris for a few days. Much to my surprise, and even more to the surprise of Ambassador

Bohlen, de Gaulle invited Mrs. Nixon and me to have lunch at the Élysée and asked Bohlen to join us as well.

After my two electoral defeats, neither I nor any American political expert believed I had a political future. Consequently de Gaulle's invitation seemed to be a very gracious and generous gesture. In his informal luncheon toast de Gaulle said that when he first met me three years earlier, he had intuited that I would play a greater role in American leadership. He stated that he stood by this view and that he saw a future role for me in "a top capacity."

It was a gracious compliment but also a sincere one. Throughout my presidency and my years in San Clemente, visiting French officials who had known de Gaulle never failed to remark to me that he had predicted I would be elected President years before it was even suggested in the American press.

During my years out of office de Gaulle received me on every trip I made to Paris, except when he was out of the city, even though he usually granted appointments only to those who were in power. I do not mean to suggest that these meetings indicate that de Gaulle had an extraordinary personal admiration for me, though I believe that our respect was mutual and that it grew over the years. He was a shrewd observer of American politics and global affairs. I think he probably surveyed the American political scene and did not see many leaders who had much of an understanding of world politics. He also probably thought that the times would require a leader who had such an understanding and that I therefore might find an opportunity to return to power. Thus, our meetings were a chance for him to cultivate a friendship with and to get his views across to a possible future leader of his most important ally.

Also, I think that he empathized with me because he saw me as another who knew what it was to be "in the wilderness."

The adversity of de Gaulle's defeats helped build the character that attracted his fiercely loyal followers. But de Gaulle wrote that a man of character also needs grandeur to be an effective leader. "He must aim high, show that he has vision, act on the grand scale, and so establish his authority over the generality of men who splash in shallow water." If he is content with the commonplace, he will be regarded as a good servant, but "never as a master who can draw to himself the faith and dreams of mankind."

De Gaulle's cause was France. Nothing inspired him more than the symbols of French glory, and nothing saddened him more than French weaknesses and failures.

"All my life I have thought of France in a certain way," de Gaulle proclaimed in the opening line of his wartime memoirs. In the stirring paragraph that follows, he elucidated a fascinating view not of the French nation-state but rather of the French nation-soul. His emotional side, he wrote, tended to envision France as a country fated either for great success or exemplary misfortunes. "If, in spite of this, mediocrity shows in her acts and deeds, it strikes me as an absurd anomaly, to be imputed to the faults of Frenchmen, not to the genius of the land." His rational side contended that France was really not herself "unless in the front rank." Only a grand national ambition that put France in the forefront of history could counterbalance the natural disunity of the French people. "In short, to my mind, France cannot be France without greatness."

"When leaders fail," de Gaulle explained to U.S. Admiral Harold Stark in 1942, "new leaders are projected upward out of the spirit of eternal France, from Charlemagne to Joan of Arc to Napoleon, Poincaré, and Clemenceau." He then added, "Perhaps this time I am one of those thrust into leadership by the failure of others." There was really never any doubt that de Gaulle considered himself the next in the long line of saviors in France. His armies marched under the flag of the Cross of Lorraine, under which Joan of Arc rallied the French centuries before. When he once said that "it was for me to assume the burden of France" after the capitulation of the Third Republic, he meant that through his decision to continue the resistance he had become the personification of France in the eyes of the French.

The inability of the Allies to comprehend this fact led to much of their antagonism toward de Gaulle during World War II. Once, when Churchill tried to get him to adjust his approach to some small matter, de Gaulle sternly refused and said, "Mr. Prime Minister, now that at last you have Joan of Arc on your side, you are still determined to burn her." President Roosevelt was incapable of understanding de Gaulle's motivations and continually joked with friends that de Gaulle thought he was Joan of Arc. Though Churchill had great sympathy and respect for de Gaulle, the British Prime Minister was often exasperated by the French leader's intransigence. In one such moment, Churchill topped Roosevelt's jibes by saying, "Yes, de Gaulle does think he is Joan of Arc, but my bloody bishops won't let me burn him."

Eisenhower, on the other hand, genuinely admired de Gaulle both as a military and political leader. He deplored the negative bias many U.S. foreign service officers had against de Gaulle and welcomed his return to power in 1958. He told me emphatically that while de Gaulle could be difficult, France would not have survived as a free country had it not been for his leadership. Years later I went out to see Eisenhower in Walter Reed Hospital before my 1969 state visit to France. At seventy-eight he was bedridden, with only a few weeks left to live. But his mind was alert and his memory keen. He said reflectively, "We did not treat de Gaulle with enough sensitivity during the war."

As President, Eisenhower treated de Gaulle with great respect, and what Eisenhower gave in common courtesy de Gaulle returned in friendship. The alarming deterioration of Franco-American relations during the 1960s was due in large part to the failure of American policymakers to recognize the simple truth that respectful sensitivity and good manners are a small price to pay for good relations between nations.

De Gaulle's greatest fear was that France would suffer the fate of those nations that once made history and now only observe it. In my arrival remarks on my state visit to Paris in 1969, I recalled Benjamin Franklin's comment that everyone is a citizen of two countries, his own and France. If one stops to consider the many contributions France has made to modern civilization in art, literature, philosophy, science, and government, the adage rings true. De Gaulle dedicated himself to making sure that it continued to do so.

The materialism of postwar Europe disturbed de Gaulle. He worried that the French were too preoccupied with their standard of living. "This is not a national ambition," he told a reporter. "In the meantime, other peoples are thinking less about their standard of living, are conquering the world, and are conquering it without even having to fight for it."

De Gaulle once commented to Eisenhower, "Unlike the British, we have not lost our taste for excellence." De Gaulle never lost that taste, but many of his people had. He often complained that the French people were the greatest obstacle in his quest for French grandeur. He strove to lead them to "the heights," but often they did not follow. In 1969 they did not respond to a televised appeal in which de Gaulle called for an end to the civil disturbances that were sweeping France. Disgusted, de Gaulle told his aides, "The French are cattle, just cattle."

It might seem strange that a man so dedicated to France as a nation could have such contempt for the French as people. Yet France, to de

Gaulle, was more than the sum of its people. His vision was an idealized vision, which he held out to the nation to try to raise and exalt its spirit. The people were simply people—mundane, imperfect, their eyes not on that crest beyond the horizon but on the ground beneath their feet.

It was imperative in his mind that France be in the front rank of nations, in the advance guard of history. His efforts to design a grand national ambition for France were unsuccessful. He toyed with the idea of forging a philosophical compromise between capitalism and communism in France, but the French as a whole were not interested. His efforts to bolster the national pride, however, were largely successful. He insisted that France develop its own atomic weapons and nuclear force. And when American administrations in the 1960s neglected to consult with de Gaulle before taking diplomatic actions, he withdrew France from the integrated command structure of NATO.

During my discussions with de Gaulle in 1967, his preoccupation with France's global role showed through both in the manner in which he conducted the talks and in the positions he took on major foreign policy issues. We met in his office in the Élysée Palace with only his translator present. I could tell that de Gaulle had a substantial understanding of English, though he never spoke it. I had enough familiarity with French from college to notice that when our translator occasionally missed the nuances of his statements, de Gaulle would rephrase his thought in very precise language, emphasizing the ideas that were misinterpreted. With his passion for perfection, he probably did not want to speak imperfect English. But I also sensed that he used only French because he thought that it should be restored to its former position as the language of international diplomacy.

He also recognized that there was a tactical advantage to conducting his half of the conversation in French. By waiting for the translations of my statements and questions, he doubled the time he had to contemplate his responses. He obviously had this in mind because he listened just as carefully to my original statements as to the translations.

We met shortly after the Arab–Israeli war of 1967 had broken out. De Gaulle had called for a summit meeting to discuss the Middle East and other trouble spots. He told me during our meeting that he believed that the Russians were "embarrassed" by developments in the Middle East and might be amenable to a settlement that would be fair to both the Arabs and the Israelis.

I asked him if the Soviet policy of supporting Nasser's aggression throughout the Mideast did not raise doubts as to the sincerity of their desire for a fair settlement. He acknowledged that the Soviets had a policy of helping "socialist" countries such as Egypt and that they had constantly tried to exploit Mideast tensions in order to gain influence and leverage in the Arab world. But he emphasized that the Soviets had not completely rejected his proposed summit.

As it turned out, the Russians had no interest in meeting with the leaders of the West. I believe that de Gaulle's desperate desire for a greater international role for France caused this rare lapse in judgment. As President Giuseppe Saragat of Italy once remarked to me, "De Gaulle is an honest and good man, but he is like the woman who looks into the mirror and does not like what she sees."

De Gaulle could not bear the fact that France, with its great history as a world power, had only a fraction of the economic and military power of the United States. He did not want the United States and the Soviet Union to make all the critical foreign policy decisions without the consultation or involvement of France. He also believed that the long experience of the French in diplomacy enabled them to contribute toward better East-West relations in ways that the inexperienced and sometimes rash Americans could not.

While his judgment about the present was faulty in this instance, he was prophetic in his analysis of the future of the Middle East. Israel, he thought, would insist on very tough terms in exchange for returning the territories it occupied. He remarked that the Israelis were an extreme people, saying, "Look at their history as recorded in the Bible." He also pointed out that the Arabs were equally extreme. "Both," he observed, "always make demands for more than they are entitled to."

He said that the United States and other countries should join together in working for a peace based on reconciliation, not vengeance. He thought such a peace was in Israel's long-term interests. "Israel has won all the wars it has fought with the Arabs to date, and will win the next one," he said. "But in the end, they cannot survive in a sea of hate."

Unlike many western leaders at the time, de Gaulle put the blame for the Mideast crisis on both sides. As a result, some unfairly labeled him an anti-Semite. Bohlen, who often was critical of de Gaulle, disagreed. "The problem," he told me, "is that he feels that the Jews are generally internationalists, and above all, he is a deep-down nationalist."

I concluded the conversation by saying that there was a need for greater consultation among the NATO powers in dealing with the Russians and that the United States should not rely exclusively on bilateral relations with the Soviet Union on major issues. With a slight smile he replied, "I will remember." And he did.

When I became President, de Gaulle and I closed the breach that had developed between France and the United States. Unlike some of my predecessors, I did not scorn de Gaulle's advice and counsel but welcomed it, for I knew I could profit greatly from his experience and wisdom in world affairs. I believe this change in attitude alone went a long way in improving the relations between our two countries.

The lessons on leadership that de Gaulle encapsuled in *The Edge of the Sword* were remarkably simple yet equally trenchant. If a leader has mystery, character, and grandeur, he can acquire prestige. If he can combine prestige with charisma, he can command authority. And if he can add prescience to authority, he, like de Gaulle, can become one of those few leaders who make a difference in history.

But the aloofness of mystery, the self-reliance of character, and the detachment of grandeur carry a heavy price. De Gaulle wrote that a leader must choose between prominence and happiness because greatness and a "vague sense of melancholy" are indivisible. "Contentment and tranquility and the simple joys which go by the name of happiness are denied to those who fill positions of great power." A leader must endure strict self-discipline, constant risk taking, and perpetual inner struggle.

De Gaulle wanted to revive his nation's grandeur and was willing to pay the personal price for it. His drawn face, with lines etched by age and events, gave him the leader's melancholy aura. His lips were pressed together in a sort of permanent frown. When he did smile, they straightened out, but never seemed to curl upward. His deep-set, icy blue eyes, with dark circles beneath them, seemed to radiate a certain sadness. His left eye, cast ever so slightly outward, could give one the impression that he was a hopeless romantic who could see his vision but who would never see it realized.

To maintain his personal aloofness, de Gaulle felt he had to shun the friendship of his colleagues. None of them ever addressed him with anything less formal than *"Mon Général."* One biographer even argued that de Gaulle purposely transferred away any aides who had worked with him for a long time in order to reduce the risk that they would become too familiar with him.

But no man could maintain this dour, austere manner at all times. The "human" side of de Gaulle occasionally crept to the surface. For instance he had great respect for the traditional values of family life. He knew by memory the names of the wives and children of the members of his staff and asked about them often.

At times sharp bursts of typically sardonic French humor lighted up his usually serious demeanor. On one occasion during his presidency, an aide was trying to get through the tangle that is the Paris telephone system. Giving up in frustration, he slammed down the receiver and exclaimed, "Death to all fools!" De Gaulle, who had come into the room without his aide noticing, remarked, "Ah, what a vast program, my friend!"

Gerald Van der Kemp, the distinguished curator of Versailles, told me of another example. When de Gaulle was taking an inspection tour of the refurbished guest quarters for state visitors in the Grand Trianon Palace, someone remarked that Napoleon's bathtub might be too small for President Johnson. De Gaulle shot back, "Perhaps, but it would be just about right for Nixon."

De Gaulle wrote that a leader cannot enjoy the simple pleasures of friendship, but in social settings he proved himself wrong. He was the very essence of courtesy. At official dinners he did not dominate the conversation, but tried to bring everybody into it, including Mrs. Nixon and Mrs. de Gaulle. I had known, of course, that he had been a great officer, but after seeing him at close hand, I knew that he was a great gentleman as well.

Many leaders are so wrapped up in the affairs of state or are so obsessed with themselves that they do not talk with or show any interest in their dinner partners. But this was not the case with de Gaulle. At the dinner we gave in his honor in 1960, Mrs. Nixon had gone to a great deal of trouble to arrange a beautiful floral display—orchids surrounding a fountain in the center of a horseshoe-shaped table. De Gaulle noticed it and commented graciously about how much time it takes for a hostess to plan and to make arrangements for an official dinner. Mrs. Nixon later pointed out that most visiting dignitaries either would not have noticed or would not have bothered to compliment the hostess for it. "The mark of a true gentleman," she observed, "is that he thinks and talks about others and not just himself."

These incidents of public warmth were the exceptions that punctuated a career characterized by frosty dignity. De Gaulle reserved his emotions for his family, and he managed remarkably well one of the most wrenching challenges a leader faces: the conflict between duty to his family and duty to his job. For those who make their way to the top, the family usually comes out second best in this competition—not because the leader loves them less, but because he knows that millions of other families depend on his decisions. Because of the long hours he has to give to his work, because of the uncertain schedules with which he must live, his family often feels neglected. Life under the relentless scrutiny of the cameras, the trailing hordes of reporters, and the ubiquitous gossipmongers is difficult at best, and the family called on to put up with these intrusions needs the father's support more rather than less. Yet usually he has less time to give.

De Gaulle compartmentalized his life, keeping work and family separate. In the Élysée his office was only a few steps across a hall from his residence, but it might as well have been across the continent, because the two were entirely different worlds. His aides knew that de Gaulle was almost completely inaccessible after he left his office at the end of the day. No one was to call him unless there was an emergency. His time with his family was his own and their own. Equally, when he was attending to affairs of state, his family did not intrude and did not expect to be consulted. But with this separation he struck a balance that few are able to—neither job nor family came second. Each was first in its own sphere.

On a typical evening he returned to the residential quarters of the Élysée at about eight o'clock. After watching the televised news and eating a quiet dinner, he would relax with his family over books, music, or conversation. The de Gaulles were not enthusiasts of any sports. Like Adenauer and de Gasperi, de Gaulle's only exercise was walking. The family was devoutly Catholic and never missed Sunday mass.

As the patriarch of the family, de Gaulle enjoyed gathering together his children and grandchildren for weekends at La Boisserie. The whole clan was always very supportive of de Gaulle and his policies.

Family support is always very important for a leader. One who rigorously separates his public and private lives and maintains an austere and distant public persona has an even greater need than others do for a warm, supportive family. He needs a place where he can relax, among those few whom he knows he can trust beyond question, where he can drop the public mask and be his private self. A General de Gaulle needs a place where the private Charles de Gaulle can live. Without cronies, he needs his family more. As de Gaulle wrote in his memoirs, "This family harmony was precious to me."

De Gaulle's wife, Yvonne, ranks very high among the first ladies in the world. She played the role very differently from such first ladies as Madame Chiang and Eleanor Roosevelt, who were public figures in their own right. Mme. de Gaulle did not seek publicity, but instead tried to avoid it. Many among the Paris elite resented her refusal to wear the latest fashions and bask in the limelight. But she remained steadfast.

She at once complemented and deferred to de Gaulle as a great pia-

nist does when he accompanies a great singer. The pianist must subli-
mate his role to that of the singer. And the greatness of the pianist is
measured not by what one remembers about how he played, but by
what one remembers about how the singer performed. Similarly Mme.
de Gaulle saw her role as solely that of making him look good, rather
than being obsessed about making herself look good.

Yvonne de Gaulle was no glamorous showboat, but she was every
inch a lady. She always dressed like a lady, acted like a lady, and
thought like a lady. From my conversations with her I could tell that her
mission in life was to make a happy home for her husband and her children. She summed up her attitude when she told me with simple eloquence: "The presidency is temporary, but the family is permanent."
She provided de Gaulle with the simple, private home life that he appreciated so much. I could tell that he had deep affection and respect
for her. As a family friend once said, "Few people realize how much the
General depends on Yvonne. She has sustained him all these years."

The de Gaulles had three children: Philippe, Elizabeth, and Anne.
One cannot always judge a leader by his family, but one can in de
Gaulle's case. If a leader's children turn out badly, it is often a result of
their inability to cope with the strains of life in the political fishbowl. If
they turn out well, it is usually because their upbringing imbued them
with the values that animated the leader's public life. De Gaulle's wife
and children reflected his old-world gallantry, his Christian values, his
great respect for women, and his love for family life. His family was one
of his most impressive legacies.

Philippe de Gaulle, who bears a striking resemblance to his father,
fought bravely with the Fighting French in World War II. He is now an
admiral in the French navy. When I met with him in Paris in 1980, he
escorted me through the quarters that his father occupied during the
years out of power. The simplicity of the general's private office impressed me. There were no ornate pieces of furniture or elegant paintings, just some rickety tables and chairs, a beat-up typewriter, and a few
mementos. I have noted through the years that great leaders do not try
to impress their visitors with huge offices. Whether it is a leader in government, business, or the professions, more often the rule is: The smaller the man, the bigger the office he insists on.

Admiral de Gaulle told me that public office did not interest him. He
said his only aspirations were to serve his country as a naval officer and
to do nothing that would be unworthy of the memory of "the General."
De Gaulle's daughter Elizabeth married an army officer and embodies
the simple grace that was the mark of her mother.

In one of my conversations with Mme. de Gaulle, she spoke movingly of the difficulties that people in public life have in raising children and giving them a normal life. Though she did not refer to it at the time, I had the feeling that she was thinking about what they had gone through with their third child, Anne, who was born retarded and died at the age of nineteen. Mrs. Nixon recalls that Mme. de Gaulle showed no interest in attending fashionable parties or seeing historical sites during her visit to Washington: She only wanted to visit children's hospitals and homes to see how they cared for the retarded.

If there was ever really any question whether de Gaulle lacked the full quota of human emotions, the sad story of Anne's life and death surely dispels it.

Yvonne de Gaulle was struck by a car shortly before the birth of her third child. She was uninjured, but may have gone into shock. When she gave birth to Anne, the doctors told the de Gaulles that their daughter was retarded and would probably never be able to speak. They went into despair. Mme. de Gaulle once wrote in a letter to a friend, "Charles and I would give anything, health, all our money, advancement, career, if only Anne could be an ordinary little girl like the rest." They loved Anne deeply and would not part with her. When it was suggested that they put her in a home, de Gaulle replied, "She did not ask to come into the world. We shall do everything to make her happy."

During her brief life, de Gaulle was the only person who could make Anne laugh. He shed all his austere dignity when he was with her. A neighbor in Colombey recalled that de Gaulle "walked with her hand-in-hand around the property, caressing her and talking quietly about the things she understood." According to biographer Jean-Raymond Tournoux, he would dance little jigs with her, do short pantomimes for her, and sing popular songs to her. He even let her play with his military cap, the very sight of which brought a gleam into her eyes. In her happiness she made almost articulate sounds and laughed like all the other children. "Then," as Tournoux wrote, "tired but happy, she would go off to sleep, with her hand in her father's."

The de Gaulles fiercely protected Anne from curiosity seekers and the press. During the wartime years in Britain, he forbade photographers from including any of his children in the publicity shots at his country house because he knew that the presence or the absence of Anne would be sure to elicit comment. Other children teased her because she was different, and her pain was compounded because she did not understand why she was different.

The de Gaulles feared that there would be no one to protect Anne after they died. Therefore they established a trust that would guarantee that Anne received proper care. Using their own meager financial resources, they bought a castle on some wooded land near Milon-la-Champelle. Nuns of the order of Saint Jacut agreed to staff the home, and it opened in 1946. De Gaulle later pledged a large portion of the royalties from his memoirs to maintain the solvency of the Anne de Gaulle Foundation.

In 1947, shortly before her twentieth birthday, Anne died of pneumonia. At the conclusion of a brief private service at the graveside in Colombey's humble cemetery, de Gaulle and Yvonne stood silently with tears in their eyes. After a few moments he took her hand and said, "Come, now she is like the others."

Seldom has history seen a leader whose personality combined all the admirable qualities that de Gaulle's did. He could be both human and superhuman. I had the honor of welcoming him to the United States in 1960 and the privilege of being invited frequently to the Élysée during my years out of office. But my most memorable meetings with de Gaulle were our last ones, when we came together as Presidents of our respective countries.

On February 28, 1969, *Air Force One* landed at Orly Airport, the next-to-last stop in my first trip abroad as President. I shall never forget the splendor of the arrival ceremony—the huge red carpet, the magnificent honor guard, the newly refurbished reception marquee. De Gaulle seemed to tower over it all as he stood at the bottom of the ramp, hatless and coatless in the freezing weather.

At first I thought he might have laid on such an impressive welcome because of the importance of the country I represented. But Vernon Walters had told me that de Gaulle insisted on providing equally splendid receptions for heads of state from smaller countries as well. His policy of treating the leaders of smaller countries with the same respect that he extended to leaders of major countries probably stemmed from the resentment he felt over the demeaning treatment he received from the Allies in World War II. The policy also was very shrewd, for it helped increase France's influence in Africa and Latin America. Diplomatic slights and lapses in protocol, whether intentional or accidental, have a far greater effect on leaders of minor powers than on leaders of major ones.

The magnificent state dinner at the Élysée and the superb luncheon at Versailles were constant reminders of the glory that was and is France. But the highlight of the visit was the ten hours of one-on-one talks we had in which he expressed his views not just on Franco-American issues but on the world scene as well. The scope of our conversation was as vast as the acres of formal gardens we could see from our meeting place in the Grand Trianon Palace. With a sweeping yet graceful gesture he said, "Louis XIV ruled Europe from this room." In the grandeur of Versailles, de Gaulle looked completely at home. He did not try to put on airs, but an aura of majesty seemed to envelop him.

During our meetings, his performance—and I do not use that word disparagingly—was breathtaking. At times eloquent, at other times coldly pragmatic, and at all times articulate—like MacArthur—he was not always right, but he was always certain.

The first subject we discussed was western policy toward the Soviet Union. Some of de Gaulle's detractors had labeled him a rigid, right-wing ideologue, but he was coldly pragmatic in urging a policy of détente with the Russians. While he knew that the Soviet threat was the central fact of life for postwar Europe, he believed that the Soviets were willing to improve relations. He explained that their traditional fear of Germany was now compounded by an obsession with China. He said, "They are thinking in terms of a possible clash with China, and they know they can't fight the West at the same time. Thus I believe they may end up opting for a policy of rapprochement with the West.

"As far as the West is concerned," he continued, "what choice do we have? Unless you are prepared to go to war or break down the Berlin Wall, then there is no alternative policy that is acceptable. To work toward détente is a matter of good sense: If you are not ready to make war, make peace."

We then turned to the problem that has plagued the Atlantic alliance from its inception and is still a burning issue today. "If the Russians made a move," I asked, "do you think they believe the United States would react with strategic weapons? And do the Europeans have confidence that we would move in answer to a Soviet attack, or a threat of an attack, by massive conventional ground forces?"

After my questions were translated, he seemed to wait for over a minute before answering. Then he replied with carefully measured words: "I can only answer for the French. We believe that the Russians know that the United States would not allow them to conquer Europe. But we also believe that, if the Russians marched, you would not use nuclear weapons right away, since it would imply a total effort to kill everyone on the other side." If both the Russians and the United States were to use tactical weapons, he went on, "Europe would be destroyed. Western Europe and the United Kingdom would be destroyed by Soviet tactical weapons, and East Germany, Poland, Czechoslovakia, and Hungary would be destroyed by American tactical weapons. The situation in Europe would indeed be tragic. Meanwhile the United States and the Soviet Union would not be harmed."

With that thought de Gaulle apparently considered the subject closed. But the next day he subtly returned to it. We began talking about the disastrous effects of World War II on the great nations of Europe. He compressed volumes of history in a single sentence when he said, "In the Second World War, all the nations of Europe lost; two were defeated." About a year before de Gaulle died, he remarked to Malraux, "Stalin said only one serious thing to me: 'In the end death is the only winner.' " Reflecting on these two comments, I believe that in our meeting de Gaulle was telling me that if there were a nuclear war, there would be no winners, only losers. In his view the only rational East-West policy was one that combines deterrence with détente.

When I asked him about the Communist Chinese, he said he had "no illusions about their ideology," but urged that the United States should not "leave them isolated in their rage." He had expressed the same view to me in 1963, and his thinking paralleled my own. I told him that in pursuing talks with the Russians I might also want "to keep an anchor to windward with respect to China." I added, "In ten years, when China has made significant nuclear progress, we will have no choice. It is vital that we have more communications with them than we have today." De Gaulle agreed and put a clever rhetorical twist on it. "It would be better," he said, "for you to recognize China before you are obliged to do so by the growth of China."

De Gaulle had little use for the United Nations, which he once contemptuously described to me as *"le machin."* Churchill's attitude toward the U.N. was very similar to de Gaulle's. The British leader once told me, "No great nation can allow an issue involving its very survival to be decided by other nations." De Gaulle once told Eisenhower, "You are very much for the United Nations because you still control it, but with this 'flowering of independences,' which you and the Soviet Union are pushing for entirely different reasons, soon you will no longer control it." He went on to say that the Soviets supported anticolonial movements to create and exploit vacuums of power and the United States did likewise because it lived "under the illusion that George Washington was an Indian chief who drove out the British landlords."

With the world's two most powerful countries pressing for an end to colonial rule, he predicted to Eisenhower, "You will lose control of the United Nations to the developing countries and the city-states, who will inevitably be easily manipulated by the Soviet Union, but by that time you will have made such a golden calf out of the U.N. that, when the day comes that they order you to do something which is contrary to common sense and the interests of the United States, you will have no choice but to obey." Though an overstatement with regard to America's willingness to bow to the U.N., it was a prophetic analysis of the problems that would develop within the United Nations.

We spent a great deal of time discussing Vietnam in 1967 and 1969. In 1967 he advised me that as a presidential candidate I should advocate an early end to the war on the best possible terms. Unlike Adenauer, de Gaulle believed that the Soviet Union wanted to end the war in Indochina. He told me that in a meeting Kosygin had lamented the problems the war caused the Soviet Union. He said the Soviet leader smashed his fist into the palm of his other hand and said, "You don't know how much trouble this war in Southeast Asia causes in the Russian budget."

I believe that de Gaulle's usually keen judgment was faulty on this issue. He believed that one of the greatest responsibilities of a leader is to keep the economy sound, keep inflation down, and retain a sound currency; he seemed to think that the Soviet leaders would look at their problems in a similar way. I did not believe that was the case then, and I do not believe that is the case now. Budget problems do concern the leaders of the Soviet Union. But the pursuit of their expansionist goals takes precedence over domestic economic problems, for they can simply turn a deaf ear to the grumbling of their populace.

In my meetings with de Gaulle in 1969, he urged that the United States withdraw from Vietnam, but not precipitously—not "*en catastrophe*," as he put it. He recognized the political difficulties withdrawal would present for me. He contended that his "cruel" decision to withdraw from Algeria—"a part of France"—had been even more difficult, but added that it had been the only course open to him.

He believed the United States had to disencumber itself of Vietnam in order to negotiate successfully with the Soviets. To an extent de Gaulle was right: Our relations with the Soviets would have been much less complicated without the war in Vietnam. But whether a simple pullout would have improved the negotiating climate is another question. Shortly before the first Moscow summit in 1972, North Vietnam launched a massive assault in the south. Most experts advised that any strong American countermove would torpedo the summit. I rejected this advice and ordered the bombing of Hanoi and the mining of Haiphong Harbor. This was language the Russians understood, and far from torpedoing the summit, I am convinced that it increased their eagerness to go forward.

While I did not always agree with de Gaulle, I was always deeply impressed by him. During those three days of meetings, he spoke without a note in front of him and without advisers beside him. No leader I met could surpass his remarkable ability to discuss any subject or any part of the world with such competence, intelligence, and at times profound insight.

After our meeting in Paris in February 1969, I saw de Gaulle again a month later when he flew across the Atlantic to join in a last tribute to his friend and wartime ally Eisenhower, who had died on March 28. We met for an hour in the White House and discussed recent international developments.

De Gaulle again urged that I take steps to put an end to the Vietnam War as quickly as possible. On the other hand, he recognized that our withdrawal from Vietnam should not be precipitous, but rather should be orderly and planned. He was convinced that the power and prestige of the United States could be greatly increased and confidence in it throughout the world would be renewed once we brought the war to an end.

I told him of our plans to initiate a withdrawal program and said that we were already in secret contact with the North Vietnamese. I added that we believed that negotiations would succeed only if they were private. He said that the North Vietnamese had given the French an indication that they might be amenable to private negotiations to try to end the war. In retrospect I believe this meeting laid the groundwork for Kissinger's secret trips to Paris, which resulted four years later in the Paris Peace Agreement and the end of American involvement in Vietnam. Without the assistance of President Pompidou, de Gaulle's successor, and the French government, the negotiations could not have been carried to a successful conclusion.

De Gaulle was greatly concerned about a British-German agreement to produce enriched uranium by the ultracentrifuge process. I told him that I felt that Franco-German reconciliation was one of the greatest achievements of his presidency; many people had believed that it could not be done, but he had made it a reality.

He appreciated the compliment, but spoke with pragmatic candor about his decision to proceed with rapprochement and cooperation with Adenauer, despite the misgivings he had about the Germans generally. While he recognized the "tremendous vitality, drive, and capacity of the Germans" and that they had a certain "bonhomie," he had proceeded with the reconciliation cautiously because he felt that deep down the Germans had a driving ambition, which, when not constantly checked, had led to bitter experiences for France and other nations. For this reason the French were determined that the Germans should never possess their own nuclear weapons. He said he was concerned about the Anglo-German agreement because, when you "have enriched uranium and you are Germany, with all of its technical capacity, it is not a far step to the production of nuclear weapons." This the French could never accept, he added.

In light of developments today—thirteen years later—his views with regard to Soviet-American relations were particularly interesting. I expressed concern about the Soviet Union's tremendous ability to increase its military forces, especially its missile capacity and its naval strength. Yet we had received indications that the Soviets would have liked to lessen East-West tensions.

I told him that I was not personally acquainted with the rulers of the Kremlin and would appreciate his evaluation of them, particularly his view about reports that there might be a potential split between doves and hawks. He expressed the opinion that while the Soviet Union had "tremendous ambitions," the Kremlin leaders were not bent on conquest in the classical sense but instead wanted to make the Soviet Union unassailable and not inferior to any other nation, particularly the United States.

Podgorny, he said, was an "old man without the drive and ardor" of Brezhnev, who was in de Gaulle's view the undisputed master of the Kremlin. Kosygin, he said, was a skillful, hardworking man who had made a career in government and was more flexible than Brezhnev and who, according to information the French had received, had been much more temperate than his colleagues on the question of invading Czechoslovakia after the popular uprising in 1968.

He said that while the leaders might differ on issues like Czechoslovakia, which they considered a small matter, they were united on the big issues and particularly on building up the strength of the Soviet Union. He had found in his talks with them that they seemed to answer forthrightly and frankly and even with sincerity, but he realized that this was largely dissimulation. He concluded by saying that the "whole world is waiting for the U.S. President to make contact with them or for them to make contact with the U.S." When I asked him whether he thought such direct contacts could be useful, his reply was categorical: "Most assuredly so."

As I escorted him to his car after our meeting, he asked me to express his sympathy and respect to Mrs. Eisenhower. De Gaulle did not often display his emotions, but I could sense in the way he talked that his affection and respect for Eisenhower were deep and his sorrow over Eisenhower's death profound.

Our meeting on the occasion of Eisenhower's funeral was the last time that I was to see him. We had already begun preliminary plans for his state visit to Washington when he suddenly resigned the presidency on April 29, 1969, and went into retirement. He did not leave office because of a great issue, but because of what appeared to be a minor one: the defeat of his plebiscite involving senate and regional reforms. Malraux later asked him why he had resigned over such an "absurd" issue. His reply was what one would expect from General de Gaulle: "Because it *was* absurd."

De Gaulle, like Churchill and Adenauer, found it difficult to prepare and build up a successor. Churchill put down Eden; Adenauer put down Erhard; de Gaulle put down Pompidou. I rate Pompidou as one of the abler world leaders I have met. To follow one of the true greats is enormously difficult. Truman, at least in historical perspective, was not able to fill Roosevelt's shoes, but he made his mark in history in his own way. No one could fill de Gaulle's shoes, but Pompidou, one of the world's premier economic experts, was a worthy successor. What particularly impressed me about him was that in our discussions of foreign policy he always thought globally rather than parochially.

When de Gaulle resigned, I sent him a handwritten note in which I repeated my invitation for him to come to Washington and told him that "scores of our cities and states would be honored if you could include them on your schedule." I concluded by writing, "Putting it in blunt terms—in this age of mediocre leaders in most of the world—America's spirit needs your presence." Vernon Walters delivered my letter to de Gaulle at Colombey. De Gaulle read it and said, "He is a true comrade." He sat down at his desk and penned a handwritten reply that same day:

Dear Mr. President:

Your gracious official message and your very warm personal letter touched me deeply. Not only because you occupy the high office of President of the United States, but also because they are from you, Richard Nixon, and I have for you—with good reason—esteem, confidence, and friendship as great and as sincere as it is possible to have.

Perhaps one day I will have the occasion and the honor to see you again; in the meantime, I send you from the bottom of my heart all my best wishes for the successful accomplishment of your immense national and international task.

Would you please give Mrs. Nixon my most respectful regards, to which my wife adds her warm wishes. For you, my dear Mr. President, the assurance of my feeling of faithful and devoted friendship.

Charles de Gaulle

This letter was the last time I heard from de Gaulle. On November 9, 1970, he died, and I joined leaders throughout the world in flying to Paris to pay our final tribute.

During his lifetime Charles de Gaulle physically towered over those around him, but the strength he projected was an inner strength. The bulbous nose, the slight pudginess, the soft, slender hands, neither enhanced nor detracted from it. It was a strength that went beyond the physical—a discipline that extended itself beyond the man, a presence that commanded silence and invited deference.

De Gaulle spoke not of doubts but of certainties. He could sometimes be wrong, but even his mistakes became a force in history.

He wanted to renew the virtues of France's past, not enshrine them. He was, in Malraux's words, "a man of the day before yesterday and the day after tomorrow."

He was a modern-day cathedral builder. The cathedral he built was a concept, a perception—real and yet unreal, visible yet invisible, tangible yet intangible. It was *France:* not merely France in a geographical or political sense, but France in a spiritual sense. De Gaulle held out to Frenchmen a vision of France as it might become, and by telling them that this was France, he helped France to become more nearly the likeness of that vision.

Just as the ancient Chinese viewed China as the "Middle Kingdom"—the center of the world, beyond which all was merely peripheral—so de Gaulle saw France as a sort of middle kingdom. The rest of the world had meaning only as it affected France. He could be cold-eyed and farsighted in analyzing the affairs of the world, but his policies were solely those designed to advance or protect the interests of France.

He was France's interpreter, protector, prophet, conscience, goad, inspiration. In a certain sense, he was France. It was not a union. It was more a oneness. He embodied France; he represented the French not only to the world, but also to themselves.

De Gaulle did not particularly like Americans, as a people; for that matter, neither was he particularly fond of Frenchmen. But this was irrelevant. He loved his family and France, and what mattered in his relations with other nations was not whether he liked their people, but what they could do for or to France. He was a statesman, not a humanist.

Throughout his life de Gaulle was embroiled in often bitter controversy. But these conclusions are clear: Without de Gaulle, France might not have survived the tragedy of defeat in World War II. Without de Gaulle, France might not have recovered from the devastation of World War II. Without de Gaulle, the Franco-German rapprochement might not have been achieved. Without de Gaulle, France would not have adopted the constitution of the Fifth Republic and might have sunk into chaos politically, economically, and socially. And without de Gaulle, the spirit of France—which for centuries has inspired the world with its vibrancy, its élan, its radiance, its unique combination of distinctiveness and universality—might have died instead of being as vital and strong as it is today.

One of my most vivid memories of de Gaulle and his era was the scene in Notre-Dame as his memorial service drew to a close. The dignitaries from all over the world began filing out. Many came up to me to express their appreciation for my having come to the service as the representative of the American people. Then, just before I reached the exit, the cathedral's great organ began booming out the stirring strains of "The Marseillaise." I stopped, and turned back toward the altar with my hand over my heart. Just then another foreign guest, oblivious of the music, reached out to grab my hand in greeting, and what might have been a supremely dramatic moment was abruptly lost. I have often thought that nothing would more fittingly have captured the spirit of Charles de Gaulle than to have had that entire assemblage of leaders from all over the world turn together toward the altar and, as the organ played "The Marseillaise," fill the ancient cathedral with their voices, singing in unison the national anthem of France.

DOUGLAS
MacARTHUR
AND
SHIGERU
YOSHIDA

East Meets West

ON A SUNNY spring afternoon in 1951, a seventy-year-old Japanese gentleman was hosting his first flower-viewing party of the season. During the party, he was given the news that had just reached Tokyo from America: President Truman had fired General Douglas MacArthur from all of his posts, including his battle command in Korea and his position as Supreme Commander of the Allied Occupation in Japan. The host looked stricken and excused himself from the receiving line. He was so upset that it took him half an hour to pull himself together.

The gentleman—Shigeru Yoshida, Japan's hard-as-nails Prime Minister—knew this was no time for sentimentality. He had brought the hammer down on enough of his own opponents to realize that politics was a rough business. MacArthur and Truman had been locked in a titanic political struggle, and MacArthur had lost. Regardless of whether Truman was right or wrong, Japanese-American relations would continue to develop without the popular general. Yoshida had to be careful not to offend the President and thus cloud the prospects for the U.S.-Japan peace treaty, which he had sought since 1946.

Yet the statement Yoshida made in a broadcast to his nation was undiplomatically profuse in its praise for his departing friend. It also resonated with emotion, which was even more unlike Yoshida. "The accomplishments of General MacArthur in the interest of our country are one of the marvels of history," he said. "No wonder he is looked upon by all our people with the profoundest veneration and affection. I have no words to convey the regret of our nation to see him leave."

Yoshida's remarks were reported in the American press, but they were engulfed and soon forgotten in the din that followed the firing and that dogged MacArthur for the rest of his life. Three decades later most Americans, when they are reminded of MacArthur, think of Korea or of the brilliance of his military leadership in World War II. But his greatest legacy was pinpointed by Yoshida in the first moments after MacArthur's career ended. "It is he who has salvaged our nation from post-surrender confusion and prostration," Yoshida said of the man who was just then being keelhauled by his critics for brash trigger-happiness. "It is he who has firmly planted democracy in all segments of our society."

His own role in the rebuilding of Japan was just as important, but the Premier was being characteristically modest. In fact MacArthur and Yoshida—victor and vanquished, Occidental and Oriental, general and politician—had together executed the swiftest and most dramatic transformation of a major nation in the history of the modern world.

MacArthur was an American giant, a man of legendary stature who embodied all the contradictions and contrasts of a legend. He was a thoughtful intellectual and a swaggering, egotistical soldier, an authoritarian and a democrat, a gifted and powerful speaker given to flights of Churchillian rhetoric that inspired millions—and sent most liberals right up the wall.

Yoshida was Japan's temperamental and obstreperous leader in its darkest hour, a puckish, cigar-smoking former diplomat who helped his country snatch economic victory from the jaws of military defeat. Because of his intestinal fortitude, his sharp tongue, and his stout figure, and because he was raised to power at an age when most men have been retired for years, Yoshida has often been called the Churchill of Japan.

In 1945 MacArthur took control of a Japan beaten in body and spirit. Two million of its people, a third of them civilians, had died. Its factories were crushed. Foreign trade, the cornerstone of Japan's strength in the 1920s and 1930s, had ceased to exist. There were critical shortages of food. Even worse, the Japanese people had invested all of their faith and energy in a war they thought heaven would not let them lose. Their Emperor had told them to lay down their arms and, for the first time in Japan's history, endure the humiliation of surrender: Soon Emperor Hirohito would publicly renounce the myth of divinity in which emperors had wrapped themselves for centuries and which was the foundation of the Japanese religious system.

Rarely had military defeat left such a material and spiritual vacuum. Yet, nine years later, when Yoshida stepped down as Prime Minister, Japan was a flourishing, vibrant democracy that was in the process of building the second largest economy in the free world.

It is widely believed that all of this was MacArthur's doing, because it was during his proconsulship, from 1945 to 1951, that most of the social, economic, and political reforms that transformed Japan were undertaken. I knew both him and Yoshida well enough, and know enough of their lives, to say that Japan was remade by both men working together in an extraordinary partnership in which MacArthur was the lawgiver and Yoshida the executive. MacArthur's edicts were cast in the form of principle. Yoshida molded them to fit Japan. The result was the transformation in a few years of a nation from totalitarianism to democracy and of a ruined economy to one that has since proved itself among the strongest in the world.

For each it was an exercise in the unexpected. MacArthur's critics had pegged him as a pompous martinet. He turned out to be one of the most progressive military occupation commanders in all history—and one of the few who were successful. Yoshida took office as a caretaker and had no experience in running for office or running a government. He became one of the postwar period's best Prime Ministers and created a model of moderately conservative, probusiness government from which Japan has yet to deviate.

MacArthur cast a long shadow, and in many accounts of the Occupation Yoshida seems to slip into it. One reason for this is the difference in personality between the two men, which is clear enough in their own writing. MacArthur's _Reminiscences_ are dramatic and occasionally self-congratulatory; in them the Occupation appears to be almost a one-man operation—MacArthur's. His only reference to Yoshida, besides the quotation of laudatory messages from Yoshida to himself, is to Japan's "able" Prime Minister. In contrast Yoshida's *Memoirs* are disarmingly modest. In them, he seems reluctant to take credit for many of his accomplishments.

Between these two versions is the truth about the Occupation, which is that Japan was run for seven years by two governments that sometimes meshed and sometimes clashed. MacArthur operated by proclamation, Yoshida by sometimes unseen and unrecorded smaller actions. Each man was as important as the other, but Yoshida was hard to see in the glare of MacArthur's enormous power and towering personality.

To make matters worse, Yoshida's seven years in office are habitually described by many scholars in negative terms. Some brand him as a disgruntled old-style conservative who spitefully reversed MacArthur's labor, education, and police reforms as quickly as he could. Others say that Yoshida's revision of these reforms was actually the work of the Americans suddenly conscious of the need for a strong anti-Communist ally in the Far East.

Yoshida was in fact a careful politician, with basically liberal instincts, who was justifiably concerned that the flurry of reform initiated by the Americans was a matter of too much, too quickly. The Japanese, probably the least xenophobic people on earth, had a long tradition of "borrowing" from other cultures, but they were always careful to regulate new influences so they would enrich Japanese society rather than disrupt it. It was no different with the concepts imported by MacArthur. He created democratic institutions and expected the Japanese to become democrats. Yoshida knew it would take time for his people to appreciate both the benefits and the responsibilities that came with their new freedom. He also knew that everything that worked in the United States would not necessarily work in Japan.

The vastly different roles MacArthur and Yoshida played required men of vastly different temperaments. My own first encounters with them reflect their differences.

I first saw MacArthur in 1951, when I was a U.S. senator and heard his "Old soldiers never die" speech to a joint session of Congress. Awash in the drama of one of the great confrontations of modern political history, he was almost Olympian in stature. His presentation was hypnotically powerful. Time after time he was interrupted by prolonged applause. When he finished with his emotional farewell—"Old soldiers never die, they just fade away"—the congressmen and senators, many of them in tears, leaped to their feet and cheered wildly. It was probably the greatest ovation ever given to anyone, including Presidents, who had addressed a joint session of Congress. Bedlam reigned as MacArthur marched majestically down the aisle and out of the chamber. One member said that we had just heard the voice of God. Another pro-MacArthur senator joked to me later that the speech had left the Republicans with wet eyes and the Democrats with wet pants.

I first met Yoshida two years later in Tokyo. When he arrived a few moments late for our first meeting, he was holding a handkerchief over his mouth and nose. He apologized profusely and said he had been attending to a nosebleed—which resulted, he added with an embarrassed chuckle, from eating too much caviar the night before. I remember thinking that few leaders would have been down-to-earth enough to admit such a thing, especially when it would have been so easy to make up some excuse about the urgency of government business.

The impressions I received from these encounters were borne out by later ones. MacArthur was a hero, a presence, an event. Those who were invited to meet with him, as I was during his retirement years in New York, listened in deferential silence as he paced around the room, declaiming upon whatever subject happened to be on his mind at the moment. Yoshida was as human and accessible as MacArthur was remote. Sitting low in a chair, his roguish grin sometimes hidden in a cloud of cigar smoke, he reveled in the good-humored give-and-take of a well-informed conversation.

They had their similarities. Both were well-read intellectuals. Both were in their seventies when they exercised their greatest power. Victorians by birth, each carried himself in public with a certain old-world dignity and austerity. But MacArthur never softened his bearing. A one-time assistant said, "Even in reproof and rebuff, he kept the lofty manners of a gentleman." Yoshida, in contrast, could be refreshingly coarse when the moment demanded it, as when he called a Socialist in the Diet a "damned fool" or when he poured a pitcher of water over the head of an annoying photographer.

If I had had to guess from my first encounters with MacArthur and Yoshida which man was the lofty idealist and which was the stubborn pragmatist, I think I would have guessed right. As it turned out, postwar Japan needed both. Without MacArthur's vision, the necessary reforms might not have taken place. Without Yoshida's meticulous attention to detail, those reforms might have jarred Japan from confusion into chaos.

In essence MacArthur was an Occidental whose life unfolded East, while Yoshida was an Oriental whose life unfolded West. They shared a vision of the way their cultures could meet on the crowded archipelago of Japan and produce a new and powerful free nation.

Douglas MacArthur was one of the greatest generals America has produced. He was also one of the most flamboyant, and as a result his personal style sometimes attracted more attention than his accomplishments. Because of his aristocratic bearing and grandiloquent speech, he made an easy target for tastemakers and satirists, who portrayed him as a vainglorious anachronism, a haughty Victorian born fifty years too late. His speeches, often composed of towering, stirring invocations of the greatness of the American system, were laughed off by many as jingoism.

But his critics found it difficult to stereotype MacArthur. His was so richly complex a personality that, great actor though he is, even Gregory Peck was unable to capture it on film as George C. Scott so ably captured another great, but less complex, general, George Patton.

I first became keenly aware of MacArthur during World War II, when I was assigned as a Navy operations officer to a Marine combat air-transport unit in the South Pacific. What I heard was uniformly negative, because it was tainted both by the press, which was generally biased against MacArthur, and by the usual Army-Navy rivalry.

For example there were two kinds of seats in the C-47 cargo and transport planes we used: the uncomfortable bucket seats that were the lot of most servicemen, and a pair of more luxurious, airline-type seats for high-ranking officers. The latter were derisively called "MacArthur seats."

As it turned out, the general's reputation was completely at variance with the facts. During the seige of Bataan and Corregidor, MacArthur insisted on living in a house above ground rather than in a bunker, thus exposing himself and his family to Japanese shelling. Yet all we heard was that his men on Bataan called him "Dugout Doug." When the situation became hopeless, MacArthur had every intention of staying on the island and dying after he had killed as many Japanese as he could with his derringer. President Roosevelt finally ordered him to leave, but all we heard was that MacArthur, when the going got rough, beat a hasty and cowardly retreat, taking along his wife, his three-year-old son, and their Chinese nursemaid.

It was ironic that MacArthur's World War II nickname was Dugout Doug, because in World War I that is where he really was—in the dugouts and trenches with the doughboys in France. As chief of staff and later commander of the Rainbow Division, he was admired, even revered, by his troops because of his tactical skill and his eagerness to face every risk they did. During more than one American charge he was the first man over the top, and in the course of a year he was wounded twice and collected seven Silver Stars for gallantry.

Throughout his career his brushes with death were so frequent as to be almost routine. During a dramatic reconnaissance mission at Vera Cruz in 1914, Mexican bullets tore through his uniform. During World War I he was gassed, his sweater was tagged by machine-gun fire, and his command post at Metz was destroyed the day after he moved out. In the midst of an earlier barrage at Metz he stayed calmly in his seat, saying to his understandably concerned staff, "All of Germany cannot make a shell that will kill MacArthur."

After the war, when his car was pulled over by a highwayman in New York, MacArthur told the man to put down his gun and fight for his money. When the man learned that he was trying to rob General MacArthur, under whom he had served in the Rainbow Division, he apologized profusely and let him go.

During World War II MacArthur could often be found staying calmly in his chair during Japanese strafing runs, peering through binoculars at the action while others wondered which way they would jump if a shell hit, and ignoring officers and enlisted men who begged him not to endanger himself. The bullets, he would say, were not for him.

He frequently combined displays of courage with strokes of drama that bordered on rashness. When he landed in the Philippines in 1945 and visited Japanese POW camps that held the malnourished and mistreated remnants of his Bataan and Corregidor forces, he turned to his staff physician and said, "Doc, this is getting to me. I want to go forward till we meet some fire, and I don't just mean sniper fire." He strode forward, past the bodies of Japanese troops, until he could hear the fire from an enemy machine-gun nest directly ahead. Then he turned and walked slowly back, daring the Japanese to shoot him in the back.

MacArthur's whole life, including the displays of fearlessness that sometimes verged on foolhardiness, was in a sense a struggle to do justice to the memory of his father, General Arthur MacArthur.

Whether by coincidence or design, the careers of father and son had much in common. In 1863 Arthur, then an eighteen-year-old adjutant in the Union Army, earned the Congressional Medal of Honor for being the first soldier to plant his division's colors on top of Missionary Ridge in Tennessee, which set the stage for Sherman's march through Georgia. Douglas, too, won the Medal of Honor, for his heroism on Corregidor. Arthur spent much of his career stationed on America's frontiers; first the Southwest, then the Philippines. Douglas, from 1935 until his recall in 1951, visited the U.S. only once.

MacArthur the Elder and MacArthur the Younger, as they were differentiated by the Filipinos, were both obsessed with the importance of the Far East and of the Philippines to the future of the West. And both men's careers were marked by dramatic clashes with civilian authority—Douglas with President Truman and Arthur with William Howard Taft, president of the civil commission in the Philippines when he was military governor.

If Arthur was the example, MacArthur's mother, Pinky, prodded him toward a lifelong compulsion to follow and even surpass it. When he went to West Point, she went with him to make sure he studied and to protect the handsome cadet from romantic entanglements that could distract him from his career. He was graduated first in his class. While thirty-eight-year-old Colonel MacArthur was fighting in the trenches of France during World War I, his mother was writing fawning letters to his superiors, including General Pershing, who had served under his father. Finally, when he was appointed the youngest Army chief of staff in history in 1930, she ran her hand over the four stars on his shoulder and said, "If only your father could see you now. Douglas, you're everything he wanted to be."

MacArthur always felt compelled to be different from those around him, and this led to certain glaring but harmless eccentricities. In the military, uniform dress is intended in part to reinforce the command hierarchy. But MacArthur wanted to stand out, not fit in. To another officer who asked about his unusual garb, he said, "It's the orders you disobey that make you famous."

At various times in World War I he wore a rumpled cap in place of the regulation steel helmet, a turtleneck sweater, a plum-colored satin necktie, and riding breeches. Once he was mistaken for a German and momentarily arrested.

When he was superintendent at West Point from 1919 to 1922, he could be seen walking across campus carrying a riding crop. Later, in the Pacific during World War II, his simple but unorthodox uniform—familiar to Americans from pictures of the general wading ashore on one South Pacific island after another—consisted of sunglasses, faded khakis, a worn cap, and a corncob pipe. He wore none of his twenty-two medals, only small circles of five stars on his shirt collar.

One would think that MacArthur's refusal to deck himself out in gold braid, brass, and ribbons would have been endearing rather than irritating, especially since by the middle of the century the age of the common man was in full swing. But MacArthur's appearance enraged Truman, for example, when the two men met at Wake Island in 1950 to discuss the Korean War. Many years later Truman blurted out that the general "was wearing those damn sunglasses of his and a shirt that was unbuttoned and a cap that had a lot of hardware. I never did understand ... an old man like that and a five-star general to boot, why he went around dressed up like a nineteen-year-old second lieutenant."

MacArthur did not have to dress bizarrely to stand out from the crowd, because he was one of the most handsome public figures of his time. He also had a powerful personal magnetism—which, abetted by his shrewd intelligence, helped him captivate audiences, inspire troops, and command absolute loyalty among the people who worked on his staff. His aide at West Point said, "Obedience is something a leader can command, but *loyalty* is something, an indefinable something, that he is obliged to win. MacArthur knew instinctively how to win it."

MacArthur had a special knack for attracting and keeping the loyalty of subordinates. Both Alexander Haig and Caspar Weinberger, prominent members of both my administration and President Reagan's, worked for MacArthur, and they still count him among their idols. Weinberger was a young captain on MacArthur's staff in the Pacific near the end of World War II. Haig, as a lieutenant on the staff of the American Occupation in Japan, was the duty officer who first informed MacArthur that the Communists had invaded South Korea.

MacArthur was almost never ill. Though his only formal exercise was calisthenics, he paced constantly, sometimes miles each day, in his office and living room, in airplanes, or on the decks of ships during attacks. MacArthur himself attributed his good health and physical condition to his afternoon naps, his near-abstention from drinking, moderate eating habits, and his ability to fall asleep almost at will. He was a profoundly religious man but not a churchgoer.

MacArthur was a totally disciplined man in thought, speech, and action. While he is best remembered for his "Old soldiers never die" speech and his farewell address at West Point, one of his best public performances was during the Senate Korea hearings. I did not participate in the questioning, since I was not a member of the committee conducting the hearing. I dropped by the first day just to see how MacArthur would handle himself under intensive questioning and expected to stay only a few minutes. His performance was so brilliant and spellbinding that I stayed for the entire three days of his testimony. Democratic senator William Fulbright and others came well prepared and asked some brutally tough questions aimed at demonstrating that MacArthur had violated presidential directives and had refused to accept the principle of civilian control of the military.

A lesser man would have crumbled under this assault. But MacArthur remained in command throughout. He was never trapped into a damaging admission; he used every question to get across a point he wanted to make in his answer; he was as quick and sharp at the end of a long, grueling day as at the beginning.

But even more impressive than what he said was how he said it. What particularly impressed me was his ability to put things in perfect, orderly English no matter how complex the issue was that he might be discussing. As was the case with de Gaulle, there were no pauses, no incomplete thoughts, no stopping a sentence and going back to start it again. It was almost as if he had written out his answers beforehand and memorized them. I was soon to see firsthand that he talked that way in private conversation as well.

It was at Robert Taft's funeral in August 1953 that I first spoke with MacArthur. I mentioned that Taft had been one of his most loyal friends. MacArthur replied expansively, "I was *his* greatest friend!"

Shortly thereafter I received a message from his aide, General Courtney Whitney, that MacArthur would like to see me the next time I was in New York. I shall never forget that day. First I had breakfast with President Hoover in his suite in the Waldorf Towers, 31A. I always profited from my meetings with the man we affectionately called The Chief. Hoover, as was his custom, asked me for my views and listened attentively as I replied to his questions about the administration's budget and the prospects for maintaining the Korean truce.

He was a man who was at peace with himself. He had been a Taft supporter, but now his only interest was in ensuring the success of the Eisenhower administration. The only uneasy moment came when he asked me to join him in smoking one of his fine Cuban cigars after breakfast. I had never smoked a cigar in the morning before, and twenty-five years passed before I tried it again.

After our talk I took the elevator up to MacArthur's suite, 37A. General Whitney met me at the door and escorted me into the drawing room. Hoover's suite was impressive in its simple, uncluttered dignity. MacArthur's, while the same size, was spectacular. The memorabilia that covered the walls, gathered during his years of service in the Pacific, gave me the feeling that he rather than Hoover had served in the highest position America could offer. He also had a fine collection of Japanese art.

MacArthur walked toward me as I entered the room and took both of my hands in his. He said, "How good of you to come" and introduced me to Mrs. MacArthur, then and now one of the most gracious and charming women it has ever been my privilege to meet. She asked me about Mrs. Nixon and the children and then excused herself.

It was the first of what would become a series of conversations I had with him over the next eight years, all of them fascinating. We usually discussed the American political scene and current foreign policy issues—or, rather, he discussed and I listened. While Hoover had always asked for my thoughts on the various topics we discussed, MacArthur almost never did. A meeting with him was like a graduate seminar in whatever subject he was discussing, and the best policy for a visitor was either to listen quietly or to take notes. One colonel booked a fifteen-minute appointment with MacArthur during the Japanese Occupation, but was so stunned by the formidability of the general's monologue that he forgot to bring up the reason for his visit. Later the colonel learned that MacArthur had judged him a "fascinating conversationalist."

As it turned out, my meetings with MacArthur were among the very few high-level contacts between him and the Eisenhower administration. I did not report on them to the President, and in fact I cannot recall ever discussing MacArthur with Eisenhower. I always had the distinct impression that any mention of MacArthur would be unwelcome.

These two great American generals had held each other at arm's length ever since the 1930s, when Eisenhower was MacArthur's aide. During the 1950s I knew that MacArthur desperately wanted to come to Washington. He would describe to me, at great length and with extensive accompanying detail, how he would trim the military budget or how he would "straighten out the Pentagon in a month" if he were appointed Secretary of Defense or Chairman of the Joint Chiefs of Staff. But the call never came.

While Eisenhower probably had good reason not to install the controversial five-star general in his administration—many in the Pentagon would have chafed at taking orders from him—there can be no doubt that MacArthur was hurt by the way he was treated. He would never speak disparagingly of Eisenhower in a direct way, but he did sometimes manage a backhanded jibe. Once, when talking with me about Eisenhower's years as his aide, MacArthur said, "He could write a brilliant paper for a position or against a position. You just had to tell him what the position was."

When Eisenhower suffered his first heart attack in 1955, setting off speculation about whether he would or should seek a second term, I received a message from MacArthur through Courtney Whitney. "General MacArthur is in the Vice President's corner all the way," Whitney told me. "He says that what should happen is that the other fellow should get out of there right away." MacArthur's message was highly inappropriate under the circumstances and would have been embarrassing to me, to say the least, if Eisenhower had learned of it. I recall thinking at the time that MacArthur was probably more eager to see Eisenhower out of the White House than to see me in it.

MacArthur resented Eisenhower's popularity. He also believed that the attention paid to Eisenhower and Europe during and after World War II encouraged Washington's neglect of the U.S. position in the Far East. Eisenhower, in turn, thought MacArthur, though a great general, was pompous and overly theatrical. While he usually kept such opinions to himself, he once wrote in his diary after receiving some strategic advice from MacArthur in 1942, "Wonder what he thinks we've been studying all these years. His lecture would have been good for plebes."

While MacArthur did not play a public role in the 1960 presidential campaign, he did take pains to let me know that he was on my side. In June I sent him a wire congratulating him on receiving an award from the Japanese government for his work promoting Japanese-American friendship. I warmly praised his "heroic" contributions to history and expressed confidence that these would leave their mark "on the heritage of free people everywhere." He wired in reply, "You have sent me a magnificent message. I have given it to the press to show my complete support of your candidacy for the presidency." Perhaps only a man of MacArthur's ego would have assumed that his releasing the text of my praise of him showed his support of me, but he seemed completely unabashed about making the assumption.

Often he made comments to me that were highly disapproving of Kennedy. Not surprisingly I appreciated them—before the election because they buoyed me up, and after the election because they helped salve the wounds. Once before the election he spoke disparagingly of Kennedy's PT boat exploit, saying that Kennedy was "brave but very rash" and that "he could have been court-martialed for his poor judgment in the episode." In June 1961, two months after the Bay of Pigs fiasco, he was brutally critical of Kennedy. He mentioned that he had recently had a conversation with Jim Farley, the legendary former Democratic National Committee chairman and FDR confidant. Farley had made the point that Kennedy had a very quick, agile mind. MacArthur's response was that he did not think that Kennedy had judgment—the kind of broad judgment that involves weighing all the factors before reaching a decision. MacArthur went on to tell me that "a commander's most important function is to separate the five percent of intelligence he receives which is important from the ninety-five percent which is not important." He said he thought Kennedy had failed that test in making his decisions on the Bay of Pigs and that, as a result of the fiasco, Kennedy had unfortunately totally lost confidence in the military and the CIA. He did credit Kennedy with being "clever" politically and attributed to politics Kennedy's having provided MacArthur with a plane for his sentimental journey to the Philippines. But he called Kennedy "just dumb when it comes to decision making." Having said that, however, he added very emphatically—he always spoke emphatically—that "Kennedy _will_ take Cuba. Now is not the time, but later he must do it and he will do it."

Nearly always MacArthur's comments got back to Asia at one point or another. He once told me that, looking back, he believed that if he had had half a million Chinese Nationalist troops under his command at the Yalu, he could have split China in two and, in one stroke, changed the world's balance of power. But that opportunity was gone. He had grown pessimistic about Asia's future because of Communist encroachments, but thought it would be a grave mistake for the U.S. to become involved in an Asian land war. His last advice to a U.S. President was his urging of Lyndon Johnson not to commit more forces to Vietnam. He felt that all we could usefully do was to continue to bluff and to support local governments against Soviet- or Chinese-supported insurrections.

His attitudes on political matters were also unequivocal. He said that living in New York and serving as board chairman of Remington Rand had given him the opportunity to study Wall Street businessmen more closely, and he had found that they had "no character" whatsoever. "They will never stand up for principle," he said. "The only guideline they follow is to pick a winner and support him regardless of what he may stand for." In the early 1960s he told me that high taxation was the major issue and that the country was turning more conservative. But before the 1964 Republican convention he emphatically expressed the view that Goldwater could not be nominated because he was too conservative.

He told me in 1961 that Kennedy had seemed "almost a Socialist" when Kennedy's father had brought him to meet MacArthur at the Waldorf in 1951. He did credit Kennedy with a "remarkable memory," recalling that when he had seen him after he became President,

Kennedy's memory of their first meeting ten years earlier had been remarkably accurate. What particularly fascinated me about this was what it showed about MacArthur's memory.

MacArthur gave me one bit of personal advice that many believe I should have followed. When I asked him whether he thought I should run for governor of California in 1962, he grasped my hand and said, "Don't do it. California is a great state but it is too parochial. You should be in Washington, not Sacramento. What you should do is run for Congress." Herbert Hoover had given me the advice just two hours earlier and six floors below.

My conversations with MacArthur are always linked in my own mind with those I had with Hoover. Both were aging, both were wise, both lived in the Waldorf Towers, and I usually visited both on the same day. Often the comments of the two offered curious parallels and contrasts.

My last conversation with Hoover was on August 10, 1963, when I dropped in to see him on his eighty-ninth birthday. His nurse told me that he had been very sick and it was a miracle for him to have recovered, but that his mind had never wavered. She said that he often got up in the middle of the night to write on his yellow pad. For years Hoover had answered each of his hundreds of birthday cards with a personal letter. His nurse said that he still read each card but was unable to answer them personally.

As she wheeled him into the room in his wheelchair, I was saddened to see how painfully thin he was. But his handshake was firm, his voice was surprisingly strong, and his comments on issues were succinct and to the point. Despite his hard-line anticommunism, he supported the test-ban treaty, which was signed that month by the U.S. and the Soviets. His view was that "at least it gives some present relief from tension." As he put it, " 'Khrush' needs friends because of the Chinese." He disagreed with Adenauer's view that we should play the Chinese against the Russians. He pointed out that they were in an early stage of communism and therefore especially aggressive. Also, he told me the Chinese were a highly emotional people who could be "bloodthirsty" both against foreigners and against their own people.

Hoover's attitude was colored by his experiences while working as a mining engineer in China at the time of the Boxer Rebellion of 1900. He and his wife had a hand in defending a settlement of foreign families at Tientsin against the xenophobic Boxer rebels. Both the Boxers and the government troops committed horrible atrocities against one another; Hoover reported seeing thousands of bodies floating in the river that ran by his settlement. To him the carnage of the Chinese revolution was just another chapter of the same story. He predicted that the Chinese people had not been changed by twenty-five years of Maoism because "a national heritage is slow to change," and said that the U.S. should have as little to do with them as possible.

He was more generous to Kennedy than MacArthur had been, commenting that "he was much better than I had anticipated."

Hoover also differed with MacArthur about Goldwater. His view was that it might be best to give the extreme right a chance to try itself and to "get it out of our system."

Although MacArthur and Hoover had very similar outlooks on a wide range of issues, I cannot recall an occasion when either one mentioned the other. At first I assumed that they rarely saw each other. But I learned later from Mrs. MacArthur that President Hoover invited the MacArthurs to his suite for private dinners five or six times a year, and that these events were the setting for some fascinating conversations between two of the most eminent leaders of our time.

MacArthur's disregard for military policy was not confined to the officers' dress code. Soldiers are supposed to obey their superiors to the letter, which MacArthur did not always do, even if the superiors in question were Presidents of the United States.

Often enough MacArthur was right and his superiors were wrong. In World War II he leapfrogged his forces across the South Pacific so expertly that he suffered fewer casualties from 1942 to 1945 than the Americans suffered in the Battle of the Bulge alone. His successes in this encouraged him to second-guess orders from Washington.

Once the Pentagon told him a plan to recapture the Philippine island of Mindoro was too risky. MacArthur went ahead anyway and succeeded. After taking the big island of Luzon, he began to take the other islands in the archipelago without authorization—losing only 820 men in the process. And in Japan his forays into social and economic reform went way beyond the letter of his authority as Supreme Commander, but his achievements were so brilliant that President Truman, who later fired him for insubordination, sent him nothing but praise.

In addition to his father's example, two factors in particular contributed to MacArthur's disregard of higher authority. First, from the beginning of his career he suspected other officers of trying to torpedo him. During World War I he mistrusted the men around General Pershing at the Allies' Chaumont headquarters in France. Later his major antagonists were officers like George Marshall, who had himself been at Chaumont with Pershing.

In a conversation with me Herbert Hoover, Jr., an admirer of MacArthur, called these officers the "Pentagon Junta." They were men whose overseas experience had been in Europe and whose outlook remained primarily European. MacArthur thought many of them, particularly Marshall, were intent upon thwarting his every move in the Pacific for both political and personal reasons. He also believed that Truman and his military advisers had not done enough to resist the Communist victory in China and that the administration's unclear Asian policy had left South Korea open to Communist invasion.

MacArthur also had contempt for desk men. He was a field commander at heart, and he felt he understood better than men in offices what needed to be done on the battlefield. Presidents of the United States, of course, are the ultimate desk men, and MacArthur was no more intimidated by them than he was by his superiors in World War I or the Joint Chiefs of Staff during World War II.

None of MacArthur's relationships with the Presidents he served from the 1930s on was ideal, though the irritants were different in each case.

With Hoover there was the famous "Bonus March" during the Depression, when 25,000 veterans and their families came to Washington demanding cash bonuses. Army Chief of Staff MacArthur questioned the marchers' motives and personally went into the field against them. Hoover sent orders to MacArthur not to send his troops into the marchers' makeshift camp, but MacArthur ignored Hoover's orders and routed the protesters.

With Franklin Roosevelt, despite a veneer of cordiality, there were disagreements with MacArthur over the Army and Air Force budget in the 1930s and the general's resentment over FDR's decision not to reinforce the soldiers on Bataan. When MacArthur learned of Roosevelt's death in 1945, he said to a member of his staff, "So Roosevelt is dead: a man who would never tell the truth when a lie would serve him just as well."

But no two American leaders had greater distaste for each other than MacArthur and Truman. As early as June 1945, Truman noted in a memorandum to himself that a big question for the U.S. after the war would be "what to do with Mr. Prima Donna, Brass Hat, Five Star MacArthur." He added, "It is a very great pity we have to have stuffed shirts like that in key positions. I don't see why in hell Roosevelt didn't order [Bataan commander Jonathan] Wainwright home and let MacArthur be a martyr [on Corregidor]." MacArthur, in turn, thought Truman was ignorant about Asia, "subject to paroxysms of ungovernable rage" (such as when he threatened physical assault on a critic who panned his daughter's singing), and inclined to lose his nerve at crucial moments. The tension between the two came to a head over Korea.

The most spectacular event of MacArthur's command in Korea, and possibly of his career, was his amphibious landing at Inchon, a classic example of his "Hit 'em where they ain't" battle strategy.

In Korea in the fall of 1950, U.N. troops were holed up at Pusan, in the southeast corner of the peninsula. Rather than risk the high casualties that might result from an assault against the North Korean Communists massed along the Pusan front, MacArthur decided to stage a surprise landing at Inchon, the port of Seoul, on the west coast of Korea. After the landing he planned to seize the South Korean capital from the Communists and seal off the enemy troops in the south in much the same way he had isolated the Japanese on islands he passed over in the Pacific.

Inchon was a treacherous place for a landing, and at first MacArthur's superiors were hesitant. In August Truman sent one of his advisers, Averell Harriman, to Tokyo to meet with the general and survey the situation in Korea. Harriman's military aide was Vernon Walters, later a close friend of mine whom I appointed deputy director of the CIA.

Over breakfast one morning in the dining room of the American embassy in Tokyo, where MacArthur lived with his family during the Occupation, the general gave Harriman a list of the reinforcements he would need at Inchon.

"I cannot believe that a great nation such as the United States cannot give me these few paltry reinforcements for which I ask," MacArthur said as Walters, fascinated, listened. "Tell the President that if he gives them to me, I will, on the rising tide of the fifteenth of September, land at Inchon, and between the hammer of this landing and the anvil of the Eighth Army, I will crush and destroy the armies of North Korea." Walters told me later, "The hair on the back of my neck stood straight up."

Harriman was also impressed. MacArthur got his reinforcements— and approval of his plan by the Joint Chiefs. On September 15, 1950, with their seventy-year-old commander watching from aboard the command ship *Mount McKinley*, troops spearheaded by the First Division of the U.S. Marines landed at Inchon and defeated a North Korean force of over 30,000, losing only 536 men in doing it. By the end of the month MacArthur had driven the Communists back over the 38th Parallel and returned Seoul to a grateful Syngman Rhee.

After Inchon the U.N. Security Council voted that the objective of

MacArthur's forces was to unify Korea, an action that echoed a policy the Truman administration had already decided upon unilaterally. But in late November, as MacArthur's forces pressed toward the Yalu River, hundreds of thousands of Chinese troops under Lin Biao—their movements had been misjudged by both the CIA's and MacArthur's intelligence teams—surged down from the hills, forcing the general to execute a humiliating but typically expert and orderly retreat.

The following spring, after learning that Truman had decided to seek a truce, MacArthur issued a military appraisal of the Korean situation that included pointed references to the inferiority of the Chinese forces and hinted that the Communists ought to come to terms. MacArthur argued later that any commander in the field had the right to issue such a message to the enemy. What was probably unwise was the contentious tone of his appraisal, which drew violent criticism in Peking and Moscow and forced Truman to delay his own diplomatic initiative.

To make matters worse, a few days before his call for the Chinese to negotiate became public, MacArthur had written a letter to House Republican leader Joe Martin, who had asked the general's opinion about whether troops under Chiang Kai-shek should be used in the war. MacArthur wrote that they should be used and added that diplomats were trying to fight the war against communism with words. Communist victories in Asia would lead to the fall of Europe, he said; "win [the war] and Europe most probably would avoid war and yet preserve freedom." He added, "There is no substitute for victory."

When Martin read this letter on the floor of the House, it created a firestorm that swept over the Capitol and down to the White House. Even the usually staid Senate, where I was then serving, was in an uproar. Although Martin had made the letter public without MacArthur's permission or knowledge, Truman announced his decision to fire the general. MacArthur suffered the additional humiliation of learning first from a news program that he had been removed from all his commands. Former President Hoover managed to reach him directly on the telephone and urged him to come home immediately and tell his side of the story to the American people—sixty-nine percent of whom, according to a Gallup poll, supported MacArthur against Truman.

After MacArthur was fired, I introduced a resolution in the U.S. Senate calling for his reinstatement. "Let me say that I am not among those who believe that General MacArthur is infallible," I said in what was my first major speech in the Senate. "I am not among those who think that he has not made decisions which are subject to criticism. But I do say that in this particular instance he offers an alternative policy which the

American people can and will support. He offers a change from the policies which have led us almost to the brink of disaster in Asia—and that means in the world."

In retrospect I believe this summary of the matter stands the test of time in that it puts the blame on both parties. MacArthur had defied the principle of civilian control of the military and had in effect interfered with the President's conduct of foreign policy. But the Truman administration's policy had been timid and equivocal. For years it had been a source of enormous frustration to MacArthur, one of the few U.S. leaders at that time who knew enough about Asia to see that ominous forces were at work there and that we courted disaster by failing to counter them resolutely.

The Martin letter and the military appraisal were not the first examples of MacArthur's comments on Washington policy decisions. Truman said later he had considered removing MacArthur from the Korea command the previous August, over a letter about the defense of Formosa that the general had sent to the Veterans of Foreign Wars, but had not done so because he did not want to "hurt General MacArthur personally."

Throughout the war MacArthur's stock with the Truman administration seems to have risen and fallen according to the administration's political requirements. After the VFW letter he was nearly fired. After the triumph at Inchon, Truman flew to Wake Island for a conference whose only apparent purpose was to generate news photographs of the beleaguered President and the popular general standing together. After the second U.N. capture of Seoul, MacArthur's convictions about total victory became an obstacle to a negotiated settlement. As Charles de Gaulle said in a speech four days after the firing, MacArthur was a soldier "whose boldness was feared after full advantage had been taken of it."

In the end the President who claimed to have cared so much about MacArthur's personal feelings did not even get a personal message through to him. MacArthur wrote, "No office boy, no charwoman, no servant of any sort would have been dismissed with such callous disregard for the ordinary decencies."

The personal clash between MacArthur and Truman was the most dramatic highlight of the dispute over Korea. But the dispute can also be explained as a struggle between MacArthur, with his predominately Asian outlook, and a U.S. foreign policy that was excessively weighted in favor of Europe.

Truman's policies in Europe—the Truman Doctrine, the Marshall

Plan, and the Berlin airlift, for example—were strong and forthright. His Asian policies, however, were curiously mixed. The idea that the Communist victory in China or the Korean stalemate presaged the fall of other Asian or Southeast Asian nations to communism seemed outlandish to many of the administration's policymakers. It seems less outlandish now.

This myopia regarding the Far East was shared by most Americans, perhaps because their roots are in Europe. MacArthur, however, spent much of his life in Asia, and many speculated that he was more comfortable with Asians than with fellow westerners. When he served in the Philippines in the 1920s and 1930s, he ignored the traditional "color bar" by which Filipinos and westerners had always been segregated. At his dinner parties in Manila in the 1930s there were often few white faces to be seen.

Now that China has once again been brought onto the world stage— and now that the threat the Japanese economic miracle poses to American economic dominance is becoming more and more obvious— Americans are beginning to realize that the history of the world for the next several generations may well be dictated by the men and women of the Orient. This lesson has taken a long time to sink in.

In 1953, my first year as Vice President, I undertook a two-month tour of nineteen Asian and Pacific countries at the request of President Eisenhower, who felt the previous administration had neglected Asia and wanted to get a firsthand report on conditions there before making major decisions that might affect the area. Along the way Mrs. Nixon and I met hundreds of leaders and thousands of people of all backgrounds. We saw the enormous potential of the region, but at the same time saw clear evidence of the ominous thrust of direct and indirect Communist aggression emanating from both Peking and Moscow. We were concerned that some countries, especially those in French Indochina, were not getting the quality of leadership they needed to meet this threat. Most of all, our visits and discussions convinced me that Asia could well become the most important part of the world, as far as U.S. policy was concerned, for the rest of the century. This was the thrust of my report to President Eisenhower and to the nation at the conclusion of my trip.

But one trip by a Vice President could not begin to change the attitudes of an entire nation. The U.S. continued to face west. In a 1967 article I wrote, "Many argue that an Atlantic axis is natural and necessary, but maintain, in effect, that Kipling was right, and that the Asian peoples are so 'different' that Asia itself is only peripherally an American concern."

A half-century before, MacArthur had made his own survey of the Far East, and he, too, fell under its spell. After leaving West Point in 1903, he joined his father on an inspection tour of Japanese positions in Asia and of European colonies throughout the Far East. The whole tour took nine months, and it was one of the most important events in MacArthur's life.

"Here lived almost half the population of the world, and probably more than half of the raw products to sustain future generations," he wrote later. "It was crystal clear to me that the future and, indeed, the very existence of America, were irrevocably entwined with Asia and its island outposts." Following his three years as the reform-minded superintendent of West Point (where he ordered maps of Asia displayed so cadets could study them), MacArthur's personal history was caught up with the history of the American presence in the Pacific for more than two decades.

MacArthur's influence over America's position in the Orient began in 1930 when, as Army chief of staff, he had responsibility for keeping the Army and Air Force ready to fight. Winning adequate military budgets during peacetime is a frustrating and difficult job, and in the Depression the going was even tougher.

In 1934 MacArthur was able to dissuade Franklin Roosevelt from making further drastic cuts in the defense budget in an explosive confrontation in the White House. "In my emotional exhaustion," MacArthur wrote later, "I spoke recklessly and said something to the general effect that when we lost the next war, and an American boy, lying in the mud with an enemy bayonet through his belly and an enemy foot on his dying throat, spat out his last curse, I wanted the name not to be MacArthur, but Roosevelt." When he left the President's office, the Secretary of War told him he had "saved the Army"; MacArthur, aghast at his own audacity, vomited on the White House steps.

In 1935 MacArthur returned to the Philippines, then a U.S. commonwealth, to take charge of its armed forces. Like his father, he believed the islands were crucial to any U.S. defense scheme in the Pacific, but his military spending requests went largely unmet. It was the first of many brushes MacArthur would have—before, during, and after World War II—with what he called "North Atlantic isolationism": Washington's neglect of U.S. interests in the Far East and its obsession with developments in Western Europe.

Though Washington finally sent MacArthur more money in 1941, the

Philippines fell to the Japanese the following year. From the island for-
tress of Corregidor, after MacArthur had directed a brilliant retreat onto
the Bataan peninsula, he promised his struggling troops that Roosevelt
was sending help, but the help went instead to the European theater—
embittering him toward Roosevelt and feeding his suspicions about the
"Pentagon Junta."

When he was Supreme Commander in Japan, he lamented to visitors
that Americans had not yet begun to recognize the importance of Japan
to Asia and of Asia to the world—or to appreciate Asia's vast potential.
After Acheson's statement in January 1950 that Formosa and South Korea were outside the U.S. defense perimeter, MacArthur concluded that
the Secretary of State was "badly advised about the Far East." He invited
Acheson to Tokyo, but Acheson said his duties prevented him from
leaving Washington—though he found time to go to Europe eleven
times while in office. In 1950 the Communists invaded South Korea,
and MacArthur was called to arms for the last time.

MacArthur's dispute with Washington over Korea must be viewed in
this context. MacArthur believed the Chinese intervention in the Korean War demonstrated "the same lust for the expansion of power which
has animated every would-be conqueror since the beginning of time." A
compromise with the Chinese would encourage further Communist
adventures in Asia and even Europe. With adequate support from
Washington, MacArthur believed he could hand the Communists a defeat that would discourage them from such adventures. At that time the
rift between the Chinese and the Soviets was still years away, and many
of us in Congress agreed with MacArthur that defeating the Chinese
Communist "volunteers" in Korea was essential to the containment of
aggressive forces that threatened all of free Asia.

MacArthur challenged Truman not because he was eager to extend
the war into China for the sake of doing so. In fact he never proposed
using American ground troops to counter the Chinese intervention and
contended until the end of his life that sending U.S. soldiers to fight on
the Asian mainland would be folly. He challenged Truman because of
his longtime suspicion that policymakers in Washington did not understand Asia and the threat that Communist expansion posed to it. He
also believed it was dangerous to let the idea get around that an aggres-
sor could safely have a small war with the U.S.

He understood from experience what Whittaker Chambers grasped
intuitively. "For the Communists," Chambers told me in urging support
for Truman's decision to commit American forces in Korea, "the war is

not about Korea but about Japan. If Korea is taken over by Communists when Japan is in a very unstable condition and trying to recover from the devastation of war, the Communist movement in Japan will be given enormous impetus."

MacArthur thought Truman already had two strikes against him in Asia. He had failed to hold China, and his ambiguous Korea policy may have encouraged the Communists to attack the south. Now, with Chinese troops in the war, MacArthur thought Truman and Acheson had once again lost their nerve. It was his fear that the administration's timorousness could eventually imperil the entire Far East, including Japan, that prompted the actions for which he was fired.

On the day of MacArthur's dismissal, William Sebald, the head of the Occupation's diplomatic section and one of America's ablest foreign service officers, received orders from Washington to meet with Prime Minister Yoshida and assure him that U.S. policy toward Japan was unchanged. By the time Sebald was ushered into Yoshida's upstairs study, the Premier—who had been dressed in western clothing during his garden party that afternoon—had changed into a kimono. He was "visibly shaken," his guest wrote later.

Sebald, upset by the news himself, feared that Yoshida would resign, both as a characteristically Japanese gesture of responsibility and because the Premier was so close to MacArthur. He told Yoshida that the Japanese people would need strong leadership in the days and weeks ahead to help them recover from the shock of MacArthur's departure. At the end of the interview Yoshida promised Sebald that there would be no resignation.

Though Yoshida remained in office for over three more years, one of postwar history's greatest partnerships had ended. Except for a brief period when Yoshida was out of office, he and MacArthur had been working together since 1946 to raise a new Japan from the ruins of the old.

MacArthur's part in this effort is relatively common knowledge. Yoshida, however, is one of the unsung heroes of the postwar world. Vigorous, compassionate, articulate, politically skilled, selfless, and deeply loyal to his country, he was a giant among postwar leaders of nations. He was also one of the few whose influence lasted beyond his retirement and death. It continues even today, for Japan is still governed in 1982 according to basic principles of moderation and restraint Yoshida established over three decades ago.

Yet in a world in which every schoolchild knows the names Churchill and de Gaulle, Yoshida, who was in many ways the equal of these men, is unknown to almost all except the Japanese, academics, and those who had the privilege, as I did, of knowing him personally.

Yoshida was as captivated by the West as MacArthur was by the Orient. Along with many other educated Japanese of the nineteenth and twentieth centuries, he was eager to find ways for Japan to advance its own interests through its foreign relations. In a sense his life was a reflection of a dichotomous nation that for centuries encouraged foreign influences without allowing them to disrupt what was fundamentally Japanese about Japan.

Since the seventh century China had exerted tremendous influence on Japan. It had been the model for Japanese governmental and military organization, land reform, religious and ethical systems, art, and literature. From the nineteenth century on, Japan has been bound up with the United States in much the same way it had been bound up with China before. This new relationship has encompassed the booming trade of the 1890s, the agonies of Pearl Harbor and Bataan, the trauma of Hiroshima and Nagasaki, and the intricate commercial and security arrangements of the postwar era.

"Japan's decisive century," to use Yoshida's phrase, began after the sight of the bristling cannons on the decks of Commodore Perry's black ships in 1854 helped convince the Japanese that they could no longer resist pressure to join the modern world. Soon a group of reformers abolished the shogunate, which had ruled Japan in the name of a powerless Emperor for 270 years. The reformers restored the Emperor Meiji, whose court had been restricted to the political backwater of Kyoto, to supremacy within the ancient palace walls in Tokyo.

The Emperor Meiji and his counselors believed modernization was the only way Japan could avoid being colonized by western powers as parts of China and Indochina had been. They also believed modern government would help bring economic prosperity. Thus, during the late nineteenth century, the Japanese began to take a long, sophisticated look at the U.S. and the West and soon borrowed principles of education, law, agriculture, and government.

The Meiji reformers created a democracy but of a decidedly limited variety, closer to Bismarck's Germany than to the U.S. or Britain. The grafting of West onto East was incomplete. Western democracy was introduced, but eastern absolutism, in the form of the Japanese Emperor, was invoked to make it work. The 1930s brought economic crises and increased international hostility toward Japan. A relatively small group of militarists was able to exploit the resulting surge of nationalism and seize the government.

When the militarists—Yoshida called them the "uniformed politicians"—took control, they commanded obedience because they, like the shoguns a century before them, had made a captive of the throne and spoke with its authority.

Yoshida was born in 1878 in the midst of the upheavals of the Meiji Restoration. Though he was born near Tokyo, his family was from Tosa, a province of Japan's smallest island. The men of Tosa were lumberjacks and sailors—brusque, rugged individualists in a society that valued consensus and politesse. The Tosans have been called "the Basques of Japan"; Yoshida, as rugged and brusque a son as Tosa ever produced, was later called "One-Man Yoshida" for his high-handed style of government.

Yoshida was the fifth son of a Tosan who was closely identified with Meiji-era politics. In Japan before primogeniture was abolished during the Occupation, sons after the first were often adopted by other families, and Yoshida's adoptive father was a family friend named Kenzo Yoshida, who died when Shigeru was eleven, leaving behind a substantial fortune.

After he was graduated from college in 1906, Yoshida began a career as a diplomat. Perhaps because of his provincial background, he was at first relegated to the China service, which was then a diplomatic slow track. He spent much of his time spending his inheritance on high living. But Yoshida married shrewdly. His wife, Yukiko, was the daughter of Count Makino, a trusted adviser of the Emperor. When Makino served as one of the Japanese delegates to the 1919 peace conference, he took the forty-year-old Yoshida along with him, which boosted the young diplomat's stature enormously.

The Japanese went to Versailles full of optimism about Wilson's Open Door foreign policy. Acting in the Wilsonian spirit, Makino proposed a clause in the treaty affirming the basic equality of the races. But the British, deeply suspicious of the Japanese and their growing power on the sea, vetoed the proposal—with the support of the United States. Yoshida found that the idealism of the Meiji Restoration and the Open Door was no match for the hard realities of postwar international relations. He went home bitterly disappointed.

I met with Yoshida for the last time in 1964, when he invited me to his estate at Oiso for dinner. Then eighty-six, the retired Premier reflected at length about his experience at Versailles. He said that he had often wondered whether the course of history would have been different if the great western powers had been more receptive to the Japanese point of view after World War I. Personally I always found it remarkable that Yoshida never let the experience sour him permanently on Britain and the United States. It was one sign that Yoshida had great character and strong convictions even as a young man.

Nevertheless the peace conference had its effect on him. As international hostility toward Japan increased—the U.S. Exclusion Act of 1924, which banned all Japanese immigration, was an example—he and many other Japanese grew more concerned about ensuring sufficient Asian markets for Japan's products and sufficient Asian raw materials for its factories. From 1925 to 1928, as Japanese counsel at Mukden, Yoshida played a significant role in preparing the ground for his country's Manchurian conquests in the 1930s.

However, Yoshida was never one to pay attention to political fashions, and he began to drift away from militarism at the same time Japan was succumbing to it. On a tour of Japanese foreign embassies in 1932 and 1933, he met a man who had also been at Versailles: Colonel Edward House, who had been Wilson's close aide and adviser during the war. House gave Yoshida the same advice he said he had given the Germans before World War I: If Japan chose violent rather than peaceful means of solving its foreign disputes, it would sacrifice everything it had built up so painstakingly since the time of Meiji.

Having been steeped in the prowestern tradition of Meiji Japan, Yoshida by now had become a vigorous proponent of internationalism in spite of Japan's increasing nationalism. He returned to Japan and began conveying House's message to everyone who would listen, a course of action that probably contributed to the "uniformed politicians" growing distaste for him.

After an attempted coup d'etat in 1936 by a group of renegade officers in Tokyo—from which Count Makino barely escaped with his life—the militarists controlled Japan. Yoshida was soon nominated to be Foreign Minister by the new Prime Minister, who hoped to hold the line against the militarists, but the army vetoed him. Yoshida was named Ambassador to Britain instead.

The appointment was lucky for two reasons. First, it took Yoshida out of Japan, where opponents of the army were in danger of harassment by the "thought police," imprisonment, and even assassination. Also, three years of constant exposure to British politics cemented his moderate, prowestern political philosophy in place. In many ways England was what Japan could have become if the dreams of the Meiji reformers had been allowed to flower: a powerful and influential island nation with a constitutional monarchy, a parliament, and a strong, competent civil service.

Yoshida became convinced that Japan could protect its economic interests in Asia without submitting to angry nationalism. He advocated aggressive diplomacy instead of military aggression. In spite of his anti-militarist views, Yoshida managed initially to stay out of jail when he returned to Japan in 1939. Yoshida was in touch with influential members of the Japanese government, and he struggled in vain to find a way to avert war with Britain and the U.S. Much later he recalled telling Tojo's Foreign Minister that if he could not "prevent a Japanese declaration of war on the United States, he should resign, an act which would hold up Cabinet deliberations and give even the army something to think about; and that if as a result of such a gesture he should be assassinated, such a death would be a happy one." After Pearl Harbor he sent an apologetic note to U.S. Ambassador Joseph Grew and made sure Grew had enough food while he was being held at the American embassy, two small gestures that took great courage.

During the war Yoshida was a member of the informal network of antimilitarist politicians known as the "peace faction." Like Konrad Adenauer in Nazi Germany, he avoided the sort of aggressive resistance that might have landed him in jail or worse, but at several points during the war he discussed with other antimilitarists the possibility of putting out peace feelers. Finally, in April 1945, he was arrested by the military police. They questioned him about his note to Grew and about his role in a written peace appeal to the Emperor, a copy of which had been discovered by a government spy on his household staff. He was then thrown in jail.

Yoshida endured his forty days in jail with characteristic good humor. With Tojo now out of office, he was confident that no real harm would come to him. His natural father had been a political prisoner at the time when his son was born, and Yoshida decided "a taste of prison life might not be so bad for me either for a change." He became popular with the other prisoners and the guards by distributing the extra food he received from home. He was transferred to a suburban jailhouse when the military prison suffered a direct hit during the bombing of Tokyo ("I was thinking how unpleasant it would be to be roasted alive," he wrote later) and was released shortly afterward. He went home to his estate at Oiso, forty miles south of Tokyo, to recuperate, assuming—

mistakenly, as it turned out—that he would spend the rest of his life there as a little-known retired diplomat.

One day early in the Occupation of Japan, Yoshida was driving on a deserted highway between Oiso and Tokyo. "Two American GIs suddenly appeared and signaled my driver to halt," he wrote later. "I imagined them to be on some kind of marauding expedition, but they turned out to be soldiers returning to Tokyo who had lost their way." Yoshida offered them a lift, and "we had not proceeded far before they were pressing chocolates, then chewing gum, and finally cigarettes upon me."

This was one of Yoshida's favorite stories. "I recall thinking at the time," he wrote, "that it was this natural way of acting on their part, and the inherent good nature of the average American, which enabled the Occupation of Japan to be completed without a shot being fired." A group of liberal Japanese intellectuals I met in 1953 seemed to agree. They told me that to the extent there was anti-American sentiment in Japan, it was not caused by the behavior of our troops.

The Americans' friendliness was certainly one reason the Occupation was a success. Another was the stoic acceptance of defeat by the Japanese and their openness to the change that came with defeat. But it was Douglas MacArthur's immediate recognition of these qualities in the Japanese that got the Occupation off to such a successful and dramatic start.

On August 30, 1945, MacArthur flew to Yokohama, where he was to establish a temporary headquarters. Nearby were some kamikaze pilots who had refused to surrender and 250,000 armed Japanese soldiers. The fighting had ended only two weeks before, and the two sides still regarded one another with a high degree of understandable suspicion.

Many Japanese expected the victorious Americans to overrun the country, plundering and raping as they went. Many Americans, in turn, worried that the Emperor would take the remnants of his army, flee into the mountains, and wage a lengthy guerrilla war. No one believed that the same army that had conducted the Philippine Death March and had fought to the last man on Iwo Jima and other Pacific islands would surrender quickly.

No one except MacArthur. In spite of his aides' warnings, MacArthur insisted on landing at Yokohama alone and totally unarmed. He even forbade his aides to carry sidearms. He was convinced that a show of absolute fearlessness would impress any recalcitrant Japanese more than a show of strength. Characteristically it was a gamble; characteristically MacArthur was right. He landed safely. Churchill called it the most courageous single act of World War II.

It was in ways such as this that MacArthur, who had already become virtually a demigod to the people of the Philippines, established a similar relationship with the Japanese—a relationship based on absolute mutual trust. He cemented this relationship for all time with one inspired decision. Many—the British, the Russians, even some in Washington—demanded that Hirohito be tried as a war criminal. The Emperor himself paid an unprecedented call on MacArthur at the American embassy and said that the ultimate responsibility for Japan's warmaking was his and his alone.

But the general saw that reverence for the Emperor, even in surrender, was what held Japan together. Hirohito's radio broadcast in August 1945, telling his people to "bear the unbearable" and surrender, was one reason MacArthur was able to land safely at Yokohama. MacArthur also took an immediate liking to the bookish, unassuming yet quietly dignified monarch. The Supreme Commander decided to keep the Emperor in place and throughout the Occupation treated him with respect. Under the MacArthur constitution, promulgated in 1947, Hirohito became a constitutional monarch whose ceremonial role was carefully circumscribed. This decision went against much of the advice MacArthur was receiving at the time. The insight behind it could only have come from a profound understanding of the history and culture of the people he now governed.

In the end MacArthur did not so much abolish absolute political authority as transfer it from the Emperor to himself. He located his own permanent headquarters across from the moat that surrounded the Imperial Palace. Throughout the five years of his rule he remained as aloof and mysterious as Hirohito had before. Each day he was seen only in his office, at home at the American embassy, or en route between the two. Between 1945 and 1951 he left the Tokyo area only twice, both times for destinations outside Japan.

Hirohito, meanwhile, toured factories and farms and appeared at baseball games, mingling with his people as never before. But although power flowed from him to MacArthur and eventually, in 1952, to the people, there was still the sense that the general, like the shoguns and the Meiji reformers before him, was simply ruling at the behest of the Emperor. One Japanese said about MacArthur, "The Emperor couldn't have picked a better man."

Although Yoshida was an advocate of parliamentary democracy, he was also fiercely loyal to the Emperor. He thought MacArthur's treatment of Hirohito was, more than any other factor, responsible for the success of the Occupation. It was also in large part responsible for Yoshida's remarkable affection for MacArthur.

When Yoshida became Japan's third postwar premier in 1946 at age sixty-seven, he did so both unexpectedly and reluctantly. As a result of MacArthur's purge of men who were linked with the militarists, the Liberal (actually conservative) party had found itself without a candidate for Prime Minister. Yoshida had already left Oiso to serve as Foreign Minister, and the leaders of the Liberal party turned to him for the top job only to find him reluctant to accept. He finally said yes, but only after warning the party that he would avoid intraparty squabbles and fund raising. He was expected to be only a caretaker Premier. As it turned out, he served over seven years and seated five cabinets.

He was a decisive and, at times, painfully blunt leader. For instance he had a wary but genuine respect for the contributions scholarship can make to society, but he was not particularly fond of scholars themselves unless they agreed with him. He publicly called one who did not a "prostitute of learning." A reference in his 1947 New Year's message to "renegades" in the labor movement helped spark plans for a nation-wide strike that MacArthur had to call off personally and that brought down Yoshida's first government. In 1953, when he called a Socialist Dietman a *bakayaro* (damned fool) in his exasperation over his opponents' attempts to prevent him from modifying some of the more unworkable Occupation reforms, his opponents were able to engineer a no-confidence vote in his government. However, he still won the next election and was able to continue his efforts.

The Churchill of Japan governed according to one of the most realistic edicts of the Churchill of England, who once wrote, "People who are not prepared to do unpopular things and to defy clamor are not fit to be Ministers in times of stress." In the confusion of postwar Japan, when public opinion was fluid and malleable, Yoshida steadfastly went his own way, governing according to his own instincts. As his father-in-law, Count Makino, said admiringly, "Shigeru may not have the most appealing personality, but he has backbone, and that's what counts."

He did not distrust the Japanese people in the same way Konrad Adenauer distrusted the Germans. He blamed only the small militarist clique for the calamity of World War II. A relative of the Premier told me, in fact, that Yoshida trusted his countrymen absolutely and was certain they would be able to rebuild their country as long as their leadership was sufficiently forthright.

Often he donned a beret and inverness and wandered through the streets of Tokyo, listening to what people had to say about him. He was seldom recognized and more than once heard himself described as the "one-man" Premier. He did not seem to take it as an insult. Most of the criticism of his tactics came from the minority parties, which bore the brunt of them, and from the anti-Yoshida press. The people themselves found him inspiring and even entertaining. Other politicians rained abuse on him for calling a Diet opponent a *bakayaro*, but an American reporter wrote that one could call a taxi driver a *bakayaro* and "earn a grin instead of a scowl" once Yoshida had sanctified the term.

Yoshida could be as hard on his subordinates as he was on his political opponents. Once he held a dinner in honor of William Sebald, and he also invited a Japanese foreign service officer who was about to take up a diplomatic post in the U.S. The foreign service officer and his wife left the party early so they could catch the last train for their home in the suburbs. A few days later Sebald learned that Yoshida had canceled the man's U.S. assignment because he had left the party before the guest of honor—an offense that Yoshida considered unconscionable both for a Japanese gentleman and a would-be representative of Japan abroad.

Despite his occasional high-handedness, Yoshida had a reputation for listening carefully to experts and advisers before making a decision. He was not the sort whose pride or stubbornness prevented him from changing his mind in the face of new evidence or effective arguments. He respected those who had more experience in a field than he did; for instance Yoshida knew he was comparatively weak in the area of economic policy. For his economic advice he was more likely, as was Eisenhower, to turn to businessmen than bureaucrats, and in fact was one of the few Japanese Premiers to appoint businessmen to his cabinets. Most important, like de Gaulle and Adenauer, he chose able Finance Ministers, such as Hayato Ikeda, a Yoshida protégé who later became Prime Minister himself.

While he acknowledged the deficiency of his economics background, Yoshida had a certain intuitive grasp of basic economic questions. For instance he was correct in believing that Japan would need to modernize its industrial base to succeed in the postwar international marketplace. "Fortunately, Japan was reduced to ashes by air raids," he once said mischievously. "If Japan introduces new machinery and equipment now, it should be able to become a splendid country with productivity far higher than the countries that have won the war. It costs much to demolish machinery, but the demolition was done for us by the enemy." While Yoshida was being facetious, he was, as it turned out, absolutely right.

In my meetings with Yoshida, from our first talks in Tokyo in 1953 through the dinner he gave for me at Oiso in 1964, I found his private persona differed markedly from his blustery public one. His wit in private was disarmingly subtle. For westerners, unaccustomed to dry Japanese humor, it was at times hard to detect. At a dinner given in our honor in 1953, Yoshida turned to Mrs. Nixon, who was sitting next to him, and remarked that a U.S. destroyer group was docked in Tokyo Bay. "Tell me," Yoshida said, "are they there to protect you from us?"

With his stern expression and severe crew cut, the Premier at first looked deadly serious. It was only when his eyes twinkled and a faint smile came to his face that we knew he was joking.

Yoshida often put humor to work in his diplomacy. After the war many Asian nations clamored for war reparations. Correctly anticipating these might be on Indonesian President Sukarno's mind during a state visit to Japan, the Premier took the offensive.

"I have been looking forward to your arrival," Yoshida said pleasantly. "Your country always sends us typhoons which have caused serious damage to Japan. I have been waiting for your arrival in order to ask for compensation for the damage caused our country by your typhoons." Yoshida laughed heartily; Sukarno, completely flabbergasted for one of the few times in his life, decided not to raise the subject of war reparations.

Yoshida governed and lived zestfully, with the aplomb that comes only with age and a certain inbred sense of superiority. By six in the morning he was walking in the garden of the Prime Minister's residence, chopping weeds from around his beloved bonsai trees with a sickle. Recreation was a good conversation—he was a gifted raconteur and a good listener—or a horseback ride. As a youth he had been one of the few children in his neighborhood to ride a horse to school. When he was Prime Minister, he used the Imperial equestrian ground.

He liked food of all kinds, except Chinese, and savored sake and cigars, which he dispatched at a rate of three a day. He enjoyed reading biographies of Japan's most illustrious diplomats. He also read French and English and was familiar with the literatures of both languages. When he suffered from insomnia, he read himself to sleep instead of taking sleeping pills.

As any proper Meiji Japanese might, Yoshida read *The New York Times* and *The Times* of London each day, marking articles and sections he thought his aides should read and sending them around to the various departments. He had less time for the Japanese mass media, which he considered unruly and overly opinionated. He did sometimes meet with individual reporters whose work he admired, but he also often expressed his attitude toward the mass media by quite unmistakable actions. Once he called the police to oust reporters from a chrysanthemum-viewing party, and frequently he was seen fending off photographers with his cane.

Yoshida loved his wife, Yukiko, dearly. She was an amateur poet whose works were praised by Japanese critics for their juxtaposition of Japanese themes against foreign settings, which she no doubt described from her memories of places Yoshida had worked as a diplomat. She died two months before the beginning of the war. When she fell ill, Yoshida was at her bedside each day throughout her three-month hospitalization. Mrs. Joseph Grew, the wife of the U.S. Ambassador, also visited Madame Yoshida daily and brought her homemade soup.

Yoshida never remarried. Once, when somebody asked him for his ideas on women, he said shortly, "Since my wife died, I have no ideas about women."

After Madame Yoshida's death, his official hostess was his multi-lingual daughter, Madame Kazuko Aso. She was sometimes called "the power behind the throne," though she scoffed at the notion. Nevertheless, before our visit to Japan in 1953, William Bullitt, who had served as Roosevelt's Ambassador to Russia and France, told me that she rated with Madame Chiang Kai-shek at the very top of his list of first ladies on the international scene. She measured up to his evaluation in every way. Highly intelligent and gracious, she was a worthy companion for her illustrious father. She once told me that many leaders were great men but not good husbands. "I would much rather have the latter," she said. But it was clear that she considered her father to be both.

By all accounts, while it was not in MacArthur's nature to reciprocate Yoshida's effusive public praise of the general, there was a strong personal friendship between the two men.

Each morning MacArthur and his son, Arthur, would romp at the embassy with their pet dogs before Arthur went off to his lessons and the general to his headquarters. A relative of Yoshida told me what happened one day when Yoshida went to MacArthur's office and found the general in low spirits. One of the dogs, MacArthur said, had suddenly and unexpectedly died.

By then Yoshida had grown to love Arthur as if he were his own son. Not telling MacArthur what he was doing, the Prime Minister managed to get a picture of the pet and gave it to his Agriculture Minister, telling him to find another dog that looked just like it. When one was located at the National Institute of Animal Husbandry, Yoshida took it personally in his car to the American embassy and gave it to Arthur while a delighted MacArthur watched.

Another time Yoshida brought MacArthur an ingenious toy horse that he had bought for Arthur during one of his anonymous walks through the streets of Tokyo. When Yoshida visited MacArthur's office again a few days later, he saw the toy still sitting on the general's desk, next to a stand containing his famous corncob pipes. Yoshida asked MacArthur why he had not yet given it to his son. The Supreme Commander answered somewhat sheepishly that he had been having too much fun playing with it himself. Later he reluctantly passed the toy on to Arthur.

Perhaps the most convincing evidence of MacArthur's regard for Yoshida was that he allowed him to remain Prime Minister. Over 200,000 Japanese, including the man whose place Yoshida took as head of the Liberal party, had been purged by the Occupation, and MacArthur could just as easily have purged Yoshida when the Prime Minister became resistant to one or another of MacArthur's wishes, as he occasionally did. Instead he was known to purge political opponents of Yoshida at the Premier's request.

Just as he did not earn the affection of the Japanese people by being polite or nonabrasive, Yoshida did not earn MacArthur's respect by being submissive. In 1946, while he was choosing the members of his first cabinet, demonstrators filled the streets of Tokyo, protesting the shortage of food. Soon he let it be known that he would not complete his cabinet appointments unless MacArthur promised massive food shipments from the United States. "The Americans," he said privately, "will certainly bring food to Japan once they see people waving red flags throughout the country for a whole month."

When MacArthur heard of this, he sent a covered jeep to fetch the new Prime Minister to his office. Yoshida returned twenty minutes later looking noticeably calmer. MacArthur had promised he would not let a single Japanese starve to death while he was in charge of Japan. Yoshida had in turn promised to complete his cabinet that night.

MacArthur still had to sell the idea to Washington, where some were self-righteously opposed to using surplus from Army stockpiles to feed America's former enemies. He wired, "Give me bread or give me bullets." Washington sent the food, and MacArthur was able to keep his promise.

As Premier, Yoshida's position was particularly difficult because it severely limited the extent to which he could exercise personal initiative. His government spent most of its time reacting to directives from MacArthur and his staff. Some reforms he accepted wholeheartedly. Others he resisted but ultimately had to accept. Still others he resisted and eventually reversed.

He was caught in the middle. His opponents called him an American patsy. When I visited Japan in 1953, Ambassador John Allison told me that some of the anti-American sentiment in Japan was actually anti-Yoshida sentiment caused by his strong pro-U.S. posture. At the same time some on the American Occupation staff thought he was a troublemaker and had tried to keep him out of office in 1948, when he formed his second cabinet.

Yoshida supported MacArthur's broad aims for Japan: demilitarization, democratization, and revitalization of the economy. The general's land redistribution program and his new constitution were among his first and most sweeping accomplishments. In swift, decisive strokes he shattered the two fundamental institutional causes of Japan's militant imperialism: the rural discontent that had filled its armies and the Emperor-centered system of government that had allowed the militarists to take power so easily.

In 1945 most Japanese farmers tilled fields owned by absentee landlords, a situation MacArthur believed amounted to "virtual slavery." Yoshida, in turn, knew that rural discontent could fuel a Communist revolution in Japan as easily as it had fueled militarism in the 1930s. Working along lines set down by MacArthur, Yoshida's government devised a sweeping land reform bill. By 1950 ninety percent of Japan's farmland was owned by the farmers themselves.

The MacArthur land reform gave farmers both a sense of individual worth and an incentive to produce more. After it was completed, communism in Japan became almost entirely an urban phenomenon because MacArthur had stolen the Communists' big rural issue. As biographer William Manchester notes, "It is ironic that MacArthur should be remembered by millions as a man who wanted to resolve the problem of communism on the battlefield."

It is also ironic that the Taiwan "economic miracle," which can be compared in character if not in size to the Japanese "miracle," was made possible in large part by Chiang Kai-shek's liberal land reform program, which he instituted soon after he came to Taiwan from the mainland. Had Chiang been able to initiate such programs on the mainland, Mao might not have been able to exploit the rural discontent that contributed to the success of the Chinese Communist revolution.

If MacArthur's most obvious target was the agricultural system, one of the trickiest was Japan's top-heavy political system. The Japanese people had no specified political and civil rights, and MacArthur granted them at an astonishing rate. He established habeas corpus. He abolished all restrictions on civil liberties and fired five thousand officers of the secret police.

He also gave women the vote, believing, as he had confided to an aide, that "women don't like war." Fourteen million women went to the polls for the first time in April 1946—many apparently thought MacArthur would reprimand them personally if they stayed away—and thirty-nine women, including one well-known prostitute, were elected to the Diet.

Some Japanese politicians, eager for democracy to get off on the right foot, thought the prostitute's election was inauspicious, and a nervous senior legislator arrived at Occupation headquarters to break the news to MacArthur. The Supreme Commander asked him how many votes she had received; the legislator sighed and said 256,000. MacArthur replied—"as solemnly as I could," he wrote later—"Then I should say there must have been more than her dubious occupation involved." He sent all the new Diet members, including the prostitute, letters of congratulations.

The textbook in MacArthur's school for democracy was the MacArthur constitution. When the pre-Yoshida Japanese government balked at rewriting the Prussianesque Meiji constitution, the general took yellow legal pad in hand and composed his own outline for the new charter. The final product, written by his staff in somewhat awkward Japanese, combined the American executive and British parliamentary systems. It abolished the peerage, renounced war as a means of settling disputes with other countries, and outlined a bill of rights. Most important, it made the Japanese people sovereign and designated the Emperor as the "symbol of the nation." After it was approved by the Diet, the Emperor proclaimed it the law of the land.

The MacArthur constitution has always had its critics, many of whom say it is illegitimate because it was written by foreigners and forced on a weakened and irresolute public. Still, Japan has so far resisted all attempts to amend it, and most Japanese apparently approve of the Emperor as a constitutional monarch.

*   *   *

MacArthur had masterfully turned back overt attempts by the Soviets to influence the conduct of the Occupation, in which they were nominally partners. When Stalin's man in Tokyo said the Russians might occupy the northernmost island of Hokkaido, MacArthur promised to throw him in jail if even one Russian soldier set foot on Japanese soil. He thus saved Japan from the anguish of being divided into a Communist north and a non-Communist south.

But domestic communism was more insidious. When Stalin finally returned Japan's World War II POWs in 1949, they had been organized into cadres and indoctrinated. Communist-inspired violence escalated the following year when the Soviets ordered the Japanese Communist party to emphasize illegal and terrorist tactics and abandon its policy of seeking a "peaceful revolution."

When I went to Japan in 1953 I felt strongly that Communist-inspired violence there justified the step of outlawing the Communist party. MacArthur, before his recall in 1951, and Yoshida had already purged party members from government and business. I was surprised to discover, however, that Yoshida—as staunch an anti-Communist as I have ever met—was against outlawing the party outright unless the threat it presented to the stability of Japan increased.

He was typically whimsical about the shift in our own attitudes about communism from 1945 to 1950. "Americans are very interesting people," he said once. "When you came here in 1945, we had all the Communists in jail. You made us let them all out. Now you tell us to put them back in jail again. That's a lot of work, you know."

Yoshida was probably reluctant to take further action against the Communists in 1953 because by then Japan's economic recovery was in full swing. Land redistribution was complete and farmers were brimming with enthusiasm and vigor, as I found during my conversations with some of them at the time. As a result, the Communist party was doing poorly at the polls.

Still, Yoshida continued to worry about the Communists. During one of our meetings in 1953 he ruminated about "our natural tendency to be sympathetic toward communism." He was concerned because young intellectuals tended to support left-wing radicals. Madame Aso added that intellectuals supported the Communists because it was the fashionable thing to do. "It just isn't fashionable to be conservative," she said. The problem was compounded by the fact that many Communist slogans, the ones about freedom and equality and the rights of workers, only sounded like slightly more strident versions of MacArthur's reforms. Yoshida believed that many Japanese, lacking an instinctive feeling for what democracy meant, had confused democracy with license and anarchy. MacArthur had set up a giant experiment in democracy, but Yoshida had to keep it from boiling over.

MacArthur, for instance, quite properly wanted to encourage a free labor movement. But his staff, which included many idealistic junior social engineers, recruited Japanese Communists to help them establish new unions, and it was no surprise that they were prone to unreasonable demands, strikes, and violence. When he could, Yoshida modified the new labor laws, over the outraged howls of the Socialist opposition. Eventually most unions turned away from the Communists.

The Americans were also intent on trust-busting—not just the giant combines, or *zaibatsu*, such as Mitsubishi, but also over a thousand smaller companies. Many on the Occupation staff mistakenly believed that big business was the root of all the evils of the 1930s, in Japan as well as in the U.S. Yoshida correctly believed that Japan would not survive without healthy commercial and industrial sectors and resisted the anti-monopoly drive. Many of the breakup schemes were finally abandoned, and in 1953 Yoshida's government modified the stringent anti-monopoly laws.

Yoshida was severely criticized by liberals in both Japan and the U.S. for resisting some of the reforms MacArthur's staff had insisted upon. But in retrospect he was right: Many of the reforms—in areas ranging from labor and business to education and law enforcement—were unsuited to conditions in postwar Japan. Yoshida's stubborn defense of his nation's interests against radical reforms at a time when Japan could least afford them was a key factor in the success of MacArthur's Occupation.

Yet, as important as Yoshida's role was in modifying some of the Occupation's more extreme domestic measures, his greatest legacy was a shrewd foreign policy that had two parts: opposition to large-scale rearmament, a domestic issue with international ramifications; and determined pursuit of a peace treaty and security alliance with the U.S. Together these policies meant that Japan could have national security without paying for it and could devote all of its attention and resources to building one of the greatest economies in the world.

As an American, I did not support the Yoshida foreign policy in its entirety. But as an observer of leaders and leadership, I can appreciate its soundness from his standpoint and the enormous boost it gave to Japan's economic recovery.

Winston Churchill, 1954. A
somber Prime Minister strides
into St. Paul's Cathedral, London,
for the funeral of a long-time
associate. *(Wide World)*

Churchill as a war correspondent in southern Africa during the Boer War. *(Wide World)*

Churchill as campaigner seeking reelection to Parliament as leader of the Opposition in 1950, a year before his return to power as Prime Minister. *(Wide World)*

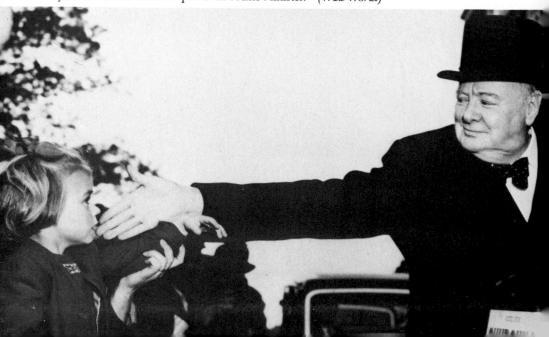

Churchill riding from the airport to the White House, accompanied by the author, during his 1954 visit to Washington.   *(United Press International)*

Churchill as a child, as an officer of the Fourth Hussars, and as a young member of Parliament.   *(Wide World photos)*

Charles de Gaulle with the author as they walk through the palace of Versailles, 1969. *(White House photo)*

President and Madame de Gaulle in London, 1960, being driven along Fleet Street in an open carriage en route to a luncheon at the Guildhall. *(Wide World)*

De Gaulle's official portrait as President of France. *(Wide World)*

The many faces of de Gaulle: his expressions as caught by the camera at a presidential press conference.   *(Wide World photos)*

Above: Douglas MacArthur with the author in 1958, on MacArthur's seventy-eighth birthday.
Below: With former President Herbert Hoover in 1957.   *(Wide World photos)*

Top: MacArthur as a cadet; with his mother, who lived near the campus during his years at West Point. *Middle:* As a brigadier general in command of the Rainbow Division during World War I; smoking his corncob pipe moments after landing in defeated Japan in 1945. *Bottom:* Speaking to a crowd in San Francisco in 1951 after being fired by President Truman; testifying during the Senate Korea hearings.   *(Wide World photos)*

Above: MacArthur waves to his troops from his landing barge at Morotai Island, south of the Philippines, 1944.   *(Wide World)*   *Below:* With General Dwight D. Eisenhower, his former aide, during Eisenhower's May 1946 visit to Japan.   *(United Press International)*

Above: MacArthur with Shigeru Yoshida in 1954, when the Japanese Premier visited the former supreme commander in New York. *Below:* Yoshida at home in 1953, dressed in a Japanese kimono. *(Wide World photos)*

Yoshida meeting Konrad Adenauer in West Germany during Yoshida's around-the-world trip in 1954.   *(Wide World)*

Left: Adenauer arrives in France in 1963 for his last meeting as Chancellor with his friend de Gaulle. The French President, as chief of state, broke protocol in order to go personally to the airport to greet the West German head of government. *(Wide World)* *Below:* The author with Adenauer in Bonn in 1963.

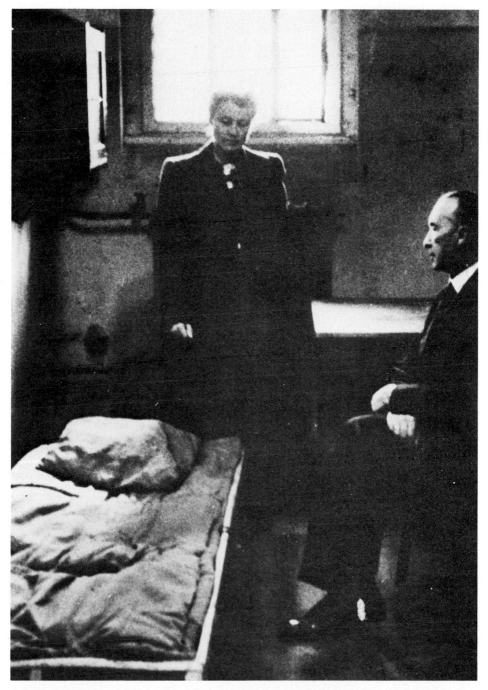

Adenauer and his wife, Gussi, pay a postwar visit to the cell in Brauweiler prison where Adenauer had been imprisoned by the Nazis in 1944. *(Wide World)*

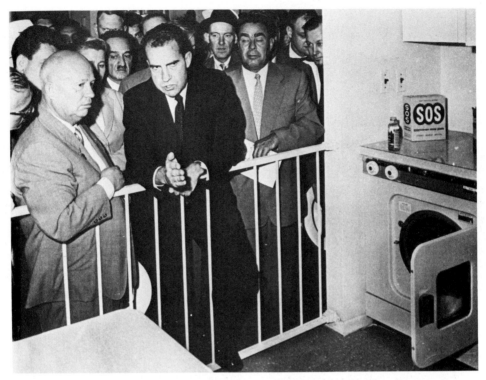

Above: Nikita Khrushchev and the author engage in their "kitchen debate" at the American National Exhibition in Moscow in 1959; the then little-known Soviet official standing behind the author is Leonid Brezhnev. *Below:* During a motorboat ride on the Moscow River, Khrushchev pauses so that he and the author can greet a group of swimmers.   *(Wide World photos)*

Above: Brezhnev stresses a point during a discussion in the study of the author's San Clemente home in 1973. *(White House photo)* *Below:* Also in San Clemente, Brezhnev tapes a televised speech to the American people, to be broadcast at the conclusion of that year's summit meeting. *(Wide World)*

Brezhnev and the author contemplating the globe in Brezhnev's office during the 1972 summit. The portrait above is of Lenin.   *(White House photo)*

Before the realities of the Cold War began to press on Japan and the U.S., MacArthur had thought Japan could become a new kind of nation: an economic powerhouse that had renounced forever the intention of resorting to war to solve its disputes with other nations. He used the phrase _Switzerland of the East_, and the idea was written into the MacArthur constitution as Article 9, the "no war" clause.

Vernon Walters once told me, "Most generals see only to the end of war. MacArthur looked beyond war." Article 9 of the Japanese constitution is the most concrete proof that MacArthur, who had seen firsthand the horrors of two world wars, dreamed of a world in which war would no longer be necessary. Unhappily his optimism was premature. By the late 1940s many Americans believed that the enactment of Article 9 had been a mistake. With the Soviet Union and, after 1949, Communist China on its western flank, Japan needed some means of self-defense. When the Korean War broke out, MacArthur took most of his troops to Korea and in their place created an indigenous 75,000-man Japanese security force—later called the Self-Defense Force. Yoshida believed that Japan had renounced offensive war but had not given up its natural right to defend itself from aggression by others. He quickly set to work, over the opposition of the Socialists and a pacifist public, to make the new force as effective as possible.

Obviously 75,000 men, however effective they were, could not defend an island nation one and a half times the size of the United Kingdom. But Yoshida resisted pressure for further rearmament, both before independence in 1951 and after. His reasons were largely economic. "Under the present economic conditions," he said, "the construction of a single battleship would upset the whole of government finance."

Truman had assigned John Foster Dulles to work out the details of a peace treaty between Japan and the Allies, and Dulles used his position to try to influence Yoshida to rearm Japan. But when he first mentioned the subject, the Prime Minister replied, "Don't talk nonsense." Nonetheless the issue remained alive in the Eisenhower administration, and it remained a concern of Dulles after he became Secretary of State.

Before I left on my 1953 trip, Dulles suggested that I address this sensitive issue publicly in Tokyo to test the reaction in both the U.S. and Japan. In a luncheon speech at the Japanese-American Society on November 19, I pointed out that the situation had become radically and dangerously different from what it had been when the U.S. imposed Article 9 on Japan. Our hopes for a peaceful world, free from the threat of armed conquest, had been shattered by the Soviet Union's aggressive actions.

Article 9, therefore, had been a well-meaning mistake, I said. "We made a mistake because we misjudged the intentions of the Soviet leaders. . . . We recognize that disarmament under present world conditions by the free nations would inevitably lead to war and, therefore, it is because we want peace and we believe in peace that we ourselves have rearmed since 1946, and that we believe that Japan and other free nations must assume their share of the responsibility of rearming." The Japanese press gave the speech banner headlines. Not surprisingly, major emphasis was put not on my call for rearmament but on my admission that the U.S. had made a mistake.

Yoshida's reaction was polite but noncommittal, and he stuck to his position until his retirement in 1954. Since then Japanese defense spending has crept upward, but it still comprises less than one percent of Japan's gross national product, whereas the U.S. spends six percent and the Soviet Union as much as eighteen percent of its GNP on defense. While the Self-Defense Force has grown substantially in sophistication and more than tripled in size, it is still ridiculously inadequate; Japan, for instance, has two-thirds fewer men in uniform than North Korea.

I believe it is imperative that Japan take on more of the burden for its own defense. However, I cannot fault Yoshida for disagreeing. One of the marks of a good foreign policymaker is the degree to which he obtains the best possible deal for his own country at the least possible cost. By this criterion Yoshida's was an excellent policy.

Like many of his policies, it was also dangerous for him politically. By opposing large-scale rearmament but supporting and encouraging the Self-Defense Force, Yoshida received none of the political benefits that a pacifist policy would have given him at a time when pacifism was widespread in Japan. At the same time, by putting Japan's security under the wing of the U.S., he incurred the wrath both of pro-rearmament rightists and of anti-American leftists.

It would have been politically easier for Yoshida to profess some form of pan-Asian neutrality. But he knew neutrality was meaningless for a weak country and reminded those who disagreed of an old Japanese adage: "The frog in the well doesn't know the dimensions of heaven and earth."

Yoshida was realistic enough to know that Japan needed protection from its enemies. He was practical enough to know that the Japanese people could not afford to pay the cost of that protection by themselves. And he was shrewd enough to know that the U.S. would pay instead.

Yoshida's security alliance with the United States became the most divisive foreign policy issue in Japan. Critics said it turned Japan into a virtual U.S. colony. Riots over its renewal in 1960 caused President Eisenhower to cancel a visit to Japan, and it remains a source of controversy twenty years later. Despite the criticism, however, the pact contributed enormously to Japan's development into an economic superpower.

If he had given in to the simplistic "Yankee go home" jingoism of his opponents and entered what they euphemistically called "an overall peace"—an arrangement that would have included China and the Soviets and deprived Japan of the protection it needed—MacArthur's Switzerland of the East might have become the Finland of the East, a Communist satellite in fact if not in name. Instead Japan was able to devote itself single-mindedly to creating an economy and a standard of living that are the envy of almost every nation on earth.

Yoshida lived another thirteen years after leaving office in 1954, and he derived enormous satisfaction from seeing his policies bear fruit. His opponents said he would make Japan "the orphan of Asia." Instead he helped make her a giant.

One reason his policies did bear fruit was that they were tended from 1957 until 1972 by his successors, first by Nobusuke Kishi and then by Hayato Ikeda and Eisaku Sato, both graduates of the "Yoshida school." I had the good fortune to know all three and found them to be world statesmen of the first rank. It is a truism of leadership that great leaders rarely groom younger men because they are so captivated by their own accomplishments that they cannot imagine anyone taking their places. Yoshida was a notable exception.

I have often been struck by remarkable similarities between Yoshida and West Germany's Konrad Adenauer. Both ruled when they were in their seventies. Both courageously opposed the totalitarians who controlled their countries in the 1930s. And both presided over the resurrection of defeated countries and their transformation into economic superpowers. In 1954, on Yoshida's world tour, the two men met in Bonn. Yoshida admitted to Adenauer that he had always imagined himself engaged in a kind of friendly competition with the German since their circumstances and backgrounds were so similar.

There was one crucial difference between them, however. Yoshida carefully prepared his Finance Minister, Ikeda, to follow in his footsteps. Adenauer treated his equally capable Finance Minister and successor, Ludwig Erhard, so shabbily that Erhard could not control his emotional distress in discussing it with me in 1959.

Yoshida was not necessarily less of an egotist than Adenauer. It is in fact the ultimate in self-gratification for a leader to see his policies continued long after he leaves the stage. The trick is for him not to become convinced that he is the only actor who can play the part. Adenauer fell into that trap. Yoshida gracefully avoided it.

I had known Sato before I became President, and I negotiated extensively with him during my presidency. The most significant outcome of our talks was the reversion of Okinawa to Japanese control in 1972, and even then it seemed that Yoshida was a party to our conversations. Sato mentioned his mentor often. When a Sato emissary came to Washington in advance of our meetings for preliminary talks with Henry Kissinger, he used a pseudonym to enhance security. The name Sato's envoy chose was "Mr. Yoshida."

Yoshida remained in touch with MacArthur until the general's death in 1964. He had hoped to see MacArthur in September 1951, when the U.S.-Japan peace treaty that MacArthur had made possible was signed, but Truman and Acheson spitefully refused to invite the general to the ceremonies at San Francisco. The State Department also told a disappointed Yoshida that it would be "inappropriate" for him to visit MacArthur in New York before returning to Japan.

When Yoshida made a state visit to Washington in 1954, he became the first Japanese leader since the war to visit the U.S. Senate. As Vice President, I was the Senate's presiding officer, and I had the distinct privilege of welcoming him. It was a measure of how much progress he and MacArthur had made since the end of the war that I was able to introduce him as "a great friend of the United States and the cause of freedom." The Senate responded by giving him a standing ovation.

Yoshida left office the following month after a no-confidence vote in the Diet against his fifth government. For a variety of reasons, many of which were beyond Yoshida's control, his popularity had reached a low point. Some members of his government were implicated in a shipbuilding scandal. Characteristically he was being criticized by some for being an American toady and by others for failing to obtain enough American aid during his visit to Washington. And finally, many conservatives who had been purged by MacArthur were now back in action and angling for power. That he held onto the premiership and accomplished as much as he did for more than a year and a half after the end of the Occupation and the political purges are testaments to his skill and resilience.

Yoshida left office reluctantly, and the circumstances of his departure were messy. He had always been undiplomatically blunt toward those who opposed or displeased him, even when he was a diplomat; once in the 1930s he advised a bothersome superior to either calm down or commit himself to an insane asylum. As Prime Minister, on visits to Japanese zoos he would call the monkeys and penguins by the names of prominent political figures. His freewheeling behavior entertained the Japanese people and helped ease the humiliation of defeat and occupation, but it also bruised the tender egos of his enemies.

They avenged themselves in the end. The late-1954 Diet debate over the no-confidence resolution was brutal. Once Yoshida paused over his notes and said in a moment of confusion, "Ah ... ah ... ah." His opponents yelled back cruelly, "Ah ... ah ... ah." In mid-December, Yoshida's leftist and conservative opponents joined forces against him and passed the no-confidence measure. It was considered unlikely that he could win yet again at the polls; Yoshida, now seventy-six years old, had finally been beaten.

No Japanese Premier except Sato has matched Yoshida's seven years and two months in office, and none has had to endure the atmosphere of sweeping, sudden change and political instability in which he governed. Yoshida held power through a military occupation and the brief burst of nationalism that followed it, the Korean War, the dizzying inflation of the late 1940s and the equally dizzying economic surge of the early 1950s, and the establishment of social and governmental reforms that shook Japan to its foundations.

For a while after leaving office he slipped into the obscurity that usually envelops a defeated politician. But his protégés, Sato and Ikeda, made regular trips to Oiso for advice and counsel. He wrote his memoirs and articles and eventually undertook occasional diplomatic missions for his successors. After a few years had passed, the extent of his vast contribution to Japan's stability and economic vigor began to be appreciated more clearly. By the time of his death, he was a respected elder statesman.

Today, almost thirty years after the end of his career, Yoshida is viewed with renewed respect by a new generation. When Japanese politicians visit me, they often tell me how much they admire not only his accomplishments but also his personal example—his courage, his absolute forthrightness, his willingness to stand up to enormous political pressures in defense of his beliefs and Japan's interests. Just as de Gaulle and Churchill will live on in the collective memories of their nations, especially in the example they will provide for generation after generation of young people, so Yoshida has taken on new life in Japan.

*   *   *

In 1960, in the midst of my campaign for the presidency, the eighty-two-year-old Yoshida was once again summoned from retirement at Oiso to serve his country. The Japanese government asked him to head a delegation to Washington to mark the one hundredth anniversary of the first Japanese diplomatic mission to Washington. We invited him and Madame Aso to our home. After dinner Yoshida gave me a carving that he said had been specially made for me by a Japanese artist. With the campaign very much on my own mind, I could not help smiling appreciatively when Yoshida mentioned, in a studiedly offhanded way, that the work's title was "Victory."

After the election that November he sent me a very gracious note describing the outcome as "sad" and saying that he hoped I would come back to lead again "at home and abroad." I particularly appreciated it then, because such gestures mean more in defeat than they do in victory, and from him, because it was a gesture he no longer had to make. During his years in office Yoshida had developed into a tough, skilled politician whose enemies accused him of being ruthless and selfish. I knew better, and I cherished the fact that in that difficult moment he showed himself to be a loyal friend.

I saw Yoshida for the last time in 1964 at Oiso, after a meeting scheduled for the spring of that year was delayed by a sadly ironic twist of fate. I was making a tour of the Far East that spring, and Yoshida had invited me to a luncheon at his home. But on April 5, four days before I arrived in Tokyo, MacArthur died, and Yoshida and Madame Aso left immediately for the United States to attend the funeral. The dinner was rescheduled for the following November, when I visited Asia again.

Our forty-mile automobile ride to Oiso, through traffic jams worse than those on the freeways of Los Angeles, was grueling, but the journey was well worth the trouble. Yoshida met me at the door, wearing a kimono. At our previous meetings he had worn western clothes and even shown a particular fondness for high Victorian collars. Seeing him for the first time dressed in traditional Japanese garb reminded me once again of the extent to which this product of Meiji Japan was an amalgam of eastern and western influences. Of all the Japanese leaders I have known, Yoshida was paradoxically the most western and yet the most Japanese. I learned later that, when he was Army chief of staff in the 1930s, MacArthur sometimes wore a kimono in his Washington office.

Yoshida's home, which had a spectacular view of Mount Fuji, was comfortably large but not ostentatious. It reflected the impeccable taste of Madame Aso, who again served as our hostess. Its decorations and furnishings reflected the usual Japanese eye for proportion and balance, but in Yoshida's case the balance was between things western and things eastern. Western books stood alongside works of Japanese art. Yoshida slept on a _futon_ mattress rather than a bed, but on the terrace, where dinner was served, he had a western-style table and chairs rather than a low-slung Japanese table. Even the meal he served us combined Japanese and western dishes.

In a conversation that ranged widely over the world scene, Yoshida reflected on his trip to Versailles with Count Makino. In discussing my 1953 statement on rearmament, one of the other guests got the date of it wrong. Before I had a chance to say anything, Yoshida quickly corrected him. I thought to myself that the speech must have made more of an impression on him than he had let on at the time.

He expressed a particular interest in de Gaulle and in my evaluation of the French leader. I told him that I did not wholly support de Gaulle's international policies, especially his ambivalence toward NATO. I suggested that de Gaulle's international "high posture," to use a characteristically Japanese term, was possible because of his domestic successes and his popularity in France. I added that in view of Japan's economic strength, the Japanese government, like de Gaulle, was in a position to play a "high posture" role in international affairs—provided Japan developed a stronger military capability. I expressed my firm conviction that "Japan must not become an economic giant and remain a military and political pygmy." As he had in 1953, Yoshida politely but firmly turned my suggestion aside.

In retrospect the most significant subject of our talk over dinner in 1964 was China. It was a conversation we had begun eleven years before, when I first met him in Tokyo. At that time Yoshida, an "old China hand" from his days as a diplomat, told me that he had made a lifelong study of Chinese culture and retained a deep respect for it. He believed that just as no invader had ever been able to conquer China permanently, the invasion of communism would inevitably fail in its attempt to overcome centuries of Confucian influence. Chinese intellectuals, though in temporary eclipse in 1953, would eventually prevail over the Communist ideologues, Yoshida said.

However, Yoshida disagreed with the then-prevalent view that Chiang Kai-shek might still have a role to play on the mainland. Yoshida argued that although Chiang was himself a Confucian scholar, he had irreparably alienated the intellectuals, and that this was politically fatal. On this point he disagreed with Emperor Hirohito, who had still been strongly supportive of Chiang when I saw him during the same visit.

Yoshida's almost instinctual philosophical affinity with the Chinese impelled him to believe that increased trade between China and the non-Communist nations of Asia would ultimately cause China to throw off communism in favor of free enterprise. Like Eisenhower, he passionately believed that trade between potential enemies could lead to peace. He also felt that China's intervention in Korea was an aberration that resulted from its concern about a possible threat to its own borders. He believed the Chinese were essentially a peaceful people who would only resist aggression, not initiate it.

His attitude toward Peking led him to hint in 1951, when the U.S.–Japan peace treaty was before the U.S. Senate, that he intended to open relations with the mainland. John Foster Dulles, who had negotiated the treaty, told Yoshida that the Senate might reject it if he recognized the Chinese—who were then fighting Americans in Korea—and the Premier dropped the idea. One of my assignments on my 1953 trip was to reiterate Dulles's warning. While Yoshida did not disagree with my prediction that there would be a strongly negative U.S. reaction to any move he might make toward the Chinese Communists, it was obvious that I had not shaken his own support of a rapprochement with Peking. Had he not retired in 1954, Japan might well have reopened relations with China in the 1950s rather than the 1970s.

I was therefore not surprised that the Chinese question was still high on Yoshida's agenda in 1964. Yoshida and his Japanese guests were worried about the opening of diplomatic relations between France and China in January of that year, a move de Gaulle had made without informing the Japanese beforehand. Yoshida asked me whether I thought the United States might do the same thing. When I replied that I could not speak for the Johnson administration, the former Japanese Ambassador to the United States, Koichiro Asakai, said that he had some bitter experiences in Washington when officials announced policy decisions affecting Japan without informing him in advance. He predicted that at some time in the future the U.S. would negotiate directly with Peking without informing Tokyo. I replied—somewhat prophetically, as it turned out—that I could not rule out that possibility.

When we conducted the negotiations that led to the surprise announcement in July 1971 that I would visit China the following year, these discussions had to be kept secret from the Japanese as well as from our other friends throughout the world. Any leak might have torpedoed the initiative. When I made the announcement, it was immediately branded in Japan as the "Nixon shock." While the U.S. opening to China is often cited as the spark for the Sino-Japanese rapprochement that came in September 1972, the Chinese and the Japanese had actually been trading and conducting informal relations for years. For some time, groups of Japanese, including politicians, had been visiting China. The establishment of official relations between the two countries was less a result of the Nixon shock than it was the culmination of the gradual reconciliation that Yoshida had envisioned two decades before.

Yoshida's preoccupation with this kind of continuity in government, through which the work begun by one leader can be finished by others, was clear in one poignant moment as he escorted me to the door at the end of my visit. I told him that I looked forward to the day when we would meet again. He laughed and said, "No, I don't think we will. I am afraid I am too old. But you are a very young man [I was fifty-one at the time]; you can provide leadership in the future."

Of all the leaders I have met, Yoshida shares with Herbert Hoover the distinction of growing old most gracefully. Part of the reason was that although he was personally out of power, his policies were being continued by men he had prepared for leadership and who still valued his counsel. He was at peace with himself because he was confident that his good works would live after his death.

He died in late 1967 at Oiso, at the age of eighty-nine. Prime Minister Sato was on a state visit to Indonesia when he heard the news. Sato immediately flew home to Japan, went to Oiso, and wept openly at the bed where his mentor lay in state. A few days later Yoshida was given the first state funeral to be held in Japan since World War II.

In a political sense the last eleven years of MacArthur's life were wasted. His intellectual powers were undiminished, but in the 1950s and early 1960s, because of a combination of circumstances, they were not put to use as they should have been.

One reason was that he had become tainted by partisan politics. While serving in Japan in 1948, he made a stab at the Republican presidential nomination, but got only a humiliating eleven delegate votes on the first convention ballot. When he returned from Korea in 1951, he addressed Congress and then campaigned against Truman's Asian policies from one end of the country to the other.

MacArthur openly favored Senator Robert Taft over Eisenhower for the nomination in 1952. He was selected to give the keynote address at the Chicago convention in July, and we in the Eisenhower camp were concerned that his speech might deliver the convention for Taft. The general himself thought the delegates might even turn to him as a dark-horse candidate.

But the speech was a disappointment. It was well written and well delivered, but somehow, as Lincoln might have put it, "it just didn't scour." Part of the reason was that the delegates were bone tired by the time he began to speak at 9:30 P.M. They grew more and more distracted as he plodded along. It was almost embarrassing. Instead of giving him the rapt attention he had received at the joint session in 1951, some of the delegates coughed, some wandered around the floor and politicked, and others left for the men's room. He kept pressing to lift them out of their lethargy, but the chemistry and magic of the "Old soldiers never die" speech were missing. Then he had risen brilliantly to a dramatic occasion. Now the memory of the brilliance remained, but the drama of the occasion could neither be duplicated nor recaptured. The inevitable result was a feeling of anticlimax and letdown. MacArthur, the first-class showman, had made an uncharacteristic mistake: He had tried to top a performance and failed. The speech was the end of his chances as a political candidate.

FDR once said to MacArthur, "Douglas, I think you are our best general, but I believe you would be our worst politician." He was right. MacArthur was not a good politician, and eventually he realized it. He quotes Roosevelt's pronouncement himself in his memoirs. His greatest political miscalculation, in fact, was to appear to be interested in politics at all, to attempt personally to convert his enormous prestige into political capital. He should have left the active politicking to those who were willing to act on his behalf.

I believe that Eisenhower wanted to be President as much as MacArthur did, but he was clever enough not to admit it. Though Eisenhower always insisted that he was just an amateur politician, he was in fact a masterly political operator. He instinctively knew that the best way to get the prize was to appear not to be seeking it. When I first met him at the Bohemian Grove in California in July 1950, the business and political heavyweights who were there were all talking about the possibility of his being the Republican candidate in 1952. All, that is, except Eisenhower. When the question came up, he deftly changed the subject to the future of Europe and the Atlantic alliance.

In May 1951 his fellow Kansan, Senator Frank Carlson, insisted that I call on Eisenhower during a trip I was scheduled to make to Europe. He felt sure that the general was going to throw his hat in the ring and he wanted me to support him if he did. I saw Eisenhower for an hour at the Allied military headquarters in Paris. He greeted me cordially. Instead of talking about himself, he complimented me for my fairness in conducting the Alger Hiss investigation and asked for my evaluation of American sentiment toward NATO. He had the rare ability to make his visitors come away thinking *they* had done well rather than that *he* had done well. As a result, most left meetings with him, as I did, enthusiastic Eisenhower supporters.

The appearance of letting the office seek him rather than the other way around enhanced his chances of winning the presidency. MacArthur, on the other hand, gave every appearance in 1948 of running for office while on active duty in Japan. The impression that he was eager politically was strengthened by his action after Truman had fired him.

This is not to say that MacArthur would not have made a good President. He had a profound understanding of foreign policy issues. In Japan he demonstrated that he could handle domestic issues, running the gamut from labor relations to educational policy, in an intelligent, evenhanded manner. He was obsessed with maintaining the stability of the currency and with the pursuit of moderate, consistent fiscal policies. In fact he grew more conservative economically as he grew older, a development I also noticed in the careers of Eisenhower and de Gaulle. During the 1950s and early 1960s, when it was clear MacArthur would probably never hold another public office, he often lectured me about balancing the budget, cutting taxes, and going back to the gold standard.

MacArthur's major problem as President would have been that of adapting to the fact that his power over the government was more circumscribed than his power over troops had been as a general or his power over Japan had been as Supreme Commander. He would have found it difficult to tolerate and then master the seemingly endless stream of petty detail that comes with the presidency. In the U.S. as in Japan, MacArthur would have needed a Yoshida to implement his imaginative and creative policies.

Aside from running up on the shoals of politics, MacArthur was the victim of shifts in popular and military fashions. In World War I he was the doughboys' hero for his daring exploits in the trenches of France. In World War II, when he was in his sixties, he was "Dugout Doug" in spite of an equally impressive record of bravery.

Between the world wars, the values MacArthur represented—valor, patriotism, love of liberty—had begun to go out of style. They were revived during World War II but weakened once again by Korea and nearly dealt a deathblow by Vietnam. Even during World War II generals like

Eisenhower and Bradley—fatherly, unobtrusive, accessible—were more palatable to the intellectual establishment and even to GIs, who were, after all, among the first fully grown products of what was being called the century of the common man. As is often the case, MacArthur's accomplishments, among them a battle strategy in the Pacific that saved tens of thousands of GIs' lives, could not outweigh the burden of his image as an aristocratic poseur.

He still managed to strike a chord with the American public, as the deafening welcome he received from coast to coast upon his return from Korea showed. But soon even the public turned from him and elected his rival, Eisenhower, to the office they both coveted. It was a choice of a man who represented unity and moderation over another who was at times blatantly partisan and unfailingly controversial.

Douglas MacArthur liberated the Philippines, rebuilt Japan, and, at Inchon and after, prevented Communist control of South Korea. He came home a subject of intense controversy and was soon a political exile in his own country. The reason was that few understood Asia, MacArthur, or what one meant to the other. Few understood that MacArthur's destiny was to protect American interests in the Far East, almost single-handedly, for two decades.

As an admirer of MacArthur, I have never fully understood how a man whose accomplishments were so vast and self-evident could be so unpopular in American intellectual circles. The vicious attacks that plagued MacArthur during most of his career could be explained in part by Lord Blake's analysis in the epilogue of his classic biography of Disraeli.

He noted that while Disraeli and Gladstone were mortal enemies, they were alike in being subjected to violent and often unfair criticism by many of their contemporaries. He wrote, "The truth surely is that both were extraordinary figures, men of genius, though in widely differing idioms, and that, like most men of genius operating in a parliamentary democracy, they inspired a great deal of dislike and no small degree of distrust among the bustling mediocrities who form the majority of mankind."

Had MacArthur retired to the Philippines or Japan, where he had lived almost without interruption since 1935, his last years would have been less empty. The Japanese revered him, and those who remember his years as Supreme Commander revere him still. When he made his sentimental journey to the Philippines in 1961, he learned that in the Philippine army his name was called at every muster, and a sergeant answered "Present in spirit!" Many Americans credit MacArthur for avenging the attack on Pearl Harbor. The Japanese, the Filipinos, and the South Koreans saw him not as an avenger but a liberator. He freed the Japanese from totalitarianism and Emperor worship, freed the Filipinos from the Japanese, and freed the South Koreans from the Communists.

MacArthur may have seemed anachronistic to many U.S. political commentators, but throughout his career in Asia he demonstrated extraordinary foresight. At the turn of the century, after his tour of the Far East with his father, he speculated that the Japanese might have hegemonic designs on their neighbors. In the 1930s he warned of the growing Japanese threat to peace in the Pacific. In Japan his progressive reforms surpassed both in scope and in vision the blueprint that had been written for the American Occupation by desk officers in Washington. And in Korea he understood that the Communists were fighting not for South Korea but for control of all Asia.

The common denominator was always Japan. He was either preoccupied by the threat it posed to the Far East or, after the war, preoccupied with the threat others posed to it. During his five years of governing Japan, two seeming paradoxes emerged. First, though a skilled man of war, MacArthur proved to be a committed man of peace. Second, he applied the tools of the absolute autocrat to the task of freeing Japan forever from autocracy.

The first, of course, is not really a paradox. The idea that soldiers and generals by nature promote constant international belligerency is only a bit of philosophical debris from the 1960s. As MacArthur said in his magnificent farewell address at West Point in 1962, "The soldier, above all other people, prays for peace, for he must suffer and bear the deepest wounds and scars of war."

No man in American history has been given absolute power in peacetime. In a democracy power is diffused among different sectors of society to prevent abuses. MacArthur, however, had absolute power in Japan for five years. The real paradox is that true democracy could not have been established there any other way.

One commentator on the Occupation wrote, "MacArthur was in control. Japan would be made a peace-loving, democratic, prosperous, industrial nation if it took violence, tyranny, and economic chaos to do it." The statement was intended to be facetious, but it was still basically true. The Japanese are quick studies, and they soon learned to mouth, as if by rote, the abstract principles of democracy. It was quite another thing to teach them to believe in democracy in their hearts.

Two hundred and thirty years ago, confronting the thorny question of how just political systems could be established, Jean Jacques Rousseau wrote:

> Men . . . do not govern themselves by abstract views; one does not make them happy except by forcing them to be, and one has to make them feel happiness in order to make them love it. There is a job for the talents of the hero. . . .

Rousseau's point was that in the earliest stages of a new society, its values must be imposed from above by some wise and forward-looking hero. In the case of Japan, MacArthur was the hero who made the Japanese feel democracy and therefore love it. Along with Yoshida he made them cherish liberty and therefore want to safeguard it. In fact no figure in modern political history has come as close as MacArthur to being the semimythical being called a lawgiver—a man of such towering political vision that he can single-handedly reinvent a society according to an ideal model.

Like Japan's own Meiji reformers, he used his privileged position to introduce sweeping political reforms, though he abolished the easily abused absolute power of the Emperor, which the Meiji system depended on. At first he took all of Hirohito's vast real and spiritual authority on his own shoulders. Then, after cracking the toughest nuts himself—a new constitution and land reform—he gradually began to shift more and more power to Yoshida, the elected representative of the Japanese people. Importantly Yoshida, both before and after the Occupation, was able to modify what MacArthur had set in place. This unique partnership produced modern Japan, a great and free nation that represents the best hope that the rest of Asia may someday share in the heritage of liberty, justice, and prosperity.

KONRAD ADENAUER

The West's Iron Curtain

IN 1963 AN aging but still formidable Konrad Adenauer was overseeing one of his last sessions of the West German Bundestag. The end of his career had come. Badly damaged politically by the Berlin Wall crisis, the eighty-seven-year-old Chancellor had barely been reelected in 1961. He had bowed to pressure from younger politicians and agreed to step down after two years of his fourth term. Fourteen years of extraordinary accomplishment were behind him. Four years of restless, bitter retirement were ahead.

A longtime Bundestag adversary, who perhaps felt he could afford to be kind now that the implacable Adenauer was being put out to pasture, rose from his chair and told the Chancellor that he had been right after all when he had engineered West Germany's admission to NATO in 1954.

Adenauer eyed the man stonily and then delivered a terse reply. "The difference between you and me," he said, "has been that I was right on time."

In those few words Adenauer himself summed up the essence of his career and in an important way the essence of all great leadership. Many, like the opposition deputy, have the gift of hindsight; Adenauer had the gift of foresight. In power during the unsettled period after World War II, when alignments of nations were set that would last for generations, he had the wisdom and courage to take action when action was needed—and the political skill to overcome the objections of those who were afraid or unwilling to act. Winston Churchill was seldom off the mark in evaluating world leaders. In 1953 he told the House of Commons that Adenauer was "the wisest German statesman since Bismarck."

Adenauer was the major architect of the postwar order of Western Europe. As a Rhinelander, he had always sought rapprochement between Germany and France, and throughout his life he cherished an ideal vision of a united Europe in which the conflicts that plagued earlier generations would never recur. He also recognized from the start that the Soviet Union represented what was bad about the old Europe, not what was good about the new. As a result he held the eastern ramparts of free Europe with rock-hard determination.

In a sense Adenauer was the quintessential Christian Democratic statesman. He believed that tyranny of any kind—that of one nation over other nations, or that of a government over its people—was the ultimate evil because it smothered individual liberty. His dream of a united Europe, born in the ashes of World War I and reenforced by the horrors of the Nazi era, stemmed directly from this abhorrence of tyranny.

After World War II, however, free Europe was threatened from without by forces far greater than those that had before threatened it from within. At first few understood the nature or the magnitude of the threat; Adenauer was one who did. After he came to power in 1949, he stood like a rock at the Elbe, the free world's eastern frontier, unmoved by the Soviets' threats and contemptuous of their sporadic, self-serving peace overtures. But he realized that Germany, unarmed and isolated, could not contain this new danger alone. During the 1950s the United

States and Great Britain were steadfast in their support of the defense of Europe and the rest of the world from the Soviet Union. But France, without which an effective anti-Soviet coalition in Europe was unthinkable, had been stung three times in seventy-five years by the might of Germany, and it remained deeply skeptical of any plan for the rearming of its neighbor to the east. So Adenauer turned once again to his dream of destroying the barriers that divided Europeans from Europeans. Before, this had been an impractical, almost poetic abstraction; now it was a matter of dire necessity, and he pursued it with redoubled tenacity.

While striving to cement a united European front against the Soviet threat, he also sought to bind Europe together with a system of economic and political interdependencies that would finally put an end to threats to the peace from within Europe. Through such initiatives as NATO, the European Coal and Steel Community, and the Franco-German friendship treaty of 1963, this was achieved to a remarkable degree. Much of the credit goes to Konrad Adenauer.

For over a decade Adenauer was our own Iron Curtain—a man of iron will yet infinite patience whose profound belief in Christian principles made him the West's most effective, articulate, and consistent spokesman against what he considered to be an empire founded on godlessness and spiritual oppression. At the same time, in spite of his outward austerity and his rigorous anticommunism, he was a warm, good-humored, gentle man beloved equally by his people and his own children, a forgiving father figure for a fatherland that had been led far astray.

In the ruins of postwar Germany, Adenauer stood out like a great cathedral. To his defeated people he was *der Alte*, "the old man," a symbol of faith and perseverance in a time of national humiliation and confusion. He reassured them by conducting himself with calm, patient dignity, if also with a certain air of schoolmasterlike superiority. Against those who stood in his way, he was a conniving and ruthless political infighter. To the rest of the world he was the trusted spokesman of the new democratic Germany. Within a decade he would transform it from an international outlaw into a dependable bastion of freedom.

Friendships between national leaders are rare. They usually meet within the swirl of events and amid the confines of protocol, immersed in history and surrounded by diplomats, aides, and translators. The specter of national self-interest that hovers over their encounters tends to inhibit friendly interaction.

During my political career, though I had friendly meetings with many foreign leaders, I could call only a few of them personal friends. Konrad Adenauer was one of those few. Our friendship spanned fourteen years, and for each of us it continued both in office and out.

In the fall of 1947, I was one of nineteen members of a House of Representatives committee, chaired by Christian Herter, that visited Europe and made recommendations for implementing the Marshall Plan, which had been announced in June. Our stops in Germany were among the most sobering experiences of my life. Entire cities had been completely flattened by Allied bombers, and we found thousands of families huddled in the debris of buildings and in bunkers. There was a critical shortage of food, and thin-faced, half-dressed children approached us not to beg but to sell their fathers' war medals or to trade them for something to eat.

One of the other congressmen on the committee, a normally reserved conservative southerner, was so moved by the sight of the children he met during one of our stops that he gave them all of his soap and candy and the sweater he was wearing. He told us later, "The last piece I had I gave to a little girl of about ten who was holding a baby that was about a year and a half old. And do you know what she did with that chocolate? She didn't eat it. She very carefully put it in the mouth of the baby and told the baby what it was and let the baby eat it. When she did that I just couldn't help myself. I went back into the train and got everything I had and gave it to the kids."

In Washington, Congress had been considering whether to give war bonuses to our World War II veterans; in Essen, I met a miner who was living in a cellar with his wife and twenty-two-year-old son. Though the son had lost a leg in battle, he received no pension or benefits at all because his disability was not considered severe enough.

During a visit to a coal mine we met workers who saved the watery, meatless soup they were given for lunch so they could take it home and divide it among their families. Germany's coal mines were producing far less than before the war with the same number of workers, because the men were weakened by hunger and malnutrition.

Still, the children who refused to beg and the men who shared what little they had demonstrated to me that Adenauer was right when he declared in late 1945 that the German people were "bowed low, but . . . unbroken."

The American military occupation authorities, led by General Lucius Clay, assured us that the Germans indeed had the strength of spirit they would need to recover. What was missing so far, Clay said, was leadership. Germany had lost a whole generation of potential leaders during the war, and thousands more had been disqualified from leadership positions because of links with the Nazis. He told us that Germany would have to develop an entirely new crop of leaders for both the public and private sectors; those from the wartime and prewar eras would not do. What was needed above all was a strong national leader, dedicated to democratic principles, who could guide his people back into the family of free nations and at the same time protect them from the new danger looming in the east.

Clay was right about the kind of leader Germany needed, but wrong in assuming that such a leader could not come from the prewar ranks.

Konrad Adenauer was born in 1876 to a father who was a court clerk in Cologne and a mother about whom little is known other than that Konrad's father gave up a promising career in the Prussian army to marry her. Both parents were hardworking and religious. Konrad was raised in the Catholic Church and remained devoutly religious all his life.

His childhood was strict and austere, but also secure and loving. The family had very little money. One year it was so scarce that the children were allowed to choose whether the family would go without meat for several Sunday dinners so there would be enough money for a Christmas tree and candles. Konrad and the others opted for the Christmas tree.

Though he did well in school, his father told him at first that the family could not afford to send him to college. Konrad accepted the ruling with inner disappointment but outward equanimity and took a job as a bank clerk. But when his father saw how miserable he was after two weeks on the job, he squeezed the domestic budget further so the boy could go to college, where he studied law. Konrad knew that his education meant sacrifice for his family, and he applied himself ferociously to his studies. To increase his study time, he sometimes kept himself awake at night by putting his feet in buckets of cold water.

Young Konrad's tenacity was matched by his audacity. Two years after graduation he went to work in a law firm owned by a leading member of Cologne's Center party, the conservative Catholic party and forerunner of Adenauer's own Christian Democratic Union. One day in 1906, the twenty-nine-year-old Adenauer learned that his employer, a man named Kausen, planned to appoint a young judge to a seat on the Cologne city council. He marched straight to Kausen's office. "Why not take me?" he demanded. "I'm sure I'm just as good as the other fellow."

This took guts and it also took self-assurance, two qualities Adenauer consistently displayed throughout his career. In fact Adenauer was a good lawyer and a hard worker, and in claiming to be as good as the other man he was probably absolutely right. Kausen gave him the seat, and Adenauer began a political career that would last for fifty-seven years.

A photograph of the young Adenauer shows him on an outing in the country with four friends. The children are buried up to their chins in a haystack, and the other youngsters are all grinning mischievously. Konrad's face bears a stern, somber expression reenforced by deep shadows under his cheekbones and his mouth. But he is waving at the camera with his left hand, which pokes out just above the top of the haystack. This was typical of Adenauer: Though displaying a studied reserve and detachment, he could also enjoy himself.

Adenauer was seventy-seven when I first met him on his state visit to Washington in 1953, and his impassive face by then was finely and evenly lined, the wrinkles resembling the thin furrows water makes through sand. While it had the same detached quietude, it was not the same face as the one in the haystack photograph. When he was forty-one, his driver fell asleep and hit a tram. With characteristic stoicism Adenauer pulled himself from the wreckage and calmly walked to the hospital, his face covered with blood. The driver, only mildly injured, made the trip by stretcher.

Adenauer suffered broken cheekbones, along with other facial injuries, and the accident left him looking even more severe. Many writers later described his face as resembling that of a Chinese mandarin. It was an oddly apt comparison; the old bromide about Oriental inscrutability was completely appropriate to Adenauer. John J. McCloy, who served with great distinction as America's first High Commissioner to Germany after World War II, put it another way. He told me, "He had the strong, stoic face of an American Indian. He looked like Geronimo."

Because of his outward seriousness, Adenauer was thought to be humorless, even coldhearted, by many of his critics and even by supporters who did not know him well. But although he was not a punster or a backslapper, beneath the surface Adenauer was a deeply compassionate man with a subtle, refined sense of humor.

Adenauer rarely wasted his energies on unimportant issues or lost causes. Similarly he usually reserved his humor for some practical purpose. In 1959 President Eisenhower gave a reception at the White House for the foreign dignitaries who had come to Washington for John

Foster Dulles's funeral. There Adenauer saw me standing with Soviet Foreign Minister Gromyko, who had flown in from the stalemated Geneva conference on Germany and Berlin. He walked over to us, and I commented to him lightheartedly that many people claimed Gromyko and I looked alike.

The Chancellor laughed and said, "That is very true, and as a result I have a suggestion for breaking the impasse at Geneva. You get on Gromyko's plane and go back to Geneva and let Gromyko stay here and be the Vice President. Then, I am sure, we'll be able to break the logjam." Even the usually dour Russian joined in the laughter.

While Adenauer's remark was facetious, he had made a telling point about the Soviets' intransigence at Geneva. Many years later, after he had left office, he used humor to indicate his disappointment with the political acumen of his successor, Ludwig Erhard. Settling down one day for an interview with a reporter, he asked, "Shall we discuss serious politics, or Chancellor Erhard?"

In 1917, while Adenauer was recuperating from his auto accident, a pair of city officials visited the Black Forest sanatorium where he was staying. The position of Lord Mayor had become vacant and the city council wanted Adenauer to take it. The delegation's mission was to involve Adenauer in a conversation about municipal affairs to determine whether the accident had scattered his brains. He quickly figured out what his visitors were up to, however, and told them, "Gentlemen, it's only outwardly that my head isn't quite right." The officials laughed and offered him the job on the spot. World War I was drawing to an end. Cologne was in shambles. Adenauer accepted immediately.

At first the forty-one-year-old *Oberbürgermeister* had his hands full finding enough food and shelter for the residents and returning soldiers and keeping the population under control in the political vacuum left by the nation's defeat and the Kaiser's abdication. But as life returned to normal, Adenauer undertook a grand plan to restore Cologne's ancient cultural and architectural splendor. He told a friend gleefully, "Times of political catastrophe are especially suitable for new creative ventures!" Already his attention was straying beyond Germany's borders. He viewed his city as a new link between Germany and Western Europe.

Even then he sometimes displayed both ingenuity and guile in getting colleagues to go along with his schemes. In 1926 he wanted to build a suspension bridge across the Rhine, but a majority of the city council wanted an arch bridge instead. He sought out the Communist councilmen and told them that suspension bridges were what gave Leningrad its rare and special beauty. Adenauer knew practically nothing about Leningrad or its bridges, but he knew a great deal about human nature and the warm spot German Communists had in their hearts for revolutionary Russia. He got his suspension bridge—and also earned a reputation as a skillful political operator.

At around the same time Adenauer turned down a chance to become Chancellor. During the Weimar Republic, Chancellors stayed in office an average of only seven months before their legislative coalitions crumbled. The leaders of the Center party thought Adenauer might be forceful enough to make a government last, and in 1926 they invited him to form one.

He was tempted. But his poker face hid a shrewd politician who steered clear of lost causes. It was not that he was unwilling to take risks. But he did follow a practice of carefully weighing the chances of success, combining close analysis with a finely tuned political instinct. After going to Berlin and testing the political climate, he concluded that the chance of beating the odds was not worth it. So he declined the offer and returned to Cologne.

The mounting economic and social pressures that were then making effective government so difficult in Germany might have overcome even Konrad Adenauer. But while his decision is understandable from a personal standpoint, I have often wondered how profoundly history might have been changed if this enormously capable political leader had become Chancellor at that time. Hitler might have met his nemesis before he seized power and brought such tragedy to Germany and the world.

Three and a half years later Adenauer was elected to a second twelve-year term as Lord Mayor. Then fifty-three, he expected to serve it out and retire. But when Hitler became Chancellor, the Nazis did not want leaders of Adenauer's national stature and independent mind in office. He made his stubborn independence plain from the outset. Within a few weeks he either snubbed or resisted Hitler three times. First he vocally but unsuccessfully opposed the Nazis' abolition of the Prussian state parliament, of which Adenauer had been a member since 1917. Later, on a campaign trip before the March 1933 elections, Hitler visited Cologne. Adenauer pointedly refused to meet him at the airport. Two days later, on the morning of Hitler's Cologne speech, he ordered city workmen to remove Nazi banners from a bridge over the Rhine and sent a contingent of policemen along to protect them while they worked.

After the elections the Nazis commanded absolute power, and Adenauer became persona non grata. He was taunted in public. Soon he was dismissed as Lord Mayor for imaginary crimes against the people of Cologne and driven from the city. While the Nazis regarded him with hostility, however, he was not high on their list of people to be eliminated. He was arrested during the Night of the Long Knives in 1934, but released unharmed when the bloodbath was over. For most of the remaining Nazi years he was left alone to tend his roses and his family at his home in Rhöndorf, near Cologne.

Most, but not all, for in 1944 he had a close brush with death. He was apparently invited to join Carl Goerdeler's courageous but ill-fated plot to kill Hitler, but turned the conspirators down after figuring the odds and deciding the plan would probably fail. After the assassination attempt did fail, he was arrested and imprisoned. He escaped transfer to Buchenwald by feigning illness. He then slipped from the hospital with the help of a friend who was in the Luftwaffe. Eventually the Gestapo found him hiding in a mill in the forest forty miles from Cologne and arrested him again. The Nazis finally let him go in November 1944 after his son Max, an officer in the German army, went to Berlin to plead for his father's release. Adenauer was at home in Rhöndorf when the Americans took Cologne the following spring.

Despite this drama the most significant period of Adenauer's life during the Nazi years was the quietest. When he was driven from Cologne in the spring of 1933, he left his family at home and entered a Benedictine abbey fifteen miles from the Rhine. He hoped that in the abbey he could at least temporarily escape the attention of the Nazis. The abbot was an old school friend. Adenauer stayed there almost a year, spending most of his time meditating, wandering in the woods, and reading. The abbey had a good history collection, and he devoured book after book.

Before Hitler took power, Adenauer was the prosperous, powerful "King of Cologne" and the stern but affectionate patriarch of a growing family. Now his power was gone, his family was separated from him, and he was quite literally living a life of monastic asceticism. Only his faith remained. As he reflected on the perils a people courted when it surrendered to militant nationalism and tyranny, he began to dwell with increasing intensity on his lifelong dream of a new European political order in which liberty and Christian principles would come first and national power and identity second.

These were the solitary idylls of a deeply disillusioned man. Fifteen years later, when he took power in West Germany, Adenauer's practical political instincts again became dominant. But when practical considerations dictated that the only way to ensure a united defense of Europe was for France and Germany to overcome their differences, Adenauer was philosophically ready. He had always wanted to bring these two nations together; now it could be a means to a great end—the defense of the West against the new Soviet empire—rather than just an end in itself.

When the Americans took Cologne in 1945, they rushed to reinstall Adenauer as mayor. But then Occupation control passed to the British. For reasons that have never been satisfactorily explained, they soon fired him and prohibited him from engaging in political activity. He believed that the British Labor government wanted the Social Democrats to take power in Germany and therefore did not want to allow a conservative to remain in as influential a position as mayor of Cologne. The dismissal was a heavy blow to Adenauer, for whom reviving Cologne was a true labor of love.

In any case, Cologne's loss was Germany's gain. Again Adenauer was thrust into the wilderness, this time by the Allies instead of the Nazis, but now theory and opportunity coincided. He spent these two months of forced retirement turning his view of Germany's destiny into a concrete plan for political action. As soon as the British allowed him to participate in politics again, he began to concentrate his energies on the Christian Democratic Union, the new conservative party. It would be the foundation of his power until 1963.

With his persuasive powers, hard work, and sheer force of will, Adenauer won control of the party and swiftly built it into a formidable national force. He also helped himself along by some carefully timed power plays. He took over the chairmanship of one important party meeting by striding in, sitting down, and announcing that he was in charge because he was the oldest man present. The other participants were too stunned to protest.

One might expect a leader who entered parliamentary politics relatively late in life to find the grind of election campaigning irritating and even demeaning. Shigeru Yoshida, a career diplomat before becoming Japan's Prime Minister after World War II, certainly did. But not Adenauer. In the spring of 1960 he gave me some shrewd strategic advice with regard to the coming American election and then asked me whether I enjoyed campaigning. I told him that I found it an ordeal. I said that after a campaign I felt the way I did after my service in the Pacific in World War II: I wouldn't have missed it, but I wouldn't want to go through it again for a while. He then surprised me by disagreeing. "I like to campaign," he said. "I like to be able to fight for what I believe, to debate the critics, to strike back at them."

In this sense he was unlike his great friend de Gaulle. Adenauer enjoyed the cut and thrust of personal political combat; he liked to get in the ring with his political opponents. De Gaulle almost imperially refused to do so. Contrary to what one might expect, the Frenchman, de Gaulle, was the introvert. The German, Adenauer, was the extrovert. Each succeeded politically, but with completely different approaches.

In the weeks before the first postwar German elections in 1949, the seventy-three-year-old Adenauer proved phenomenally effective and energetic on the stump. He had the staying power of a man half his age and an unexpected knack for communicating with voters about what mattered to them. His frustrated opponents, the Social Democrats, who immediately after the war had expected to be the dominant party in West Germany, resorted to bitter personal attacks, but he rarely responded in kind. In the election the CDU received 7.36 million votes, 400,000 more than the Social Democrats. By one vote the newly formed Bundestag elected Adenauer as the first Chancellor of the German Federal Republic.

As leader of an occupied nation, Adenauer's actual powers were severely limited. In dealing both with the Allies and with opponents in the government, he had to rely heavily on his common sense and his tenacious, steely patience. In negotiations and debates his customary approach was not to try to dominate them from the beginning, but rather to listen first to what everyone else had to say. When he finally spoke, his gambler's instincts helped him avoid points on which his position was weak and concentrate on points he knew he could win.

Essentially the secrets of his formidability were simply being right, being reasonable, and being prepared. He thoroughly studied each topic on the agenda. He was seldom caught offguard; he made sure he could respond quickly and effectively to opponents' arguments. Sir Ivone Kirkpatrick, the British High Commissioner, said that Adenauer "was always quick to detect any weakness in the opponent's armor and to drive his weapon through the chink."

He had other weapons besides the cold steel of logic, however. When a cabinet meeting grew difficult, he would sometimes suspend debate for a while and pass around a bottle of wine. After a few glassfuls and some friendly small talk, he would resume the meeting. The opposition would then be substantially less resolute.

Adenauer was a connoisseur of fine wines. He loved not only his native Rhineland but the rich wines from its vineyards. Sometimes at luncheons he would serve both a Rhine wine or a Moselle and a Bordeaux, but he would leave the French wine entirely to his guests. John McCloy told me of an occasion at a small dinner party when he had served what he considered to be a good German table wine that he had obtained from a PX. He noticed that Adenauer drank only half a glass. The next day he received from the Chancellor a case of Bernkasteler Doktor, a Moselle and one of the world's finest wines. Incidentally it is also one of my favorites; I sometimes served it at White House state dinners.

One of Adenauer's greatest assets was that even in his seventies he seemed tireless. The best politician, he once told me, is the one who "can outsit the rest." Willing to let meetings run far into the night if necessary, he would sit patiently as one sleepy opponent after another came around to his point of view.

Like every successful leader I have known, Adenauer was an intensely competitive man in virtually every activity in which he engaged. Just as Eisenhower, despite his disarmingly genial and easygoing manner, was a fierce competitor on the golf course and at the bridge table, Adenauer gave no quarter in his favorite game of boccie—Italian lawn bowling. McCloy, a fine athlete who in his youth had been a world-class tennis player, found him to be a tough competitor. He told me that Adenauer played boccie with great skill and total concentration and was determined to win even when he was playing with a close friend. He would not have agreed with the old saying "It isn't whether you win or lose that counts but how you play the game." Adenauer played fair, but he always played to win.

The same was true of his political style. Like Churchill, Adenauer was a brilliant parliamentarian. During the 1949 session of the Bundestag in which he spelled out his program, Adenauer showed that he had another key political skill: the ability to keep his wits and his good humor under stress.

Since it was essentially the inaugural address by the winner of the first legitimate German election in sixteen years, the moment ought to have been solemn and dignified. Adenauer knew the whole world was watching to see whether the Germans had learned how to be democrats. But in the middle of the speech his Communist and Social Democratic opponents began to heckle him. A man who was really as pompous as Adenauer was supposed to be might have shown outrage that the occasion had been sullied; a man as humorless as he was thought to be might have icily ignored the hecklers. Instead he bested them. When a Communist Bundestag deputy named Heinz Renner called out sarcastically that the section of Adenauer's speech about the

Soviet Union had been "drafted by an expert" on the subject, Adenauer paused for a moment and said, "Herr Renner, you are an envious man!" The remark brought down the house.

Adenauer's use of high-handed tactics and his skill as a political infighter earned him a reputation for ruthlessness that he did not seem to resent. Once, accused of running roughshod over opponents, he countered modestly, "That is not altogether true." Adenauer and the postwar leader of another former Axis power, Japan's Yoshida, developed a strong mutual admiration. This may have been enhanced by the fact that both were firmly committed to democracy, yet each had a certain penchant, in practice, for one-man rule.

Unlike some, Adenauer was generally patient with the press, but he did not suffer fools gladly and refused to bear the perennial politician's burden of dignifying a bad question with a good answer. To one correspondent he barked, "I'd flunk you from the diplomatic service for that question."

The Allied Occupation lasted for six of Adenauer's fourteen years as Chancellor. He often told me that he could never have achieved what he did had it not been for our Marshall Plan assistance and for the wise counsel and support he received from four remarkable Americans: Dean Acheson, Lucius Clay, John McCloy, and John Foster Dulles. Another reason he succeeded was his willingness to compromise with the Allies if compromise allowed him to inch a step closer to his objectives of securing Germany's independence, economic recovery, and integration with the rest of Western Europe.

Like Yoshida, Adenauer knew that being cooperative with the Allies was a far cry from being submissive, although sometimes, when he became exasperated by the stridence of some particularly impatient Germans, he would say, "Who do they think lost the war, anyway?" In 1949, before becoming Chancellor, he delivered a major address to an international group in Berne, Switzerland, in which he made a stinging attack on a number of Occupation policies. He also said that Germans would need a new sense of national pride—he was careful not to say nationalism—if they were to rebuild and defend their country.

After the speech many critics, including newspapers in Allied capitals, huffed that the Allies were confronting an unrepentant German nationalist. But Adenauer's relationship with the military governors themselves, who knew him well, was not changed. Meanwhile his reputation among his countrymen was enhanced. By his bold independence he projected a personal dignity that was a tremendous boost to the Germans, who desperately wanted to have their national dignity restored.

I first met Adenauer at National Airport in Washington in April 1953 on a dark, rainy morning as he arrived for talks with President Eisenhower and John Foster Dulles. Dulles and I were at the airport as Eisenhower's representatives.

The Chancellor's visit had great significance for two reasons. First, no German Chancellor had ever come to the United States. In fact Adenauer was the first official visitor from Germany since before World War I. But the occasion was also important because it came only eight years after the end of World War II. The manner in which Adenauer was received in the United States, both by political leaders and by the people themselves, would show whether the bitterness unleashed by Hitler and the Nazis had eased.

U.S. support for Adenauer's foreign policies was by no means certain. Many influential Americans were suggesting that the U.S. should refuse to involve itself in the defense of Europe, and this isolationism would be encouraged if our talks with Adenauer were unproductive or unfriendly. Our small, soggy ceremony at Andrews would be the source of millions of first impressions, both among the American people and in Europe.

When I first saw Adenauer emerge from his airplane, I was struck by his massive six-foot-two-inch frame, his stiff, straight posture, and most of all his sharply angled, sphinxlike face. Some men's faces automatically betray their feelings. Other men, like Adenauer, bear completely controlled expressions that reveal nothing. In politics and international relations one participant has an advantage if he can guess correctly what another is thinking or feeling by studying his expression. Adenauer's was one of quiet, almost stoic self-control. It concealed his thoughts completely.

The key message I wanted to get across in my welcoming statement was that Adenauer's visit marked the rebirth rather than the birth of the productive relationship between our two countries. Because of the two world wars, the image of the goose-stepping, nationalistic, militaristic Prussian-Nazi had become a part of American folklore; it was commonly asserted that "the Hun is either at your throat or on his knees." I knew, however, that there was another side to Germany and German-American relations. Mrs. Nixon's mother had been born in Germany. My own mother had majored in German in college and had always spoken highly of the accomplishments and standards of the great German universities. At Duke Law School I had learned from Professor Lon Fuller of the profound influences German scholars had had on the development of western legal principles.

In welcoming Adenauer, I wanted to invoke the memory of an earlier time and remind Americans that Germans had helped build our country from the very beginning. I told Adenauer that only a few steps from Blair House, where he was to stay in Washington, there stood a statue of Baron Friedrich Wilhelm von Steuben, the Prussian army officer who had served with George Washington at Valley Forge during the winter of 1777–1778 and who had taken over the training of the Continental army with spectacular results. I said that Americans would never forget the contributions Von Steuben and millions of other Germans had made to this nation.

In his response Adenauer turned to me and said, "You just mentioned Baron Steuben. I wish to thank you for the generous manner in which you have paid tribute to the friendship between America and Germany without mentioning the last few decades." His authorized biographer wrote later that he was visibly moved by the welcome. The next day he laid a wreath at Von Steuben's statue.

Adenauer's domestic and foreign policies were formed by the most basic lessons of his life. Raised in a political and cultural atmosphere in which loyalty to things German was balanced by instinctive affection for things French, he sought a Franco-German rapprochement that would use the ancient rapport between the two nations as a strategic wedge in the modern world of East-West confrontation. Trained as a devout, freedom-loving Catholic, he sought partnerships between nations and interest groups in society—government, business, and labor—that would prevent one nation or group from establishing a tyranny over the others. And above all, since he loved liberty and considered it crucial to the survival of the human spirit, he was prepared to fight to protect his and other free societies from the threat posed by communism and the Soviet Union.

While his thinking was neither complex nor original, it was sound and comprehensive and it gave him the unity of purpose that a great leader needs. Unity of purpose and good sense, of course, do not always go together. I have met some leaders who were effective technicians but who had no discernible idealism. I have met others who were starry-eyed idealists but did not have the foggiest notion of how to achieve their ideals. Adenauer was one of those rare leaders whose practical political intelligence matched his idealism. He was the master of a rare alchemy by which he turned his profound spiritual belief into a basis for effective political action.

Adenauer understood that democracy's roots are in Judeo-Christian ethics. In fact what he feared most from both communism and Nazism was that people could be forced to sacrifice their spiritual selves on the altar of materialism. But he was not a modern crusader out to convert the non-Christian world. To him the essence of good Christian government was that it left each person alone to make his accounting to God in whatever way he wished.

With the protection of the liberty and dignity of each individual as their highest imperative, Adenauer's Christian politics were also at the heart of Germany's economic miracle. In this case his instincts were an adequate substitute for technical know-how. He did not know much about economics and did not participate in the drafting of specific fiscal and monetary policies, leaving the details to his superb Finance Minister, Ludwig Erhard. But Erhard operated according to Adenauer's "principle of distributed power." Twelve years of German fascism and his knowledge of the Soviet Union had schooled the Chancellor in the dangers of allowing too much power to gather in either public or private hands. He opposed both nationalized industry and monopolies and both strikes and unfair management practices.

An historic meeting in 1951 between Adenauer and Germany's leading labor leader produced an agreement that allowed workers to sit side by side, and vote one for one, with management on industrial supervisory committees. This partnership gave West Germany three decades without significant labor unrest.

Because of this agreement and Erhard's shrewd management of the economy, and because Adenauer in 1949 persuaded the Allies to reduce drastically their plans for dismantling German industry, West Germany enjoyed breathtaking economic growth for almost three decades. Today its per capita GNP is higher than that of the United States, and its industrial output is one and a half times that of the larger, undivided Germany before the war.

Just as Adenauer's concept of partnership brought prosperity to West Germany, it helped bring peace and economic unity to Western Europe. "In my opinion," Adenauer once wrote of the postwar scene, "no single European country could guarantee a secure future to its people by its own strength."

With French Foreign Minister Robert Schuman, Adenauer agreed to an international authority that put most European steel and coal production under joint control, an unprecedented arrangement that led, under the guidance of the brilliant French economist Jean Monnet, to the European Common Market. His dream of a European army to which each nation would supply troops died when the French Parliament, because of its lingering distrust of the Germans, refused to consider it. But Adenauer overcame his initial disappointment, and with the help of Churchill and Anthony Eden he arranged West Germany's entry into NATO in 1954 and its complete independence from Allied control in 1955. He and Charles de Gaulle capped the reconciliation by making triumphant visits to each other's countries and by signing a friendship treaty in 1963.

Adenauer was sometimes compared with Charlemagne, the towering figure who through force of personality and faith united Europe briefly under one Christian empire in the late eighth and early ninth centuries. The comparison was apt in more than one sense. Both Charlemagne and Adenauer were big men physically. Both, though men of profound faith, also enjoyed the good life. And while both were known as men of action rather than as great thinkers, each was enthralled by the same dream and possessed of the means and ability to make it real.

Charlemagne's empire was divided among his three grandsons in the ninth century. Since then France and Germany, the two largest parts of the divided empire, have periodically been embroiled in hostility. During his years in the wilderness, as he studied and reflected, Adenauer grew increasingly convinced that the people of Europe could once again be brought together under friendly governments united in their commitment to Christian values. After the war his priority became a free Europe united against Soviet despotism.

Ironically this dream of unity had a dark side. After World War II many Germans thought he was not really interested in reuniting the divided German nation. When Adenauer faced toward Western Europe, they saw him as turning his back on his seventeen million countrymen in East Germany. To an extent this was true.

Adenauer was born in the Rhineland, part of the "middle kingdom" between medieval France and Germany. Many Rhinelanders are born with a kernel of ambivalence: They are both German and a little French at once. Some of his critics charged that he was more pro-Rhineland, or even more pro-France, than he was pro-Germany. While his patriotism was never legitimately in doubt, it is true that his heart always remained in the Rhineland and that he had none of the Prussian German's antipathy toward the French.

John McCloy was a close personal friend and admirer of the Chancellor. Once in talking with me he used a quotation from Goethe to describe Adenauer: "Two souls dwell, alas! in my breast." One of these souls was German, the other European. One soul loved the fatherland, the other was repelled by its episodes of militarism and totalitarianism. Adenauer wanted the West German capital located in the Rhineland; this was one way to disassociate his new Germany from its Prussian past. Bonn is closer to Paris than it is to Berlin.

Ultimately Adenauer's distaste for Prussian Germany probably caused his downfall. When the East Germans began building the Berlin Wall in August 1961, he did not travel to Berlin for nine days, a delay that earned him loud and partially justified criticism. His presence at the outset of the crisis would have been a great comfort to the people of both halves of the city.

When he finally did arrive—and was coolly received by the Berliners and their mayor, Willy Brandt—he walked determinedly toward the barbed wire fence at Potsdamer Platz and stood four or five yards away from it, staring over to the other side. East German officials jeered at him through loudspeakers, but he stood his ground. It was an impressive moment of silent defiance, but it was not enough to dispel the bitterness many West Germans felt at his not having gone sooner. In the following month's elections, Adenauer's CDU lost its absolute majority in the Bundestag.

Throughout his chancellorship, though Adenauer always said he was dedicated to uniting the two Germanys, there was always uncertainty about how deeply he believed his own words. He once said that there were three kinds of Germans: the schnapps drinkers of Prussia, the beer drinkers of Bavaria, and the wine drinkers of the Rhineland. Only the Rhinelanders, he said, were sober enough to rule the rest. And there is the possibility that this shrewd politician may have been concerned that more liberal East German voters in a united German nation might have jeopardized the margin of victory that had given him the chancellorship.

The more fatalistic historians define a capable leader as one who manages to conform his policies to the unchangeable flow of history. Putting it simply, they believe that history makes the man rather than the other way around. According to this theory West Germany drifted toward Western Europe and away from the Communist East because of the strong current of the Cold War and the antagonism between the U.S. and the Soviets. Adenauer was simply a rudderman who could make small adjustments.

That sort of theory is cherished by theoreticians, who deal with the abstract. It wins little respect from statesmen, who deal with the concrete and who know from experience how a leader's decisions can change events. In fact, during those troubled early postwar years, the prospects for Franco-German rapprochement, the key to European unity, often seemed slender. Three times in less than a century the French and the Germans had slaughtered each other in bloody combat. The hatred and distrust each had for the other seemed too deep to root out. The reconciliation finally came to pass only because of Adenauer's persistence, the confidence he inspired in other key leaders such as Schuman and de Gaulle, and the new sense of urgency created by the Soviet threat.

At several points during the 1950s, as when the French Parliament vetoed the idea of a European army, a different German leader might have allowed Franco-German relations to drift back into hostility for another generation. Adenauer swallowed his frustration. "I believe patience is the strongest weapon in the armory of the defeated," he once said, "and I possess a great deal of it. I can wait."

For a long moment after the war Europe tottered on a thin edge between alliance and isolationism. In a moment like this, when events can move in one direction as readily as another, a great leader can be the decisive element. Adenauer, with his vision of modern Europe based on the Europe that existed at the dawn of the Middle Ages, was prepared to be such a leader and executed his role perfectly.

After his 1953 trip Adenauer came to Washington six more times before 1961. One reason he came so often was that his talks with Dulles and President Eisenhower were unusually productive. He found the American government more consistently receptive than either Great Britain or France to his ideas about the defense of Western Europe. After the French rejected the European army in 1954, Adenauer told Dulles that he found the "best Europeans" were in the U.S.

He was very close to Dulles, with whom he had much in common. Both were deeply religious. Both had legal backgrounds. Both were devoted to their families. Most important, both were dedicated internationalists, unabashedly committed to combatting the advance of tyranny. As Adenauer biographer Terence Prittie wrote, "Perhaps the strongest bonds which united them were their dutiful belief in God and their hatred of communism."

Adenauer never recognized the legitimacy of the Communist government in East Germany, which he continued to call "the Soviet zone" until the end of his life, and he did not believe the Soviets when they said they wanted an independent, unified, and neutral Germany with a democratically elected government. First, Adenauer knew the Soviets had never allowed free elections in East Germany. Second, he believed no nation in postwar Europe that chose to remain neutral would remain independent for very long. "One cannot sit between two chairs," he said.

At home Adenauer drew heavy criticism from opponents who insisted that he should be more responsive to the Soviets' occasional overtures on unification. In Dulles he found reinforcement for his own strong convictions. As he wrote in his memoirs, "Dulles and I were agreed on one key principle; no concessions without concessions in return. We were accused of being obstinate and static, and the whole world wrote that we should be more flexible."

One day in Bonn, C. L. Sulzberger, the distinguished *New York Times* correspondent, asked Adenauer to name the greatest man he had ever encountered. Adenauer walked to his desk and picked up a framed photograph of Dulles taken during Dulles's last visit to Germany in 1959. This had been the last time Adenauer had seen his friend alive.

The Chancellor handed Sulzberger the photograph and said "There." When Sulzberger asked why he had picked Dulles, Adenauer replied, "He thought clearly. He thought ahead, with visions of what was coming; and he kept his word. He kept his promises."

Some critics argue that Dulles and Adenauer became so close that each hardened the other's unreasonable inflexibility toward the Russians, and that Dulles's personal friendship with the German leader effectively put the U.S. State Department at the service of Adenauer's foreign policy. It is closer to the truth to say that their unique friendship grew from their complete agreement on the issues that mattered to them most, especially their nations' best position vis-à-vis the Soviets.

In February 1959 Dulles learned that he had incurable cancer. One of the first people he told was Adenauer. Dulles died in May, and the eighty-three-year-old Chancellor flew to Washington and marched in the funeral procession.

Dulles's funeral in 1959 drew dignitaries from all over the world to Washington. They came in record numbers. Some hated him; some feared him; all respected him. Adenauer was among the few who loved him.

Like the absurd claims that the British lack a sense of humor and the Japanese cannot see straight, the idea that Germans are by nature stoic and unemotional is a myth. It has been my own experience that despite outward appearances most Germans are deeply emotional. Adenauer certainly fit this mold. Tears came to his eyes as he spoke to me about his affection and respect for Dulles. "There is no figure on the world scene who will be able to fill his shoes," he said.

Just as many found Adenauer cold and unemotional, many others— seeing the straightforward, almost organic unity of his thinking and his programs—thought him to be a simple man. Austria's able and usually perceptive Prime Minister, Bruno Kreisky, once went so far as to say that Adenauer was uncultivated and had said hardly anything. It is true that Adenauer's speech was not peppered like MacArthur's with literary and philosophical references. Nor was he an accomplished writer like de Gaulle and Churchill. In fact he told me that writing his memoirs was a burden that he endured only out of a sense of duty to history.

But he was nonetheless a cultured, well-informed man. Contrary to Kreisky's impression, he read constantly, particularly works of history; I knew this from my own conversations with him. When he went on vacation, he took along his large collection of classical recordings, of which his favorites were works by Schubert, Haydn, Beethoven, Vivaldi, and Mozart. He was well known as an accomplished amateur horticulturist. But few realized that he was also an authority on the Dutch masters. The head of Washington's National Gallery once said admiringly that if he had to pick his own replacement, it would be Adenauer.

The morning after Dulles's funeral, Adenauer and I met in my office in the Capitol, and that evening Mrs. Nixon and I hosted a dinner for him at our home in Washington. In our talks Adenauer never spoke English, but I could tell that he had a considerable understanding of it. Like de Gaulle he sometimes corrected his translator when he felt that the nuance of what he had said had not been properly conveyed.

During dinner our conversation turned to the rigors of campaigning and of international travel. Suddenly he asked me, "How well do you sleep?" I told him I found it very difficult when I had a lot on my mind. Adenauer said he had slept poorly since early in his life. I asked him what he did about it. "I take sleeping pills," he replied. "I've been taking them for thirty years."

I asked him what he did when the pills did not work. He smiled and said, "I go to the doctor and get different ones."

His authorized biographer said Adenauer's insomnia began in 1933, when he became a fugitive from the Nazis. When he was Chancellor he would rise at six, long before the rest of his family, and sit on the terrace or in his garden, listening to the birds and watching the light of the rising sun play on the tops of the Eifel Mountains. This, he claimed, made up for his sleepless nights.

Adenauer sometimes took a pencil and paper into the bathroom with him in the morning, because he often got his best ideas while shaving. After breakfast, the morning papers, and a few moments with his family, he would emerge from his house at 9:50, walk briskly down a flight of fifty-three stone stairs and past his lilac and magnolia bushes, cheerfully greet any reporters, guards, and gardeners who might be waiting for him, and step into his limousine. Like Pope Pius XII, Adenauer liked to drive fast. He was usually at his office in Bonn in ten minutes. His neighbors could set their clocks by his precise morning routine.

Like de Gaulle and Yoshida, Adenauer was an exceptionally devoted family man. His life was struck twice by profound personal tragedy. His first wife, Emma, died in 1916 in Cologne after a lingering illness. For months before her death Adenauer sat by her bedside at midday and during the evening, talking and reading to her until she fell asleep. In 1919, at forty-three, he married twenty-five-year-old Gussi Zinsser, a cousin of the wife of John McCloy. In 1944, when Adenauer was in hiding from the Nazis, they arrested Gussi, installed her in a cell full of prostitutes, and then brutally questioned her about where her husband was. She relented only when the authorities threatened also to jail her teen-age daughter, Libet.

Gussi died in 1948 of leukemia, and a deeply bereaved Adenauer never married again. He raised his seven children as he had been raised himself: with strong doses of discipline and affection. One of his sons said, "Father leaves democracy at the door. He rules our family with a strong hand. If a rose tree must be transplanted, he decides when and where. If my sister wants to bake a cake, he must say yes or no. This is not unusual in Germany, you know; this is how it should be."

After Gussi's death one or more of Adenauer's children often accompanied him on his trips to the United States. His son Paul and daughter Libet were with him in 1959 when he joined Mrs. Nixon and me at dinner in our home.

Adenauer had visited Moscow in the fall of 1955 for talks with Khrushchev, and I was preparing for my own trip in July. I had consulted with many experts on Russia—including Dulles, whom I had seen in his hospital room four days before his death—and at dinner that night I especially wanted Adenauer's thoughts. Not surprisingly they were very similar to those of Dulles.

Adenauer had gone to Moscow hoping to soften the Soviets' belligerence toward the Federal Republic and perhaps to loosen their grip on East Germany. He had found Khrushchev totally intransigent on these issues, but he did obtain the release of ten thousand German POWs who had been held by the Soviets for ten years. In exchange, he agreed to diplomatic relations between the Soviet Union and West Germany.

He undertook his mission with a sense of dread. To Adenauer the Soviet Union represented institutionalized godlessness the likes of which the world had not seen since the time of Constantine. Khrushchev's boorishness heightened Adenauer's horror. He told me that he had to steel himself to avoid being physically ill in the Soviet leader's presence.

Khrushchev was indeed his usual bullying, insulting self with Adenauer, shouting at one point that "capitalists roast Communists and eat them—what's more, without salt!" Adenauer faced him down with his usual steely patience, but so little progress was made during one session that he ordered his airplane back from Frankfurt—though an aide made sure the order was given over an open and presumably monitored telephone line. Believing the Germans were about to pull out, the Soviets softened up considerably.

Khrushchev was then relatively new to power and unfamiliar with the leaders he would be confronting in the free world. He was clearly intent upon testing Adenauer's mettle. During one banquet he proposed a seemingly endless series of toasts to see whether the seventy-nine-year-old Adenauer, so intractable at the negotiating table, could be worn down by liquor. Though he preferred wine to vodka, Adenauer had a stomach as well as a will of iron. After fifteen toasts he was still both upright and alert—alert enough, in fact, to notice that Khrushchev had been drinking water. The next morning Adenauer confronted Khrushchev with the tongue-in-cheek suggestion that any man who would do such a thing could not be trusted. Surprised to find that he had been caught in the act, Khrushchev could only laugh.

Throughout their week of confrontations, Adenauer matched Khrushchev blow for blow. When the Premier said in response to one German proposal, "I will see you in hell before I agree with you on that!" Adenauer shot back, "If you see me in hell, it will only be because you were there before I got there!" Another time, when Khrushchev shook his fist in anger, the Chancellor popped to his feet and shook both fists.

The Russians were at their self-righteous best as they recited atrocities the Nazis had committed against the Soviet Union during World

War II. Adenauer refused to don the mantle of abject guilt that the Kremlin had fashioned for him. He told Bulganin and Khrushchev that many Germans had opposed the war and added that his country also had suffered at the hands of Russian troops.

This point triggered a typical outburst from Khrushchev, who asserted that Adenauer's charge of Russian atrocities was "offensive." "After all, who is responsible?" said Khrushchev haughtily. "We did not cross any frontiers. We did not start the war."

Adenauer stood firm. He reminded Khrushchev that he had been jailed by the Nazis both before and during the war and that as a result he had had plenty of time to consider the motives of those nations that were supporting Hitler. Khrushchev, his moralistic bubble burst by this pointed reference to the Molotov-Ribbentrop pact of 1939, backed down, and the conversation proceeded for a while more genially.

Over dinner that night in 1959 Adenauer recounted his verbal battles with Khrushchev with great relish. But he cautioned me that despite the Russian's bumptious behavior it would be a deadly mistake to underestimate him. "He is highly intelligent, tough, and ruthless," Adenauer said.

Still, Adenauer had evidently enjoyed jousting with Khrushchev. I could see that, unlike some leaders, he did not shrink from unpleasant combat. On the contrary, he welcomed it. It was the same spirit he displayed when he later described his enjoyment of political campaigning. Throughout his life he always wanted to be in the arena rather than in the stands.

At the time of that 1959 visit to Washington, Adenauer had recently announced his decision to seek the West German presidency. He hoped to turn the office, until then a largely ceremonial one, into something similar to the French presidency under Charles de Gaulle. He would be able to make policy without the draining day-to-day political squabbles of the chancellorship.

The decision was not a wise one, but it was understandable. Adenauer had built the Federal Republic of Germany, and by his tenth year as Chancellor he had come to identify himself with it and wonder what would happen to it when he was gone. After the Nazi era Adenauer had never again fully trusted his countrymen. He once called them "carnivorous sheep." Near the end of his life he told a reporter, "The German people seriously worry me. The only thing I can say for them is that they have lived through too much. They have not found peace of mind and stability since the war of 1914–1918."

Because Adenauer never believed the German people were fully grown politically, he struggled to retain power longer than he should have and in fact to expand his power when he should have been quietly preparing the way for others to take over after him. During the presidential crisis of 1959 Adenauer reached too far.

Once again stories about his authoritarianism were trotted out, this time in connection with his handling of his cabinet. Many of them were close to the mark. According to one perhaps apocryphal story, after a cabinet debate on his landmark agreement giving "co-management" rights to factory workers, he was asked, "When are you going to grant co-management to your ministers?"

As what became known as the "presidential crisis" developed, Adenauer grew bitter because the leaders of the CDU, who had originally suggested that he seek the presidency, insisted on backing Ludwig Erhard to succeed him as Chancellor. Adenauer considered Erhard politically naive. He finally withdrew his candidacy for the presidency, deciding instead to keep the chancellorship himself in order to keep Erhard out of it. The former Finance Minister persisted, however, and he eventually became Chancellor upon Adenauer's retirement in 1963.

In his eighties, though still an energetic, healthy man who accomplished as much in a day as a man twenty years younger, Adenauer occasionally became defensive about his advancing years. Once, though the subject of his eyesight had not come up, the Chancellor took off his glasses and held them out to show a visitor that they were not reading glasses but were designed only to deflect ultraviolet rays from his small, sensitive eyes. He took a nap daily but was loath to admit it; if someone asked how he had slept, he would snap, "I didn't sleep, I was busy."

This was not mere vanity. Adenauer believed that he was indispensable to the survival of West Germany. When the matter of his inevitable departure from office was timorously raised one day by some friends, he replied perfunctorily that, yes, it was possible he could be killed in an auto accident. During an interview on Adenauer's ninetieth birthday in 1966, after he had left office, a reporter reminded the former Chancellor that he had also interviewed him on his eightieth birthday and said that he looked forward to doing so on his one hundredth. Responded *der Alte*, "Certainly. I will tell my secretary to make a note of it."

Churchill and de Gaulle also found it difficult to think of anyone else in their places, let alone to prepare successors. In this respect they all differed from Yoshida and Eisenhower. The day Eisenhower selected me as his running mate in 1952, he told me of his shock when he found

Truman was not adequately prepared to take over as President because Roosevelt had kept him in the dark on major issues. Eisenhower was determined not to make that mistake and assured me he would keep me completely informed so that I would be adequately prepared to take over if I should succeed him.

Few great men groom successors, but fewer still are as hard on their successors as Adenauer was. He sniped at Erhard in interviews and even to representatives of other nations who came to visit him in retirement. In one meeting I had with Erhard in my vice presidential office in the summer of 1959, he choked up and, with tears in his eyes, told me how deeply hurt he was by Adenauer's treatment of him.

It was soon after he returned to West Germany from Dulles's funeral that Adenauer announced he would remain as Chancellor. Though he had mentioned the subject only in passing during our meetings, the decision must have been weighing heavily on his mind. Despite this he found time for a personal gesture that reveals the warm human qualities he rarely displayed in public.

Since childhood Adenauer had been an avid horticulturist. As a youngster he was given to experimentation until an attempt to produce "creeping pansies" led his father to admonish him, "One must never try to interfere with the work of God." Later, working in his rose garden gave Adenauer comfort from the anguish of the Nazi years and relief from the constant pressures of the chancellorship. Professional flower growers were admirers of his work, including Mathias Tantau of Uetersen, who bred a new rose and named it after a delighted Adenauer in 1953. A full, dark-red flower, the "Konrad Adenauer" can still be seen in gardens all over the world, a living testament to a great professional politician and an equally great amateur gardener.

The rules of protocol often made Mrs. Nixon his dinner partner at the White House and on other diplomatic occasions. They got along famously. He once asked me what her background was. When I told him that she was half German and half Irish, he snapped his fingers, smiled broadly, and said, "I could have guessed it. The Irish-German combination produces the most intelligent and beautiful women in the world."

In their conversations he learned that she shared his interest in flowers. When he came to our home the day after the funeral, he asked to see our modest backyard garden. A few weeks later one hundred rose bushes arrived by air from West Germany.

The following March, Adenauer made his seventh visit to the U.S. He sent word ahead that he wanted to meet with me, and we made an appointment for six o'clock one evening at our home. Fifteen minutes ahead of time Mrs. Nixon suddenly saw the Chancellor's limousine pulling up in front of the house. When she opened the door, he announced that he had come early to see how his rose bushes had survived the winter. When I arrived for our six o'clock meeting, I was astonished to find him standing in our garden, discussing the state of the roses with her as intently as he would later be discussing the state of the world with me.

Adenauer's visit to our home attracted a great deal of attention, especially because he was trailed by photographers and West German newsreel cameramen. One columnist, Ruth Montgomery, wrote, "The friendship between the eighty-four-year-old German Chancellor and the forty-seven-year-old American fascinates official Washington. The two politicians have met and huddled on at least a half-dozen previous occasions, but the most recent one was certainly the chummiest." She added, "Should Nixon capture the White House, Adenauer seems to have laid the groundwork for another intimate liaison like the one he used to enjoy with the late Secretary of State John Foster Dulles."

For years Adenauer had been a master at using the press as a tactical political weapon. That June he was reported as believing that Senator Kennedy did not have enough training or experience in foreign affairs to be President. Meanwhile Franz-Josef Strauss, Adenauer's Defense Minister, had ordered his ministry to assess what a Kennedy administration might mean in the international arena. A copy of the ministry's report—it became known as the "Strauss indiscretion"—was leaked to the Baltimore *Sun*, which headlined the story "Nixon More Acceptable to Germans." According to an Adenauer biographer, "It was perfectly true, as far as Adenauer and the CDU were concerned...."

Adenauer's practical interest in cultivating my friendship was clear from the political advice he gave me as the 1960 campaign approached and also from his uncomplimentary remarks about Senator Kennedy. By the mid-1950s he knew that I might become President, and he wanted to begin building a working relationship with a dependably conservative possible successor to Eisenhower.

But after Kennedy won and I lost in November, he made clear that his motives were also more personal. Adenauer had been inviting Mrs. Nixon and me to West Germany since the mid-1950s, but the usual range of pressures and duties had always made it impossible for us to accept. Shortly after my defeat in the election, I received a very warm letter from Adenauer in which he wrote sympathetically of what he knew must be my feelings and renewed his invitation to Mrs. Nixon and me to visit Bonn.

It was not until ten years after I first met Adenauer that I finally was able to accept his invitation. In the summer of 1963 Mrs. Nixon and I and our two daughters took a six-week vacation that included a stop in Germany. I visited Adenauer in the Chancellor's office in Bonn, and we talked for over an hour with only his trusted interpreter present.

I gave him my impressions of Europe in general and described my dismay at my first glimpse of the Berlin Wall. We were to visit France next, and Adenauer particularly asked me to give his best wishes to his friend de Gaulle, for whom he had developed unbounded affection and respect since they first met in the 1950s. He expressed guarded support for the nuclear test-ban treaty, which was to be signed the next month. But he warned that the Soviet Union's willingness to sign the treaty in no way reflected a change in its expansionist aims.

To my surprise, however, this uncompromising foe of communism expressed the view that the U.S. should not "put all its eggs in one basket" and should move toward rapprochement with Communist China as a buffer to Soviet expansionism.

As we talked, I was saddened to see that for the first time he had lost some of the buoyant zeal that had always been so evident before in our talks. After his party had been battered in the election that followed the Berlin Wall crisis, he had bowed to pressure from younger leaders and promised to step down after two more years. Now that time was approaching. He would soon be out of power, he had very little confidence in his successor, and he would be leaving the stage before he had fully realized his dream of a unified, steadfast free Europe.

In October 1963 Adenauer made his farewell speech to the Bundestag. When he was finished he gathered his papers, stepped from behind his chair on the cabinet bench, and walked, stiff-backed and solemn, to the desk assigned to him on the floor of the parliament. His bearing was dignified and his face characteristically impassive as he gave up the power of the chancellorship, but his heart was in turmoil. Though he had spent fourteen years laying the foundations of a prosperous, free, and secure West Germany, he was leaving office a deeply troubled man because he was afraid that what he had built might not last.

His successor, Ludwig Erhard, though a brilliant economist, had little foreign policy experience. At the same time developments that Adenauer thought ominous were unfolding on the international scene. Within the last month the United States and Canada had announced plans to sell $750 million worth of wheat and flour to the Soviet Union. Only two days before his farewell to the Bundestag, he had urged President Kennedy not to approve such sales without wringing something from the Soviets in return, such as concessions on the Berlin question. That summer he had told me of his fears of just such a development; when he mentioned the word *détente,* he shuddered visibly. "I am tired and frightened by this talk of détente," he said.

He was concerned, as I was, about the tendency of some naive leaders and opinion makers in the West to view détente as an alternative to deterrence rather than insisting, as we both did, that there could be no détente without deterrence.

Our last meeting was during a fact-finding tour of Europe I made in 1967 prior to the 1968 presidential elections.

Having stepped down as Chancellor in 1963, Adenauer had also given up the presidency of the CDU in 1966. He had been given a small office in the Bundeshaus as a courtesy. When I entered it, I was shocked at his appearance. For the first time *der Alte* really *was* an old man, stripped of his power and no longer able to direct the destiny of his country. He was almost painfully thin, and his ramrod-straight posture had deteriorated into a noticeable stoop. But this ninety-one-year-old man had lost none of his mental alertness. He walked across the room as I entered and embraced me. Then he stepped back and, with his hands still on my shoulders, said, "Thank God you are here. Your visit is like manna from heaven."

On the wall I saw a painting of the Acropolis of Athens, which Adenauer said was a gift from the man who had painted it—Winston Churchill. I also noticed the photograph of Dulles that he had shown Sulzberger eight years before. After exchanging pleasantries, we embarked on an intense discussion of international politics.

He expressed great concern about the future of France after de Gaulle, saying, "De Gaulle is not anti-American; he is pro-European." He pointed out that a recent poll had indicated that forty percent of the French people favored better relations with the Soviet Union. Only de Gaulle, he believed, could hold the line against the left; once he was gone, the left would inevitably prevail in France.

John McCloy told me that Adenauer's admiration for de Gaulle approached hero worship. After a visit he made to the French leader's home at Colombey, he said to McCloy with awe in his voice, "Do you know who came to the door when I knocked? Not an aide or a servant, but de Gaulle himself." In his mind I imagine he envisioned Charles de Gaulle as the lineal descendant of his own ninth-century hero, Charlemagne—or Charles the Great, as he is sometimes called.

Like Adenauer and Dulles, Adenauer and de Gaulle were alike in some ways. Both were big, impressive men in every way. Both were profoundly religious. Both were devoted family men. Both had great inner strength and outward dignity. Both were men of vision.

But in other ways they were quite different. While de Gaulle was a fine writer, Adenauer was not. De Gaulle, though known primarily as a military leader, was basically an introspective intellectual and a creative thinker. He was essentially a man of thought; Adenauer was essentially a man of action. Adenauer would often lighten up serious discussions with humor and pleasant banter; I cannot recall a time when de Gaulle did so.

What matters most is that these two postwar giants respected each other and worked together to heal centuries-old conflict between France and Germany. Neither would have been able to do it alone. That they exercised power at the same time in their respective countries was one of the fortunate accidents of history.

Adenauer told me that he disagreed with his friend de Gaulle's view that the U.S. should withdraw from Vietnam. He asked rhetorically whether the Germans, for example, would feel confident of our continued support if we let the South Vietnamese down. But he added that if we stayed in Vietnam, we would be doing precisely what the Soviets wanted. "The Russians are not going to try to help you get out of Vietnam," he said. "They want you to stay there. They want to drain you white and consequently they aren't going to help you unless some other factor changes the situation so that it is in their interest to do so."

He scoffed at the suggestion being made by some political and business leaders in Germany and the United States that increased trade between the West and the Soviet Union would bring peace. His cryptic comment was that "business is business." I had to agree. Trade alone does not assure peace. In both world wars, trading partners had suddenly found themselves bitter enemies.

His main concern now, as it had been when I had first met him fourteen years before, was the Soviets' aggressive policies. He was concerned that they were building four more access routes to Berlin. He pointed out that their first target would be Germany and then France. On the other hand, he said they recognized that their greatest enemy was the United States. "Make no mistake about it," he said, "they want the world. The whole world. Most of all they want Europe, and to get Europe they know they must destroy Germany. We need you to keep us strong and free. But you also need us."

He was skeptical about the nuclear nonproliferation treaty, which was then being negotiated. He pointed out that the Morgenthau Plan would have resulted in the permanent destruction of German industry. The Marshall Plan had built it up. Now the nonproliferation treaty would in effect limit Germany's potential to become a world power. The Soviets certainly recognized this; in a rare moment of candor Aleksei Kosygin had admitted to the Danish Prime Minister, "Only if the Germans sign is the treaty important to us."

Adenauer criticized German Foreign Minister Willy Brandt's policy of *Ostpolitik:* trying to ease tension by making a series of "small steps" toward better relations with the Soviet bloc. Like his old friend Foster Dulles, he warned to his dying day against being taken in by Russian "peace" overtures. In his view a Communist peace offensive was just that: a tactic calculated to split the West and win total victory without war.

He spoke at some length about Soviet-Chinese relations. He recalled that Khrushchev had expressed almost pathological concern about the threat of the Chinese in the long run. Khrushchev had told Adenauer, "Twelve million Chinese are born each year and each one exists on a bowl of rice." He had cupped his hands as he made this point. Khrushchev, he believed, had a mortal fear that once the Chinese acquired atomic weapons, they would be a threat not only to the Soviet Union but to all nations of the world.

From a geopolitical perspective Adenauer could see few fundamental differences between the Chinese and the Russians. "They both want to rule the world," he said. But he made the point again, as he had in 1963, that the U.S. should tilt toward the Chinese as long as the Soviets presented the greater military threat.

A little over a month after our conversation, Adenauer died at his home in Rhöndorf. His son Paul later told Terence Prittie that Adenauer "worried a lot at the end, but never about himself. He was worrying about Europe's disunity and impotence, about the dangers of nuclear war, about people becoming the victims of their illusions. He wanted to go on fighting." I learned later, from his daughter Libet, that I had been the last American to see him, just as I had been the first American to welcome him to the United States in 1953.

*　　　*　　　*

It is one thing to have an idea. It is another thing to have the idea at the right time. And it is still another thing to be the kind of man who can make the idea work. These were the three components of Adenauer's greatness.

His idea was a partnership among nations in the face of a common enemy, the Soviet Union, and partnership within West German society in the pursuit of prosperity and the protection of liberty. Within Europe he aimed at recapturing the ninth century's brief moment of unity in order to prevent a repetition of the twentieth century cataclysms that had resulted from hatred between nations. At home the idea was to replace nationalism with Europeanism and to prevent tyranny, either of the right or the left, by keeping any one sector of society from gathering enough power to smother the liberty of individuals.

The rightness of his policies becomes clearer with each passing year. In 1954 many of Adenauer's critics said West Germany did not need to rearm and join NATO; now it is difficult to imagine a free Europe without West Germany's divisions. Skeptics scoffed at his belief that France and Germany, after three wars in less than a century, could become allies and friends. Yet Adenauer and de Gaulle, two giants on the European stage who stood head and shoulders above their critics, were able to consummate their rapprochement with the Franco-German treaty of 1963. Throughout the 1950s Adenauer was criticized for failing to unify the two Germanys; now the suggestion that the Soviets would at that time have allowed an independent, united, free Germany sounds incredible. Until his retirement he was criticized for not seeking a détente with East Germany and the Soviets such as the one Willy Brandt and his successors have sought through *Ostpolitik;* now it is clear that *Ostpolitik* by a West Germany less strong and prosperous than the one Adenauer built through an alliance with the West would have been folly, and that *Ostpolitik* as practiced has not lived up to its architects' overly optimistic hopes.

In the 1960s, as the Cold War eased, it became fashionable in West Germany and elsewhere to "take the Russians at their word"—that is, to be more receptive than Adenauer had been to their overtures on such issues as Berlin and the German unification question. Many argued that the Soviet empire in Eastern Europe was no more than a buffer against aggression from the West, and that peace—and possibly even freedom for the people of Eastern Europe and East Germany—would be assured if we could only prove our own peaceful intentions to the Soviets. Khrushchev, with his talk about Nazi atrocities against the Russians, had tried to sell this line to Adenauer in 1955, but the Chancellor was not buying. Nonetheless this attitude has increasingly colored the East-West policies of his successors. Despite *Ostpolitik*, however, the Soviet empire remains, and Soviet adventurism has escalated rather than diminished.

As a leader in free Europe today, how would Adenauer view the world? I am certain that he would view it differently than some of those who succeeded him in office. In Afghanistan in 1979 he would have seen not a minor flare-up in a remote corner of the Third World, but a brazen bid by the Soviet Union for access to the riches of the Persian Gulf. He would not have taken the parochial view, as many Europeans did at the time, that a threat to the oil that fuels Europe was beyond the scope of the European alliance's legitimate interests. It was to deal with such situations, in fact, that Adenauer had struggled for the creation of NATO. He knew that if the perimeters of the West were breached, its center would soon collapse.

Similarly, in Poland in 1981, Adenauer would have seen not an internal political problem but an unconscionable effort by the Soviets to perpetuate their subjugation of an independent-minded, Christian people of Europe. He would have viewed the Polish crackdown as an act of international criminality and responded accordingly; to today's West German leaders it is a regrettable inconvenience that may go away if they look long enough in another direction. Ironically one of the goals of *Ostpolitik* was to find a way for West Germany to compensate the people of Poland for the wrongs they had suffered at the hands of the Nazis. Now that the Poles are suffering at the hands of a new master, the West Germans can only wring theirs.

These hypothetical considerations, of course, beg the question. With leaders like Adenauer in Western Europe, the Soviets would have been less confident of getting away with their adventures with impunity. Adenauer was always known as a "Cold War warrior," and he heartily approved of the designation. If he were alive today and could survey Europe, with all its disunity and moral listlessness, he would not agree that the Cold War has ended. He would say that one of the combatants has stopped trying to win it.

If he could hear the talk of neutralism, so reminiscent of the Europe of the 1930s, he would hang his head in shame. He believed that Europe could break its back trying to "sit between two chairs"; the backbone that remains in Europe today is there in large measure because of the efforts of Adenauer and his partners in France. The fact that European unity seems frighteningly fragile whenever a crisis develops, such as those in Afghanistan and Poland, is evidence that Adenauer's successors have forgotten the urgency of his message to Europe: that it confronts a danger greater than any it has ever faced before.

More than anything else, Adenauer would have been shocked by the state of affairs within the alliance. In 1955 Adenauer and a majority of his countrymen considered it an honor to be admitted to the European alliance so soon after the end of World War II. Today many members of NATO, including West Germany, quibble over how much they will spend to support the alliance or waffle over whether they will allow its missiles—which restrain the Soviets from moving beyond Poland and East Germany—to be placed within their borders. Meanwhile *Ostpolitik* continues; soon, even as the Soviets edge closer to the Persian Gulf, Russian natural gas may be flowing into West German homes.

Adenauer's reaction to all of this would have been simple. He would deplore the suggestion, implicit in *Ostpolitik*, that the United States presents as great a threat to Europe as the Soviet Union. He would warn that in reaching east, the Europeans are in danger of breaking their lifeline to the West. And he would say that no policy is worth pursuing if it makes you lose those friends you do have while courting those friends you do not have, especially if your new friends turn out to be your deadliest enemies.

In comparison with the two other titans of postwar Europe, Churchill and de Gaulle, Adenauer is sometimes described as being relatively colorless and uninteresting. Apart from being superficial and unfair, this description misses two important points. The first is that France and Great Britain were the winners in World War II, and Germany was the loser. De Gaulle's hauteur and dashing theatrics were appropriate qualities in the founder and leader of the Fifth Republic, but they would have been dangerously inappropriate in the leader of the defeated Germany. Similarly Adenauer, though possessed of a sharp wit himself, could not have gotten away with deploying it as broadly as did Churchill, especially when the Allies were still calling the shots in occupied Germany.

But those who found Adenauer uninspiring also missed the point that there are different styles of leadership. Churchill, the wry, sometimes cantankerous intellectual, could deflect criticism from an opposition MP or a journalist with a single well-timed, finely crafted barb. De Gaulle's dignity was simply impenetrable. But Adenauer, with his patient, calculating lawyer's mind, was the kind of leader who prevailed because he was willing to work harder, reason more closely, and sit longer than those around him. He dominated issues by mastering them and overcame critics by outguessing and outthinking them. A central tenet of his Catholic philosophy was that good things resulted only from hard work. He did not expect West Germany to blunder into respectability, sovereignty, security, and prosperity. He expected that these things would come about only as a result of a concentrated struggle to bring them about.

Adenauer's greatest strength, his vision of a European colossus united against the Russian colossus, was also the source of his greatest weakness. Flowing from the same spring as his affection for the French and his commitment to the European ideal was a lingering suspicion that eastern Germany did not belong. To him Berlin stood on the threshold of Asia and was tainted by a kind of modern barbarism. Prussian leaders had too often acted the part of Oriental despots and too seldom encouraged peace or cared about the liberty of their people. Charlemagne's empire, and thus enlightened European civilization, ended at the Elbe. In a way it was the same with Adenauer's Europe.

As a German and as a man, he cared for each East German and longed for his freedom. He welcomed and protected those who managed to escape. But as a historian and Rhinelander, he believed Soviet East Germany was lost to Christian civilization. In the depths of his soul its loss may have seemed inevitable and possibly even permanent.

In the end, as a result of the postwar policies of the Soviet Union, this deep-set philosophical bias did not matter. No diplomatic overtures during the Adenauer era could have changed the Soviets' intention to make East Germany their western outpost. Such overtures, therefore, could only have lost ground for the West in its battle to protect its freedom and ideals. Adenauer's personal commitment to rapprochement with the West was the direct result of his background and his faith in God. Coincidentally it was also his only rational choice as a statesman if he was to protect the liberty of his defeated people.

Adenauer's monument is the free democratic Federal Republic of Germany, just as de Gaulle's monument is the French Fifth Republic. After being humiliated and degraded by Hitler, Germany has again become a respected member of the family of nations.

My most vivid personal memory of Adenauer, however, will always be not of one of the premier political leaders of the postwar period but of Adenauer the man: a man who was inflexible in adherence to principle but shrewd and subtle in tactics; a man outwardly stiff and austere but who, to those fortunate to be his friends, was cherished as a warm and sensitive human being with a captivating sense of humor; a man who deeply loved his family, his church, and his people, each equally but in different ways; a man one could always count on to stand firm as a rock no matter how great the risks or desperate the odds.

Rarely has a private man been so perfectly suited for public responsibility.

NIKITA
KHRUSHCHEV

The Brutal Will to Power

NIKITA SERGEEVICH KHRUSHCHEV was ebullient as he clinked glasses with guests at a diplomatic reception in Moscow in late 1957. As a boy, he had herded pigs for two kopeks a day; now, at the height of his power, he was the undisputed master of Russia. With the buoyant self-confidence of a man who had defeated the last of his rivals for power, he turned to a group of western reporters among the guests and enthusiastically recited a fable.

"Once upon a time," Khrushchev began, "there were some men in a prison. There was a social democrat, an anarchist, and a humble little Jew—a half-educated little fellow named Pinya." They decided to elect a leader to distribute the food, tea, and tobacco, he went on. The anarchist, who opposed putting anyone in authority, contemptuously proposed that they elect lowly Pinya, and they did. Soon they decided to try to escape by tunneling beyond the prison walls. But they realized that the guard would fire at the first man through, and no one seemed willing to lead. "Suddenly," said Khrushchev, his voice building with the plot, "the poor little Jew, Pinya, drew himself up and said, 'Comrades, you elected me by democratic process as your leader. Therefore, I'll go first.'

"The moral of the story," Khrushchev continued, "is that no matter how humble a man's beginnings, he achieves the stature of the office to which he is elected." The Soviet leader then paused for a moment and added, "That little Pinya, that's me."

Like all analogies, the story of Pinya is accurate in some respects but misleading in others. Khrushchev, of course, was neither democratically elected nor reluctantly thrust into leadership. For forty years he had fought and clawed, intrigued and double-crossed, bullied and murdered, his way to the top of the Soviet Union. Pinya's rise to power from humble origins is not nearly as astonishing as Khrushchev's. A pig tender, a coal miner, and a pipe fitter before joining the Bolsheviks in 1918, Khrushchev had no formal education until he was in his twenties. He was underestimated by his colleagues and the world throughout his career. But by 1957, when he consolidated his grip on power, this peasant-czar could be ignored or disparaged only at one's peril.

Of all the leaders I have met, none had a more devastating sense of humor, agile intelligence, tenacious sense of purpose, and brutal will to power than Nikita Khrushchev. His successes and failures, more than those of any other leader, dramatically and decisively altered the course of history in the post–World War II era.

He was the man who built the Berlin Wall—the first wall in history whose purpose was not to keep enemies out, but to keep his own people in.

He was the man who so brutally suppressed a people's revolt against Communist rule in Hungary that I denounced him in 1956 as the "Butcher of Budapest."

He was the man who put nuclear missiles on Cuba and who, even as he backed down and removed them, extracted American pledges to pull U.S. missiles out of Greece and Turkey and to refrain from supporting those who might threaten Fidel Castro's sanctuary in Cuba.

He was the man who started the great Soviet offensive in black Africa and throughout the developing world by trying to take over the Congo through his protégé Patrice Lumumba.

He was the man who began the massive Soviet buildup in strategic nuclear weaponry that would eventually turn the fifteen-to-one Soviet disadvantage during the Cuban Missile Crisis into a significant Soviet advantage today.

He was the man who signed the Limited Test Ban Treaty with President Kennedy, who began removing the shrouds of Stalinist secrecy that enveloped the Soviet Union, and who took significant steps toward making Russia a European country through his policy of "peaceful coexistence."

He was the man who defrocked Stalin and thus permanently shattered the unity of the Communist movement.

Above all, he was the man who was primarily responsible for communism's greatest setback and the most significant geopolitical event since World War II: the break between the Soviet Union and Communist China. His foreign policy, despite its successes and initiatives, probably will be remembered for its greatest failure: Khrushchev lost China.

Of all the leaders I have met, I disagreed with none more vehemently than Nikita Khrushchev. And yet none earned my grudging respect for his effective exercise of raw power so consistently. That he was the Devil incarnate, many would concede. That he was an ominously able Devil, few could dispute.

I was Vice President when Khrushchev first emerged in the elite of the Soviet leadership in 1953. Many in the West were quick to judge him, and their first impressions were often far off the mark. They were accustomed to Soviet leaders like Stalin: austere, secretive manipulators who controlled events by pulling the strings from offstage. When Khrushchev's rotund figure bounded to center stage, he broke the pattern so completely with his uninhibited behavior, indiscreet statements, and bombastic pronouncements that many did not take him seriously.

Life labeled him "an unimportant little man"; a *Newsweek* columnist dubbed him "an unimpressive civil servant" and "an undistinguished work horse"; and *Time* called him "a *Vydvizhenets*," one who has been "pushed forward" by events despite a lack of education or training. Most western observers did not think Khrushchev was fit to shine Stalin's boots, much less fill them. His behavior when he traveled to Belgrade on one of his first trips outside the Soviet Union did little to improve his image. He was crude, unpolished, and drunk, clearly out of place in the international social set. The press delighted in describing his alcoholic binges and wrote that, compared to Stalin, he was a light-weight who would not last long.

The foreign policy dilettantes in the Washington social circles and even some members of the career foreign service also underrated Khrushchev. One of them commented to me at the time that he did not think very highly of Khrushchev because the Soviet leader drank too much and spoke "bad Russian." These observers simply did not under-stand that Khrushchev's garbled syntax, unfashionable clothing, and unrefined tastes did not lessen his effectiveness as a leader. Overly im-pressed by style and education, they forgot that elegant manners do not make a strong leader. In statesmanship what counts is not the sur-face but the substance of the man. No matter how well polished the veneer of his personality, a statesman will not succeed unless he has a well-tempered, visceral strength underneath it.

Khrushchev was a sort of Russian Senator Claghorn in public. During the May Day military parade one year, the members of the Soviet elite impassively watched as their armed forces passed before them. But when a squadron of jet fighters roared overhead, Khrushchev bounded around the reviewing stand, slapping Premier Nikolai Bulganin on the back and beaming with the joy of a little boy with a new set of toys. Khrushchev did not maintain Molotov's icy dignity as he watched the jets, but that did not mean he would be any less ruthless in using them.

Khrushchev's personality was forged on the anvil of Stalin's years of absolute power. Stalin had two kinds of subordinates: the quick and the dead. Second only to Mao Zedong, Stalin was responsible for killing more of his own people than any man in history. Anton Antonov-Ovseyenko, in his book *The Time of Stalin: Portrait of a Tyranny*, puts the number at one hundred million, including Stalin's own wife and Lenin's widow. Only men with a talent for ruthlessness and an instinct for intrigue stayed alive and rose to the top in those years. To fight his way through the ranks, Khrushchev had to have had intelligence, stam-ina, and iron determination. John Foster Dulles recognized this. At a National Security Council meeting just after Khrushchev took power, he said, "Anyone who survives and comes to the top in that Communist jungle is bound to be a strong leader and a dangerous enemy." He was right. One perceptive western diplomat said Khrushchev was a flabby-looking man "with a core of steel."

I first encountered Nikita Khrushchev when I traveled to the Soviet Union to open the American National Exhibition in Moscow in 1959, and I met with him again when he visited the United States later in the same year.

Shortly before I left for Moscow in July 1959, Congress passed the Captive Nations Resolution, as it had every year since 1950. Eisenhower issued the proclamation provided for in the resolution urging Americans to "study the plight of the Soviet-dominated nations and recommit themselves to the support of the just aspirations of those captive nations."

Khrushchev had returned to Moscow from a trip to Poland only ninety minutes before I arrived from the United States. The Polish people had treated him with cool contempt, and Soviet relations with their satellite countries in general were strained. On his return Khrushchev went directly from the airport to give a speech furiously denouncing the Captive Nations Resolution. When my plane touched down, the reception was cool and correct. The Deputy Premier, Frol Kozlov, delivered a long, loud welcoming speech, but there were no bands, anthems, or crowds. The Captive Nations Resolution obviously had rubbed an open sore.

The next morning at ten o'clock I arrived at Khrushchev's office in the Kremlin for our first meeting. As I entered, Khrushchev was standing in the far corner of the room, examining a model of the Lunik satellite that the Soviets had fired at the moon several months before. It looked like an oversize baseball in his small hands as he put it back in its place.

He approached me in an unrhythmic stride. He was shorter than I expected, standing at no more than five feet six inches. His wide girth, stumpy legs, and Stakhanovite shoulders gave him a stocky, awkward build. When we shook hands for the photographers, the sixty-five-year-old Soviet leader's clasp was robust, giving me the impression of a man with enormous vitality, great physical strength, and bull-like energy.

While the reporters and photographers were present, Khrushchev chatted amiably, his tiny, sharp eyes darting around the room. His round face, with its heavy lips, firmly set jaw, pug nose, and high cheekbones, was animated. He praised the address I had delivered at the Guildhall in London about eight months before. He said that he welcomed the kind of peaceful competition I had described in it. Then he waved the photographers out and gestured for me to take a place opposite him at a long conference table.

Abruptly the atmosphere changed. Speaking in a high-pitched voice and frequently pounding his fist on the table, Khrushchev launched into a tirade about the Captive Nations Resolution, declaring it a serious "provocation" and a stupid, frightening decision. He demanded to know whether war would be our next step. "Heretofore, the Soviet government thought Congress could never adopt a decision to start a war," he said. "But now it appears that, although Senator McCarthy is dead, his spirit still lives. For this reason the Soviet Union has to keep its powder dry."

I explained to him that the resolution was an expression of American opinion and not a call to action. I tried to go on to other subjects, but Khrushchev would have none of it. Finally I said, "At the White House we have a procedure for breaking off long discussions that seem to go nowhere. President Eisenhower says, 'We have beaten this horse to death; let's change to another.' Perhaps that is what you and I should do now."

Khrushchev remained impassive during the translation, but he decided to have one more go at it. "I agree with the President's saying that we should not beat one horse too much," he said, "but I still cannot understand why your Congress would adopt such a resolution on the eve of such an important state visit." By now he was flushed with anger. He shouted some words that I could sense were rather rough. Oleg Troyanovsky, his translator, who later became Soviet Ambassador to the United Nations, blushed. Obviously embarrassed, he looked at Ambassador Llewellyn Thompson, who knew Russian and was smiling broadly. After a few seconds he finally made the translation: "This resolution stinks. It stinks like fresh horse shit, and nothing smells worse than that!"

Khrushchev eyed me during the translation. I decided to call his bluff, and in his own terms. I recalled from my briefing materials that Khrushchev had worked as a pig herder in his youth. I also remembered from my childhood that horse manure was commonly used as fertilizer—but that a neighbor had once used a load of pig manure, and the stench was overpowering. Looking straight into Khrushchev's eyes, I replied in a conversational tone: "I am afraid that the Chairman is mistaken. There is something that smells worse than horse shit—and that is pig shit."

For a split second after the translation, Khrushchev hovered on the borderline of rage, the veins at his temples seemingly ready to burst. Then he suddenly broke into a broad smile. "You are right there," he said, "so perhaps you are right that we should talk about something

else now. However, I must warn you that you will hear about this resolution during your visit here." On this subject, if on few others, Khrushchev kept his word.

I seldom prepared myself so thoroughly for a series of high-level
meetings as I did for those with Khrushchev in 1959. But after our first
encounter in his Kremlin office, I realized that no amount of work
would have completely readied me for Nikita Khrushchev. He was totally unpredictable. Courtesy, protocol, and itineraries meant nothing to
him. Through the course of my visit, he would harangue me and ridicule the United States before the cameras of a model of an American
television studio, threaten the West with nuclear missiles before the
washing machine of a model American kitchen, and transform a social
lunch into a five-and-a-half-hour foreign policy debate before the astonished eyes of Mrs. Nixon, Mrs. Khrushchev, and the other guests.

When I reflected on my encounters with him just after they ended, a
picture of Khrushchev, the man, formed in my mind. Always on the offensive, he combined an instinctive feeling for his adversary's weaknesses with an almost compulsive tendency to press an advantage—to
take a mile when his opponent gave an inch and to run over anyone
who showed even the slightest sign of timidity. He was colorful in word
and deed and had a tendency to be a show-off, especially when he had
a gallery.

He was a man who did his homework and prided himself on knowing as much about his opponent's position as he did about his own. He
was particularly effective in debate because of his resourcefulness, his
ability to twist and turn and change the subject when he was forced
into a corner or an untenable position. Despite the appearance of being
highly emotional, he demonstrated to me that when anything of importance was being discussed, he was sober, cold, unemotional, and analytical.

Khrushchev amused and bemused the world for eleven years. He
came up quietly from the ranks of Stalin's lieutenants in 1953 and went
out with a bang when his colleagues unexpectedly deposed him in
1964. The world was left with three images of Khrushchev in power: the
bombastic clown, who had been publicly drunk more often than any
other Russian leader of modern times; the gambling pragmatist, who
had not been bound by dogma but who had tried to solve his country's
problems with ill-considered panaceas instead of long-term remedies;

and the Communist totalitarian, who had climbed to power over the corpses of his rivals and countrymen and had stayed there by exiling all who challenged him—until he himself fell victim to his own methods.

In my encounters with Khrushchev I found that the clown in him wore two faces. At one moment he could be boisterous, jolly, outgoing, exuding friendship and an almost seductive charm. With a broad grin on his face, he came with a peasant's saying ready for every occasion. He sometimes grabbed my lapel when addressing me as if to ensure himself a similar grip on my attention. He would often lean over toward me, checking discreetly to both sides to see who might overhear him, and then in a hushed voice divulge some "secret" about Soviet military plans.

A moment later, particularly if he had an audience, he could become rude, domineering, tempestuous, the master of a very personal brand of high-decibel diplomacy. During his harangues he came toe-to-toe with me and poked me in the ribs with his index finger, as if his verbal needling required this physical needling for emphasis. He would narrow his eyes as a machine gunner does in lining his sights. He then would let fly a barrage of argument, bombast, and profanity. After my meetings with him ended, I could not help thinking that many of the things Khrushchev had said in his flashes of rage would have been sufficient to provoke a declaration of war in the age of polite diplomacy. In our age they only made the translator blush.

The clown in Khrushchev could use his histrionics expertly, as I discovered when the two of us came to the display of a model television studio on our tour of the American National Exhibition. A young technician asked us to record greetings that could be played back to visitors throughout the run of the exhibition. Khrushchev seemed suspicious at first, but the sight of a crowd of Soviet workmen emboldened him. In no time he had clambered onto the platform and was talking for the cameras and playing to the audience.

"How long has America existed? Three hundred years?" he asked me. I replied that the United States was about one hundred eighty years old. "Well, then, we will say America has been in existence for one hundred and eighty years, and this is the level she has reached," he said, taking in the whole exhibition hall with a broad wave of his arm. "We have existed not quite forty-two years, and in another seven years we will be on the same level as America." The audience was enthralled with his boasting, and their delight seemed to egg Khrushchev on. "When we catch up with you, in passing you by, we will wave to you," Khrushchev said. Carrying off this final taunt with flamboyant gestures, he peered over his shoulder with wide-eyed earnestness as he waved good-bye with his chubby little hand to an imaginary America fading in the distance.

A photo album of some of Khrushchev's other antics would be not only fascinating but also revealing. The snapshots would catch him at his best and at his worst. For instance he could use his clowning to show remarkable sensitivity to the national and personal prestige of his hosts. When his official car got a flat tire during a tour of the Yugoslavian countryside in 1956, the sixty-one-year-old Khrushchev sportively challenged his fifty-nine-year-old deputy, Anastas Mikoyan, to an impromptu roadside wrestling match. The playful contest created a diversion for newsmen while Tito's men worked on the car. Flabbergasted by the spectacle, the reporters all led their dispatches with accounts of the roadside bout between the Communist heavyweights instead of the embarrassing flat.

But most of the photographs would be unflattering, for they would show Khrushchev to be a shameless bully. During the crisis over Berlin in 1959, British Prime Minister Macmillan visited Moscow and proposed that the Berlin dispute be taken up at a foreign ministers' meeting. These meetings were futile in Khrushchev's mind because foreign ministers lacked the necessary decision-making authority. To illustrate how inconsequential foreign ministers were, he blurted out to Macmillan that if he told his chief diplomat, Andrei Gromyko, to take off his trousers and sit on a block of ice, Gromyko would have to do so.

Macmillan had not heard the last of Khrushchev's crudity. In a speech to the United Nations in 1960, Khrushchev proposed several reforms for the international organization, including one to move its headquarters to Switzerland, Austria, or the Soviet Union. When the General Assembly rejected his suggestions, he began harassing other delegates by shouting and laughing during their speeches. He reached the height of his boorish behavior during Macmillan's address. Before representatives of almost all the countries of the world, the Soviet leader took off a shoe and pounded it on his desk like a gavel.

Khrushchev was a crude bear of a man, an earthy chunk of mother Russia, a typical muzhik who was short-tempered and long-winded. But while his clowning came naturally, he was a clown only when he wanted to be. He used indiscretion and bombast as tactics.

During Khrushchev's rule the Soviet Union was vastly inferior to the United States in power. What Khrushchev lacked in military power he sought to make up for with willpower. He rattled his nuclear sabers and proclaimed that "your grandchildren will live under communism" in order to make the West fear Soviet might. He did not fool most western leaders, but his bellicosity made much of the public believe that while he professed to want "peaceful coexistence," he would have no qualms about unleashing a world war.

He was in typical form for a speech he made while visiting Britain in 1956. He told the audience that from his motorcade he had seen a few people protesting his visit, but had noticed one man in particular who shook his fist at him. "My return gesture was this," he said, shaking his fist for effect, "and we understood each other." The audience laughed, but Khrushchev added placidly, "I would remind that man of the fact that attempts have been made in the past to speak to us in those terms. . . . Hitler shook a clenched fist at us. He is in the grave now. Is it not time that we become more intelligent and not shake our fists at each other?"

History also probably will remember Khrushchev as a pragmatist of sorts. He was not a theoretician of the Marxist-Leninist creed who knew by rote every dit and twiddle of the Communist scriptures. He believed in the cause of communism and the inevitability of its victory, but he worshiped at the altar of theory on Sundays only. I find it difficult to imagine him ever actually reading all three burdensome volumes of Marx's *Das Kapital*. In this respect he differed from Stalin, who read widely and wrote copiously about Communist theory.

Khrushchev prided himself on his pragmatism. He and I were once discussing his Deputy Premier, Frol Kozlov, whom I had welcomed to New York when he opened the Soviet National Exhibition. Kozlov was an apparatchik who slavishly followed every twist and turn of the party line. Khrushchev commented with obvious contempt, "Comrade Kozlov is a hopeless Communist." Khrushchev was also an irredeemable Communist, but he refused to be bound by the dogma itself.

He frequently chastised the "rhetoricians" of Marxism-Leninism, whom he considered "parrots" who "learned by heart" archaic theoretical passages "not worth a kopek" in the modern age. "If Marx, Engels, and Lenin could rise from their graves," he once exclaimed, "they would ridicule these bookworms and quoters who, instead of studying modern society and creatively developing theory, are attempting to find among the classics a quotation on what to do with a machine-tractor station."

His belief in the tenets of Communist doctrine was not acquired but instinctive. He carried in his mind the stereotypes that derive from

Communist ideology, yet he paid little heed to its intricacies. He did not go along with Stalin's dictum that "if the facts and the theory don't agree, change the facts." But no one could ever accuse him of missing any opportunities to forward his cause or, as he might put it, "to give history a push."

Khrushchev was in top form as he took me for a boat ride on the Moscow River during my visit to the Soviet Union. On eight occasions he stopped the boat to greet nearby swimmers with handshakes and to shout to them, "Are you captives? Are you slaves?" The bathers, obviously all members of the Communist elite, would answer with a chorus of *nyet*'s. He would then elbow me in the ribs and exclaim, "See how our slaves live!" Meanwhile Soviet newsmen took down every word. When we disembarked, Khrushchev was beaming. "You know, I really must admire you," I told him. "You never miss a chance to make propaganda." "No, no, I don't make propaganda, I tell the truth," he retorted—though he had never in his life told the truth when a lie would serve his purpose.

He continued to peddle his version of the truth throughout my travels in the Soviet Union. The thousands of people Mrs. Nixon and I met in Leningrad, in Sverdlovsk, and in the Siberian city of Novosibirsk greeted us with exceptional warmth. We were impressed by the fact that the Russian people were strong, hardworking, and friendly, and that the great majority seemed genuinely to like Americans. But at every stop at a factory or a marketplace Khrushchev had arranged for a Communist functionary to harass me with a well-rehearsed political question. The questioner would step forward and introduce himself as "a plain Soviet citizen." Then, almost by rote, he would ask, "Why is the United States blocking efforts to stop atomic testing?" or "Why does America want war?" or "Why does the United States threaten us with military bases on foreign soil?"

Harrison Salisbury, the dean of American correspondents in the Soviet Union, summarized Khrushchev's orchestrated heckling in *The New York Times:* "Vice President Richard M. Nixon preached the virtues of free speech to several hecklers. It was one of the rarest experiences in Soviet life—a free and easy interchange between a leading personality and challengers who appeared from the crowd. The similarity of the questions directed at Mr. Nixon and the tactics of the questioners suggested a central source of inspiration."

A pragmatist in the sense that he did not let dogma constrict him, Khrushchev was a strangely impractical one. He approached the problems of the Soviet Union as a reckless gambler does a roulette wheel, with less forethought than enthusiasm. Impatient with strategy and susceptible to hunches, he wagered his assets with daring abandon, and more often than not he left empty-handed.

Quick in thought but quicker in action, he often let the latter run ahead of the former. He delighted in trying to solve major national problems with a single adventuresome stroke. He pushed through one grandiose program after another. He opened up vast tracts of marginal land to cultivation, only to have them ravaged by dust storms; he expanded the planting of corn for fodder, only to waste tens of thousands of acres whose soil was unsuited to it; he exalted in the virtues of using reinforced concrete and prefabricated construction, only to neglect to increase the production of cement.

It was through these and similar programs, Khrushchev boasted, that the Soviet Union would surpass American production levels in seven years. But like anyone else who traveled to the Soviet Union in the 1950s, I noted that its primitive transportation system alone rendered Khrushchev's statement hopelessly unrealistic.

Khrushchev genuinely sought to bring prosperity to the Soviet Union. But he failed to understand, or perhaps understood all too well, what this would require. He would have had to drastically overhaul the entire Soviet economic and political system in ways that would have loosened the Communist party's control over the people—something he was unwilling and unable to do. Instead he put his hopes into grand schemes that were more like a magician's tricks than an economist's programs. When none of the tricks seemed to work, his audience in the Presidium grew restless and finally yanked him off the stage, condemning him among other things for blind pursuit of "harebrained schemes." Khrushchev had tried to have his cake and eat it, too—to retain complete control over the economy and to seek prosperity as well—but in the end lost the chance to do either.

The bombastic clown and the misdirected pragmatist were important aspects of Khrushchev's personality, but after my first encounter with him I could tell that the totalitarian in him dwelled at the core and animated his being. Only thinly veiled even in his good moods, his cold ruthlessness was always present in his merciless dark-blue eyes, which seemed to turn coal black when he was emphasizing a point.

Odd though it may seem, the totalitarian in him was very much apparent in his sense of humor. The jokes he told at diplomatic receptions often had unmistakably sinister overtones. Many were about the activities of the Cheka, the earlier Russian secret police agency. He seemed to enjoy these in particular because of the obvious parallels between the Cheka and his own police apparatus.

One of his favorites was an old joke about a review of troops in Moscow. A soldier in the ranks sneezed. The Cheka officer present asked whoever it was to step forward. No one responded. The first row of soldiers was lined up and shot. The officer asked again who sneezed. No one replied, so the second row of troops was executed. The officer asked a third time who sneezed. "I did," answered the timid voice of a soldier in the back. "Gesundheit," said the Chekist.

Khrushchev also appreciated macabre humor in others. During our lunch at Khrushchev's dacha outside Moscow in 1959, Mikoyan commented on Stalin's peculiar work habits, saying that Stalin often summoned his subordinates in the middle of the night. "We sleep much better," Mikoyan said, "now that Comrade Khrushchev is our Premier." After doing a double take at what he had said, Mikoyan commented with a smile, "I guess you can take that in more ways than one." Khrushchev, who was seated across the table from Mikoyan, beamed with pleasure over the double entendre.

Khrushchev was renowned for his colorful quips and sharp retorts. It would have taken a Churchill in his prime to match him in this respect. But Khrushchev's humor, unlike Churchill's, was almost always combative, aggressive, intimidating, designed not so much to evoke laughter as to issue an unspoken challenge or threat. Churchill's wit was sharp, but Khrushchev's was always brutally blunt.

To Khrushchev, humor was a bludgeon for clobbering adversaries. While scolding a group of farmers for not selling their livestock for slaughter, he told them that they were "not zoo keepers who collect animals for show." Asked if Russia would remain Communist forever, he said that it would not abandon Marxism-Leninism "until the shrimp learns to whistle" or until "you can see your ears without a mirror." At an art exhibition Khrushchev, whose dislike for modern art was intense, listened impatiently as a poet explained to him that the "formalistic tendencies" in certain abstract art would "be straightened out in time." To this Khrushchev shot back indignantly, "The hunchbacked are straightened out by the grave!"

After Khrushchev and I left the American National Exhibition's model television studio, he kept needling me about my background as a lawyer, implying that I was a slick and dishonest manipulator of words, while he was an honest miner and worker. As we passed a model

American grocery store, I mentioned to him that my father had owned a small general store in which my brothers and I had worked while going to school. "All shopkeepers are thieves," Khrushchev snorted with a wave of his arm. "Thieving happens everywhere," I responded. "Even in the market I visited this morning, I saw people weighing food after they had bought it from the state." For once Khrushchev was stumped and sought to change the subject.

Khrushchev seldom indulged in self-deprecating humor, but when he did, he almost always used it to make a point he truly did not believe. After the kitchen confrontation I was walking with Kliment Voroshilov, who was serving in the figurehead office of President of the Soviet Union. Khrushchev was walking a few steps behind, and I beckoned him to join us. "No, you walk with the President," he told me. "I know my place."

Khrushchev's sinister jokes and insulting jibes provided a glimpse of the man who had learned to rule as an apprentice to Joseph Stalin. Under Stalin, the cruelest of taskmasters, only the fittest survived. His understudies had to be not only ruthless but clever. Former Ambassador Foy Kohler, one of America's few top Soviet experts, described Khrushchev as the embodiment of the Russian adjective *khitryi*. "According to the dictionary," he wrote, "it means sly, cunning, artful, intricate, or wily. But it really means more than this; it also means unscrupulous, smart, clever, quick-witted. Roll all these adjectives into one and you have the *khitryi* Khrushchev—a bootlicker or a bully as circumstances required, a demagogue and opportunist always."

Khrushchev joined the Bolsheviks in 1918 at the age of twenty-four. In 1928, while working as a minor party official in Kiev, he caught the eye of Lazar Kaganovich, the Communist party boss of the Ukraine. When Kaganovich returned to Moscow in 1929, he took Khrushchev with him as his loyal first lieutenant. In the 1930s the two benefited greatly from the purges. They were more Stalinist than Stalin and their political stars streaked upward. As construction supervisor of the Moscow subway, Khrushchev won a reputation for being a tough, reliable functionary who was not afraid to get mud on his boots or blood on his hands. With that on his résumé Khrushchev was appointed the boss of the Ukrainian Communist party in 1938.

No assignment in the Soviet Union was more difficult. The embers of Ukrainian nationalism still glowed, and fanned by Stalin's farm collectivization, during which several million Ukrainian peasants had been killed, they could ignite at any moment. Khrushchev's mission was to extinguish them by purging the Ukrainian Communist party of any members with nationalist sympathies and by accelerating the Russification and communization of the province's forty million inhabitants.

The Great Purges were at their height when Khrushchev became Stalin's viceroy. In six months his predecessor had liquidated almost seventy percent of the Ukrainian Central Committee that was selected in 1937. Stalin replaced him with Khrushchev in order to step up the pace. Khrushchev did not disappoint his boss. Soon only three of the 166 members of the 1937 committee remained. He also purged a fifth of the local party secretaries and thousands of rank-and-file members.

When Hitler's armies invaded the Ukraine in the Second World War, its people joyously welcomed them as liberators. It was Khrushchev from whom they were being freed. In 1943 German Occupation forces excavated ninety-five mass graves containing a total of ten thousand corpses. Artifacts found with the bodies identified them as victims of the Communist political purges from 1937 to 1939.

In 1940 Khrushchev supervised the Soviet takeover of eastern Poland when it was partitioned in accordance with the Hitler-Stalin pact. After the Germans attacked the Soviet Union, he served as a lieutenant general—not as front-line officer, but as a political commissar whose task it was to ensure that Stalin's orders were being followed. After the war he returned to the Ukraine to kill those who had collaborated with the Germans. He was soon boasting to Stalin that "half the leading workers have been done away with."

Stalin died in March 1953, but his influence did not die with him. It lived on through the imprint his years in power had left on the men who had helped him rule and who were now taking over. The lessons of Stalinism were brutally simple. Instinct counseled Khrushchev that if he was not at the top or moving toward it, he would be at the mercy of those who were. Wisdom advised him to compromise with an adversary only if he did not have the power to crush him or if he needed his help to vanquish someone else. Experience taught him the value of one of Lenin's sayings: "The important thing is not to defeat the enemy, but to finish him off."

The struggle for succession began immediately after Stalin's death. When Khrushchev secured the position of First Secretary of the Communist party, other members of the Presidium scorned him. Lavrenti Beria, the head of the secret police, called him "our potato politician." Kaganovich was known to dislike his lieutenant's rise to prominence.

Georgi Malenkov, the Prime Minister, and Vyacheslav Molotov, Stalin's formidable Foreign Minister, dubbed Khrushchev *"nedostoiny"*—"unworthy."

Khrushchev remembered everything and forgave nothing. He set about using the patronage powers of his office to undermine his rivals much as Stalin had done to his thirty years before. Khrushchev combined his intimate knowledge of the party machinery with an uncanny gift for timing, a ferocious tenacity of purpose, and a ruthless approach to power, and he won preeminence by 1957.

He vanquished his competitors for power. As a result, Beria, the man most feared after Stalin's death, was arrested and executed. Kaganovich, the man who most advanced Khrushchev's career, labored at an unspecified post in the provinces. Malenkov, the man Stalin had designated as his successor, managed a small power plant in Siberia. And Molotov, the man who had negotiated the Hitler-Stalin pact, clinked glasses with the diplomats of Ulan Bator in Outer Mongolia.

Stalinism had made Khrushchev a totalitarian by temperament as well as conviction. He was wholly intolerant of opposition, whether it came from his colleagues in a struggle for power or from me in a debate. He would bide his time if confronted with equal force. But the moment he sensed that he had gained an advantage, he pressed it to the limit.

In all my discussions with him he was totally inflexible, never giving an inch of ground or leaving any room for negotiation. In his mind he was always completely right and I was always irredeemably wrong. When I responded in his own terms at our Kremlin meeting, he backed off. When I let his bombast go unanswered at the model television studio, he took this restraint as a sign of weakness and exploited it to the maximum.

After his aggressive performance before the television cameras, our next stop on the tour was the model American home. As we walked up the center hall of the house, looking into the rooms on both sides, he continued to push on the offensive. We stopped at the kitchen, where we began discussing, of all things, washing machines. After he delivered a rambling statement about why having only one model of a washing machine was better than having many, I said, "Isn't it better to be talking about the relative merits of our washing machines than the relative strengths of our rockets? Isn't this the kind of competition you want?"

When he heard the translation, Khrushchev appeared to turn angry, jammed his thumb into my chest, and shouted, "Yes, that's the kind of competition we want, but your generals say they are so powerful, they can destroy us. We can also show you something so that you will know the Russian spirit. We are strong, we can beat you. But in this respect, we can also show you something."

He had thrown down the gauntlet. It was time to call his bluff. "To me you are strong and we are strong," I said, pointing my finger at him to drive my message across. "In this day and age to argue who is stronger completely misses the point. If war comes, we both lose." Khrushchev tried to laugh off my point, but I pressed it home. "I hope the Prime Minister understands all the implications of what I have just said," I went on. "When you place either one of our powerful nations in such a position that it has no choice but to accept dictation or fight, then you are playing with the most destructive thing in the world."

He struck back furiously, seeming at times to lose control of his emotions. But as I noted later, Khrushchev "never loses his temper—he uses it." Now he was using it to try to make me look like a villain, sternly warning me not to threaten him and vehemently denying that he had ever issued an ultimatum himself. "It sounds to me like a threat," he shouted. "We, too, are giants. You want to threaten—we will answer threats with threats."

I said that our side would never engage in threats. He then accused me of threatening him indirectly. "You are talking about implications," he said, deliberately misconstruing the way I used the word. "I have not been. We have the means at our disposal. Ours are better than yours. It is you who want to compete. *Da, da, da* . . ."

I said that we were well aware of the power of the Soviet Union, but emphasized that in the nuclear age marginal differences either way were immaterial. Khrushchev soon realized that he could gain nothing more by these means and sought to end the discussion. Halfheartedly he said, "We want peace and friendship with all nations, especially with America."

Suspicion was central to his nature. After we left the model house, Donald Kendall, international president of Pepsi-Cola, offered him a glass of his company's product. He eyed it suspiciously and would not drink it until I tried it first. After I tasted it, he gulped down a glassful without taking a breath.

My encounter with Khrushchev in this so-called "kitchen debate" convinced me that he was a brutal totalitarian to the bone. He was never content simply to say his piece and to let me say mine. He compulsively created disputes in order to try to bully me into submission and intimidate me into silence, not through the logic of his arguments or the eloquence of his words but through the power of his bombast and the gravity of his threats.

This characterization may seem harsh to those who best remember Khrushchev as the man who initiated the period of slightly relaxed censorship known as the "thaw" and who exposed the unjust killings of the Stalin years. But neither of these episodes disproved the characterization. They both reaffirmed it.

During the "thaw" Khrushchev permitted greater freedom of expression in literature and the arts, but reserved for himself the privilege of determining what could be criticized and what could not. Many of the horrors of the Stalin era were fair game, but those that continued into the Khrushchev era were not. Khrushchev enforced his literary rules strictly; he knew how difficult it was to allow the intelligentsia a little bit of freedom without the process snowballing. He once told a group of writers that the revolution in Hungary in 1956 could have been forestalled if the government had simply shot a few writers who were stirring up discontent. If a similar situation arose in the Soviet Union, he said as he eyed the writers stonily, "my hands would not tremble."

Similarly, in his "secret speech" delivered at the Communist party congress in 1956, Khrushchev did not denounce Stalin's reign of terror because of some newly discovered moral revulsion. He did so as part of a calculated political gamble. Choosing his words carefully, Khrushchev never condemned Stalin's brutality itself. He noted approvingly that Lenin "resorted ruthlessly and without hesitation ... to the most extreme methods." He even went so far as to list the liquidation of the "right deviationists" as one of Stalin's great "services" to communism. He denounced only those crimes in which his political rivals could be implicated. In effect, by skewing the history of Stalin's purges, he was able to use it to conduct his own.

Exiled dissident Vladimir Bukovsky reported that while Khrushchev was denouncing Stalin's crimes in a speech at a Communist party meeting, a note from someone in the audience was handed to him. It asked, "Where were *you* at the time?" Khrushchev read the note over the public address system and shouted, "Who wrote this note? Please stand up!" After a moment or two it was clear that no one was going to come forward. "All right," Khrushchev said, resolving to answer the question, "I was where you are now."

The anecdote may well be apocryphal. Whether fact or fiction, it poignantly illustrates that Khrushchev kept the Stalinist system basically intact even as he defrocked Stalin himself. And though he exorcised

Stalin from the nation's soul, he never succeeded in cleansing Stalinism from his own.

After our heated debate in the model kitchen, Khrushchev transformed himself into a friendly, convivial host. At a luncheon in the Kremlin he urged us to join him in the Russian tradition of throwing our champagne glasses into the fireplace after drinking our toasts. He also stopped insisting that we fly on Russian airplanes for the remainder of our trip and offered to allow us to use our own.

These incidents were examples of Khrushchev's disarming change of pace. Though he never gave an inch on substantive issues, he could be very generous in personal relations. He considered this a small price to pay if he believed it could give him even a slight edge in the discussions of major issues. He was a living testament to one of the ironclad rules of statesmanship: Good personal relations do not necessarily lead to better state relations.

But Khrushchev knew that this was all show. In using geniality and charm as weapons, one of the most coldly brutal leaders of all time, Joseph Stalin, could be effusive. When Khrushchev, and later Brezhnev, treated me similarly, I better understood how Harry Truman could have once referred to Stalin as "good old Joe." With none of them, however, did these calculated displays of warmth mean that substantive concessions would follow.

Khrushchev continued to ply me with his charm during the official dinner the American Ambassador gave for him. Midway through the evening he began describing in eloquent detail the beauties of the Russian countryside. Suddenly he insisted that we must not wait to see them. Our schedule called for us to go to his dacha in the morning, but he quickly arranged for us to make the twenty-two-mile drive after dinner so that we could spend all of the next day there.

I was glad to leave the oppressive drabness of Moscow behind as our limousines sped down deserted roads toward Khrushchev's summer house. As I looked out on the night, I reflected on the colorless streets and facades of the Soviet capital. I thought to myself that the color we associated with communism should not be red but gray.

Khrushchev's dacha was set deep in the woods that surround Moscow. Before the 1917 revolution it had been a summer home of the czars. It became Stalin's a few years after the red czars took over and devolved to Khrushchev upon his ascension to the throne. The dacha was as luxurious an estate as I have ever visited. The mansion, which was larger than the White House, was surrounded by pristinely kept grounds and gardens. On one side a marble staircase descended to the banks of the Moscow River. I thought to myself that the Bolsheviks had come a long way since the ascetic days of the revolutionary underground.

At about noon Khrushchev and his wife drove up in their limousine. Khrushchev sported a dazzlingly embroidered shirt. Bubbling with the energy and enthusiasm of a cruise social director, he lined us up for pictures. He then ushered me off for the boat ride on the Moscow River. When we returned we joined the ladies for lunch, after which, I assumed, we would excuse ourselves and proceed with our official talks.

Khrushchev took us to a long table standing underneath a canopy of magnificent birches and pines, which were originally planted in the days of Catherine the Great. The table was laden with every manner of Russian delicacy and soft and hard drinks. Despite his well-deserved reputation for drinking heavily, Khrushchev only sampled the array of vodka and wine. He appreciated good food and drink. But just as his famed temper was always his servant and not his master, his drinking on this occasion was strictly for pleasure and was never permitted to interfere with business. He was cold sober throughout our long afternoon of talks.

The conversation at the beginning of the luncheon was lighthearted and cordial. While the first course was being served, Deputy Premier Mikoyan began to talk across the table to Mrs. Nixon, who was seated next to Khrushchev. The Soviet Premier interrupted Mikoyan and scolded him: "Now look here, you crafty Armenian. Mrs. Nixon belongs to me. You stay on your side of the table." He then proceeded to trace a line down the middle of the table with his finger and proclaimed, "This is an iron curtain. And don't you step over it."

Meanwhile I had a pleasant conversation with Mrs. Khrushchev, over whom the Soviet leader did not try to exercise proprietary control. She had all her husband's energy but none of his boorishness. Her outgoing warmth was a welcome contrast to Khrushchev's often harsh demeanor. And unlike her more rough-hewn husband, she had refined interests—classical music, the ballet, French and Russian literature—and spoke of them knowledgeably.

One of the first courses was an unusual delicacy, a frozen white fish from Siberia. It was served raw, sliced into thin strips, and spiced with salt, pepper, and garlic. "It was Stalin's favorite dish," Khrushchev said, urging me to taste it. "He said it put steel in his backbone." Khrushchev took a double portion and I made sure to do likewise.

Moments later, as the plates were cleared for the next course, Khrushchev swung the conversation dramatically from diplomatic small talk to military big talk. He began bragging about the potency and accuracy of Soviet missiles, citing statistics about their payloads and ranges. But then he added in a hushed voice, almost as an afterthought, that about a month earlier a malfunctioning Soviet ICBM overshot its course and headed toward Alaska. Though it carried no warhead and eventually fell in the ocean, Khrushchev said that he had feared a "fuss" if it had crashed on American territory.

Warming up to the conversation, Khrushchev displayed a repertoire of gestures that a conductor of a brass band would envy. He would give a quick flip of the hand to try to ward off a statement as he would a fly. If that failed, he swatted it away with a peasant's saying. He would raise his eyes impatiently to the sky if he felt he had heard enough of an argument to anticipate the rest. When he spoke emphatically he cupped the hands of his outstretched arms as if they held self-evident truths for all to witness. When angered he would wave both arms over his head in unison, as if exhorting his band to play louder.

I asked him if he planned to replace his bombers with missiles because of their greater accuracy. He replied, "We almost stopped production of bombers, because missiles are much more accurate and not subject to human failure and human emotions. Humans are frequently incapable of dropping bombs on their assigned targets because of emotional revulsion. That is something you don't have to worry about in missiles."

He said that he felt sorry for the navies of the world. Except for submarines, their vessels were simply "sitting ducks" for missiles and could only provide "fodder for the sharks" in a future war. I asked him about his submarine program. "We are building as many submarines as we can," Khrushchev answered. Mikoyan gave him a warning glance and said, "The Chairman means we are building as many submarines as we need for our defense."

Khrushchev professed ignorance when I inquired about Soviet development of solid fuels for underwater missile launches. He said, "Well, that is a technical subject which I am not capable of discussing." Mrs. Nixon expressed surprise that there was any topic that the head of a one-man government could not discuss. Once again Mikoyan came to the rescue of his boss, saying, "Even Chairman Khrushchev does not have enough hands for all he has to do, so that is why we are here to help him."

I then told Khrushchev that his bombastic statements about his military might were making it impossible to reduce international tensions or to negotiate lasting agreements. He seemed to agree to curb this practice, but not ten seconds later proceeded to break his word. He said he had superiority in rocketry and that no defense against missiles was possible. He then laughingly referred to a quip about a pessimist and an optimist that he said was current in England. The pessimist said only six atomic bombs would be needed to wipe out the United Kingdom, while the optimist said nine or ten would be required.

I changed the topic to Soviet efforts to subvert the governments of non-Communist countries. I told him that I hoped he was not so naive as to think that the United States was unaware of the directives the Kremlin was sending to Communist movements in other countries. I then pointed out that in a speech in Poland he had declared support for Communist revolutions throughout the world.

"We are against terror against individuals," he replied, "but if we go to the support of a Communist uprising in another country, that is a different question." He added that if the "bourgeoisie" did not surrender peacefully, violent revolutions might become necessary.

"In other words, you consider that workers in capitalist states are 'captives' whose liberation is justified?" I asked.

He said *captives* was a vulgar term, not at all "scientific." He added that it was not interference in another nation's domestic affairs if the Soviets were supporting a genuine internal revolution.

I asked him why the Soviet press had approved of the attack against Mrs. Nixon and me by a Communist-led mob in Caracas, Venezuela, in 1958. Khrushchev was thrown off stride for a moment. Then he leaned over and said in a low, emotional voice, "We have a saying 'You are my guest, but truth is my mother,' so I will answer your very serious question. You were the target of the righteous indignation of the people there. Their acts were not directed against you personally, but against American policy—against the failure of your American policy."

I pointed out that the military might of a superpower and the fervor of revolutionaries were a dangerous combination. If he did not exercise extreme caution, I added, events could spiral out of control.

I told him that Eisenhower and he should meet to address East-West differences on a basis of give and take, emphasizing that both sides would have to make concessions. "You say the United States is always wrong, and the Soviet Union is never wrong," I said. "Peace cannot be made that way."

This fired him anew. He began a harangue on the Berlin and German questions that lasted for almost an hour. I could not get a word in edgewise. When he simmered down, I tried to find out whether there was any room for negotiation in his position. "Suppose I were the President of the United States sitting here across the table from you instead of the Vice President," I asked. "Is your position so fixed that you would not even listen to the President?"

Khrushchev said that this was a "fair question," but that he could only reply in terms of what the Soviet Union could not accept. He then said simply that with or without a summit conference he could never allow the perpetuation of the Occupation regime in West Berlin. He ominously implied that there would be a confrontation between the superpowers if his terms were not met.

I told him that he could not expect President Eisenhower to go to a summit conference merely to sign his name to Soviet proposals. He seemed to agree, yielding only slightly for the first time all afternoon. But he added that he could not attend a summit simply to ratify American proposals, saying, "I would much rather go hunting and shoot ducks." At this point he was obviously not interested in further debate. Everyone seemed a little dazed. He soon rose to indicate the luncheon was over—well over five hours after it had begun.

Khrushchev left me with the impression of a man of exceptional energy, discipline, and stamina. Like a strong but unartistic boxer, he stood his ground resolutely, ready to take the verbal blows as well as he gave them. His tempo never slackened. He bobbed and weaved as he probed my defenses in search of an opening for a jab, a combination, an uppercut—anything that might score a point, lower my guard, or set me up for a knockout. If one line of argument did not work, he tried another. If it failed, he tried a third and fourth. If I backed him into a corner, he would either come out swinging or squirt out along the ropes with a change of topics. He was a master at fighting his own fight, never letting me set the grounds of debate and always reinterpreting my questions to his advantage. Ambassador Thompson was overly generous when he later observed, "They had a heavyweight in their corner, and we had a heavyweight in ours. They fought to a draw."

I felt a deep sense of depression as our plane took off from Moscow and headed for Warsaw, because I realized that the Soviet people, most of whom had welcomed us so warmly, almost certainly would never escape from under the blanket of oppression that smothered them. But even so, I was soon to see why Khrushchev exhibited such sensitivity about the Captive Nations Resolution.

I had an inkling that things might be different in Warsaw as our motorcade left Babice Airport. The Polish honor guard, which had used the Russian goosestep in its marching review, applauded and cheered as we drove past them. I could not help thinking that Khrushchev would have to think twice before relying on these men in a war with the West. The Polish government, sensitive about the comparison that would be drawn between my welcome and Khrushchev's cool reception only a few days before, did not publish our motorcade route. But Radio Free Europe broadcast it, and word of mouth spread like wildfire.

Mrs. Nixon and I have received some warm welcomes in our many years of world travel—in Tokyo in 1953, Bucharest in 1969, Madrid in 1971, Cairo in 1974—but none approached in intensity the spontaneous greetings we received in Warsaw that day. An estimated 250,000 people overflowed the sidewalks and pressed into the street, stopping the motorcade time after time. Some were shouting, others were singing, and many were crying.

Hundreds of bouquets of flowers were thrown into my car, into Mrs. Nixon's car, and even into the press vehicles that followed. Some newspapermen who ventured into the crowd were told, "This time we bought our own flowers." The Polish government had declared a holiday when Khrushchev had visited, transporting children and government workers to the motorcade route, and had bought the flowers for the people to throw in their "spontaneous" welcome. Many had saved the flowers from that day to use when we arrived. As we inched through Warsaw streets, the crowd shouted "Niech zyje America"— "Long live America"—and sang "Sto lat"—"May you live a thousand years."

In light of this experience, it came as no surprise to me when millions of Poles rose up en masse against communism in 1980. Never has there been a system of government that has had greater success in extending its domination over other nations and less success in winning the approval of the people of those nations.

Our overwhelmingly moving reception in Warsaw that day reinforced the convictions I have long had with regard to the Communist-controlled countries of Eastern Europe. However, no matter how much compassion we feel for them, we must be careful not to encourage the people of the oppressed nations into provoking the kind of armed repression that Khrushchev inflicted upon the Hungarian people in 1956. At the same time we must constantly work to keep the lines of communication open with the peoples of Eastern Europe and the Soviet Union and must be careful that we do nothing to snuff out their flickering hope of one day lifting the deadly weight of Communist oppression from their backs. As John Foster Dulles said a few months before his death, "Communism is stubborn for the wrong; let us be steadfast for the right."

After the luncheon at the dacha I took Khrushchev aside for some private words. We discussed the invitation he had just received from President Eisenhower to visit the United States. I told him we wanted him to receive a courteous welcome and that he could assure this if there was some progress in the deadlocked talks on Berlin at Geneva. Khrushchev was coldly noncommittal, and Gromyko remained as intransigent as ever in Geneva.

Eisenhower's decision to invite the leader of the Communist world to the United States had provoked a storm of controversy. Hard-line conservatives and Americans of East European ancestry vehemently opposed it. They believed the visit would confer on the Soviet Union the illusion of moral equality and thus erode the will of the American people to fight communism. I disagreed with this view. While Americans were naturally trusting and friendly, they were not about to collapse in their opposition to communism merely because its leader waved to them from an open car in a motorcade.

I believed the visit was a sound idea, provided it did not lead to euphoria. Many, for example, believed that if only we repeatedly assured Khrushchev of our peaceful intentions, the Soviet leader would soften his rigid stance and settle the outstanding East-West issues. Some in the media, and even a few in the administration, were so naive as to think that if Eisenhower treated Khrushchev with respect, lavished courtesies on him, and plied him with his famous charm, real progress could be made on resolving our fundamental differences.

I disagreed with this approach. Based on my experience, I felt that Khrushchev might misinterpret excessive geniality for softness. I did not expect any significant progress on resolving basic differences. What was vitally important was for Eisenhower to impress him both as a courteous and reasonable host and also as a strong leader who could not be pushed around.

In my mind the Khrushchev visit was primarily important for the educational effect it would have on him. He knew that the United States was militarily and economically powerful. But his ideology told him that injustices plagued capitalist society and sapped its strength. The secondhand descriptions Khrushchev received from his aides tended to reinforce this view, telling him what he wanted to hear instead of what he needed to know. In effect Khrushchev relied on the hopelessly outdated picture of capitalism that Karl Marx had painted over a hundred years ago and that was fundamentally wrong even then. Khrushchev had repeated the lies about the evils and weaknesses of free societies so often that he actually believed them. I felt that a tour through the United States would thoroughly disabuse Khrushchev of these illusions. He would come to appreciate the basic strength of the country and the will of its people.

When Khrushchev arrived in Washington in September 1959, he became the first Russian leader in history to set foot on American soil. He was highly aware of the significance of this event. But he was also more obsessed with any slight deviation from protocol than any other visiting dignitary I ever met. He interpreted any deviation from the official schedule as an attack on his country's honor. He was a man who constantly carried a huge chip on his shoulder. And if someone else did not knock it off, he would do so himself.

Several days before his arrival I made an off-the-cuff remark to the effect that the Soviets had launched three Lunik moonshots, not one, as they claimed, because they kept missing the moon and had to try again. Khrushchev heard about this comment and chose to regard it as an insult to Soviet prestige and an indication that I wanted to see his trip to the United States fail. During his visit, he proclaimed that he would "swear on the Bible" that this was not so and challenged me to take a similar oath if I truly thought that my account was correct. He also attacked the statements I made about Soviet-American relations in a speech to the convention of the American Dental Association. He ignored the addresses I delivered at the conventions of the American Legion and the Veterans of Foreign Wars. Both organizations were on the verge of issuing condemnations of the Khrushchev visit. They reconsidered only after I had strongly impressed upon them the importance of a courteous welcome for Khrushchev.

When Eisenhower invited me into the Oval Office to sit in on the summit's first preliminary meeting, Khrushchev did not smile as he shook hands with me. He referred to our debate in Moscow with bitter sarcasm. Eisenhower tried to mollify him by saying that he had seen the footage carried on television from Moscow and thought that each of us had handled himself well and had treated the other courteously.

Khrushchev then complained that I was opposed to his visit and was trying my best to spoil his welcome, pointing to one of my recent speeches as evidence. "After having read that speech," he said, "I am surprised to find on arriving here that people in the United States welcome us with such tolerance and obvious friendliness. In the Soviet

Union there would have been no welcome whatsoever if I had, in advance, publicly spoken against the visitor." I reminded him of the vitriolic attacks he had made on me in speeches upon my arrival in Moscow. Khrushchev claimed that mine were worse and then asked Eisenhower to be the referee in deciding whose speech had been more provocative. Eisenhower and I signaled to each other that matters would be better off if they were alone, and I soon found an excuse to leave.

When we were planning Khrushchev's tour around the United States, I felt it was imperative that his escort be someone who could effectively answer the outlandish attacks that Khrushchev was bound to make on our policies. Eisenhower enthusiastically agreed with my recommendation that our Ambassador to the United Nations, Henry Cabot Lodge, was the best man for the job. He was a skillful diplomatic speaker who had handled himself well in East-West debates in the United Nations, and he had a sufficiently high rank to act as Khrushchev's official escort. Lodge did a highly effective job. At almost every stop he was called on to blunt one of Khrushchev's arrogant statements, and he did this in a hard-hitting but always courteous manner.

After his tour was over, Lodge told me that Khrushchev was the "Harry Truman of the Soviet Union." While both men were simple, direct, and earthy, I am sure that neither would have appreciated the comparison. Lodge felt that Khrushchev had received a real education during his cross-country trip. He told me the Soviet leader's lower jaw hung open when he saw the thousands of workers' automobiles in the parking lots of California factories and the tremendous productivity of the cornfields of Iowa. It is no wonder that after his visit he warned Mao that the United States was not a paper tiger.

After Khrushchev's tour of the country, he and Eisenhower went to Camp David to try to hammer out some agreements on bilateral issues. Eisenhower asked me to sit in on the conference's first plenary session in the living room of Aspen Lodge. Khrushchev, who clearly had no intention of reaching any agreements, quickly zeroed in on me. Looking directly at me, he said that many members of the Eisenhower administration wanted to improve relations with the Soviet Union, but that others hoped to continue a policy of confrontation. The implications of his unbroken stare were unmistakable, but he gave me no reason to respond. Therefore Eisenhower broke in to say that he believed that his administration was united behind the current foreign policy.

Khrushchev's uniquely Russian sense of inferiority and his obsession about Soviet prestige made him constantly see slights to his honor where none could have possibly been intended. At the luncheon following the plenary session, I tried to lighten up the conversation by asking Khrushchev about his vacation preferences. He said that he liked to go swimming in the Black Sea or hunting in the country. Eisenhower remarked that he liked to get away for fishing and golf, but that he found it difficult to escape the constant interruptions of phone calls. After hearing the translation, Khrushchev took umbrage, saying, "We have telephones in the Soviet Union too. As a matter of fact, we will soon have more than you have in the United States." Eisenhower, who realized that his guest was serious, could hardly suppress his smile.

After the lunch Eisenhower and I agreed that I should return to Washington in the hope that with me out of the picture, he and Khrushchev might have some constructive talks. The President did his best to win over the Soviet leader with his reasonable attitude and contagious charm. But Khrushchev was feeling cocky about the recent Soviet successes in space exploration and needled Eisenhower more than he negotiated with him. By the time Eisenhower concluded his discussions with Khrushchev, the President recognized that all the toasts, dinners, and nice diplomatic talk in the world would not budge Khrushchev an inch on the adamant positions he was taking. Khrushchev at least learned, however, that beneath Eisenhower's outward geniality was a man of steel.

The last time I saw Khrushchev was at the reception he gave at the Soviet embassy shortly before returning home. I told him that I believed his visit had gone well and that he had received a very courteous and often very warm welcome. He indignantly snapped back, "If it has gone well, it isn't because you wanted it to. From the reports I have had, you wanted the visit to be a failure."

I sensed that there might be purpose behind this continual belligerency. Khrushchev was aware that a presidential election was coming in 1960 and that I was probably going to be a candidate. The surge in my popularity following the "kitchen debate" obviously galled Khrushchev. The way he fought back is a tribute to his skill.

First of all, he tried to undermine the reputation of the Eisenhower administration. He was right in concluding that he could affect my popularity through Eisenhower's. If the American people believed the President could make progress in relations with the Soviet Union, he must have reasoned, they would see his chosen successor as their best bet. If the President appeared ineffective, the American people might reject me. When his military shot down an American U-2 spy plane over

Russia in 1960, he aborted the four-power Paris Conference and shame-lessly exploited the incident to try to make Eisenhower look like a fool. It obviously served his interest to embarrass the United States, but he was also not one to pass up an opportunity to damage an adversary's electoral chances.

Some may argue that Khrushchev was genuinely upset by the viola-tion of Soviet airspace. But except for the U-2 incident, I cannot remem-ber his ever adopting the sanctimonious hypocrisy that the Soviet Union did not engage in espionage. During the lunch at his dacha in 1959, he whispered to me that he had acquired a copy of the "United States Operational Plans for War" and that he suspected our spies had obtained the Soviet plans as well. He even joked about espionage. Dur-ing the White House dinner in Khrushchev's honor in 1959, he was in-troduced to Allen Dulles, the director of the Central Intelligence Agency. Khrushchev quipped that "I read the same reports you do" and then proposed that our two countries save money by combining intelli-gence networks "so we don't have to pay twice for the same informa-tion." I could not resist the temptation to introduce the Soviet leader to J. Edgar Hoover. Upon hearing Hoover's name, Khrushchev, with a leer in his eyes, said, "I imagine that we know some of the same people."

His perpetual bellicosity toward me also served a purpose. He made sure the press heard of the antagonism between us, and soon many stories appeared about how "Khrushchev just doesn't like Nixon." These stories had the intended result. Shortly before the election, Mrs. Christian Herter, the wife of the Secretary of State, urged me to do something about them. She said her friends were telling her that they might vote for Kennedy because he could "get along" with Khrushchev, whereas I could not. After the election Khrushchev openly bragged to newsmen that he had done everything within his power to contribute to my defeat. Years later he even claimed to have told Kennedy, "We made you President."

Whether Khrushchev's strategy actually helped Kennedy and harmed me is a matter of speculation. But in an election as close as that of 1960, small numbers of votes could have made a big difference in the outcome. And almost all observers agreed that Khrushchev's actions did not help me, and they certainly were not intended to.

Khrushchev's foreign policy could be as subtle as his meddling in American politics or as straightforward as a division of Soviet armor. His goal—world conquest—remained constant, inspired as much by his Russian heritage as by his Communist ideology. As Konrad Adenauer told me, "There's no question but that Khrushchev wants to rule the world. But he does not want war. He does not want a world of ruined cities and dead bodies."

Khrushchev paraded around the world under the banner of "peaceful coexistence," but the sincerity of his desire for peace was always dubious. Ambassador Charles Bohlen once told me that, after the Geneva Conference in 1955, many American officials were greatly mistaken in believing that Khrushchev was "sincere" in his desire for peace. I asked if this meant Khrushchev did not want peace.

"That isn't the question," he replied. "Khrushchev wants the world. But he knows the consequences of modern war as well as we do. He wants to accomplish his objective without war. In that sense he wants peace. The mistake is saying he is sincere. We are idealists. They are materialists." Pointing at a coffee table in front of us, he added, "You can no more describe Khrushchev or any other Communist as being sincere than you can describe that coffee table as being sincere. He is for peace not because he is sincere but because he believes that his objective, world conquest, can best be furthered without war—at this time."

Perhaps the best explanation of Khrushchev's doctrine of peaceful coexistence came in my last meeting with John Foster Dulles, four days before he died of cancer. I was preparing for my trip to the Soviet Union in 1959, and I went to Dulles's bedside in Walter Reed Hospital to seek his counsel. I told him that a number of people had urged that I try to convince Khrushchev that we had no aggressive designs on the Soviet Union and that we sincerely wanted peace. I asked him what point he believed I should emphasize to Khrushchev above all others.

Dulles usually paused to think about an answer before starting to speak. This time he waited longer than usual. He then said, "Khrushchev does not need to be convinced of our good intentions. He knows we are not aggressors and do not threaten the security of the Soviet Union. He understands us. But what he needs to know is that we also understand him. In saying that he is for peaceful competition, he really means competition between his system and ours only in our world, not in his. The peaceful coexistence which he advocates represents peace for the Communist world and constant strife and conflict for the non-Communist world."

Probably no other comment I have ever heard captured quite so trenchantly the nature of Khrushchev's policy of "peaceful coexistence." He zealously played the game of power politics in the free world, but considered the countries of the Communist bloc to be strictly out of bounds. The rules of Khrushchev's game were fundamentally unfair, but unfortunately he had the military might to enforce this self-proclaimed rule.

Khrushchev's bombast covered but did not conceal a pervasive sense of insecurity. But that self-uncertainty was also peculiarly Russian, with antecedents in the days when Peter the Great opened up Russia to Europe, only to demonstrate that his nation was centuries behind in virtually every area. The Russians have been trying to catch up ever since.

British Prime Minister Harold Macmillan had told me before my trip that Khrushchev took a particular pride in showing off Russian state treasures, especially the jewels and gold of the czars. Macmillan sensed that Khrushchev desperately wanted to be "admitted to the club"—accepted and respected as a major world figure in his own right and not simply because he controlled the great military power of the Soviet Union. We agreed that he should be admitted into "the club," but only if he agreed to abide by the rules.

Khrushchev and his successor, Brezhnev, have gone a long way toward making Russia a truly European country. It could be said that Stalin, like Mao, was basically a nationalist, and that Khrushchev, like Zhou, was an internationalist. Stalin rarely left the Soviet Union, but Khrushchev was a world traveler, taking fifty-two journeys abroad in his eleven years in power. Stalin was an Asian despot looking east, but Khrushchev and Brezhnev both looked to the West. In his discussions with me about China, Brezhnev often would lean toward me and say in a low voice, as if we were confidants, "We Europeans must join together in building barriers against potential Chinese aggression."

I think that much of Khrushchev's attraction to the West resulted from his enormous respect for its economic success. He desperately wanted economic progress for the poverty-stricken Soviet people. He also knew that without this progress his goal of world domination would be a pipe dream. But while he wanted western progress, he insisted on retaining Communist policies. The two are simply irreconcilable, as he discovered when he tried to incorporate western economic ideas into the rigid Soviet ideological system. He wanted the progress of the West, without its ideas. As a result, he got neither.

Khrushchev's political career ended with an abruptness matched only by his personal style. In October 1964, shortly before the launching of a three-man crew at the Baikonour space center, Khrushchev telephoned the cosmonauts to wish them good luck and tell them of the grand welcome he was preparing for their return. After Khrushchev hung up, Leonid Brezhnev also called the crew to wish them luck, an unprecedented act for a Khrushchev subordinate.

Midway through the spaceflight, Khrushchev talked to the cosmonauts in the *Voskhod* spaceship by radiotelephone. He signed off with strangely prophetic words: "Here is Comrade Mikoyan. He is literally pulling the telephone from my hands. I don't think I can stop him." When the three cosmonauts returned from their seven-day flight, Khrushchev was conspicuously absent from the festivities. He had been ousted into the oblivion of the pensioner's life of a disgraced politician.

There were two basic reasons why Khrushchev's colleagues deposed him. First, even though almost all of them owed their success to him, they were increasingly uncomfortable with his erratic, unpredictable management of the country. Whenever Stalin adopted a dramatic new set of policies, he wiped the slate clean of all those who had supported the old ones. Khrushchev's own purges lacked the finality of those he himself had helped to carry out for Stalin. Party bureaucrats might lose their standing but rarely lost their heads. "In the end," observed Soviet expert Robert Conquest, "he antagonized his subordinates without sufficiently terrorizing them, a fatal lapse."

Second, the Russian leadership was simply ashamed of him. His clowning and his insulting of foreign guests amused them for a while and delighted the hierarchy for a time. But the Russians, with their deep sense of inferiority, wanted acceptance on the international scene. Khrushchev, as several Soviet officials implied to me during our summit meetings, was seen as tarnishing their prestige. "Thank God we're rid of that idiot," one Soviet diplomat said when he heard of Khrushchev's ouster. "He was making us look like fools all over the world."

From absolute leadership of the second most powerful nation in the world, he was reduced to the status of what the Soviets call a "nonperson." Khrushchev lived under perpetual house arrest, confined to his nondescript apartment or modest country residence except for brief and closely supervised auto trips. Being out of power was difficult for many great leaders, but for Khrushchev it was a fate almost worse than death. When he appeared in public occasionally, it was obvious that the pensioner's life was torture for him. He had lost his electric dynamism; his eyes had lost their sparkle. His voice was little more than a whisper, trailing off to nothing before he completed his sentences.

While I was in Moscow on a personal trip in 1965, I was having dinner with my two Soviet guides when a Canadian newspaperman suggested

I call on Khrushchev at his apartment. My guides were supposed to stay with me at all times. But I told them I was going to the men's room, and my Canadian friend and I slipped out the back door and took a cab to the shabby apartment house where Khrushchev lived. When we arrived, two big, burly women barred the door. One had a pail of water in one hand and a mop in the other. I asked if I could see Khrushchev. She answered through my friend, who was acting as my translator, "He's not here. I don't know where he is." As far as she was concerned, he could have been on the moon with his Lunik.

I left a handwritten note for him, saying that I hoped someday we would meet again. I assumed that he probably never received it. Years later, after his death in 1971, I learned that Khrushchev had been told of my attempt to see him and that he regretted very much having missed me.

While Khrushchev and I were engaged in our heated "kitchen debate," I felt someone bump into me as he pushed through the crowd to take a spot along the railing separating the kitchen from the hallway. I glanced at him momentarily as he listened attentively to the debate. He reacted to our exchange only once. He nodded his head vigorously when Khrushchev shouted, "We, too, are giants." I did not think twice about him at the time. But the man's name, I would later learn, was Leonid Brezhnev. Thirteen years later we met again—not in another chance encounter, but in a summit conference as leaders of the two most powerful nations in the world.

Brezhnev greeted me in the same Kremlin office where I had first met Khrushchev. He was cordial as we shook hands. His square, wide face with its icy blue eyes was impassive except for a fixed and rather wary smile. Just as Khrushchev had done, he gestured for me to take a seat opposite him at a long table at one side of the room. He then began by complaining about our actions in Vietnam, but he spoke in an almost perfunctory manner. He warmed perceptively after this pro forma statement. He said it was necessary for us to develop a personal relationship like the one between Roosevelt and Stalin during World War II.

I said that after studying the history of the relationships between the Allied leaders, I found that during the war disagreements between lower-level officials were often overcome by agreements at the top. "That is the kind of relationship that I should like to establish with the General Secretary," I added.

"I would be only too happy, and I am perfectly ready on my side," he responded with obvious delight. I then remarked that if we left all the decisions to the bureaucrats, we would never resolve anything. "They would simply bury us in paper!" he replied, laughing heartily and slapping his palm on the table. On that pleasant, hopeful note—a stark contrast to my first meeting with Khrushchev—we ended our first, brief encounter.

Brezhnev, with whom I would hold three summit conferences as President, became the fourth absolute ruler of the Soviet Union. Born in 1906 in a working-class slum in the Ukraine, Brezhnev was an adolescent during the rule of Lenin, a rising Communist functionary during the purges of Stalin, and a trusted lieutenant during the ascendancy of Khrushchev. An organization man rather than a visionary and a technician rather than an ideologue, he is nonetheless a dedicated, ruthless Communist who has led the Soviet Union in its first sustained bid for world dominance.

Brezhnev and his blustery predecessor made an interesting study in contrasts. Khrushchev wore plain-cuffed shirts and ill-fitting suits, while Brezhnev wore French cuffs and gold cufflinks to go with his well-tailored silk suits. Khrushchev almost always rode in the front seat of his limousine with his chauffeur, while Brezhnev sank into the plush upholstery in the backseat without even a nod in the direction of his driver.

Even when the two men shared an interest, they differed greatly in the way they went about it. Both, for instance, enjoyed hunting. Khrushchev loved every facet of duck hunting, from the quiet sound of water lapping against the side of his boat to the anticipation of the sudden rush of birds' wings. Brezhnev told me he prefers boar hunting, but he decidedly lacks his predecessor's sportsmanship. Brezhnev simply sits on his country porch, waits for his prey to wander into a special area that has been baited with corn meal, and guns the animals down with the aid of a telescopic sight.

Hunting is not Brezhnev's only indulgence. He has a fascination for technical gadgetry such as automatic doors and fancy telephone consoles. Illustrating his typically Russian combination of discipline and laxity, Brezhnev once showed me his fancy new cigarette case with a built-in timer that was designed to cut down on his chain-smoking. Every hour he would ceremoniously remove the allotted cigarette and close the box. Then, minutes later, he would reach into his jacket and take another cigarette from an ordinary pack he carried to tide him over until the timer permitted him another virtuous cigarette.

Brezhnev, the leader of the world's first "workers' state," also collects the finest luxury cars the capitalist world has to offer. When we flew to Camp David during our summit in 1973, I presented him with the official gift commemorating his visit, a dark-blue Lincoln Continental. He insisted on trying it out immediately, jumping behind the wheel and motioning me into the passenger's seat. He gunned the engine and we sped down one of the narrow roads that run around the perimeter of Camp David. Brezhnev was used to unobstructed driving in the lane reserved for VIPs in Moscow. I hated to think what would have happened if a Secret Service or Navy jeep had suddenly turned onto that one-lane road.

At one point on the road there was a very steep slope with a sign at the top reading Slow, Dangerous Curve. Even when driving a golf cart down this decline, I had found it necessary to use the brakes to avoid going off the road at the sharp turn at the bottom. Brezhnev was driving at more than fifty miles an hour as we approached the slope. I reached over and said, "Slow down, slow down," but he paid no attention. When we reached the bottom, there was a squeal of rubber as he slammed on the brakes and made the turn.

After our drive he said to me, "This is a very fine automobile. It holds the road very well." I replied, "You are an excellent driver. I would never have been able to make that turn at the speed at which we were traveling." Diplomacy, I thought to myself, is not always an easy art.

Brezhnev believes in living the good life and enjoys yachting, thoroughbred racing, and the company of pretty girls. At Camp David during the summit in 1973, as I approached Brezhnev's cottage for our first meeting, a very attractive, quite full-figured young woman was leaving. In introducing her to me, Brezhnev's translator said that she was his boss's masseuse. As we shook hands, I recognized the scent she was wearing. It was Arpège, one of the finest of French perfumes, which happens to be Mrs. Nixon's favorite.

Brezhnev is not alone among the world's leaders in his love of luxury and comfort, but is the first Soviet leader to indulge his rich tastes so shamelessly. In a long conversation I had during my trip to China in 1976, the Vice Chairman of the Congress kept reiterating to me that the Soviets, unlike the Chinese, were revisionists because the members of the political and cultural elites lived privileged lives. He said, "Just consider this: The leaders of the government and the party, artists, scientists, et cetera, have become millionaires and are acting like millionaires—that is the trouble with the Soviet Union today!" Though he understated the stratification of Chinese society, he was right on target about the Soviets.

Brezhnev and his colleagues have formed nothing less than a "new class"—separate and remote from the average Soviet citizen and totally oblivious of his concerns. In fact, during all my trips to the Soviet Union, I could not help but think that the Communist elite more closely resembles Marx's definition of a ruling class than any group of capitalists ever did.

A joke I once heard about Brezhnev illustrates the contradiction perfectly. One day he took his mother on a tour of his elegant dacha. After he led her proudly through the opulent gardens, gilded hallways, and posh bedrooms, she turned to him in wonderment and said, "Leonid, it is all very beautiful, but what will you do if the Communists come back?"

Brezhnev may be a "new czar" in his private life, but his foreign policy is a throwback to the expansionism of the old czars. If he had been a leader under the Old Regime, he would be called "Leonid the Great," earning the laudatory appellation for his success in expanding Russian influence throughout the world. Under his leadership, the Soviet Union and its Communist allies have seized control of South Vietnam, Cambodia, Laos, Ethiopia, South Yemen, Angola, Mozambique, and most recently Afghanistan, the "turnstile of Asia's fate." In addition Moscow is ominously expanding its Communist bridgehead in the Caribbean and Central America.

When Khrushchev fell from power, the players may have changed, but the game remained the same. Brezhnev's goals are identical to Khrushchev's: to increase Soviet power, to extend Soviet control, and to export communism at every opportunity. Khrushchev was a master of bluff and bluster because he had to be. He held few trump cards in his hand. Brezhnev can afford to be cordial because he has dealt himself some aces through his massive buildup of armed might.

In their personal diplomacy Khrushchev and Brezhnev were similar to Lyndon Johnson. They felt compelled to reinforce their words with some sort of physical contact. Khrushchev's tactile diplomacy was almost always menacing, whether he was trying to intimidate me through proximity or attempting to harass me with sharp pokes in the ribs. When Brezhnev reached out to touch or grab my arm, he sought to implore, not to bully. But should these gentler means fail to persuade me, Brezhnev could also apply sheer muscle.

What struck me most about Brezhnev was his emotional versatility. At one moment he would speak with what seemed to be perfect sincerity about his deep desire to leave a legacy of peace for his grandchildren. In the next he would assert with unequivocal determination his right to control the destinies of other nations all around the world.

The ease with which Brezhnev would shift from friendliness to ruthlessness was remarkable. During our summit in 1972 he enthusiastically took the members of our party for a boat ride on the Moscow River. As we cruised along, Brezhnev kept nudging me playfully as he pointed proudly at the speedometer, which showed we were moving at ninety kilometers an hour.

After this pleasant excursion Brezhnev sat us down for a meeting before dinner. I momentarily thought of Dr. Jekyll and Mr. Hyde when Brezhnev, who had been jocularly slapping me on the back moments before, started angrily denouncing my efforts to end the Vietnam War and accusing me of trying to pressure him through our new relationship with China. His sally was only the first in a prolonged attack. For three hours Brezhnev, Aleksei Kosygin, and Nikolai Podgorny took turns launching blistering verbal assaults, spelling each other like KGB interrogators working over a difficult suspect.

Yet a few moments after this session ended, we went upstairs and had a perfectly cordial conversation over dinner. I made my usual joke about not giving Kissinger too many drinks because he had to negotiate with Gromyko later. The quip amused the Soviet leaders greatly, and they proceeded to pretend to ply Kissinger with vodka. It was as if the acrimonious session downstairs had never happened.

Brezhnev, like many Soviet leaders of his generation, became especially emotional when speaking of the suffering of war. In World War II the Soviet Union lost over twenty million people, and the memory of those catastrophic days is as fresh as if they had ended only yesterday.

When I addressed the Soviet people on radio and television in 1972, I told the story of Tanya, a twelve-year-old girl whose diary chronicled the loss, one by one, of the members of her family during the Siege of Leningrad. I concluded by saying, "Let us do all that we can to ensure that no other children will have to endure what Tanya did." Brezhnev told me later that my conclusion had brought tears to his eyes. When I included the same message in a toast to him at a private dinner in my home at San Clemente the following year, Brezhnev's eyes welled up with tears. He rose from his chair, walked around the table, and embraced me.

Brezhnev once leaned over to me and said, "I am an emotional man, particularly about death in war." But no one should mistake that emotionalism for mush. He had a strong, deep voice that radiated a great deal of animal magnetism and personal drive. He gestured emphatically and often rose from his chair and paced about the room. He once joked about this habit by telling me, "Everytime I get up, I make another concession." He sometimes talked too much and too imprecisely, but was adept at subtly directing a conversation away from points on which he was vulnerable. And he could be every bit as forceful, shrewd, and devious as Khrushchev.

In 1973, during our second summit, we had retired early one evening because Brezhnev said he was feeling the effects of the three-hour time change from Washington. A few hours later, however, a Secret Service agent came to my room with a message from Kissinger: Brezhnev wanted to talk. I arranged for us to meet in my upstairs study. "I could not sleep, Mr. President," Brezhnev said with a broad smile as he filed in with Gromyko and Soviet Ambassador Anatoly Dobrynin. I replied that this was a good opportunity to talk without interruptions or distractions.

For the next three hours Brezhnev pummeled me on the Middle East. He adamantly insisted that together we had to impose a settlement on the Israelis and the Arabs. At the very least, he said, we had to agree on a set of "principles" that would govern a settlement, citing as examples the withdrawal of Israeli troops from all the occupied territories, the recognition of national boundaries, and international guarantees of the settlement.

I responded that neither side in the dispute would or should accept a dictated settlement and that we should instead try to get talks between the two parties started. I pointed out that I would be prejudicing Israel's rights if I agreed to any of his "principles." And if we were to lay down controversial principles beforehand, I insisted, both parties would refuse to talk—in which case the principles would have defeated their purpose.

At one point Brezhnev made a show of looking at his watch and furrowing his brow. "Perhaps I am tiring you out," he said. "But we must reach an understanding." He left no doubt that our agreement must heavily favor the Arabs. He loudly insisted that without such a settlement he would be leaving the summit empty-handed and then ominously implied that he could not guarantee that war would not resume. "If there is no clarity about the principles," he said, "we will have difficulty keeping the military situation from flaring up."

The emotional intensity of this midnight session almost rivaled that of the dacha meeting on Vietnam during our first summit. I continued to reject his proposals for superpower condominium, reiterating that a

lasting settlement could come only through direct talks between the Israelis and the Arabs. After an hour and a half of near-monologue by
Brezhnev, I brought the discussion to a conclusion, saying that we
should concentrate on the peaceful settlement of the Arab-Israeli dispute this year because "the Middle East is a most urgent place."

Throughout this discussion I remained determinedly unemotional in
responding to Brezhnev's outbursts. Unlike Khrushchev, Brezhnev was
far more impressed by a facade of stoic control than by bombast. We
were unable to come to any agreements because we were working
toward different ends. Put bluntly, the U.S. wanted peace, and the Soviets wanted the Middle East. But as our meeting broke up, I sensed that I
had strongly impressed upon Brezhnev my commitment to Israel and
to a just, negotiated settlement.

Four months later, on October 6, I received word from Israeli Prime
Minister Golda Meir that Syria and Egypt were in the final countdown
to war. I immediately thought back to the summit meeting in which
Brezhnev alluded to the possibility of war resuming in the Middle East
and wondered whether even then he had committed himself to supporting an Arab attack.

Both the American and Israeli intelligence services had failed to detect Arab military preparations until the attack was imminent. As a result, Israel was highly vulnerable, particularly because the invasion
came on Yom Kippur, the holiest Jewish holiday, and many of its soldiers were on leave. The Israelis suffered grim reversals in the first days
of the war, losing more men by the third day than they had in the entire
war in 1967.

Within a few days weapons and supplies on both sides were beginning to run low. We had begun making arrangements to resupply Israel
when we received reports that the Soviets had undertaken a massive
airlift of material to Syria and Egypt. They were sending their clients
seven hundred tons of equipment and supplies daily. Meanwhile, our
airlift was having trouble getting off the ground. It was stalled in the
Pentagon, where critical hours were lost trying to decide such matters
as how many and what kind of aircraft should be used. Kissinger told
me that the Pentagon wanted to send only three C-5A military transports in order to cause fewer political difficulties with Syria, Egypt, and
the Soviets. I asked him how many airplanes were available, and he answered about thirty. Then I told him, "I'll make the political decisions.
We'll take just as much heat for sending three planes as for sending
thirty." Later, after still more bureaucratic delays, I told Kissinger to tell

the Pentagon to send "everything that can fly." The next day thirty C-130 transports were bound for Israel, and within a week the operation had become bigger than the Berlin airlift of 1948–49.

By the end of the first week of fighting, the Israelis had moved on to the offensive. With Soviet hopes for a quick Arab victory squelched, Brezhnev sent me a letter asking that I have Kissinger go to Moscow for direct talks. They drew up a set of proposed terms for a cease-fire, which Israel, Egypt, and Syria agreed to put into effect on October 21. It broke down quickly, but the belligerents agreed to another cease-fire three days later.

Brezhnev had not thrown in the towel, however. On October 24 our intelligence services picked up some startling information: Seven Soviet airborne divisions, numbering fifty thousand men, had been put on alert; and eighty-five Soviet ships, including landing craft and ships carrying troop helicopters, were now in the Mediterranean. Shortly thereafter, Egyptian President Anwar Sadat publicly requested that Brezhnev and I send a joint peace-keeping force to the Middle East, an idea Brezhnev would obviously back because it would give him an opportunity to reestablish a Soviet military presence in Egypt. We soon picked up rumors that the Soviets were maneuvering in the U.N. for nonaligned nations to sponsor a resolution calling for a joint U.S.-U.S.S.R. force in the Middle East.

I sent Sadat a message warning him of the dangers of inviting a great-power rivalry in this volatile region. A few hours later, a message from Brezhnev arrived. He asserted that Israel was still violating the cease-fire and therefore urged us to join him in sending military contingents to the region. He called for an immediate reply and added, "I will say it straight that if you find it impossible to act jointly with us in this matter, we should be faced with the necessity urgently to consider the question of taking appropriate steps unilaterally. We cannot allow arbitrariness on the part of Israel." This message represented perhaps the most serious threat to U.S.-Soviet relations since the Cuban Missile Crisis eleven years before.

I had my White House chief of staff, General Haig, and Kissinger gather together our key national security officials to formulate a firm reaction to this scarcely veiled threat. Words were not making our point— we needed action. My national security advisers unanimously recommended that we put all American conventional and nuclear forces on military alert, and we did so in the early morning hours of October 25.

When we were sure the Soviets had picked up the first signs of the alert, I sent a message to Brezhnev, in which I stated that I had studied his message the night before but found his proposals for sending Soviet and American military forces to the Middle East unacceptable. I denied that there were any significant violations of the cease-fire taking place and stated that in this light we viewed his "suggestion of unilateral action as a matter of the gravest concern involving incalculable consequences." I said that I would be prepared to agree that some American and Soviet personnel go to the area, but not as combat forces. Instead, they might be included in an augmented U.N. force. I then put our point in unequivocal language: "You must know, however, that we could in no event accept unilateral action."

Later that morning, a message arrived from Sadat that stated he understood our position and that he would ask the U.N. to provide an international peace-keeping force. Then a message from Brezhnev came in. Now he just wanted to send seventy individual "observers" to the Middle East. Though this was a far cry from the military contingent he described in his earlier letter, I again expressed firm opposition, suggesting that the Secretary-General of the U.N. should decide the composition of the cease-fire observers.

The alert worked. Brezhnev sent no military personnel to the region, and it became possible to start working toward a peaceful solution to the conflict. The alert had succeeded for two reasons. First, Brezhnev knew that we still had a slight edge over the Soviet Union in nuclear weaponry. Second, he knew that we were determined to defend our vital interests and to stand by our allies, as we had shown through the decisive actions we had taken in Vietnam the year before. My cold words on the Moscow–Washington hot line during the crisis were reinforced by my steadfast refusal to cave in to his demands on the Middle East during our late-night meeting in San Clemente. Thus, during the October crisis, Brezhnev realized that he was up against an adversary who had credible military power and the will to use it, and he backed down.

When Brezhnev and I met again in Moscow in 1974, he expressed bitterness toward the Israelis, blaming them for all the tensions in the Middle East. He also heatedly denied that the Soviets had directly urged the Arabs to launch the 1973 war. Through the tone of his protestations, I sensed that he was pained that our exchanges during the October crisis had been so tough. But he also made it clear that he did not want to venture that close to the brink of war again.

Brezhnev was always a realist in his diplomacy. But as Dobrynin once told Kissinger, Brezhnev and the entire Soviet leadership had one "neuralgic point": China. It seemed that no summit meeting was complete until Brezhnev had made an appeal in one form or another for us to join with him in an alliance against what he called the "yellow peril."

During our second summit I told him that I thought his concern about the Chinese was exaggerated. They would not acquire a sufficient nuclear capability to risk aggression against the Soviet Union for at least twenty years. Brezhnev shook his head in disagreement, so I asked him how long he thought it would take China to become a major nuclear power.

He held up his two hands with fingers outspread and said, "Ten, in ten years, they will have weapons equal to what we have now. We will be further advanced by then, but we must bring home to them that this cannot go on. In 1963, during our party congress, I remember how Mao said, 'Let four hundred million Chinese die; three hundred million will be left.' Such is the psychology of this man." Brezhnev then implied that the entire Chinese leadership was instinctively aggressive and would remain so even after Mao's death.

Our three summits produced a number of important agreements, including the first treaty limiting the Antiballistic Missile Treaty of 1972 and the first strategic arms limitation agreement, SALT I. But both Brezhnev and I considered the personal relationship we developed to be as important as any of the specific pacts. By getting to know each other, we substantially reduced the most dangerous and least recognized danger to peace: miscalculation.

In the nuclear age no sane leader will deliberately step over the brink of war between the superpowers. But leaders who do not meet, who do not talk out their differences, who do not understand each other, run the risk of inadvertently pushing each other over the brink—not because they want war, but because they miscalculate what actions will provoke war. In our meetings Brezhnev and I found that each was the other's equal in resolution. Each, therefore, would think twice before testing the other. It became clear that if we were to go forward in our areas of dispute, we would have to do so together and with mutual respect. That is the major reason why both then and now I believe that annual summit meetings between the leaders of the two superpowers are essential if we are to limit the miscalculation that can lead to war.

In the past thirty-six years I have had an unusual opportunity both to examine firsthand the strategy of the international Communist movement and to take the measure of the Communist leaders.

In 1947 I witnessed the Communist effort to exploit the agonies of war-ravaged Western Europe.

In that same year I helped conduct a congressional investigation that exposed Communist espionage reaching into the highest levels of the United States government.

In the 1950s I saw hundreds of thousands of refugees who had risked their lives to flee the oppression of Communist rule in East Germany, Hungary, North Vietnam, North Korea, and Communist China.

In 1958 Mrs. Nixon and I were attacked and almost killed by a Communist-led mob in Caracas, Venezuela.

In the early 1970s I developed with Brezhnev a closer personal relationship than any other pair of Soviet and American leaders has had since Stalin and Roosevelt.

On visits to the Soviet Union, China, Romania, Hungary, Poland, Czechoslovakia, and Yugoslavia, I have seen the effects of Communist rule. Also, some of the shrewdest insights into Soviet behavior that I have been given have come from the leaders of other Communist countries.

While this experience is substantial, I would not presume to know with certainty what every aspect of our policy toward the Soviet Union should be. At best such policies contain a large measure of guesswork. In *The Real War* I have written at length about the approaches I believe we should take.

If experience does not make clear all that we should do, however, it does give clear guidance about some of the things we should not do.

In dealing with the Soviet Union, we are dealing not just with a great power, but very specifically with that relatively small handful of men who control that great power. By understanding Khrushchev, Brezhnev, and their likely successors, we can better understand how the Soviet Union is likely to react to various policy alternatives.

Debate in the United States often seems to oscillate between two extremes, both well-meaning, both patriotic, and both misguided.

On the one hand there are the superhawks. They contend that because the Soviets lie, cheat, grab anything they can get away with, and are so implacably determined to defeat the West, we should have nothing to do with them. They argue that we should increase our nuclear capability until we have unquestioned superiority. They assert that because the Russians threaten us, we should have no cultural exchanges, no trade, no negotiations. They believe that if we follow this course, the jerry-built economies of the eastern bloc will inevitably collapse, taking the Communist regimes down with them.

At the other extreme there are the superdoves. They argue that the leaders of the Kremlin are old, conservative, cautious men who will pose no threat to us if we do not threaten them. They suggest that if we set an example by unilaterally reducing our nuclear capabilities, the Soviets will follow suit and use those resources instead to build a better life for their people.

Both of these views miss the mark. The Soviets will not allow the United States to regain nuclear superiority; as leaders of a totalitarian state, they can pour into armaments whatever portion of their resources they choose. To refuse to negotiate to reduce the danger of nuclear war is reckless. To suggest that isolating the Soviet Union will bring about its collapse is unrealistic, and can even be counterproductive. External conflict can sometimes strengthen a dictatorship, and relaxation of tensions can sometimes weaken it. Without the détente of the 1970s, the conditions that allowed Solidarity to emerge in Poland might never have developed.

On the other hand, to apply the Golden Rule to our dealings with the Soviets is dangerously naive. President Carter, with the best of intentions, tried unilateral restraint in the hopes that the Soviets would follow suit. The result was disastrous. As he cut back on American arms programs, the Soviets stepped up theirs. Consequently, President Reagan has had to institute an arms buildup to restore the nuclear balance of power.

There are two kinds of détente: hard-headed and soft-headed. Hard-headed détente is based on effective deterrence. This kind of détente encourages the Soviets to negotiate, because it makes the cost of Soviet aggression too high. Soft-headed détente, by contrast, *discourages* negotiation, because it makes the cost of Soviet expansion so low that the Soviets find the rewards of aggression too tempting.

Hard-headed détente, backed by the force to make deterrence credible, preserves peace. Soft-headed détente invites either war or surrender without war. We need détente, but it must be the right kind of détente.

If there are things we cannot do, however, there also are things we can do. It would be folly to give up in despair and say that because we cannot do everything, we should do nothing.

The Soviet leaders are hard, cold, tough realists who understand the arithmetic of international power.

For us the first essential must be to preserve the freedom of the West and to make clear to the Soviet leaders that we are determined to take whatever measures are necessary to do so. The more luminously clear we make this determination, the less likely it is that they will put it to the ultimate test.

This means restoring the military balance of power so that we can deter war and prevent defeat without war. When the United States enjoyed superiority in nuclear weapons, these forces were on the side of peace. If the Soviets threatened aggressive action, we could put our nuclear forces on alert, as we did in October 1973, and our adversary would back down. But today the threat would not be credible because superiority has shifted to the Soviets in both theater and strategic land-based missiles. In the hands of an aggressive power like the Soviet Union, this superiority becomes an ominous threat. Thus, in the interest of peace, we must spend the dollars that are needed to restore the balance of power.

The Soviet leaders want military superiority and want to use it to rule the world, but if we convince them that we are going to deny them that superiority, then there is a real chance that they will negotiate seriously about mutual arms limitation and even reduction.

Today, there are many who propose that both sides agree to freeze the current levels of nuclear weapons, arguing that this would reduce the risk of war and promote arms control. Ironically, just the opposite is true. Under a freeze, the Soviets would maintain their current advantages, which would increase the possibility of war and of nuclear blackmail. A freeze would also eliminate any chance for an arms control agreement that would reduce the number of nuclear weapons because it would remove any incentive for the Soviets to negotiate. The men in the Kremlin may be old and sick, but they are not fools. We cannot get something from them unless we have something to give.

As a panacea for the nuclear dilemma, the freeze proposal is as empty as it is facile. It rests on two fallacious premises. The first is that somehow we can escape the dangers of the nuclear age. But as long as these weapons exist, the peril will remain great. Even if both sides agreed to reduce their arsenals by half, each would still have enough firepower to destroy the other and the world many times over.

The second fallacy is that armaments and arms races cause wars. If we want to save the world from destruction, runs the argument, we must stop the arms race. But historically it is not the existence of arms that brings war, but rather it is the failure to resolve the political differences that might lead to the use of arms. Arms are the result, not the cause, of political tensions. And no well-worded resolution about disarmament can solve these profound political disagreements.

We cannot escape the nuclear dilemma, but must learn to live with it. We must leapfrog the sterile question of arms control and focus on the heart of the problem: the fundamental differences between the United

States and the Soviet Union. We must develop a process for resolving those differences at the conference table instead of on the battlefield. But before we can do this, we must induce the Soviets to negotiate, and they will do this only if our strength makes them fear our enmity. Brezhnev understands this, even though he resists it. We have to continue to make clear to him and his successors that we understand it too.

We must also resist the aggressive adventurism of the Soviets in other parts of the world vital to our interests. We cannot be the policeman of the world, but we also cannot afford to stand idly by as the Soviets and their proxies subvert and attack our allies and friends. We must be prepared to project our power to blunt Soviet thrusts in distant regions of the world, for that is where the fate of the world is being decided.

Additionally, it is time for us to use our massive economic power to affect the international behavior of the Soviet Union. We may be behind in some areas militarily, but we have a huge advantage economically. They desperately need their trade with us, and this gives us leverage, provided that we structure our trade to maximize their vulnerability to economic pressures and minimize our own.

Brezhnev and his colleagues in the Kremlin will scoff at the suggestion that they need a deal, but they do. We should give them one—but for a price. They must be made to understand that if they continue to engage in direct and indirect aggression in areas affecting our interests, the deal is off. Lenin said that capitalists would line up to sell Soviet Russia the rope it would later use to hang them with. We should sell them rope, but in ways that it will bind their hands if they attempt to reach out to enlarge their conquests.

While containing Soviet force, we also can and must press for change within the Soviet world. The way to achieve this is not by a lot of pious talk about it—Brezhnev and company dismiss such talk with contempt—but by giving added impetus to the forces already at work to bring about change.

The Communist world is not going to collapse in some sudden cataclysm. But it has changed, it will continue to change, and we can accelerate that change. It is in this process that the West's hope lies.

Some dismiss the idea of reform in the Communist world through peaceful change as hopeless, throwing up their hands and saying it will take forever. They forget how much has changed already.

Britain's former Prime Minister Macmillan once reminded me that a hundred years elapsed between the reign of Queen Elizabeth I, who beheaded her counselors when they fell out of favor, and that of Queen

Anne, who, because of public opinion, could only send hers into exile. He made that comment in 1958, five years after the death of Stalin, who had executed his real and imagined enemies by the millions. When Khrushchev purged his rivals, he could only banish them to the provinces. And Brezhnev could only send Khrushchev to the outskirts of Moscow.

The pace of change is desperately slow and seems even more so to a people as impatient as Americans. We have to muster enough patience to recognize that slow change is better than no change, and to stick with the long-term policies that are sometimes needed to keep slow change going.

People-to-people contacts and cultural and informational exchanges may not accomplish as much as some of the dewy-eyed advocates claim, but they do help; they are an important incremental part of the process. So, too, is trade in nonstrategic goods, provided that it, like arms control, is linked to Soviet behavior in other areas. Trade can be structured so that it gives us leverage—so that the interdependencies it builds can work to our advantage. Ideas have a force of their own, and we can force these through the barriers. A Polish Pope dramatically represents the power that religious faith can marshal. Our biggest asset is the plain fact, patently obvious on both sides of the Iron Curtain, that communism does not work. Even its most abject apologists increasingly fall back on justifications other than its miserable results.

The Russian people are strong, and so are those of the countries of Eastern Europe. Ultimately, in the contest between East and West, their strength will be among the West's strengths, because the West's adversaries are their oppressors.

Leaders during the decades ahead will have to adapt to a situation in which the superpowers face one another in a sort of uneasy standoff. Whatever one thinks of the term *détente*, the condition is a fact of life— and a fact distinctly preferable to its alternatives. Détente is not a love feast. It is an effort to find ways of living with differences rather than fighting over them. As long as the Soviet Union persists in its expansionist aims, there can be no détente without deterrence. But deterrence is both easier and more effective with détente than without it.

The United States will have to be strong militarily, strong economically, firm in its will, and it will need the cooperation of strong allies—with strong leaders. The Soviet Union is a very real threat; meeting that threat is the first responsibility of western leaders. But precisely because it is so great a threat, we must continue to be creative in finding ways to reduce our differences, to resolve them by negotiation where that is possible and to talk across them where resolution is not possible.

The Russian leaders will respect us if we stand firm and if we are strong enough to back up our words with force, should that become necessary. They will treat us with contempt if we act weakly. But if they see that they must negotiate with us, and if they see that we will negotiate, then they, too, will negotiate.

The Kremlin leaders have a compulsive drive to protect and expand their power. But they are not madmen. They will take what they think they can get away with, but *only* what they think they can get away with. If they think they have to retreat on one flank in order to protect their position on another, they will.

Our task is to increase the pressures that lead to change and to hold out the hope of reward when such change occurs.

In my Guildhall speech that Khrushchev praised when I first met him nearly twenty-five years ago, I issued a call for peaceful competition all across the board, in the spiritual as well as the material realm. This is a competition in which the West holds all the cards. We should remember that and continue to play out these cards.

ZHOU
ENLAI

The Mandarin Revolutionary

THE STORY OF China during the past half century is, to an extraordinary degree, the story of three men: Mao Zedong, Zhou Enlai, and Chiang Kai-shek. As Mao consolidated his rule on the mainland after defeating Chiang's forces, the Chinese Communists portrayed the conflict between Mao and Chiang as, in effect, a war between God and the Devil. Mao saw himself as the modern-day equivalent of the first Emperor of Ch'in, the ruler who first unified China over two thousand years ago. He wove a cult of personality that gave him the status of a deity. Zhou stayed largely in the shadows, the loyal functionary who made the machinery run. On Taiwan, Chiang ruled with an authoritarian hand but without Mao's extravagant self-glorification, preserving his dignity, working an economic miracle, and nurturing his people's hopes for a return to the mainland.

Of the three, I knew Chiang the longest. I considered both him and Madame Chiang friends in a way the others were not. Our bonds were personal and also a product of shared beliefs and principles. But it was Mao and Zhou who won the war for the Chinese mainland, and of those two, it was Zhou whose vision had the greater staying power. Zhou was also, quite simply, one of the most extraordinarily gifted people I have ever known, with an incandescent grasp of the realities of power. All three are dead, but Zhou's is the legacy that is increasingly ascendant in modern China.

Seven months before my first visit to China in 1972, I sent Henry Kissinger on a secret mission to Peking to negotiate arrangements for it. During his two days in Peking on that initial secret trip, Kissinger spent more than seventeen hours in direct, far-ranging discussions with Zhou. On his return he reported to me that he would rank Zhou equally with de Gaulle as "the most impressive" foreign statesman he had ever met.

Though given to occasional hyperbole, as we all are, Kissinger is seldom that lavish in his praise of people who are out of earshot. After meeting Zhou and negotiating with him for a week, I could understand why Kissinger had been so unusually laudatory in his assessment of Zhou.

At the conclusion of my trip to China in 1972, I said in my final toast, "We have been here a week. This was the week that changed the world." Some observers felt I had been carried away by the drama of the visit and had overestimated its significance. I believe history will demonstrate that if this first step had not been taken toward the normalization of relations between the United States and the People's Republic of China, the balance of power with the Soviet Union would now be weighted almost fatally against us. Both men and events contributed to the diplomatic breakthrough that was formalized by the Shanghai Communiqué of 1972. The one man who deserves the primary credit was Zhou Enlai.

Zhou was a Communist revolutionary and a Confucian gentleman, a devoted ideologue and a calculating realist, a political infighter and a grand conciliator. A lesser man thrust into these crosscutting roles would have ended up confused in thought and action. But Zhou could assume any one of the roles or combine qualities of each without giving the slightest impression of hesitancy or inconsistency. For him these were not masks to be donned cynically at the appropriate moments.

They were facets of a very complex, subtle man that in large measure explained the length and richness of his political career.

The ruthlessness of the Communist ideologue allowed him to capitalize on historical opportunities and to endure political setbacks and physical hardships. The personal qualities of the Confucian gentleman allowed him to excel in personal diplomacy and to become "our beloved leader" to millions of Chinese. The shrewdness of the realist allowed him to assess accurately the underlying forces in domestic politics and international diplomacy. The stealth of the political infighter enabled him to ensure that his policies would outlive him and would extend into the post-Mao era. The tact and courtesy of the conciliator allowed him to keep the country together when the actions of more cataclysmic figures worked to pull it apart.

The interplay of all these qualities allowed Zhou to lead a career in the highest reaches of Communist leadership that lasted longer than that of Lenin, Stalin, or Mao.

Zhou's early life is a textbook case of the political evolution of a revolutionary leader. He was born in the town of Huai'an, about two hundred miles northwest of Shanghai, in the province of Jiangsu. When his mother died and his father proved unable to provide for him, the Zhou clan took over his upbringing, shuttling him among a host of uncles. His traditional Mandarin family trained Zhou in the Chinese classics from his infancy. But when he stayed with an aunt and uncle in the Manchurian city of Shenyang, he attended an elementary school sponsored by Christian missionaries for several years until he was fifteen years old. It was in this period that he learned "the new knowledge" brought from the West.

After completing his elementary education, Zhou sought to enroll in a program that would have sent him to the United States for college, but was bitterly disappointed when he failed to rank high enough on the entrance examinations. Instead he attended the antitraditionalist Nankai Middle School in Tianjin and spent two years in Japan, where he read for the first time about the ideas of Karl Marx. In 1919 Zhou returned to China and attended Nankai University. Political agitation preoccupied him more than academics, however. For his role in organizing student strikes and demonstrations, Zhou spent four months in jail.

Zhou was twenty-two years old when he was released from prison in 1920. He then traveled to Europe to continue his education. He visited

England and Germany, but spent most of his time in France. His reputation as a strike organizer had preceded him, and radical groups of Chinese students abroad welcomed him. He enrolled in classes, but political agitation still consumed most of his energy. Zhou was soon receiving a stipend from the Comintern.

In 1924 Zhou returned to China to join Sun Yat-sen's revolutionary Kuomintang party, with which the Communists were then in alliance. He was appointed deputy director of the political department of the Whampoa Military Academy, whose commandant was a young officer named Chiang Kai-shek. Impressed by Zhou, Chiang retained him as chief commissar on the Kuomintang's military campaigns and sent him with other officers to organize an uprising in Shanghai to facilitate its armed capture.

In 1927, when Chiang took Shanghai, he turned his guns on the Communists within his ranks, whose growing strength he now feared. Zhou barely escaped with his life. He then organized several unsuccessful urban insurrections against the Kuomintang before Chiang's army forced the remnants of Zhou's on to the Long March. During the six-thousand-mile trek, Zhou became a trusted aide of Mao. When the Kuomintang and the Communists formed a united front against the Japanese in World War II, he served as Mao's liaison to Chiang, and afterward he was the chief Communist negotiator in the talks to try to end the civil war. After the Communist victory in 1949, Zhou served as the Premier, the Foreign Minister, and sometimes both for over a quarter of a century.

The unique personality of Zhou Enlai was one of the most vivid impressions of my trip to China in 1972. Through the many hours of plenary sessions and informal meetings, I came to know him well and to respect him greatly. *Enlai* translates as "coming of grace," a name that succinctly captured his presence and disposition. Zhou was unassuming but quietly strong. He conveyed immense charm and poise through his graceful movements and erect, easy stance. He faithfully observed the old Chinese rule in personal and political relations of never "breaking the surface."

Zhou's appearance gave the impression of personal warmth, absolute forthrightness, complete self-possession, and unmistakable intensity. In the plenary sessions he was calculatingly restrained. Wearing a neatly tailored gray Sun Yat-sen suit with a "Serve the people" ideograph pinned to the flap of his pocket, he sat motionless across the table from me. He leaned forward slightly, setting his arms on the table and clasping his hands together before him. His right arm was notice-ably wizened, a permanent reminder of an injury sustained during the Long March. At age seventy-three his brushed-back black hair was only slightly gray. Its single wave was uncharacteristic for a Chinese, as was his dark, almost Mediterranean complexion.

His sharply sculpted features remained impassive during the formal sessions. When listening, Zhou would hold his head slightly to one side while looking directly into my eyes. Henry Kissinger once likened Zhou to a cobra that sits quietly, poised to strike, and then springs at the op-portune moment. The phrase that was often used to describe Charles Parnell, the great nineteenth-century Irish patriot, could well have been applied to Zhou Enlai: He was a volcano under an ice cap.

Zhou seemed to understand what I was saying before he heard the translation, which was not surprising because he once had a working knowledge of English, as well as French, German, Russian, and Japa-nese. Occasionally he even corrected the translation of his own state-ments to capture better the nuances of his thoughts. When speaking, he used no notes and only rarely brought any of his aides into the dis-cussion. He was logical and earnestly convincing. To add power to his statement, he would lower his voice, providing emphasis with a dis-creet nod of the head.

Though he might have appeared frail because of his thin frame, Zhou's stamina surpassed that of many of his younger associates. Be-cause of his enormous workload—at the time he was both Prime Minis-ter and Foreign Minister—he was reputed to rise early and work long into the night. Often he received foreign visitors at odd hours of the morning and conducted conversations that lasted until sunrise, always finishing them as fresh and incisive as he was at the outset.

As we became better acquainted in the more informal settings of ban-quets and sight-seeing, Zhou's gestures became more expansive and his face more animated. He would often sit back in his chair and use his expressive hands to great effect, sweeping an arm before him when adding scope to a statement or generalizing and pushing his hands to-gether at the fingertips when weaving the strands of an argument into a conclusion. The silent chuckle at the wordplay in the formal sessions gave way in social conversation to easy and sometimes uproarious laughter at friendly jokes. The merriment brought out the light in his eyes, while his broad smile deepened the creases in his skin and seemed to evince a very genuine pleasure.

At the state dinners Zhou and I toasted each other with *maotai* in-stead of champagne, which is the traditional drink at such affairs. *Mao-*

tai, a 106-proof rice wine, is a fiery brew. It has been humorously said that a man who drank too much of it exploded when he lit an after-dinner cigarette. At one point Zhou put a match to a cup of *maotai* to demonstrate its combustibility, and the liquid was instantly consumed in flames.

When we moved around the banquet hall to clink glasses with over fifty high-level officials, I noted that he was sipping his drink gingerly, barely letting it touch his lips as he toasted each guest. We were both still on our first glasses by the time we returned to our table. Then we downed the rest. Given the drink's potency, I was astonished when Zhou told me that on special occasions during the Long March he drank as many as twenty-five cups of it in a day, though his age had since limited him to two or three cups. I remembered reading that on the Long March, when the Red Army overran the village of Maotai, where the drink originated, the troops had drunk the place dry. Zhou remarked to me with a snake-oil salesman's glint of the eye that on the Long March *maotai* was "a cure for everything."

Our conversation ranged from politics to history to philosophy, in all of which Zhou was completely at home. Zhou was a scholar-turned-insurrectionist who never lost the scholar's keenness of mind and depth of thought. The categories into which his ideology sometimes channeled his thinking, however, could distort his reading of history. In our talks, for example, he referred to the French troops who fought with the colonists in the Revolutionary War as "volunteers." The French forces, in fact, except for a few like Lafayette, were actually trained, professional soldiers serving a political purpose in opposing the British armies.

Zhou also told me that Lincoln waged the Civil War in order to free the slaves and won because "the people" supported him. In fact, Lincoln, who is one of the few true giants in history and of whom the Chinese spoke with great respect, waged war not to free the slaves but to bring the states of the South back into the Union. His Emancipation Proclamation was a tactical maneuver that freed the slaves only in the rebelling states, but not in the border states that had remained within the Union. Lincoln was unalterably opposed to slavery, but his first priority was to save the Union.

Though he was a dedicated revolutionary, Zhou looked not at all out of place amid the splendor of the palaces of old Peking, moving about them with a calm and grace worthy of a sage of the dynastic periods. No one would have guessed after seeing him in these surroundings that he was a leader of a movement whose professed mission was nothing less than conquering the world, reforming civilization, and changing human nature. The ornamentation was oddly respectful of China's past. The palaces were decorated with extravagant paintings of Chinese landscapes and with ancient artifacts of silver, gold, and jade. There was not a trace of the raucous exhortations of the propaganda posters that lined the streets of Peking.

The subtlety of the art and ornamentation was matched by the subtlety in Zhou's personality and his handling of affairs of state. This subtlety, which Zhou possessed to a greater degree than any other world leader I have known, is a distinctly Chinese character trait. It has resulted from centuries of development and conscious refinement of Chinese civilization. It was present in conversation, where Zhou carefully drew distinctions between shades of meaning; it was present in negotiations, where he skirted contentious points through indirection; it was present in diplomacy, where he sometimes conveyed important messages through seemingly trivial events.

Zhou and all the Communist Chinese leaders I spoke with took particular delight in reminding me that an exchange of Ping-Pong teams had initiated the breakthrough in our relations. They seemed to enjoy the method used to achieve the result almost as much as the result itself. Mao, for example, said that China had been "bureaucratic" in insisting that all major issues be settled before relations could be improved. "Later on," he said, "I saw you were right, and we played table tennis."

Zhou also had the rare ability to pay meticulous attention to detail without getting bogged down in it. On our third night in Peking we were taken to the gymnastics and table tennis exhibition. It had begun to snow, and we were scheduled to visit the Great Wall the next day. Zhou left his seat briefly, and I assumed that he had gone to the rest room. Later I found that he had personally gone to see to it that the people were sweeping the snow off the road to the Great Wall. The next day the road was pristine. This incident was typical.

I discovered that Zhou had personally assembled the members of the honor guard that welcomed us at the airport; they were all strong-looking, very tall, and immaculately turned out. He had chosen the songs for the band to play during dinner. I knew he had done his homework on my background because he had selected many of my favorites, including "America the Beautiful," which was played at my inauguration. After the trip, Secretary of State William Rogers told me that before one of his meetings with Zhou a young lady came and handed Zhou the galleys of the next day's newspaper, which he proceeded to arrange for the front page.

In Zhou's case there is almost certainly some truth in the adage that greatness is the accumulation of attention to detail. Yet, though he tended personally to each tree, he always was able to see the forest.

Zhou also possessed another distinctly Chinese quality, an unshakable self-confidence that the Chinese have acquired from enjoying cultural supremacy in their region for millennia. But the awareness by the Chinese of their cultural heritage cut two ways.

On the one hand it combined with a natural resentment of the national humiliations China suffered in the past two centuries to create a heightened sensitivity to diplomatic indignities. The Chinese attitude toward the outside world was graphically described by my friend the late Harold Lee, an Oxford graduate and a resident of Hong Kong, who had an almost uncanny understanding of both Chinese and western psychologies. In 1965 I asked him how the Communist Chinese would react if the United States recognized the government in Peking. His reply was characteristically blunt: " 'You will recognize *us*?' they would ask incredulously. 'You have it all wrong. The only question is whether *we* will recognize you.' " An incident at the Geneva Conference on Vietnam in 1954 illustrated Zhou's sensitivity to slights of Chinese national honor. Zhou was representing China and Secretary of State John Foster Dulles the United States. Dulles had told a reporter that there was one condition under which the two would meet: "Only if our automobiles collide!" By chance they encountered each other when both arrived early for one morning session. Zhou reached out to shake hands. Dulles shook his head and walked out of the room, thoroughly humiliating the Chinese Foreign Minister. Six years later Zhou still winced when he recounted the incident to his friend Edgar Snow. In the context of those times, Dulles's snub was understandable. Thousands of Americans had been killed by Communist Chinese "volunteers" in the Korean War; Chiang Kai-shek's government on Taiwan would soon sign a mutual defense treaty with us; and mainland China and the Soviet Union were united in their belligerency toward the United States. I knew how deeply the incident had offended Zhou, however. Therefore, when I reached the bottom step of the airplane ramp on my first arrival in Peking, I made a point of extending my hand as I walked toward him. Our handshake produced the most memorable photograph of the trip.

On the other hand, in our dealings with the Chinese their self-confidence allowed them to turn their critical scrutiny inward without becoming insecure about their shortcomings. Zhou continually referred in our talks to their need to understand and overcome their imperfections. In our first meeting he noted the great contrast in the average age of their party and ours, saying, "We have too many elderly people in our leadership. So on this point we should learn from you." Similarly, later in the visit, he apologized for an incident during our visit to the Ming tombs, in which a lower official had provided some children with colorful clothing and instructed them how to act when our group arrived: "Some people got some young children there to prettify the tombs, and it was putting up a false appearance. Your press correspondents have pointed this out to us, and we admit that this was wrong. We do not want to cover up the mistake on this, of course, and we have criticized those who have done this." Throughout my visit I could not help thinking of Khrushchev's bombast and how much healthier the Chinese approach was. Khrushchev's crude boasting was obviously a cover for an inferiority complex. Zhou's subtle self-criticism was clear evidence of a mature self-confidence. Yet I knew that this was basically only a way of approaching things and that in fact the Chinese were absolutely convinced of the ultimate superiority of their culture and philosophy and that these would triumph in time over ours and everyone else's.

Zhou's intellectual power and personal magnetism entranced many people who did not realize that these qualities went hand in hand with those of a ruthless political actor. Journalist Fred Utley said that Zhou was "hard to resist . . . witty, charming, and tactful." Theodore White admitted to a "near total suspension of disbelief or questioning judgment" in his presence. A Chinese newspaperman in Japan said, "I should say he is the most impressive public figure I have ever met."

Those who saw the ruthless politician and who were not taken in by him painted an altogether different portrait of Zhou. Walter Robinson, an assistant secretary of state for Far Eastern affairs during the 1950s, once told me that Zhou, charming though he was, had killed people with his own hands and then departed calmly smoking a cigarette.

A United States official who had dealt with Zhou in the 1940s said, "You pronounce his name like Joe, and—well, that's the kind of a guy he seemed to me, like a guy named Joe. I thought for a while we could split him away. Then all of a sudden I knew I was wrong. He wouldn't agree that Monday was Monday unless it would help him."

And a high-ranking Kuomintang negotiator once said, "At first, I was completely convinced that he was right, and there perhaps should be more concession on both sides of the negotiation. Then, as the days went by, I began to wonder if this man, however sincere he might be, was not totally blinded by his political prejudices. Finally, I came to recognize that there was not a grain of truth in him. . . . But in the end, I realized that it's all acting. He is the greatest actor I have ever seen. He'd laugh one moment and cry the next, and make his audience laugh and cry with him. But it's all acting!"

The two images interlocked, of course. Zhou would always act in accordance with the interests of his country and ideology, and ingratiating himself with foreign diplomats and journalists almost always furthered those interests. But should his interests require him to break a trust irreparably, he would part company unsentimentally. In our relationship Zhou faithfully kept to the letter and spirit of our agreements. He did not do so, however, for the sake of simple friendship. Rather, he formed the friendship for the sake of his interests.

Writing years after having known Zhou in Yan'an and now realizing that his absolute faith in Zhou had been misplaced, Theodore White brought both images into focus, stating that Zhou was "a man as brilliant and ruthless as any the Communist movement has thrown up in this century. He could act with absolute daring, with the delicacy of a cat pouncing on a mouse, with the decision of a man who has thought his way through to his only course of action—and yet he was capable of warm kindness, irrepressible humanity and silken courtesy."

Combining as it did the personal qualities of a Confucian gentleman and the ruthless political instincts of a Leninist revolutionary, Zhou's personality was ideally suited to his political role. Like an alloy of several metals, its fusion of elements was stronger than any one element would have been individually. The Communist system rewards masters of intrigue, but often consumes practitioners of compromise. Zhou's political genius was that he could play successfully the roles of both infighter and conciliator.

A journalist once asked Zhou if, as a Chinese Communist, he was more Chinese or more Communist. Zhou replied, "I am more Chinese than Communist." Zhou's colleagues were all Chinese nationals, of course. But most of them were Communists first and Chinese second. Zhou deeply believed in his ideology as well, but it was not his nature to carry this belief to extremes.

Zhou's Mandarin background also set him apart from his colleagues. His family had been rooted in the ways and manners of old China, its members maintaining their social position for centuries by training their children in the Chinese classics and placing them in positions in the imperial bureaucracy. Zhou renounced the philosophical corner-stones of Chinese society in his adolescence, but he could never rid himself of their cultural imprint, nor did he wish to. He always retained a certain respect for China's past—for those elements of the "old soci-ety" that deserved preservation.

Unlike most Communist Chinese, he acknowledged repeatedly his indebtedness to his past and to his family. In 1941 he was speaking to a small crowd during a break in the negotiations to restore the alliance between the Communist and Kuomintang parties against the Japanese. For the Chinese in his audience, he struck a reverberating emotional chord when in a hushed voice he remorsefully expressed a personal desire to defeat the Japanese so that he could pay his respects at his mother's grave: "As for me, the grave of my mother, to whom I owe ev-erything that I am and hope to be, is in Japanese-occupied Zhejiang. How I wish I could just go back there once to clear the weeds on her grave—the least a prodigal son who has given his life to revolution and to his country can do for his mother."

Also during the war with the Japanese, Zhou's father, who seemed to fail in every venture he undertook, wrote to his now-famous son asking for money. Zhou obligingly sent him a portion of his meager salary. When his father died in 1942, Zhou ran an obituary in the Communist party newspaper in the manner required by family tradition, an act that must have raised more than a few eyebrows among his revolutionary cohorts.

Many years before our historic meeting in 1972, Zhou told a reporter that it was the fault of the United States that no formal relations existed between our two countries. Any American would be welcome in China, he said, but there would have to be reciprocity. He added, "There is a Chinese saying which runs: 'It is discourteous not to pay a return vis-it.' " This, he underscored, was said "by Confucius, who was not a Marxist."

It may seem discordant for a Communist Chinese leader to cite Con-fucius as an authority, but for Zhou the incident was wholly in charac-ter. His upbringing had imbued him with the qualities Confucius ascribed to the "gentleman" or "superior man" who ruled society—in-telligence, dignity, grace, kindness, resolution, and forcefulness.

These qualities made Zhou remarkably effective in the personal rela-tions of politics and helped him coexist with his rivals for fully half a century. According to Zhang Guotao, a one-time member of the Com-munist Chinese politburo, Zhou's resiliency in intraparty politics and his success as a conciliator owed much to the fact that he was a "round" man: "He belongs in this category as one who is smooth in his dealings with society, who is good at making friends, who never goes to extremes, and who always adapts himself to the existing situation."

His Confucian virtues also earned Zhou the abiding affection of the Chinese people. He was the only public figure who earned the appellation "our beloved leader." His popularity was a unique force in Chinese politics, which became most evident at the time of his death. When a television newsreel showed Jiang Qing, who was Mao's wife and an ultraleftist, disrespectfully refusing to remove her cap as she viewed Zhou's body, a crowd at a neighborhood television set in Canton began chanting, "Beat her up!"

In his funeral oration Deng Xiaoping, who was Zhou's chosen deputy, praised the fallen Premier so effusively that the speech became a political issue. The ultraleft called for a condemnation from Mao in a poster that read, "The verdict should be reversed." Although Mao sympathized politically with the left at that time, he is said to have answered, "The people will surely oppose any attack on Zhou Enlai. The verdict on the memorial speech given at Zhou's funeral cannot be changed. The people do not support the reversal of the verdict."

As a Leninist revolutionary, Zhou often exercised power ruthlessly and cruelly. A friend from secondary school who met Zhou many years later observed that "his eyes were far colder; they had become the eyes of a man who could kill." The history of Chinese politics and government is filled with bloodshed, but the tyranny of the Communist regime is in a category all its own. Mao, Zhou, and their comrades have been directly or indirectly responsible for the killings of tens of millions of their own people.

I became painfully familiar with the utter brutality of the Chinese Communists during an around-the-world trip I took as Vice President in 1953. I was riding along the border area between Hong Kong and Communist China and stopped to talk to a farmer. He told me, "My wife and two children and I walked one hundred miles to freedom in the new territories in Hong Kong." I asked why they went to such great lengths to leave Communist China. He replied, "My only brother was blind and had a farm next to me. Because he was blind he could not produce as much as the Communists required in order to pay taxes. The Communists took him away and shot him. We began walking to freedom."

My interpreter told me a similarly sad story about a seventy-year-old woman who frequently crossed the waterway that runs along the border between the Hong Kong territories and China because she had land on both sides. "One day when she crossed, a Communist shot her down," he said. "The first shot only wounded her. He walked up to her and pumped three bullets into her back."

The Communist ideology inured Zhou to such heartless cruelty. Marxism-Leninism has a determinist view of history. Its adherents believe that history will inevitably lead to world communism and that it is their job to hurry history along. By viewing themselves in this way, they sidestep all considerations of morality because all the crimes they commit are simply deemed necessary for the furtherance of history.

A problem arises for the Communists, however, when they disagree among themselves. There is still no room for morality. There is also no room for compromise. This leaves a lot of room for violence. In a disagreement both sides cannot be right, and whichever one is wrong is "impeding the forces of history." And that high crime often carries the penalty of death.

Yet Zhou preferred using his tactfulness instead of his ruthlessness in both his policies and his politics. As Prime Minister, Zhou carried out vast economic reforms, some of which were beneficial and many of which were harmful, without the social convulsions his rivals so often produced by forcing too many changes too quickly. Against the opposition of radicals who demanded the achievement of the millennium by the next week, Zhou pushed consistently for a program of gradual economic modernization.

In the shifting alliances of Chinese politics, Zhou used power quietly but to great effect. He never gave his colleagues the impression of wanting more power than he had. When a coalition formed around a hardliner who had Mao's blessing, Zhou would work with his rival despite the distaste he felt for the new policies. He would lie low until the coalition degenerated into a deadlock in which his support became pivotal. At that point he would switch to an opposition faction with a more moderate line.

But if others escalated intraparty battles to violence, Zhou would follow suit. A morbid example occurred shortly after the announcement of the diplomatic rapprochement between the United States and China. It became evident that Lin Biao, who was the leader of the Red Army, had mobilized opposition to the summit. Zhou and his allies fought to suppress them. When it became apparent to Lin that he had lost, he boarded an airplane and tried to flee from the country. During our discussions, Zhou told me that Lin's plane had been headed toward the Soviet Union, but had disappeared en route. He added that they had not been able to find it since. And then he just smiled.

The Cultural Revolution in the 1960s and early 1970s was perhaps the most trying ordeal Zhou endured in his years in power.

Mao feared that since the Communist victory in 1949 the nation's revolutionary spirit and vigor had eroded and that the young people had gone soft. He decided that only in upheaval could China retain his revolutionary values. He called on the youth of China to struggle against the system, declaring, "When we started to make revolution we were mere twenty-three-year-old boys, while the rulers of that time ... were old and experienced. They had more learning but we had more truth."

The young people, many of whom were bitterly frustrated by the lack of opportunities in education and in the economy, responded with a vengeance, burning down schools and factories by the hundreds. Rephrasing the cliché that "revolutions always devour their children," philosopher Lin Yutang commented, "In China it is the children who are devouring the revolution."

The vaguely defined mission of Mao's Red Guards was to disrupt the political and bureaucratic order. Zhou sat at the top of that order as Prime Minister. At the height of the Cultural Revolution, nearly half a million Red Guards surrounded the Great Hall of the People, virtually imprisoning Zhou. With customary aplomb he engaged his captors in a series of marathon meetings lasting three days and two nights, which aired their grievances and calmed their tempers. Soon thereafter the throng started disbanding.

When Kissinger returned from his secret trip to China in 1971, he told me that Zhou could barely conceal his anguish when speaking about the Cultural Revolution. This was not surprising. Zhou was a first-generation Communist leader who had fought in the revolution to achieve an egalitarian vision; he was also a leader who pushed for a program of gradual economic modernization. Therefore, part of him sympathized with the aims of the Cultural Revolution; the other part of him knew that if China was to meet even the most basic needs of its people and its national defense over the next decades, it would have to modernize its economy.

"A builder, not a poet," as Edgar Snow once described him, Zhou must have anguished as he saw the fury of the Red Guards destroy his meticulously laid groundwork for modernization.

China may remember Zhou as the grand conciliator who held the party and country together, but the world will best remember him as China's principal diplomat. He was his country's Metternich, Molotov, and Dulles. An instinctive agility in negotiations, a command of the principles of international power, and a moral certitude derived from ardent ideological beliefs combined in Zhou with an intimate understanding of foreign countries, a long-term historical vision, and a wealth of personal experience to produce one of the most accomplished diplomats of our time.

Mao gave Zhou a fairly free rein in foreign affairs. Referring to specific international issues, Mao said at the outset of our meeting in 1972, "Those questions are not questions to be discussed in my place. They should be discussed with the Premier. I discuss the philosophical questions." Our talks then touched on the whole range of issues on the summit's agenda, but from a philosophic point of view. Most interestingly, throughout the rest of my meetings with Zhou, he often referred to what Mao had said as a guide for his own positions in negotiations.

Zhou was a central participant in two key diplomatic events that more than any others created today's global balance: the Sino-Soviet split and the Chinese-American rapprochement. The controversy that brought about the break between China and the Soviet Union really boiled down to one major question: Who was going to be number one in the Communist bloc? The Soviet Union, as the first great Communist power, had enjoyed supremacy within the international Communist movement since 1917 and was doggedly determined to retain its preeminence. China may have been the second great Communist power, but, as Chinese, Mao and Zhou were certainly not willing to accept the rank of second.

The issue of primacy existed on the levels both of substance and of symbolism. When the Soviet Union was the only Communist country with nuclear weapons, its leaders could demand that the Chinese go along with their diplomacy because China depended on the Soviet nuclear umbrella for its protection. They also used their nuclear monopoly as a not-so-subtle threat; in the Communist world, the umbrella the Soviets hold over their allies is accompanied with a sword. It is not surprising, therefore, that the Chinese wanted to develop their own nuclear weapons. They asked the Soviets for technical aid, which the Soviets granted only reluctantly and later revoked.

On the level of symbolism the Chinese leaders felt that anything short of equality with the Soviets constituted kowtowing to the barbarians. After a meeting in Moscow in 1957, Zhou complained vehemently that

Khrushchev should learn Chinese so that their talks would not always have to be conducted in Russian. "But Chinese is so difficult," begged Khrushchev. "It's no harder for you than Russian was for me," Zhou replied angrily.

The bitterness of the dispute became known at the congress of the Soviet Communist party in 1961. Khrushchev sought a denunciation of Albania, which had stubbornly stuck in its Stalinist ways despite the Kremlin's new line. As the official observer of the Chinese Communist party, Zhou opposed him. He may have reasoned that if independent-minded Albania were denounced today, China might be denounced tomorrow.

Khrushchev responded by pushing a collective denunciation of Stalinism through the congress. Zhou then laid a wreath at Stalin's tomb with an inscription reading, "The Great Marxist-Leninist." Khrushchev, never one to be outdone in such matters, delivered a final slap by engineering passage of a resolution for the removal of Stalin's body from the Lenin Mausoleum. Zhou walked out of the party congress, and the schism between the two countries became irreparable. "The ghost of John Foster Dulles," Zhou said some years later, "has now taken up residence in the Kremlin."

As a result of the Sino-Soviet split, China found itself isolated and surrounded by hostile powers by the late 1960s. Before making my final decisions on moving toward an accommodation with Peking, I tried to put myself in Zhou's place. In virtually every direction he looked, he would see actual or potential enemies.

To the northeast he saw Japan. While the Japanese posed no military threat to China, their economic might gave them an awesome potential to do so in the future.

To the south he saw India. He had nothing but contempt for the Indians after China routed their armies in a series of border clashes. But he knew that India was the world's second most populous nation and that with Soviet support it could be a dangerous threat.

To the north he saw the Soviet Union with the capacity to knock out China's minuscule nuclear force in a thirty-minute surgical strike and with over forty fully modernized divisions on the Chinese border, having more than tripled those forces in less than ten years.

Across the Pacific he saw the United States. As a Communist, he regarded the U.S. as his most deadly ideological enemy. As a Chinese, however, he recognized that of all his neighbors in Asia and the Pacific, the U.S. was the only one that had no designs, present or future, against

China. And most important, the United States was the only nation that had the power to hold the ring against his mortal enemy to the north.

The table was set, therefore, for a rapprochement—not because either of us liked the other's philosophy, but because preserving the delicate balance of power was essential to both our interests. They needed us and we needed them. When Zhou began receiving our signals about reopening relations, he moved to "seize the hour and seize the day," as one of Mao's poems put it.

Vyacheslav Molotov, Stalin's formidable Foreign Minister, once warned an American negotiator, "If you think we are difficult to deal with, wait until you come up against Zhou!" When we did, I found that Zhou was not the intransigent negotiator Molotov had described. As a dedicated Communist, he considered us ideological enemies. But as a pragmatic Chinese, he recognized that he needed us.

Our differences were great, but our common interests were greater; our task was to mute the differences, not exacerbate them. The Chinese leaders wanted to mitigate the hostile encirclement in which their break with the Soviet Union had put them. We believed that it was imperative to end the "angry isolation" of the Chinese government; we also saw an opportunity to help contain the Soviet Union through triangular diplomacy. Though a common interest in rapprochement existed, we had to define our relationship in a communiqué and resolve a great many technical matters.

In our negotiations I realized that it was politically impossible for Zhou to abandon abruptly the diplomatic positions that his ideology dictated. But I knew he was a realist who valued national interest over ideology, for as he had told Kissinger, "The helmsman must guide the boat by using the waves."

When we were discussing the American military presence in Japan and the Pacific, I knew this problem was particularly sensitive. I noted that the Chinese were calling for the withdrawal of American troops from Japan and the abrogation of our mutual defense treaty. I then pointed out that our policy was in China's national interest even though it contravened the dictates of its ideology. Alluding to the Soviets, I said, "The United States can get out of Japanese waters, but others will still fish there." Japan, I went on, either would seek an accommodation with the Kremlin or would rearm.

I knew that Zhou, as a realist, probably agreed with my analysis, but that Zhou, as an ideologue, could never do so explicitly. He responded with characteristic subtlety. He was silent for a moment and then changed the subject without comment. But nobody in the room could mistake his silence for anything other than agreement.

I met with Zhou for over fifteen hours of formal one-to-one negotiations, apart from the many hours we spent together at lunches, dinners, and other public events. Four things made an indelible impression on me: his stamina, his preparation, his negotiating skill, and his poise under pressure.

His stamina was remarkable. I noticed that in some of our longer meetings the younger men on both sides became drowsy as the hours unfolded and the translators droned on. But the seventy-three-year-old Zhou was quick, tough, and alert throughout. He never wandered from the subject at hand, never filibustered, and never asked for a break. If our afternoon sessions failed to resolve a disagreement about the wording of the communiqué, he did not leave the problem to his aides, but met personally with Kissinger for the rest of the day and night to iron it out. The next morning he would look as if he had just returned from a restful weekend in the country. He thrived on hard work involving great issues. Power and responsibility kept him young.

He was as well prepared as any leader I have ever met. He had done his homework and turned to his aides only for an elaboration of highly technical points.

Kissinger had told me that I would be amazed by Zhou's negotiating skill, and he was right. Most negotiations involve symbolic issues as well as substantive ones. After my meeting with Mao, Zhou and I sat down for our first plenary session. Zhou brought up a symbolic issue to test my resolve subtly and to see whether I was renouncing my strongly held views of the past by coming to China.

"As you said to Chairman Mao this afternoon, today we shook hands," he said. "But John Foster Dulles didn't want to do that."

"But you said that you didn't want to shake hands with him," I countered.

"Not necessarily," Zhou replied. "I would have."

"Well, *we* will shake hands," I said as I reached across the table to shake hands once again.

Zhou seemed to warm to the subject, and he continued: "Dulles's assistant, Mr. Walter Bedell Smith, wanted to do differently, but he did not break the discipline of John Foster Dulles, so he had to hold a cup of coffee in his right hand. Since one doesn't shake hands with the left hand, he used it to shake my arm." Everyone laughed, and then Zhou added, "But at the time, we couldn't blame you, because the international viewpoint was that the Socialist countries were a monolithic bloc, and the western countries were also a monolithic bloc. Now we understand that that is not the case."

"We have broken out of the old pattern," I agreed. "We look at each country in terms of its own conduct rather than lumping them all together and saying that because they have this kind of philosophy they are all in utter darkness. I would say in honesty to the Prime Minister that my views, because I was in the Eisenhower administration, were similar to those of Mr. Dulles at that time. But the world has changed since then, and the relationship between the People's Republic and the United States must change too."

Zhou was tough and tenacious, but was flexible in working out our differences. We were miles apart on the section of the communiqué dealing with Taiwan. We would not and could not abandon Taiwan; he would not and could not relinquish his unequivocal claim to it. He wanted to use our communiqué to assert that claim. It was a remarkable achievement, one for which Kissinger and he deserve the major credit, that we reached a compromise through which each side stated its position in noninflammatory language. Zhou—his eyes always on the main issue—knew that the new relationship with the United States was more important than prevailing on the issue of Taiwan.

During all our talks he never lost his poise. In stark contrast to the antics of Khrushchev and the theatrics of Brezhnev, Zhou never raised his voice, never pounded the table, never threatened to break off talks in order to force a concession. I told Zhou's wife in 1976 what particularly impressed me about her husband was that he was always firm but courteous and that he spoke most softly when he "had the cards." I attribute his poise in great part to his training and background, but it also reflected his mature self-confidence. He never felt it necessary, as the Russian leaders so obviously did, to prove his manhood before his aides.

Zhou's conversation was not as colorful as Mao's, but at times he would make his points with vivid imagery. When we were driving from the airport to the guest house in Peking, he said simply, "Your handshake came over the vastest ocean in the world—twenty-five years of no communication."

Zhou was an accomplished poet and sometimes used a poem to make a substantive point. Alluding to the presidential election in 1972 and his hope that I would win it, Zhou spoke of a poem of Mao's entitled "Ode to a Plum Blossom." "In that poem," Zhou said, "the Chairman meant that one who makes an initiative may not always be one who stretches out his or her hand. By the time the blossoms are full-blown, that is the time they are about to disappear." Zhou continued, "You are the one who made the initiative. You may not be there to see its success, but of course we would welcome your return."

During our last long session in the guest house in Peking, Zhou again turned to poetry to illustrate a point. He said, "In your dining room upstairs we have a poem by Chairman Mao in his calligraphy about Lu Shan mountain. The last sentence reads, 'The beauty lies at the top of the mountain.' You have risked something to come to China. But there is another Chinese poem which reads, 'On perilous peaks dwells beauty in its infinite variety.' " Zhou's poetic turn of mind, as well as Mao's, is not unusual among great leaders. Politics, at its best, is more poetry than prose.

Zhou's negotiations with Chiang and the American mediators during the Chinese civil war were indispensable to the Communist victory. His delaying tactics bought valuable time for the Red Army to grow in strength, and his feigned desire for compromise immobilized Chiang's American guarantors.

A Kuomintang official in Taiwan went as far as to say, "If we had only had Zhou on *our* side in the civil war, today it might be Mao who was in exile in Taiwan—and *we* would be in Peking." However much he may have overstated his case, the Kuomintang official made a valid point: Mao's role in the revolution has been overrated. Mao could not have conquered and ruled China alone. Whether he could have done so without Zhou is an open question. The important point to remember is that he did not: It was the partnership between Zhou and Mao that won China.

A peasant, Mao, who revolted against the oppression of landlords and warlords, and an intellectual, Zhou, who fought against inequality and foreign encroachments, they represented the two key elements in Chinese society that united in the Communist revolution.

Historically significant as their partnership would be, it got off to an inauspicious start. Zhou was a failed urban insurrectionist when he came to Mao's Jiangxi province base in 1931. Zhou promptly took over the military command. Mao said years later that during this period he "had no voice at all" in party affairs. After the Kuomintang army chased the Red Army out of the Jiangxi and on to the Long March, the two cooperated in charting their winding course and planning their battle tactics. Midway along the six-thousand-mile trek, Zhou threw his political support behind Mao and helped elevate him to the position of Communist party chairman, and the partnership took the form the world would know for forty-two years.

Once in power, the partnership wavered between antagonism and symbiosis. Mao saw a world filled with contradictions and in a constant state of flux; he valued struggle above all else. The more pragmatic Zhou placed more emphasis on using struggle selectively to attain concrete ends. Zhou pitted his remarkable administrative talents and seemingly inexhaustible personal energy against the overwhelming inertia of China's fifty million bureaucrats and achieved a degree of control that allowed Mao to preoccupy himself with a detached, spiritual leadership of the country.

Prime Minister Kakuei Tanaka of Japan said that Zhou "behaves in front of Mao like a clumsy secretary attending an outstanding congressman." It is hard to imagine the graceful Zhou resembling anything clumsy, but he did step into the background in Mao's presence, probably at least partly by design. He realized the danger of pretending to Mao's throne.

This does not mean that their partnership was without mutual loyalty or affection. It was not Mao's habit to extol his subordinates publicly, but two incidents illustrate the friendship between the two leaders. At one point during the Cultural Revolution, a group of Red Guards labeled Zhou "the rotten boss of the bourgeoisie, toying ambidextrously with counterrevolution" and wanted to put him on trial. To their request Mao reportedly answered, "Agreed, as long as I stand with him." Nine years later, when Zhou lay dying, Mao, who for years had been largely a recluse, went to the hospital to be with Zhou during his last hours. Mao was the last person except Zhou's doctors to speak with him.

The remarkable partnership of these two great leaders of China in the twentieth century reached its zenith in 1972 with the end of the Cultural Revolution and the success of the Sino-American rapprochement.

As Zhou escorted me into Mao's book-strewn study for our meeting, I remembered what Malraux had told me during our White House dinner just a few days before my departure for Peking: "You will be dealing with a colossus, but a colossus facing death." Mao and I did not negotiate. He was taking my measure, as I was taking his. He wanted to know if I had a global view that was compatible with his. He was trying to discern whether American affluence had made us soft and whether our troubles in Vietnam had sapped our strength of will.

The fragility of his health was striking. His secretary needed to help him to his feet as I entered. He apologetically told me that he could not talk very well, which Zhou later attributed to an attack of bronchitis but which I assumed was actually the aftermath of a stroke. His skin had no wrinkles, but its sallowness made it seem almost waxen. His face was benign, but unexpressive. His eyes were distant, but could be piercing. His hands seemed as if they had never aged. They were not tough, but very delicate. Age had affected his stamina, however. The Chinese had scheduled our meeting to run only about fifteen minutes. Mao became thoroughly captivated by the discussion, so it stretched into an hour. I noticed that Zhou glanced at his watch with increasing frequency as Mao began to tire.

The difference between the two was striking. Zhou looked, talked, and acted like a highly civilized, debonair diplomat. Mao was robust, earthy, exuding an animal magnetism. Mao was chairman of the board; even in his declining years he still was recognized as the leader. But Zhou was the chief operating officer.

Mao had a casual, elliptical manner that gave me the impression of a man juggling a dozen thoughts in his mind at once. He set forth his views in a calm, flat voice that made him impressive in a small meeting, but would have failed as oratory.

He liked to sound outrageous even when making serious points. "I voted for you during your last election," he proclaimed with a broad smile. I said that he must have been choosing the lesser of two evils. "I like rightists," he responded with obvious enjoyment. "People say that you are rightists—that the Republican party is on the right—that Prime Minister Heath is also to the right." I tossed in de Gaulle's name. Mao demurred that de Gaulle was a different question and then continued, "They also say the Christian Democratic party of West Germany is to the right. I am comparatively happy when these people on the right come into power." Referring to our diplomatic rapprochement, I brought the point home by saying, "I think the most important thing to note is that in America, at least at this time, those on the right can do what those on the left can only talk about."

He also frequently indulged in self-deprecation to make a point obliquely. While the photographers did their work at the outset of our meeting, we engaged in light repartee. Kissinger mentioned that as a professor at Harvard he had assigned Mao's writings to his students. Mao responded, "These writings of mine aren't anything. There is nothing instructive in what I wrote." I said that his writings had moved a nation and changed the world. Mao replied, "I haven't been able to change it. I've only been able to change a few places in the vicinity of Peking."

When I returned to China in 1976, Mao's condition had deteriorated considerably. His speech sounded like a series of monosyllabic grunts and groans. But his mind remained quick and incisive. He understood everything I said, but when he tried to answer, the words just would not come out. If he thought the translator had not understood him, he would impatiently grab a note pad and write out his comments. It was painful to see him in this condition. Whatever one may think of him, no one can deny that he was a fighter to the end.

In those days the United States was suffering from the Vietnam syndrome and was shirking its responsibilities as a world power. Mao asked me the key question: "Is peace America's only goal?" I replied that our goal was peace, but a peace that was more than the absence of war. "It must be a peace with justice," I told Mao.

We must keep this point in mind when dealing with the Communist Chinese. They are revolutionaries who believe their interests and ideals are worth fighting and dying for. If we answer Mao's question with a discourse that exclusively emphasizes the need for peace and friendship, the Chinese will consider us to be wrong; even worse, they will consider us to be fools. After all, they will say, if peace is really our only goal, we can attain it any time we wish simply by surrendering. Thus, we must reiterate to the Chinese that we, too, have values for which we will struggle.

The onset of Parkinson's disease had stiffened all of Mao's movements. He had never been physically graceful. But at age eighty-two the peasant's shambling stride had become an old man's slow shuffle. Mao, like Churchill in his old age, was still proud. At the end of our meeting his secretaries lifted him out of his chair and helped him walk with me toward the door. When the television lights and cameras came on to record our final handshake, however, he pushed his aides aside and stood there on his own for our farewell.

"Mao's outward jerkiness was not misleading," wrote Ross Terrill in his biographical study *Mao*. "The balance in his being, if it existed, came from a clash of opposites. He was part tiger, he said of himself, and part monkey. The ruthless side and the quixotic side each took its turn." Unlike Zhou, Mao did not weave the strands of his personality together, but instead let each of them pull him in a different direction.

As the arbiter of government policy, Mao was impulsive. He rose late in the day and worked through the night. Like Stalin, he frequently called members of his staff at odd hours of the early morning for trivial matters. He withdrew from day-to-day affairs for long periods of lonely introspection. He would cross-examine policy experts for hours and then stroll into his garden to ask a guard for advice on the same policy questions.

Malraux said to me that there was "something of the sorcerer" in Mao, a man "inhabited by a vision, possessed by it." Mao envisioned a Chinese society that would resemble a large family. When he was told that his son had been killed in the Korean War, Mao responded placidly: "Without sacrifices there will not be victory. To sacrifice my son or other people's sons is just the same." But if the monkey in Mao was possessed by this vision, the tiger in him convulsed China in trying to realize it. Mao wanted spontaneity among the people. But he would tolerate it only as long as it conformed to his vision. When they diverged, he tried to reach his goal through the use of legal restraints and brutal police power of the state. To the last, Mao never seemed to comprehend that such coercion created a hierarchy, stifled initiative, and crushed spontaneity.

As the Marx, the Lenin, and the Stalin of the Chinese Revolution, Mao made his mark on history through strategic insight, tactical agility, and staggeringly cruel violence. He revised Marxism by making the peasantry the revolutionary class instead of the industrial workers. He revised Leninism by waging revolution with soldiers organized into an army instead of insurrectionaries grouped into conspiratorial cliques. He mocked those who compared his rule with the bloody reign of Chin Shih-huang, whose tyranny went unequaled among the emperors: "You think you insult us by saying that we are like Chin Shih-huang, but you make a mistake—we have passed him a hundred times!"

Mao could not have succeeded with insight and callousness alone. A charisma that attracted fanatical followers and a power of will that disdained large odds were also necessary. With Mao his strength of will produced his charisma. When I met him I had the sense that his willpower was somehow a physical characteristic. His most vivid poetry was written during and after the battles of the Long March. When he wrote of the exhilaration of struggle, especially violent struggle, he seemed to refer to the exercise of will in the manner that others speak of the exercise of their muscles. With this quality he could inspire his comrades to such epic tasks as the Long March because it made him, and thus them, seem unconquerable.

*   *   *

In 1972, with a sweeping gesture that might have encompassed either our meeting or all of China, Mao told me, "Our common old friend Generalissimo Chiang Kai-shek doesn't approve of this." Moments later he added, "The history of our friendship with him is much longer than the history of your friendship with him." In 1953, during my first meeting with Chiang, the Generalissimo made a similar sweeping gesture when speaking of China that made it clear that his statements pertained to the mainland as well as his redoubt on Formosa.

I detected something of the Emperor in the way both spoke of their country. Their gestures and statements seemed to suggest that each man had come to identify his country's fate with his own. When two such leaders meet in history, they do not compromise, they collide. One becomes the victor, one the vanquished.

Oddly, perhaps, the two men were similar in many ways. Both were men of the East. Mao left China only twice, to meet with Soviet leaders in Moscow in 1949 and 1957; Chiang traveled outside of Asia only twice, once to go on a mission to Moscow in 1923 and once to meet as one of the Big Four in Cairo in 1943. Both often withdrew for long periods of solitude. Mao took this time to write poetry; Chiang spent it reciting classical poetry as he walked in the mountains. Both were revolutionaries. Mao rebelled against the tyranny of his father and the social system as a whole; Chiang revolted against the domestic corruption and international weakness of the Manchu dynasty and, incidentally, cut off his queue—the symbolic gesture of rebellion—seven years before Mao did.

Their differences were both superficial and profound. Mao slouched in his chair as if he were a sack of potatoes carelessly thrown there; Chiang sat up ramrod-straight as if his backbone were made of steel. Mao had a relaxed, uninhibited sense of humor; Chiang, in my meetings with him, never attempted humor of any kind. Mao's calligraphy was chaotic, its irregular characters falling into undisciplined rows; Chiang's was rigid, its square characters all falling perfectly into line.

More profoundly, they revered China differently. They both loved the land, but Mao sought to erase the past while Chiang sought to build upon it. In victory Mao simplified the characters of the written Chinese language, not only to facilitate his literacy campaign, but also to destroy the history that each of the complex characters encapsulated. In defeat Chiang made room in the refugee flotilla for nearly 400,000 pieces of ancient Chinese art, even as many loyal aides and soldiers remained on the mainland.

In my first meeting with Mao he mentioned that in a recent speech Chiang had called the Communist leadership "bandits." I asked him what he called Chiang. Mao laughed, and Zhou replied, "Generally speaking, we call them 'Chiang Kai-shek's clique.' In the newspapers sometimes we call him a bandit; he calls us bandits in turn. Anyway, we abuse each other." The relationship between Zhou and Chiang had been like a roller-coaster ride. Zhou had worked as Chiang's subordinate at the Chinese military academy in the early 1920s, and Chiang reportedly said that Zhou was a "reasonable Communist." A few years later Chiang would put out an $80,000 bounty on Zhou's life. On the whole, however, I was surprised to find that Zhou and several other officials who asked about Chiang were curiously ambivalent in their attitude toward him. As Communists, they hated him; as Chinese, they respected and even admired him. In all my discussions with Chiang he never expressed any reciprocal respect.

I first met with Chiang Kai-shek, the third great leader of China's twentieth century, in 1953. I stayed in touch with him as Vice President and as a private citizen, and we formed a personal friendship that I valued greatly. That is why the rapprochement with Peking was such a profoundly wrenching personal experience for me.

Chiang and his wife often welcomed me to their magnificent residence in Taipei. His wife served as our interpreter, though she would occasionally participate in the discussion as well. It would have been impossible to find a better interpreter than the Wellesley-educated Madame Chiang. In addition to her easy eloquence in both Chinese and English, she knew her husband's thinking so thoroughly that she could interpolate accurately when an expression or term in one language had no precisely corresponding form in the other.

Madame Chiang was much more than her husband's translator, however. It is often fashionable to put down the wives of leaders as historically and personally insignificant because their prominence resulted wholly from their marriage. This view not only ignores the behind-the-scenes role the wives of leaders often play, but also it denigrates the qualities and character that they often possess. I believe Madame Chiang's intelligence, persuasiveness, and moral force could have made her an important leader in her own right.

The contrast between Madame Chiang and Jiang Qing, Mao's fourth wife, was even more striking than that between Chiang and Mao. Madame Chiang was civilized, beautifully groomed, very feminine, yet very strong. Jiang Qing was tough, humorless, totally unfeminine, the ideal prototype of the sexless, fanatical Communist woman. Whittaker Chambers once told me, "When you meet a Communist couple, you will usually find that the wife is the red hot of the two." This was certainly true as far as Jiang Qing was concerned. I have never met a more cold, graceless person. As we sat together at a propaganda cultural program she had arranged for my visit, she showed none of Mao's warmth or Zhou's grace. She was so intense that beads of perspiration appeared on her hands and forehead. Her first comment was typical of her abrasive, belligerent attitude: "Why did you not come to China before now?"

Zhou's wife, Deng Yingchao, was quite different. I met with her in 1972 and in 1976, shortly after Zhou's death. She displayed much of the same charm and sophistication I had seen in him. Apart from her relationship to Zhou, she was and is a dedicated Communist playing her own independent role in the party. But unlike Mao's wife, she had not allowed her Communist ideology to destroy her femininity. It is interesting to note that while Zhou had only one wife in his lifetime, Mao had four.

The sad end to which Madame Chiang's family came captures in a nutshell the divisiveness that China's civil war wrought. Charles Soong, who had become wealthy as a manufacturer and distributor of Bibles, had three daughters, Ai-ling, Mei-ling, and Ch'ing-ling. Ai-ling married the director of the Bank of China and fled to the United States after the fall of China. Mei-ling married Chiang, fought with him against the Communists, shared his exile on Formosa until his death, and now lives in the United States. Ch'ing-ling married the founder of China's revolutionary movement, Sun Yat-sen, and joined the Communists during the civil war. She became a revered symbol of the revolution in later years and received a state funeral in Peking when she died in 1981.

When Chiang proposed marriage to Mei-ling, there was opposition within the Soong family because Chiang was not a Christian. If he wanted to marry Mei-ling, her family insisted, he would have to become one. Chiang, not a man who took his religion lightly, said that he would be a poor Christian if his faith were not freely chosen. He promised to undertake a serious study of the Bible after he married Mei-ling, and the Soong family consented. Chiang was converted three years later. From then on Chiang and his wife would often pray together for an hour in the morning. Chiang was not naturally trusting or affectionate, but he was won over completely by Mei-ling and grew very close to her. She was his closest confidante in matters of state and traveled repeatedly to the United States as his personal emissary during and after World War II. Her charm and gracious manner made her an international celebrity and tended to soften Chiang's more harsh image.

Chiang's immaculately kept black cape and his shaven skull complemented an austere and reticent manner in private meetings. His habit of uttering a quick *"Hao, hao"*—meaning "Good, good"—after my statements made him seem slightly nervous. But his eyes radiated self-confidence and tenacity. They were black but would occasionally flash with light. Their gaze would dart about the room until our discussion began. Then his eyes would fix themselves on mine for the duration of our talk.

In their personal habits Chiang and Mao were a study in contrasts. Everything about Chiang was orderly—his dress, his office, his home. He was a disciplined, organized individual in every way. The adjectives *tidy* and *neat* do not overstate the impression he gave. Mao was the exact opposite. His study was littered with books and papers. If the test of a good executive is the cleanliness of his desk, he flunked. Mao was as disorganized as Chiang was organized and as undisciplined as Chiang was disciplined. The adjectives *unkempt* and *sloppy* would not overstate his appearance.

Chiang was an example of that rarest of political animals: the conservative revolutionary. The American Revolution succeeded in founding an orderly and free society because its leaders were essentially conservatives. They fought for freedoms that they had once possessed, but which had been taken away. The French Revolution foundered as it did partly because its leaders sought to achieve a purely intellectual and abstract vision that had no foundations in their national history.

Chiang's intentions resembled those of the Americans more than those of the French. He wanted to revivify Chinese tradition. He rejected its corruption by the old order. He fought against pervasive opium addiction and the still-common practice of foot binding. But he was not a democrat, even though he did introduce constitutional government. The problem, as he saw it, was not too little freedom but too much. China needed discipline, for as Sun Yat-sen had stated, "We have become a heap of sand." The discipline Chiang sought, however, would release the creative and productive abilities of the Chinese people.

When implemented on Taiwan, his ideas produced an economic miracle. Though he received American economic aid through 1965, the amounts were so small that they cannot account for the country's explosive economic growth. Economic statistics can never capture the tragedy that the Communist victory was for the Chinese people, but they do make some important points. The Communists collectivized agricultural production, and today the mainland produces less rice per capita than it did before the revolution. Chiang paid the landlords for their land and distributed it to the peasantry. The former landlords invested much of their money in industry while the government encouraged foreign investment. Today, Taiwan has a per capita income five times as great as that of the mainland. And the eighteen million Chinese on Formosa export about fifty percent more than the one billion on the mainland.

Chiang was a man of action who had been right so many times in his turbulent career that he developed an absolute faith in his own judgment. He was fond of reading the Confucian philosopher Wang Yangming, who stated that "to know and yet not to do is in fact not to know."

Not even the debacle of 1949 could shake Chiang's self-confidence. It was only another temporary setback to him. Every time I saw him, he talked of reconquering the mainland. And even when some of his associates had given up hope, he never lost faith.

The name he chose for himself, Kai-shek, translates as "immovable stone," and in light of his temperament it was a most appropriate choice. I greatly admired his resolution. He never believed in bowing to the "inevitable" simply because it seemed inevitable. There are always those who will tell a public figure that his goals are impossible to achieve. They lack creative vision. Too often they consider something to be impossible just because it has never been done before. Chiang understood this. As he once wrote, "I have always been surrounded and sometimes overpowered by enemies. But I know how to endure."

Notwithstanding his tenacity, Chiang had his faults, but a tragedy like the fall of China is never one man's fault. Chiang was a brilliant political and military tactician, but his "by the book" rigidity made him a mediocre strategist. Chiang's mind was quick and decisive when operating within a given set of strategic assumptions. He played by the rules as he found them. If these assumptions remained stable, few were his match. He was less able to step outside of these assumptions and innovate a new strategy that challenged the old one. Many historical figures have challenged the assumptions of their era. History is filled with footnotes on those whose innovations were inappropriate to their times; history is made by those whose innovations exploited the opportunities of their moment. It was Chiang's misfortune that Mao Zedong was among the latter.

When Chiang's army set out on the Northern Expedition to attempt to unite China militarily, some parts of the country were in the hands of foreigners, some in the grip of warlords, some in the throes of anarchy. As he progressed, Chiang slowly amassed the most powerful army in China and after several years was proclaimed the ruler of a united China.

The unification was more verbal than actual, however. Chiang subdued his rivals but did not subjugate them. He allowed his enemies to follow the traditional Chinese strategy of yielding to superior force and to save face by becoming his allies. This was perhaps his greatest error. Machiavelli would have admonished Chiang that by allowing the warlords to remain in power and in command of their armies, Chiang would never be sure of his conquests, for certain loyalty comes only through dependency.

Here, Machiavelli would have been right. Chiang never succeeded in gaining full control of China. His forces were pinned down just maintaining national unity. If he had to commit additional forces to one part of the country, the regional warlord in another part would threaten to go his separate way. As a result Chiang repeatedly had to put down challenges from various warlords. He could never demobilize his armed forces and devote adequate attention and resources to economic modernization and reform. Still worse, he could never deploy the full strength of his army against the Communists. His strategy, in a word, saved face but lost China.

The lesson was not lost on Mao, who followed through on his own victory, establishing Communist party control at every level of society in every region of the mainland. In fact history will probably rank this accomplishment as Mao's greatest.

Zhou's historical accomplishments are much more difficult to pin down. He contributed greatly to the Communist victory in the civil war. But after 1949 Zhou was only one of several lieutenants vying for Mao's ear. Zhou wanted to temper ideology with pragmatism by following a policy of gradual economic modernization. But Mao's quixotic swings in policy continually frustrated Zhou's efforts. Zhou also stood almost alone in trying to soften the harshness of life in Communist China, to allow a small degree of free discussion, to infuse Chinese society with what Burke called the "unbought grace of life." But again, his efforts failed.

Zhou will earn high marks for his diplomacy. He steered a nation whose potential power was far greater than its real power, but nevertheless made a mark on history by exploiting the opportunities that were presented to him. When I met with Zhou's widow shortly after his death in 1976, I told her there was no need to build a monument to his memory because historians would regard his actions in preserving the global balance of power as testament to his greatness. I then tried to sum up Zhou's remarkable career by saying, "What you cannot see is often more meaningful than what you can see."

Zhou Enlai in 1972, photographed during a break in meetings with Canada's Foreign Minister. *(United Press International)*

Arriving in Peking for the first time in 1972, the author reaches out for his historic handshake with Zhou.   *(United Press International)*

Zhou in 1936, returning to Yenan during a break in negotiations with the Kuomintang. *(Wide World)*

Mao Zedong and Zhou in the late
1950s. *(Wide World)*

Mao with the author in 1972, at Mao's home. *(Wide World)*

Left: Sukarno with one of his six wives in 1947 at a reception celebrating Indonesia's independence from the Dutch. *Below:* Sukarno the orator. *(Wide World photos)*

Khrushchev and Sukarno model sarongs during the Soviet leader's 1960 state visit to Indonesia. *(Wide World)*

Above: Jawaharlal Nehru and his daughter, Indira Gandhi, with Mrs. Nixon and the author in New Delhi in 1953. *(Ed Clark,* Life *magazine,* ©Time Inc.*)* *Below:* Nehru in conversation with the author.

Above: A contemplative Chiang Kai-shek prepares to deliver a speech to Taiwan's national assembly in 1972; *inset:* Chiang in 1943, as Acting President of China.   *(Wide World photos)*
Below: Madame Chiang with Mrs. Nixon in Taipei.   *(Wu Chung-yee)*

Alcide de Gasperi announcing that his Christian Democratic party has won a decisive victory over the Communists in the 1948 Italian general elections. *(United Press International)*

The author talks with Kwame Nkrumah during the 1957 festivities marking Ghana's independence from Great Britain.

Above: Ramon Magsaysay at the wheel of his jeep in the Philippines in 1956. The author is at left; Mrs. Nixon and Mrs. Magsaysay are in the backseat. *Below:* An exuberant Magsaysay following his landslide election as President in 1953.   *(Wide World photos)*

Left: Golda Meir as an eight-year-old immigrant to the United States. *Right:* As Prime Minister of Israel. *(Wide World photos)*

Left: Meir arriving at the White House for a state dinner in her honor in 1969. *Below:* With the author during the same state visit. *(Wide World photos)*

Right: David Ben-Gurion. *Below:* The author with Ben-Gurion in the former Prime Minister's cluttered study in 1966.   *(Wide World photos)*

Gamal Nasser, far right, in Cairo with Zhou and Sukarno in 1956.   *(Wide World)*

Anwar Sadat during a press conference in London before making his last visit to the U.S. in August 1981.   *(Wide World)*

Marching in the Shah's funeral procession in Cairo in July 1980; from left to right: Empress Farah, the Shah's widow; the author; Crown Prince Reza Pahlevi; President Sadat.   *(United Press International)*

Above: The Shah of Iran with the author during their first meeting in 1953 in Tehran. *(Wide World)* *Below:* The Shah escorts Mrs. Nixon to dinner during his visit to the U.S. in 1958. *(United Press International)*

Above: King Faisal during the author's 1974 visit to Saudi Arabia. Alexander Haig, then White House chief of staff, is second from left. *(White House photo)* *Below:* De Gaulle with Faisal at the Elysée Palace in 1967. *(Wide World)*

Lee Kuan Yew and the author confer in the Oval Office in 1969.   (White House photo)

Robert Menzies and
Nehru in New Delhi in 1950.
(Punjab Photo Service)

Menzies visits Churchill at 10 Downing Street in 1952.   *(Wide World)*

In my conversations with Zhou and Mao, both spoke almost fatalistically about the large amount of work that remained for them to do and the small amount of time in which they had to do it. They kept returning to the question of age, and I sensed that they knew that the end was near.

In his last year Zhou received a poem from Mao that captured the distress they both felt:

> Loyal parents who sacrificed so much
>   for the nation never feared the
>   ultimate fate.
> Now that the country has become Red,
>   who will be its guardian?
> Our mission, unfinished, may take a
>   thousand years.
> The struggle tires us, and our hair
>   is gray.
> You and I, old friend, can we just
>   watch our efforts being washed
>   away?

Their distress may have been common, but their visions and missions were not.

Nor were their final years spent in the same pursuits. It is believed that the faction later known as the "Gang of Four" forced Zhou from power, maybe with Mao's tacit support, during Zhou's last year. By then Zhou had quietly positioned supporters of his policies in as many key positions as possible in anticipation of the struggle for power that would follow Mao's death. Mao spent his last years lurching unpredictably from one side of the political spectrum to the other, doing incalculable damage to China in the process. For a time he would support a moderately pragmatic faction, then become impatient, then launch a mini–Cultural Revolution by allying himself with the ultraleft, and then reverse himself.

The two great leaders of Communist China died within nine months of each other in 1976. Neither had achieved his goals. But Zhou's policies have outlived him, while Mao's successors in power have raced to abandon Maoism.

Without Mao the Chinese Communist movement would have lacked the mystique that not only attracted the intensely fanatical supporters who conquered China, but also inspired millions throughout the world. But Mao, like most revolutionary leaders, could destroy but could not build.

Zhou also could destroy. But he had the talent, rare among revolutionary leaders, to do more than rule the ruins: He could retain what was best in the past and build a new society for the future.

Without Mao the Chinese Revolution would never have caught fire. Without Zhou it would have burned out and only the ashes would remain. Whether it will survive and in the end do more good than harm depends on whether the present Communist Chinese leaders decide, as Zhou did, that they are going to be more Chinese than Communist. If they do, China in the twenty-first century will not need to be concerned about the Soviets to the north, the Indians to the south, the Japanese to the northeast, or even the Americans to the east. China—with one billion of the world's ablest people and with enormous natural resources—can become not only the most populous, but also the most powerful, nation in the world.

A
NEW
WORLD

New Leaders in a Time of Change

IN 1943 WENDELL WILLKIE, who had lost the presidency to Roosevelt in 1940 and expected to run again in 1944, published a book, which he called *One World.* The book's contents have since been largely forgotten, but not the title: In two words it summed up one of the key realities of the modern age. For the first time we really had been living in "one world," with no part of it so remote as to escape the turmoils of the rest.

In the four decades since Willkie wrote *One World,* greater changes have taken place in the world than during any comparable time in history. Such a global survey today might well be called *A New World.*

The new world in which we live is one of new people. Seventy percent of all the people living in the world today have been born since World War II.

It is a world of new nations. When the United Nations was founded in 1945, it had fifty-one members. Now it has more than one hundred fifty. Twenty-seven of those have a population less than that of San Jose, California.

It is a world of new ideas. There was a simplistic tendency during much of the postwar period to divide the world in two parts: the Communist world and the free world. Today, with the bitter split between the Soviets and the Chinese, the Communist world is no longer a solid bloc. Neither is the free world. A whole spectrum of political, economic, and religious beliefs competes for the loyalty of people in new nations.

It is a world in which the nature of war has been changed by the advent of nuclear weapons. All-out war between the major powers has become virtually obsolete as an instrument of national policy. The very concept of world war, and with it the thought of victory or defeat in such a war, has become almost unthinkable. But as the danger of world war has receded, the danger of smaller wars has increased. No longer can one major power credibly warn another that if it engages in aggression in peripheral areas, it also runs the risk of nuclear retaliation.

The leaders featured in this book have belonged to a particular, unique period. World War II was one of the cataclysmic events of modern history. It unleashed forces that permanently changed the world. It ushered in the nuclear age. It ended the sway of Western European powers over the rest of the globe, and it set in motion the dismantling of the old colonial empires. It locked Eastern Europe under Soviet control and established a predatory Russia as one of the world's two superpowers. It set the stage for a titanic struggle between those value systems that today we somewhat inaccurately label "East" and "West"— between the democratic ideals rooted in the culture of Western Europe and the totalitarian system developed in Moscow.

Before the war Churchill was a lonely voice in opposition, dismissed as an eccentric; de Gaulle was a lonely voice seeking in vain for an audience; Adenauer was a fugitive in his own country. Each had the same qualities that later served his country so well, but those qualities were either not recognized or not wanted. For each the time had not yet come.

Churchill, de Gaulle, Adenauer—leaders such as these are rare, not only because as individuals they tower above the crowd, but also because the circumstances that bring them to the fore are rare. World War II and its aftermath not only demanded extraordinary leadership, but also provided a stage on which great dramas could be played.

But besides these postwar giants, hundreds of other leaders have played a part in the shaping of the new world. They are less known and their lives are less studied, but in many ways they are just as important. Nkrumah, Sukarno, and Nehru were leading examples of revolutionaries against the European colonial powers. Ramon Magsaysay of the Philippines could have become one of the brightest stars in the Far East had he not died long before his time. David Ben-Gurion and Golda Meir were pioneers, raising a new nation from the ancient deserts of Palestine. And four other Mideast leaders—two kings, the Shah and Faisal; and two Egyptians, Nasser and Sadat—were among those who struggled to bring their nations into the new world without being overcome by the forces of the old.

There are also leaders whose names would, in other circumstances, have resounded through history, but who are little known because they led in quiet times or because they led less powerful countries. Lee Kuan Yew and Robert Menzies, for instance, would have ranked with Gladstone and Disraeli had they been Prime Ministers of Britain rather than Singapore and Australia. Their lives invite a world of speculation about what might have been: How different might the history of postwar India have been if Nehru had had Lee's understanding of economic realities? How different might have been the course of Europe if Menzies had been among the Prime Ministers of postwar Britain?

And finally, others who deserve to be remembered are instead forgotten because they led not in quiet times but in quiet ways. We often remember the flamboyant demagogue more vividly than the quiet conciliator or the careful, meticulous builder.

THE "GOOD MAN" WHO SAVED ITALY: DE GASPERI

One of the most impressive of the leaders from this last group was also the first one I met: Italy's postwar Prime Minister, Alcide de Gasperi.

Italy after World War II was desperately poor, even more so than much of the rest of Europe. Italy's grand Renaissance palazzi may have survived in all their splendor, but the people needed food. A bit of pasta, a slice of bread—this was wealth in postwar Italy.

In desperation, people often grasp at extremes. Italy's poverty was Stalin's opportunity. Moscow pumped money into the coffers of the Italian Communist party, trying to strengthen the party as a vehicle through which to seize Italy. For a time it looked as though Moscow would win. But the slight figure of Alcide de Gasperi stood in its way.

I met de Gasperi in 1947, when I visited Italy as a member of the Herter committee studying the reconstruction needs of Western Europe. Italy's most important elections since the war were less than a year away. Its Communist party was the largest and most heavily financed outside the Soviet bloc, and commentators in both Europe and the United States were predicting a Communist victory. Italian aristocrats were making their plans to flee the country if the Communists did come to power. The elections would be a crucial turning point, one way or the other. We knew it. De Gasperi knew it. The Soviets knew it.

De Gasperi had been Premier since December 1945. Each of us on the committee was struck by his strength, his intelligence, and his determination. But none of the adjectives so commonly attached to great men—such as *towering, visionary, masterful*—described de Gasperi. He had a certain bookish air about him. In fact he was a bookish person who had spent much of the Fascist period either in jail as a political prisoner or clerking and writing in the Vatican library after he was released. He was tall and thin, with a broad forehead, intense blue eyes, round spectacles, and a wide mouth whose thin lips seemed to form a faint frown even when his lively eyes announced that he was not at all unhappy. His hair remained thick and barely gray until his death in 1954 at the age of seventy-three.

Between de Gasperi and the other of the two major Italian leaders that I met on that 1947 trip, Giuseppe di Vittorio, the contrasts were striking. Di Vittorio, a Communist, was Secretary General of the Italian Labor Confederation and one of the nation's most powerful postwar leaders. I called on him at his office. It was lavishly furnished with period furniture, luxurious red draperies, and thick red carpeting. He was vibrant, bouncy, and hospitable as he greeted me when I came into the room. He smiled, joked, and laughed easily. He exuded warmth—at first. But when the conversation turned to the United States and the Soviet Union, his geniality disappeared. He became icy and belligerent. He wore a red flag in his lapel, and he left no doubt, either by word or by manner, that he was completely loyal to Russia and completely hostile to America.

De Gasperi's office by contrast was comfortable but not lavishly furnished. When he received the members of our committee, he was courteous but at the same time quietly reserved. Just as di Vittorio was a typical extrovert, de Gasperi was a typical introvert. I could not have imagined him slapping people on the back, engaging in light and loud talk, or resorting to lusty humor. He had an almost melancholy look in his eyes that day. This is not an unusual characteristic of leaders. De Gaulle and Adolfo Ruiz Cortines, Mexico's greatest postwar President, often had such a look.

A superficial observer might have bet that di Vittorio would defeat de Gasperi hands down in a political campaign, because di Vittorio, when he wanted to, could project the kind of outgoing personality that would appeal to the warmhearted Italian people and de Gasperi could not. But after a few minutes all of us, including even hard-bitten, isolationist political pros on our committee, were struck by a quality we could not really describe but that we all agreed he had. De Gasperi radiated inner strength, and the more quietly he talked, the stronger he sounded. One could sense that he had profound faith in his people, in his country, and in his church.

The flashy performers often do win in political campaigns. But this quiet, unassuming man, a mediocre orator who had no visible charisma and to whom political geniality came with difficulty, had the strength, intelligence, and character that mark a great leader. It is fortunate that the Italian people were able to sense these qualities. Had they not done so, Italy today might well be Communist, and what Churchill used to describe as the soft underbelly of Europe would have been fatally pierced.

De Gasperi's demeanor was modest, yet he was sure of himself and his abilities. He was known for his willingness to compromise with his political foes, but he could also be counted upon to uphold fundamental moral and political standards. He was called "the most unremarkable remarkable man of our time," yet he was the greatest popularly elected Italian leader since the fall of the Roman Republic two thousand years ago.

Rebuilding a country after its defeat in war is one of the most difficult tasks a leader can face. But often the upheavals of war and defeat push to the fore leaders of exceptional ability. Just as MacArthur and Yoshida were the indispensable men for postwar Japan, and Adenauer for Germany, de Gasperi was the indispensable man for rebuilding defeated Italy.

Like West Germany's Adenauer, de Gasperi was able to bring Italy back into the family of nations because it was clear to the rest of the world that, in the words of one Italian, "He is a good man. He means what he says." His quiet, unimposing manner also contrasted sharply with the melodramatic bombast of Italian politics during the Fascist era and provided a welcome relief both to his own people and to the rest of the world.

Mussolini had subjected the Italians to a rhetorical regimen that was as rich as de Gasperi's was bland. De Gasperi recognized his own limitations as a speaker, but he also suspected that the Italian people would prefer to be lectured by *Il Professore* after having been exhorted for twenty-three years by *Il Duce*. His oratory was rambling, sometimes a bit befuddled. Rather than wide, dramatic sweeps of the hand, de Gasperi used small, even cramped gestures; rather than florid metaphor, he filled his speeches with careful, impeccable reasoning. He would sometimes pause at the podium to search through his papers for just the right figure to bolster his case. If he could not find it after a few moments, he would sigh and mutter, "Never mind. Let us proceed."

De Gasperi made up for his shortcomings as a speaker with his brilliance as a vote juggler. As an associate said during the parliamentary crises that rocked the Italian government in the first years after the war, "A vote of confidence is worth a hundred epigrams." De Gasperi managed the votes of confidence that held his successive governments together.

Postwar Italian government was an exercise in perseverance. In West Germany and Japan final authority was in the hands of Allied Occupations, which gradually returned sovereignty to the elected governments. Thus national officials had assistance in dealing with food shortages, labor unrest, and the machinations of political extremists. They also had a "foreign devil" who could at least share the blame for the people's discontents.

Unlike these nations, Italy was left to its own devices almost immediately. Yet de Gasperi, in spite of severe economic problems and the often savage tactics of the Communists, was able to stay in office from 1945 until 1953, a period in which he formed eight successive cabinets based on coalitions dominated by his Christian Democratic party.

One reason for his success was that he was not easily alarmed by political crises. One day he was working in an anteroom near the Chamber of Deputies when a panic-stricken master-at-arms interrupted with news that a debate was getting out of hand. The Prime Minister continued to make notes, unperturbed. Finally the aide said, "Mr. Prime Minister, they are throwing inkwells! ... But, Mr. Prime Minister, they are even throwing the drawers of their desks at each other!" De Gasperi looked up. "Oh?" he asked, with mild interest. "How many?"

Initially de Gasperi's cabinet included the Communists. He had earned a reputation as a compromiser and a skilled parliamentarian. But it eventually became clear to him that the Communists were intent on paralyzing the government from within, and in 1947 he formed a new cabinet without them.

It was a stunning and courageous move. It was also a grave risk to the stability of his government. De Gasperi had been an avid mountain climber until he was fifty-four, when a mishap during a climb in the Dolomites left him dangling for twenty long minutes by a single rope over a deep chasm. He held on and eventually swung to safety. He held on with similar tenacity after he had expelled the Communists from government. The result was that in those crucial elections of 1948 the Italian people gave his Christian Democratic party, and thus his anti-Communist coalition, a twelve-million-vote landslide victory in the fall general elections. After 1948 he held his government together through skillful coalition-making in which all but the neo-Fascists and the Communists were welcome. Thus a wide array of interests, ranging from peasants to industrialists, was directly represented in the government.

One key factor in the 1948 elections was Pope Pius XII's decision to mobilize Catholic Action volunteers in all of Italy's 24,000 parishes in support of de Gasperi and anticommunism. I met Pius twice, in 1947 and 1957, and found that, like de Gasperi, he combined intense human compassion with a realistic understanding of secular political affairs. Many criticized his decision to throw the authority of the Vatican behind de Gasperi's anti-Communist coalition, but Pius believed he was acting according to his responsibilities as Pope. I could see that he considered communism as much a threat to the Church as it was to the political freedom of Italy.

But the margin of victory in 1948 was too wide to be explained simply by the intervention of the Church. Without de Gasperi, who was able to campaign as an honest, progressive proponent of democracy and freedom, the Christian Democratic party could easily have lost the election, the West could have lost Italy, and Italy could have lost its freedom.

De Gasperi understood his people. When we visited Italy, he spoke movingly to us about their plight, especially their urgent need for food. For their part the Communists spoke to the Italians of little else. But de Gasperi believed his nation needed more. La Scala, the great Milan opera house and an important symbol of Italy's cultural heritage, had been partially destroyed during the war. Although the Italian government could have used all of its funds and more just for food, enough was siphoned off to restore La Scala. De Gasperi spoke with pride of the restoration project; he knew that at this critical time sustenance was needed for the spirits of Italians as well as their bodies. On our visit we attended a performance at La Scala. The American flag had been hung over our box. The spotlight was turned on us, and the orchestra struck up "The Star-Spangled Banner." The house exploded in a tremendous, emotional ovation. I knew in that moment that de Gasperi had read his people right, and the Communists had read them wrong, and I gained a new measure of confidence that he would win the next year's elections.

Even when he was Prime Minister, de Gasperi lived a life of simplicity and devotion. When he first took office he had to get an advance on his salary so that he could afford a new suit.

Like many other leaders, de Gasperi began his day with a walk. He took along his press secretary for briefings and a pocketful of candy for the children he met as he walked through the foothills of Rome. He worked until 9:30 at night and often turned out the lights in the government's offices himself. For several years after he came to power, he, his wife, Francesca, and their four daughters lived in the same small apartment that had been their home when he was a Vatican clerk and that he had furnished on the installment plan. The only decorations in his bedroom were a crucifix and a picture of the Madonna.

During the first years of de Gasperi's premiership, his neighbor across the hall was an elderly countess who blamed the fall of the Italian monarchy on de Gasperi personally. (He had been the principal advocate of republicanism in the 1946 referendum in which the Italians chose their form of government.) She pursued her grudge against the Prime Minister by leaving her trash can in the hall in the hope that he might trip over it and by banging on her piano far into the night. De Gasperi put up with these inconveniences with bemused good humor.

De Gasperi's power brought him and his family comfort but never opulence. When I visited Italy after de Gasperi's death, I called on his widow and found her living in a modest apartment on the outskirts of Rome.

An ardent Catholic, de Gasperi founded Italy's Christian Democratic party while working in the Vatican library. Especially after the Church backed him against the Communists in 1948, he was sometimes accused of taking orders from the Pope. His associates usually replied that his thinking was so pervasively Catholic, and had been so since early in his life, that it was not necessary for the Vatican to remind him to uphold Christian doctrines.

In both Italy and West Germany, leaders arose after the war who raised the banner of Christian democracy and who were dedicated to restoring and preserving individual liberty above all else. To both de Gasperi and Adenauer, Christian politics were by nature centrist politics in which limited state intervention in society was not only permitted but desirable so long as it did not interfere with the liberty of the individual to think, act, and pray as he chose.

De Gasperi attended mass daily, often visiting small churches very early in the morning so that he would not attract attention. His Catholicism had always been an all-consuming variety, the "spirit and heart of things" both public and private.

In any case de Gasperi proved his independence of the Church in 1952, when it favored a coalition between the Christian Democrats and all other non-Communist parties, including the neo-Fascists, to keep the Communists from taking over the Rome city government. On this de Gasperi defied the Pope and ruled out the neo-Fascists.

De Gasperi was as passionately committed to the European ideal as was Adenauer. De Gasperi came from a border province, as did Adenauer, and had the same gut-level sense of Europe's common heritage. Each believed that a unified Europe was the only way to protect the liberty of their peoples from encroachment by their Communist enemies to the east, as well as a way to reduce the internal threat to peace in Europe that resulted from nationalism and xenophobia.

De Gasperi was a staunch supporter of the European economic community and NATO. He had an enormous investment in the European Defense Community, through which the nations of Western Europe would have contributed to one federated European army. In August 1954, when he had been out of office for a year, the seventy-three year-old de Gasperi broke down and wept during a telephone conversation in which he begged his former Interior Minister and the current Premier, Mario Scelba, to keep Italy committed to the idea. Some believed that when he died of a heart attack a few days later, his heart had really been broken by France's continuing reluctance to approve the plan.

His success at putting Italy solidly in the Western European community lived after him. During several visits to Europe after he left office— including one while I was President, in 1969—I found that in times when NATO was experiencing internal dissension, the Italians could always be counted on to be the most consistently loyal Europeans. It is not surprising that Italy's Manlio Brosio proved to be one of NATO's most effective Secretary Generals. Except for the fact that he was a member of a small party, Brosio might have been another great Italian Prime Minister.

*   *   *

De Gasperi did not look like a hero or sound like a hero. But he was one of the heroes of the postwar world. He showed that a statesman does not need bombast or even eloquence; that a leader can lead quietly, without thundering; that good men can prevail.

At the end of the war Italy faced a perilous political vacuum. The Fascists had come to power in 1922; Italy's young adults knew no other form of peacetime government. De Gasperi gave the Italians what they needed most: moderate, consistent government based on pragmatism instead of ideology and liberty instead of coercion. In spite of the intrigues of the best-organized Communist party in the West, de Gasperi was able to establish a republic and make it stick.

When de Gasperi took office in 1945, industrial and agricultural production were perilously low and unemployment was rampant. At one point Italy's warehouses contained only enough grain to last two weeks. Yet, after six years of his leadership, the agricultural sector had almost completely recovered and industrial output was higher than it had been before the war.

He also fully restored Italy's respectability among nations, establishing lasting links with both the United States and the nations of Western Europe. It is in large measure because of de Gasperi that Italy's national government is still dominated by the Christian Democrats and that its relations with the rest of the free world are still friendly. In fact Italy remains one of the most dependable members of what has become a very troubled alliance.

As 1982 began, the Polish crisis was testing the character of western leaders. It would have been impossible to imagine a Churchill, a de Gaulle, an Adenauer, or a de Gasperi reacting as did some of Europe's political and intellectual leaders when confronted with the Soviet-directed crackdown on Poland's stirrings of freedom. They simply did not have room for the sort of temporizing, equivocating, hope-it-all-goes-away avoidance that seems increasingly to characterize European politics generally and the Western European response to the Soviet threat specifically. De Gaulle could be imperious, and his stubborn independence was often a thorn in the American side. But at the time of the Cuban Missile Crisis, he sent President Kennedy a message: "If there is a war, I will be with you. . . ." De Gaulle, Adenauer, and de Gasperi were all leaders whose political principles were rooted in deep religious faith. They were not men who could be intimidated.

There has lately been a concern in the United States about the nature and cohesiveness, even the dependability, of the western alliance, a growing feeling that we may have to go it alone rather than risk depending on unreliable European allies. The Europeans, for their part, increasingly describe the United States as trigger-happy or impulsive or alarmist, finding one excuse after another to avoid any action to meet the Soviet threat. Europe in the 1980s chillingly resembles Europe in the 1930s in this regard. The question is whether the lessons of the 1930s will be learned in the 1980s—and learned in time.

ANTICOLONIAL REVOLUTIONARIES: NKRUMAH, SUKARNO, NEHRU

For the nations of Western Europe the postwar period meant the end of empire. For many of their former colonies it meant an abrupt immersion in the uncertainties of independence and, for the leaders of those former colonies, a formidable test that some would pass and others would fail. Three who particularly captured the world's imagination were Ghana's Nkrumah, Indonesia's Sukarno, and India's Nehru. All were charismatic, all were successful at throwing off colonial rule, all ventured ambitiously into the maelstrom of international Third World politics. Both the similarities and the contrasts among their records show how vastly different are the requirements for leading a revolution and for building a nation.

When I visited Europe in 1947 as a member of the Herter committee, I found leaders struggling desperately to retrieve their countries from the ashes of destruction so vast that it staggered the imagination. They needed help to rebuild; they also needed food to keep millions from starving. But they were not creating new nations out of the jungle. They could summon the accumulated wisdom of centuries of advanced civilization. They could speak to the spirit, and it would respond again as it had in one crisis after another. Beneath the ruins was a highly competent work force that was experienced in operating a modern industrial economy. All that was necessary was to give them the tools and they could do the job.

Ten years later I visited Ghana, representing the United States at the ceremonies marking that country's independence. While Ghana did not have the trained work force and industrial base of the European countries, the briefings I received indicated that it had an excellent chance to succeed as it embarked on self-government.

Ghana was the first black African colony to win independence. It had acquired independence through a peaceful rather than a violent revolution. The leader of its independence movement, Kwame Nkrumah, had been educated in the United States, at Lincoln University and the

University of Pennsylvania. Ghana was hailed at the time as an example of Britain's policy of "creative abdication." As they had in other colonies, the British, to their great credit, had carefully prepared the country for independence by training Ghanaians in the civil service and promoting them to positions of responsibility. Ghana also had a robust economy and an educated elite. With the world's largest cocoa crop, it had ample foreign reserves and a favorable balance of trade.

Today Ghana has become an economic and political disaster area, and one of the principal reasons for its tragedy is Kwame Nkrumah. He is a prime example of the man who succeeds brilliantly at leading a revolution, but then fails utterly at building a nation.

Delegations from all over the world attended the independence ceremony. I vividly recall our first night in the new hotel that had been built for the visiting delegations and for the tourists that were expected to follow thereafter. We were kept awake practically the whole night by people chanting, singing, and dancing the "Hi-life" in the streets.

The Duchess of Kent represented the British crown. She arrived at the parade grounds in a Rolls-Royce and seemed impeccably cool and regal despite the oppressive heat. When she read the speech for the crown at the opening of Parliament, the Ghanaian ministers and representatives of what was then an opposition party wore white British wigs. The ceremony was carried off with great dignity.

The reception given by the British Governor-general, Charles Arden-Clarke, was a gala affair. Dignitaries from all over the world went through the long receiving lines. An hour had passed by the time Mrs. Nixon and I came to the head of the line. I felt sorry for Arden-Clarke. A heavy man, he was sweating profusely under the heavy woolen dress uniform that the British required their foreign service personnel to wear, even in the tropics. As we shook hands, he said, "This is a good time to take a break," and escorted us into an air-conditioned reception room, where we were served ice-cold lemonade. I asked him whether he thought the Ghanaian experiment would work. Arden-Clarke, who had overseen much of the preparation for independence, considered my question for a moment and shrugged as he replied, "The chances of success are about fifty percent. We have prepared them as well as we possibly can. On the other hand, you have to remember that it was only about sixty years ago that we carved an area of warring tribes out of the jungle. It may be that those people you heard dancing in the streets last night are getting their independence too soon. But we are forced into it by world opinion."

Winston Churchill once commented to me that he thought Franklin

Roosevelt, in his anticolonial fervor, had pressured Britain, France, and other colonial powers into withdrawing too soon from Africa and Asia. He believed eventual self-government was the right of every nation, but he added, "A democracy is the most difficult kind of government to run. It requires years of preparation for a people to be able to handle the problems they face in a free, democratic society."

Still, in 1957, like virtually all the Americans attending the independence ceremony, I was caught up in the optimism of the moment. This was the first time I met Martin Luther King. We talked for over an hour one night about the prospects of Ghana's future. I was deeply impressed by his highly intelligent and coolly objective appraisal. But his eyes flashed when he told me passionately, "Ghana just has to make it. The whole world is watching to see if the first black African country to receive its independence can successfully govern itself."

I thought Ghana was starting out so auspiciously that it would take a genius to ruin it. I had not reckoned with the extent to which Nkrumah would prove such a genius. In fact, at that time, I found him very impressive both in his demeanor and in what he said.

Nkrumah professed a deep admiration for American democracy and all that it had achieved. When I presented him with the official gift of the U.S. government, a complete technical library, he seemed delighted and said that it would help him put the scientific advances of western civilization to work in Africa. He also told me that Abraham Lincoln was one of his heroes, and that he was determined to carry out Lincoln's principles in a way that would fit Ghana's political, economic, and social conditions.

Nkrumah was born in 1909 in a remote section of British West Africa. His father was the village goldsmith. He attended Catholic mission schools and Achimota, a famous college in the Gold Coast, and was such a brilliant student that his uncle, a diamond prospector, decided to send him to study in the U.S. He earned a Bachelor of Divinity degree at Lincoln University, then did further study both in the U.S. and in Britain. He returned to the Gold Coast in 1947 with two graduate degrees and a strong interest in socialism and pan-Africanism. He soon formed his own political party, the People's Convention party, and—like Sadat and Nehru—ended up serving time in prison for his proindependence activities. He was released by Arden-Clarke in 1951 when the People's Convention party won the general elections by a landslide. The following year he became Prime Minister.

Since his youth Nkrumah had shown a knack for public speaking, and with his soaring voice and brooding good looks he could hold crowds enthralled. I saw him cast just such a spell over those who gathered in 1957 for the independence ceremonies. Though soft-spoken in private, when he moved among the people and addressed them, he was a different man. With a few words he could send them into a frenzy of excitement. His people were obviously devoted to him, and when I talked to him, it seemed that he was devoted to his people.

But after the warm glow of the independence ceremonies wore off, Ghana lurched from one disaster to another. Nkrumah spent profligately, much of it on those projects backward countries see as the symbols of modernism: a huge dam, an airline, an airport. Determined to make Ghana economically independent, he set out to eliminate imports by producing locally everything Ghana needed, and to Nkrumah this meant production by the government—no matter that the government might not be competent or that the locally produced goods turned out to be more expensive than the imports had been. He nationalized industries, plantations, and stores, with catastrophic results. He saw himself as the father not only of his country but of African independence, and in vain he spent heavily for a headquarters for the Organization for African Unity, which was eventually located in Ethiopia instead. He poured his country's money into independence movements elsewhere in Africa.

Nkrumah's anti-western paranoia and militant pan-Africanism escalated during a period when Ghana would have benefited enormously from closer ties with the industrialized West. He developed a cult of personality and lavished his government's rapidly dwindling funds on elaborate monuments to himself.

In the mid-1960s the price of cocoa—still Ghana's principal export—collapsed, and Ghana no longer had any reserves to fall back on.

As the economy ran down, instead of focusing on the hard measures needed to turn it around, Nkrumah tried to reach out and impose his own distress on others. Guinea, to the north, was a country blessed with enormous natural resources, including gold and diamonds. Guinea's leader, Sekou Toure, came to Washington in 1960, and I escorted him to the White House. He came across as a warm and charming man. But he was a devout Marxist and had tried to impose Marxist principles on Guinea with the predictable result. If anything, Guinea, despite its abundance of natural resources, was even worse off than Ghana. But while Nkrumah, like Sukarno in Indonesia and Nasser in Egypt, was unable to cope with the problems within his own country, he developed an insatiable appetite for foreign adventures. He tried unsuccessfully to unite Ghana and Guinea.

As the years passed, Nkrumah became more and more detached from his people, calling himself "Redeemer" and ruling from within a heavily guarded compound. In 1964 all opposition parties were outlawed and many of Nkrumah's critics jailed. Two years later, when the Ghanaian economy was staggered by the fluctuations in the price of cocoa and the effects of his expensive development projects, Nkrumah was overthrown by the military while he was on a visit to Peking. In 1972 he died in exile in Guinea.

In its first quarter century of independence, Ghana had five military coups and three civilian governments. Its cocoa crop, still the staple of its economy, is barely more than half what it was before independence. Its gold production is down by two-thirds. Tobacco production on the nationalized plantations is a tenth what it was eight years ago. Food production has diminished. Of the country's paid work force, eighty-five percent are paid by the state.

Nkrumah's legacy is one of monuments to himself, corruption plaguing virtually the entire government establishment, and a bankrupt economy. It will take many years for the damage done by Nkrumah to be rectified by one who is a nation builder rather than just a destroyer.

In some respects Ghana represents a tragedy of good intentions. In the zeal of his drive for independence Nkrumah probably believed that he could work miracles. But in power he was consumed by megalomania. Those in the West who pressed the pace of decolonization did so for reasons of idealism. But in retrospect those who were more cautious may have been more realistic.

The world was going through a phase in which, in dozens of colonial outposts, the people were ripe for plucking by self-serving, exploitative new leaders. The cracking of the old colonial structures opened the way to a new struggle for power, for control, in many cases for extraordinary wealth for those who seized the levers of power. As these former colonies got their independence, many got the trappings of democracy without the experience of democracy. The result was tyranny, or impoverishment, or both.

What makes Ghana's plight doubly tragic is that it was unnecessary. One of the best testaments to that is Ghana's neighbor, the Ivory Coast. The Ivory Coast presents a stark contrast to both Ghana and Guinea. Now it is apparently on the verge of a new boom from the development of offshore oil reserves. Heretofore, however, it lacked the mineral resources of Guinea, and its economy before independence was not as rich as that of Ghana. But it had a leader, Felix Houphouet-Boigny, who had a firm grip on reality. Houphouet-Boigny had held a number of posts in the French cabinet, including Minister of State under de Gaulle. While he identified strongly with his people's yearning for nationhood, he argued that the sudden establishment of "absolute independence," as he put it, would plunge the new nation into chaos. When the Ivory Coast received its independence from France in 1960, he cut some of its ties to France, but not the essential ones. Instead of driving out the French and other Europeans, he invited them in. Instead of driving toward nationalization, he put his primary faith in private enterprise. As a result, the Ivory Coast became the most prosperous country in West Africa, with a growth rate of eight percent annually and a per capita income over three times that of Ghana—and nine times that of Marxist Guinea.

Politically the country's progress toward a democratic society has not yet been as great or as rapid as many might have wished. But neither has the Ivory Coast fallen into the trap of seeking too much too soon, losing everything as a result. Certainly of all the countries of black Africa, the Ivory Coast has done more with less, in terms of natural resources, than any other.

Houphouet-Boigny insists that the economic progress that his country has made under his leadership has laid the foundation for political progress in the future. Only time will tell. But progress on one front is far better than failure on both fronts, and anyone betting on the future of Africa would have to rate the prospects of the Ivory Coast better than those of its neighbors.

A lively debate is under way in the world about the need for a massive transfer of resources from the wealthy, industrial north to the underdeveloped, impoverished south. Enthusiastic advocates of this concept say that we need a Marshall Plan for the poor nations of Africa, Latin America, and Asia. This answer is well intentioned but completely naive. The total economic assistance provided to the countries of Western Europe under the Marshall Plan was $12 billion. The U.S. provided only $2.3 billion for Japan. Because of their industrial capacity, these advanced countries would have recovered without any outside aid. The aid only hastened the process.

This is not the case with the underdeveloped economies of the Third World. Since World War II the U.S. has provided almost $90 billion in economic aid to these countries. Some of this money has been wisely used. Much has been wasted. On the whole the results have been disappointing, and dramatically so when comparisons are made with Europe and Japan. As the tragedy of Nkrumah's Ghana testifies, the lesson for the future is to recognize that technical know-how and the kind of stable government that encourages private investment are indispensable to economic progress.

Like Ghana's Nkrumah, Indonesia's Sukarno was an immensely charismatic leader who led a successful struggle for independence. Also like Nkrumah, Sukarno proved a disaster once independence was secured. Both could destroy; neither could build.

Handsome and well aware of it, self-assured to the point of cockiness, Sukarno had an electrifying presence that worked magic on crowds. However, he was a revolutionary leader who allowed revolution to become a religion—an end in itself rather than a means to an end.

During the 1930s Sukarno was repeatedly imprisoned and exiled by the Dutch, and the experience left him with resentments he never overcame. Even after the Republic of Indonesia was established and secure, he continued his own personal revolution against his former colonial masters by stirring up trouble with Dutch New Guinea.

When I first saw him in 1953, he spent most of our meeting talking not about the awesome problems of his own country but about his territorial designs on Dutch New Guinea—or West Irian, as the Indonesians call it. I was not surprised. Sukarno's obsession with Irian was legendary. In Canberra just a few days earlier Australia's Prime Minister, Robert Menzies, had warned me to expect a lecture on the subject. I kept trying to guide my conversation with Sukarno back to his own political and economic problems, but he would have none of it, though he did manage to lecture me on Vietnam and the wickedness of the French. When I asked him what we should do in Vietnam, he bluntly said, "Nothing. You have spoiled that by not supporting Ho Chi Minh."

In the early 1960s Sukarno ordered raids on Dutch New Guinea and eventually seized it. But his "splendid victory" was a Pyrrhic victory. Within a few years he was out of power. While he was busy fulminating over Irian, the Communists, encouraged by Indonesia's poverty and domestic unrest, its increasingly friendly relations with mainland China, and Sukarno's willingness to admit Communists to his government, had become stronger and stronger. He claimed he was an anti-Communist himself. "I don't worry about the Communists," he boasted to me when he visited Washington in the mid 1950s. "I am strong enough to handle them." But in 1965 they staged a coup d'etat attempt that was brutally suppressed by the military, which seized all power from Sukarno and put him under house arrest in 1966. He died four years later.

Sukarno was the best example I know of a revolutionary leader who could tear down a system expertly but could not focus his attention on rebuilding it. The raw materials were there: Indonesia, next to India and the United States the most populous nation in the non-Communist world, had more natural resources than any other Southeast Asian nation, but not the proper leadership. Sukarno temporarily distracted his people from their problems, but he never even began to solve them.

Sukarno's people were desperately poor in spite of the richness of their land. He sought to sustain them, not on material prosperity, but on what he called "the richness of symbological fantasy." His 5,100-page economic plan, which was never put into effect, was divided into 8 volumes, 17 chapters, and 1,945 items—in commemoration of the day Indonesia achieved its independence from the Dutch, August 17, 1945. Meanwhile, like Nkrumah, he spent his country's money wildly and foolishly; as a result, Indonesia had the worst inflation rate in the postwar world.

Sukarno was consumed by passions, both political and physical. He talked about revolution in the same sensual way that he talked about the beautiful women who filled his palace in Djakarta when I visited him in 1953. He saw revolution as a cathartic national spasm that was in itself an absolute good despite the damage it could do, and believed that it should be perpetuated indefinitely. He said once:

> I am fascinated by revolution. I am completely absorbed by it. I am crazed, am obsessed by the romanticism ... Revolution surges, flashes, thunders in almost every corner of the earth ... Come ... Brothers and sisters, keep fanning the flames of the leaping fire.... Let us become logs to feed the flames of revolution.

While I was in Indonesia, I watched as Sukarno addressed a rally attended by thousands of people. He held them spellbound for over an hour and then ended with a ritualistic repetition of the word *Merdeka!*—the battle cry of the Indonesian Revolution and a word that stood for freedom, dignity, and independence. The crowd chanted *"Merdeka!"* back at him over and over again and then fell into a frenzy that was almost beyond belief. I looked over at Sukarno: His excitement was palpable. He glowed with satisfaction.

Sukarno was a strikingly handsome man who knew that he exerted a magnetic hold over people. Some of the most stirring political orators I have met are quiet-spoken, even shy, in private settings. I had the sense that their public charisma was a quality they held in reserve for those situations in which it was needed. But Sukarno was all of a piece: There was not even a hint of artifice or calculation about him. The fervor of a crowd was his sustenance, as important to him as food and water. A revolution unleashes passion and leads people to act with reckless abandon, and Sukarno sought to continue his revolution indefinitely. I was not surprised when I read in Khrushchev's reminiscences that when Indonesia began requesting aid from the Soviet Union, Sukarno immediately asked Khrushchev for money to build a giant stadium. The Soviet Premier was puzzled; he had expected to be asked for food or perhaps for weapons. But Sukarno wanted a place where he could continue to hold his giant public rallies.

One of the principal problems Third World nations face is the absence of a large middle class. Therefore opulence and abject poverty frequently exist side by side. But nowhere have I seen such a contrast between rich and poor as in Sukarno's Djakarta. In 1953, as we drove through the city from the airport, we saw open sewers and miles and miles of miserable huts. Yet President Sukarno lived in a palace set amid hundreds of acres of lush gardens. When we arrived at the main entrance, he was waiting for us outside at the top of the steps, wearing a brilliant, impeccably tailored white suit. The palace itself, also pure white, gleamed so in the bright sunlight that it strained our eyes to look at it directly.

Sukarno was a dignified host who showed not a trace of the obsequious manner that many leaders of smaller nations lapse into when they greet the representatives of major powers. Unlike them, he had no inferiority complex whatever. On the contrary, he gave the impression that he considered himself not just equal but superior. He spoke excellent English and was almost condescendingly charming as he showed us through the palace, which was filled with priceless Indonesian art— and with beautiful Indonesian women. Dinner that night was exquisite. We ate by the light of a thousand torches, near a large artificial lake whose shimmering surface was covered with white lotus blossoms. Our meal was served on gold-plated dishes.

Yet Sukarno still cared for the simpler things. He told me that in the guest bathroom were both a modern shower and an old-fashioned bucket. He said he preferred the latter. Despite the excesses of his lifestyle he also retained a remarkably empathetic relationship with the poorest of his people. Throughout my political career I always enjoyed stopping along the route of motorcades to shake hands and talk with the people. Some of the leaders I met in other countries, as well as many of our foreign service personnel—particularly in Asia—thought this was undignified. But not Sukarno. He did the same thing as we traveled through the Indonesian countryside, which was even more poverty-stricken than the sections of Djakarta we had seen. We stopped in one peasant's home and watched him fry sweet potatoes for his dinner. We also visited a village coffee shop and chatted with the proprietor. While the people seemed surprised to see an American Vice President among them, they hardly raised an eyebrow at the sight of their own President. He periodically made trips into the countryside, mingling with his people and spending the night in rundown village huts.

Sukarno's charisma worked on Americans as well as Indonesians. In 1956 I escorted him when he arrived in the United States for a state visit. As part of the welcoming ceremonies, we went to the District Building, the capital's city hall, where Sukarno was to receive the key to the city. He was gracious and good-humored, and he struck a dashing figure with his khaki uniform, Muslim *pitji* cap, and ivory-inlaid swagger stick. Suddenly, to the horror of our security detail but the delight of the crowd, he plunged across the police lines, shaking hands with the men, striking up animated conversations with the children, and kissing the women, most of whom squealed with delight when he did so.

Sukarno's political self-indulgence had a parallel in his physical self-indulgence. Recently I mentioned Sukarno to President Habib Bourguiba of Tunisia, who himself had been a revolutionary leader of the same era but was also a nation builder. When I commented that Sukarno had been a great revolutionary leader, Bourguiba frowned and shook his head. No, he said. First he protested that Sukarno had been put in power by the Japanese, with whom he had collaborated during World War II as a means of getting the Dutch out of Indonesia. But then he added another objection: "I recall so well," he said, "when Sukarno came to this country. We had a great many important things to talk about. But the first thing he asked me for was *'une femme.'* "

Sukarno was married at least six times. Throughout his time in power, his sexual prowess and sexual appetite were the subject of countless rumors and stories. The State Department briefings I received before my 1953 trip stressed this side of his character and suggested that he appreciated flattery along these lines. It was clear that both sex and revolution fulfilled in him the same need to be adored, to have others abandon themselves to him. Unfortunately this is precisely the opposite of the quality that an effective leader of a developing country needs. The enormous and pressing needs of his people, not his own, should have been paramount to Sukarno. Yet he allowed government to become an obsessive exercise of his own political and physical virility. To him Dutch colonialism was a personal disgrace and humiliation, a challenge to his manhood. He spent his twenty years in power reaffirming his manhood by living an undisciplined personal life and making threatening noises in the direction of Dutch New Guinea. Eventually these passions engulfed him.

Sukarno and Nkrumah together illustrate one of the unfortunate truths about leadership: that those best able to reach the people on an emotional level often have the worst programs.

Demagoguery works. Precisely because he lacks a sense of responsibility, the demagogue is free to craft his appeal solely in terms that have the strongest emotional force and reach the audience's basest instincts. Fear and hate are powerful forces; demagogues can mobilize these. Hope is also a powerful force, and demagogues are skilled at raising false hope, at conning those who so desperately want to believe, into investing their future in a fantasy.

Sukarno had one program—freedom from colonial rule—around which he built his appeal. Beyond this his rule was a disaster for the people of Indonesia. But he held them in his hand, partly because of the emotional force of *merdeka*, partly because of his own animal magnetism and oratorical flair, partly because his swaggering ways appealed to the hero-worshiper in them.

Perhaps it was no coincidence that, as colonialism ended, so many of the new leaders of the new nations were essentially demagogues. Throwing off colonial rule was the sort of one-issue campaign that is especially suited to demagoguery and to which demagoguery is especially suited. It requires a high degree of emotional mobilization, in effect turning the nation into a citizen army or at least presenting the credible threat that it can be turned into a citizen army. It requires none of the careful, intricate balancing that is the essence of successful democratic rule. It simply requires molding the populace into a force sufficiently threatening to persuade the ruling power that it would be either dangerous or futile to try to retain control any longer.

India's Jawaharlal Nehru was what Nkrumah and Sukarno were not: a charismatic revolutionary leader who was also a nation builder. He also shared with them, and with Sukarno in particular, a critical flaw. Nehru's obsession with Kashmir paralleled Sukarno's with West Irian, and his concern with his own role in Third World politics often seemed to overshadow if not to eclipse his concern with India's needs.

Nehru was brilliant, haughty, aristocratic, a man of quick temper and enormous ego. He was also passionately devoted to India and to the ideals of both independence and national unity. Unfortunately for India, like so many intellectuals of the time, he also developed a gripping attraction to Socialist theory. India has paid an enormous price ever since for his and his daughter's determined efforts to impose this theory arbitrarily on the teeming sprawl of India, with its centuries of resistant tradition and its millions living a hand-to-mouth existence.

Nehru was born in 1889 in Allahabad, in what is now part of Pakistan. His father was a wealthy Kashmiri Brahmin and one of India's most prominent attorneys. His ancestral tie to Kashmir was probably at least partly responsible for his later obsession with the Kashmir question: for his fierce determination to make Kashmir part of India and equally fierce resistance to letting the people of Kashmir themselves decide the issue, a decision that almost certainly would have favored Pakistan rather than India.

Nehru himself had an English gentleman's education at Harrow and Cambridge and was admitted to the English bar in 1912. Returning to India, he practiced law there for a while. But he was inflamed by the British massacre of Indian troops at Amritsar in 1919 and from then on devoted himself to the cause of Indian independence. A disciple of Mahatma Gandhi, he nevertheless moved to the left of Gandhi politically and was less committed than Gandhi to nonviolence; he preached nonviolence for others, but was not above using force himself when it suited his or India's purposes. He could be a tireless campaigner. Before the 1937 elections, as chairman of the Congress party's executive committee, he traveled 110,000 miles in 22 months and in a single week made 150 speeches.

During the 1930s Nehru was repeatedly imprisoned for his resistance activities, and he was jailed again in World War II when he opposed aiding Great Britain unless Britain immediately gave India its independence. He did some of his best writing in prison, including his autobiography and also a history of the world in the form of letters to his daughter. At the end of the war he took part in the negotiations that led to the division of the subcontinent and the creation of the independent nations of India and Pakistan. He became India's first Prime Minister in 1947 and held that post until his death in 1964.

A man of moderate height, about five feet ten inches, Nehru had regular features, an aquiline nose, and rather somber brown eyes that were capable of great intensity. He carried himself with an aristocratic grace. His English, both written and spoken, was impeccable and restrained. He could also be an enormously effective charismatic speaker. While I never heard him address a crowd, his ability to mesmerize huge audiences was legendary. He was said to have once held a crowd of a million people spellbound. The hundreds of thousands who could not hear his words were captivated simply by his presence.

Of all the world leaders I have met, Nehru would certainly rank among the most intelligent. He could also be arrogant, abrasive, and suffocatingly self-righteous, and he had a distinct superiority complex that he took few pains to conceal.

He also faced challenges that would have staggered a lesser man.

The last time I saw the Shah of Iran, when I visited him in Cuernavaca, Mexico, in 1979, he discussed some of the problems that had confronted Nehru and all other Indian leaders. He contrasted India with China. "The Chinese," he said, "are one people. They may speak different dialects, but their written language is universal. They have a sense of community wherever they live, either in China or outside China, which draws them together. They may violently disagree with each other on political matters, but in the final analysis they all consider themselves to be Chinese and are proud of their Chinese heritage." India, he noted, "is a vast jumble of races, religions, and languages. There is no basic Indian language. The only way Indians can understand each other in their parliament is by speaking English."

He pointed out that the people of the Indian subcontinent represent six major religions and speak fifteen major languages and thousands of minor languages and dialects, and that India's history is so complex that racial and other ethnic groups cannot even be counted. He noted that India had not been a nation before it was brought together by the British under their colonial rule. He also observed that India was a country that had too many people and too few resources, while China, despite its huge population, has enormous resources and the potential to feed and clothe itself.

The Shah's point was that India was almost impossible to govern and that anyone who succeeded in holding it together had to be a political genius. Nehru did this. He also, to his great credit, insisted on the retention and development of democratic institutions, despite enormous economic and social problems and the consequent temptation to turn toward dictatorship.

*   *   *

Before I met Nehru in 1953 in India, some people told me he was anti-American. Others told me that he was anti-British. Still others told me that he was just antiwhite. There may have been a grain of truth in each of these charges, but based on my own conversations with him I would agree with the late Paul Hoffman, who told me that Nehru was simply passionately pro-Indian.

Despite the years he spent struggling against British rule and languishing in British jails, Nehru continued to enjoy English poetry and sometimes spent holidays in Britain. He pushed himself forward as a spokesman for the Third World and architect of "nonalignment," but he gave every indication of wanting India to be taken seriously as a major power. Proud man that he was, he must have bitterly resented the second-class treatment Indians received from their British rulers. But the condescension and hauteur with which he later addressed the rest of the world seemed to come naturally, from within. These probably were increased by the adulation he received from the Indian people. As his popularity grew during the 1930s, his wife and daughter sometimes playfully teased him. "O, Jewel of India, what time is it?" they would ask, or "O, Embodiment of Sacrifice, please pass the bread."

When I met with Nehru in 1953, he spent less than a quarter of the time talking about U.S.-Indian relations. He spent more than half the time lecturing me about what he claimed were the dangers India faced from a militaristic Pakistan. Though his words concerned Pakistan's supposed threat to India, his demeanor foreshadowed the time eighteen years later when India's Soviet-supplied army, under his daughter's leadership, dismembered and threatened to extinguish Pakistan, a goal I may have helped to deny them by "tilting" U.S. policy in the conflict toward Pakistan.

This, in retrospect, was his great weakness: diverting so much of his undeniably superior talents and energy to India's conflict with Pakistan. Nehru was able enough and strong enough that, if he had lived, he might have bitten the bullet on the Pakistan issue and resolved it peacefully. Unfortunately, however, he could not bring himself to do this during his life. The Indo-Pakistan conflict is one of the most tragic examples of senseless military spending in postwar history. For decades two of the world's poorest nations, with hundreds of millions of people living in abject poverty, have spent billions of dollars a year for arms aimed primarily not at defense against the threat of aggression from the north but against each other.

Nehru did, however, make one point in our talks that I think had merit. He argued that India with its four hundred million people was trying to achieve prosperity, progress, and justice through democracy. China with its six hundred million people was trying to achieve these goals through dictatorship. He therefore insisted that it was in the interest of the United States and the West to do everything possible to ensure that India succeeded, so that as others in the Third World embarked on self-government they would see that the democratic experiment, not the Communist experiment, was the one that worked. This argument served Nehru's purposes. He wanted more aid. But it also had a substantial measure of validity.

One reason for the persistence of India's economic woes, of course, was Nehru's own stubborn adherence to socialism. While it was true, as Nehru argued, that China and India represented competing tests of totalitarianism and democracy, India was not a test of free enterprise. Nehru read Marx in prison; by the mid-1930s he was preaching socialism and urging that his followers organize into workers' and peasants' unions. His initial attraction to Socialist doctrine is hardly surprising. He was a child of privilege raised with a social conscience. The India he grew up in was not an industrial or even an agricultural democracy. It was a rigidly stratified caste system in which enormous wealth supported legendary opulence for some while millions of others could look forward to nothing more than the sort of grinding poverty from which early death might even be a form of deliverance.

India needed productivity from the bottom up. Instead, on the economic front, it got ideology from the top down, with layer upon layer of flypaper bureaucracy to snare the feet of anything that moved. The United States alone has provided India with more than $9 billion of aid since independence. But this has gone to remedy the results of Socialist failure rather than to build the foundation of a self-sustaining economy.

Nehru's romance with socialism and his obsession with Pakistan were, unfortunately, among the prejudices that he passed on to his daughter, Indira Gandhi. She was an interested bystander and listener in the conversations that I had with Nehru in 1953, and she served as his hostess for Mrs. Nixon and me. She was gracious and thoughtful throughout our visit. When I encountered her years later, however, when she was Prime Minister and I was President, there was no doubt that she was her father's daughter. Her hostility toward Pakistan was, if anything, even stronger than his.

Jawaharlal Nehru was without question a great revolutionary leader. In my own talks with him I could sense why he had such a powerful appeal to the Indian people. He had an almost otherworldly quality of mysticism, but I could see that he also combined this with a shrewd knowledge of the elements of power and the willingness to use power—even use it to the hilt—when necessary.

His legacy is India. It also is the persistent bitterness of India's conflict with Pakistan.

Only an immensely powerful man could have held India together during those critical early years, maintaining it as a single nation against all the forces pulling it apart. For, as the Shah's comments indicated, it was no more in the natural order of things for all India to be one country than it was for all Europe to be one country; linguistically, ethnically, and culturally, India is even more diverse than Europe. But whether this accomplishment benefited the Indian people is another question. Unity is sometimes more important to the unifiers than to the unified. If less energy had been dissipated in combating the country's natural centrifugal forces, perhaps more could have been done to improve the people's living conditions.

It has become a cliché to speak of India as "the world's most populous democracy." Whether or not India would have been better off as several nations, Nehru made it into one, and he made it and kept it a democracy. His daughter has resorted at times to dictatorial devices to keep power or regain it. Whether Nehru himself would have done so I seriously doubt. He impressed me as being firmly dedicated to retaining and expanding democratic institutions and procedures. Considering the magnitude of the tasks that he faced, his success at doing so has to rank as one of the most extraordinary achievements of the postwar era.

A PHILIPPINE NATION BUILDER: MAGSAYSAY

History is filled with tantalizing questions of "What if. . . ?" and "What might have been?" To me one of the saddest of these is what might have been if Ramon Magsaysay, the President of the Philippines, had not been killed in a plane crash in 1957 at age forty-nine.

Of all those who emerged as leaders of new nations after World War II, Magsaysay was among the most impressive. He had not led his country to independence, as Nkrumah, Sukarno, and Nehru led theirs. The Philippines was freely given independence by the United States in 1946. Magsaysay became its President in 1953. At the time of his death he was on the verge of what promised to be a landslide reelection victory.

Perhaps this was one reason for his success. He had not been a revolutionary leader; he had neither a psychological nor a political need to manufacture a continuing revolution or to create its substitute in foreign adventuring. The whole focus of his extraordinary talents was to bring security, stability, and progress to the people of the Philippines.

In pursuing these goals, however, Magsaysay had staked out as tough a fight as any faced by a postwar leader. MacArthur had liberated the Philippines from the Japanese but not from the devastations of war. Both its economy and its spirit had been ravaged by war and the Japanese Occupation. After it was granted its independence in 1946, it embarked on a struggle for survival as dire as those of the defeated nations of World War II. A free-trade agreement between the U.S. and the Philippines helped, as did over $800 million in American aid between 1945 and 1955. But the government had to contend not only with a ruined economy but also with a nation divided by bitter political disagreements.

In certain key respects the postwar Philippines resembled postwar Italy. Both nations had been ravaged spiritually and economically by the war. Both faced threats from the Communists that were substantially more dangerous than those in Japan, West Germany, or any other European nation. Both were essentially on their own after the war's end, so that they had to deal with the Communist threat themselves, without turning to the ultimate authority of an occupying power. And both nations had leaders at critically important times—de Gasperi in Italy from 1945 to 1953, Magsaysay in the Philippines from 1950 to 1957, first as Defense Minister and then as President—who met the challenges courageously, imaginatively, and forthrightly.

When the Communists promised to deliver the Italian people from poverty and despair, de Gasperi could not, as Adenauer could, simply gesture across the border and tell his people that the proof of Communist promises was in the East German pudding. He had to outwit and outmaneuver the Communists and at the same time show the Italians that his was the way to prosperity and freedom. His task was on two interrelated but often separate levels: beating the Communists, and feeding, clothing, and inspiring his people.

When his turn came in the Philippines, Magsaysay also waged a two-pronged fight against communism. His nation had been as emotionally drained by the war and the Japanese Occupation as Italy had been by the war and fascism. In fact, MacArthur once pointed out to me that a larger percentage of the Filipino people had died in the Pacific war than of any other nation. De Gasperi had to contend with a well-organized, well-funded Communist party; Magsaysay had to fight a powerful group of insurgent Communists, the Hukbalahaps, and at the same time invigorate his exhausted people and, like de Gasperi, give them a productive alternative to the alluring siren song of communism. Though he died before he could complete his work, he made tremendous progress in a short time, and his example shone like a beacon throughout free Asia.

Magsaysay was one of those rare leaders who combined immense popular appeal with boundless energy and also with plain good sense. When I first met him in 1953, he was still President-elect. I was struck at once by his size. At nearly six feet, he was very tall for a Filipino. He had natural presence, great personal charm, and a pure animal magnetism that showed itself dramatically whenever he appeared before a crowd. On that 1953 visit I addressed twenty thousand Philippine Junior Chamber of Commerce members one afternoon in Manila. When Magsaysay strode in, even though it was only to sit on the platform, the crowd went wild at the sight of him. The electricity that surged between Magsaysay and the throng in front of us was like a lightning bolt.

Magsaysay was active in the resistance movement in World War II, a guerrilla leader throughout the Japanese Occupation. He caught MacArthur's attention, and in 1945 the general made him military commander of Zambales province. But it was his successful fight against another enemy, the Huks, that made him a major national hero.

Within a few years after the war, the Huks had become so strong that they were able to maintain openly a headquarters in Manila. By 1950 there were over sixteen thousand Huks, and in some parts of the Philippines they actually collected taxes to pay for their own schools and factories.

Morale in the Philippine army was desperately low, and the army provided little effective defense against the Huks. Conditions in the countryside were abysmal. MacArthur once commented that if he were a Philippine peasant, he would probably be a Huk himself. One source of the Huks' strength was their promise of land reform. Those who worked the land paid an average of seventy percent of their meager income from crops to a hereditary landowning class.

Magsaysay, then a member of the Philippine Congress, was made Minister of Defense in 1950, and he quickly and vigorously embarked on a two-pronged initiative against the Huks. First he revitalized the army, flying between scattered camps for surprise inspections and firing negligent officers. He captured the top Communist leadership. But he also launched an ambitious resettlement program for farmers. Thus he executed a kind of political pincer movement that destroyed the Huks' power base. "I don't know where to put all the Huks that have surrendered," he said proudly at one point.

When I saw him in 1953, he explained his approach to the Huks. "Guns alone are not the answer," he said. "We must provide hope for young people for better housing, clothing, and food, and if we do the radicals will wither away." Yet despite his belief that guns alone were not the answer, he was not one of those naive idealists who believe that no guns are necessary to resist totalitarian aggression. He strongly supported our mutual defense efforts, defeated the Huk terrorists in battle, and was unswerving in his commitment to using force whenever necessary to fight the Communists. "Between our way of life and communism," he declared, "there can be no peace, no paralyzing coexistence, no gray neutralism. There can only be conflict—total and without reconciliation."

When I first met Magsaysay, he had just won the presidency by an overwhelming margin. When he was nominated by the Nationalist party (after turning aside party leaders' suggestions that he lead a military coup), he had opened his campaign with what must be the briefest acceptance speech on record. He stood up and said, "I am a man of action; therefore, I am not a speechmaker," and sat down. On my second trip to the Philippines, in 1956, I saw him in action as a speechmaker. Half a million people were gathered in Manila's Luneta Park for a ceremony celebrating the tenth anniversary of Philippine independence. I spoke first, representing the United States. Then, just as Magsaysay stepped to the podium, the gray skies opened in a tropical cloudburst, and it began to pour. Aides rushed to his side with umbrellas. He pushed them away. He had brought a prepared text, which lay on the podium in front of him. The rain soaked it through, leaving it useless. He set it aside and delivered virtually the entire speech extemporaneously. When the rain started, I had expected the crowd to scatter. Many did, but thousands more stayed in place, their eyes fixed on Magsaysay, ignoring the rain, enveloped by his voice, his cadences, his words, his presence. When he finished, still ignoring the rain, they erupted into an ecstasy of applause. It was one of the most stunning oratorical tours de force I have ever seen.

Magsaysay broke the rules of Philippine politics. In a country where corruption was rife, he was stubbornly incorruptible. In the elections of 1951, as Defense Minister, he fought to reduce the influence of local bosses and the military in politics (in one town, the police forces had gone so far as to murder opposition voters) and he prevailed; the elections that year were honest. As President, he opened his palace in Manila to everyone and listened patiently to the complaints of peasants and workers. He distrusted the opinions of so-called experts on issues and preferred to travel to the barrios and villages to find out for himself what the people felt and needed. As he drove along, he would reach out and touch the hands of the Filipinos who had come out just to see him drive past.

The Philippines' great statesman-author-educator Carlos Romulo always demonstrated a keen but also whimsical appreciation of his country's politics. On one of my visits to Manila a member of the Philippine Senate had made a vicious attack on the U.S. I asked Romulo about him. He replied, "He's a great friend of the U.S." "Well," I said, "he sure has a strange way of showing it." With a twinkle in his eye Romulo responded, "You don't know Philippine politics. The basic rule for a successful politician here is 'Give the Americans hell and pray that they don't go away.' " Another time he told me, "You Americans taught us much too well. We took all the excesses of the American political system and magnified them."

Magsaysay was an exception. It may have been partly because of his deep inner confidence, but I think it was also because of his total dedication to his country and its people. In what he sought to achieve he was an idealist. But he had also seen war at firsthand and outfought the enemy, both the Japanese invaders and the Communist terrorists. He understood how difficult the balance was between order and liberty. He saw through the masks of the new totalitarians. He was determined that they would not prevail in the Philippines. He was a realist, aware that there was a long way to go, with much hardship and many disappointments along the way. But he pressed his country forward, steering a careful course between too little hope and too extravagant promise. He felt passionately that he had a mission to provide honest, progressive government for the masses of the Philippine people.

During my 1956 visit Magsaysay took me on an eerie tour of the dark tunnels on the island of Corregidor, where MacArthur had lived with his family during the seige of Bataan. Despite the fact that Magsaysay had fought the Japanese, he had a statesman's understanding that the Japanese were destined to play a major role in Asia again. He told me that the Japanese were a great people and that he believed the Filipinos, who suffered more at their hands than any other nation, would be able to accept them into the Asian community.

He took me to Corregidor on his presidential yacht. It had been a long day, and the two of us went below and stretched out on a pair of bunks. He was tired but seemed relaxed, and he clasped his hands behind his head and looked at the ceiling and talked reflectively about the successes he had had and also the failures. Land reform was proceeding. Many farmers had been moved from the crowded island of Luzon and had been given land and houses on other islands. He had embarked on an ambitious plan to clean up government. It was all going to take time. But he still had irrepressible vigor and optimism about the future.

He also knew that what he was doing had importance beyond the Philippines. "Everywhere in Asia," he said, "people look at the Philippines and realize that American values are being tested here. I feel that if we can succeed here in bringing prosperity and freedom and justice to our people, our example and through us the American example will be a powerful magnet for others in this area and in other parts of the world as well."

The next year he was dead, killed in a plane crash that many believe may not have been an accident. His loss was a tragedy for the Philippines and for all of Asia. He was a charismatic leader who understood the difficult art of nation building, whose leadership his country needed and whose example the world needed.

ISRAELI PIONEERS: BEN-GURION, MEIR

The same years of the twentieth century that saw the dismantling of the old colonial empires, the emergence of competing nuclear superpowers, and the shrinking of the globe into a day's journey or an instant direct-dial telephone call also saw a sometimes cataclysmic transformation of the Middle East. New nations emerged there, old nations regained full independence, age-old rivalries flared. Impatient modernizers clashed with fierce defenders of ancient ways. Cultures collided. Sullen resentments simmered, subsided, and erupted.

The Middle East is the crossroads of the world, the cradle of civilization; its shrines are holy to three great religions. Today it is an area of nomads and scholars, bazaars and laboratories, oil fields and kibbutzim, parliaments and Ayatollahs. In some places farmers till the same stony fields their ancestors tended centuries ago. In others smartly dressed women read the latest magazines from Cairo or London on their way to modern offices. The Middle East is volatile, vulnerable, crucial to the conflict between East and West, and caught in shifting political crosscurrents that can be more explosively emotional than those in almost any other part of the world.

In its time of extraordinary change, the region has brought forth some extraordinary leaders.

One of the most remarkable was David Ben-Gurion, the founding father and first Prime Minister of Israel. Ben-Gurion devoted his whole life to a cause that shook the Middle East and, in its own particular but fundamental way, changed the world.

President Eisenhower used to refer to two men as "Old Testament prophets": John Foster Dulles and Ben-Gurion. I found this ironic in both cases. Dulles was a devout American Protestant who carried the doctrines of the New Testament engraved in his heart and mind. Ben-Gurion was a scholar of the Scriptures, but he described himself as secular rather than religious. "Since I invoke Torah so often," he once explained, "let me state that I don't personally believe in the God it postulates. I mean that I cannot 'turn to God,' or pray to a superhuman Almighty Being living up in the sky. . . . Yet, though my philosophy is secular, I believe profoundly in the God of Jeremiah and Elijah. Indeed, I consider it part of the Jewish heritage. . . . I am not religious, nor were the majority of the early builders of Israel believers. Yet their passion for this land stemmed from the Book of Books." He described the Bible as "the single most important book in my life."

However ironic, Eisenhower's description was also apt. Both Dulles and Ben-Gurion drew from the Bible a sense of mission that was each man's strongest characteristic. Dulles's mission was the protection of liberty from totalitarianism. Ben-Gurion's was to reestablish the Jews in their historical homeland of Palestine.

Ben-Gurion was a short man, only five feet three inches, but he gave an impression of massive size. It was partly his square build, his huge head, his ruddy face, and his great bursting crest of white hair. But it was also his imposing presence, magnified by a jutting lower lip, a determined jaw, and the sweeping way that he moved. Some people make waves. Ben-Gurion was one of those who part the waves.

Ben-Gurion moved from Poland to Israel in 1906, the same year in which Golda Meir emigrated from Russia to the United States. Arriving at Jaffa as a twenty-year-old illegal immigrant, he went to work as a farmer in the Galilean village of Sejera. If the Zionist movement was his life, he insisted that farming—making the desert bloom—gave him his greatest pleasure. When he finally retired, he returned to the desert to live out his life on the land.

Throughout his life, Ben-Gurion also read voraciously and wrote voluminously. When he was in his fifties he learned Greek, so that he could read Plato in the original. He also studied Hinduism and Buddhism. He spoke nine languages. In 1966, together with Mrs. Nixon and our daughters, Tricia and Julie, I visited him at his home, which was then on the outskirts of Tel Aviv. He took me to his study. All four walls were lined with books, in a close-packed clutter that seemed almost overflowing. I was reminded of that room when I visited Mao in 1972 and 1976. His room, too, had books and manuscripts piled and tumbling all over the place. In each case they were obviously not for show but were a much-used part of the man's daily life, unlike those I have seen in so many of the formal libraries in fashionable great houses, where the books are often dusted but seldom opened.

Over forty years passed between the time Ben-Gurion landed at Jaffa and the day in May 1948 when he stood before a microphone in the Tel Aviv Museum and read Israel's Scroll of Independence to the world. During those forty years he struggled under Turkish, British, and international rule to bring his dream to life. However, unlike other revolutionary leaders, Ben-Gurion could not celebrate peace when independence came. Within a day of his announcement, Egypt, Syria, Lebanon, Jordan, and Iraq went to war against the new country.

Militarily Israel's toughest battles did not precede independence; they followed it. In that sense Israel's was a continuing revolution—first against British rule, then against the hostility of its Arab neighbors. Fortunately for Israel, Ben-Gurion showed that he had the capability not only to lead a successful revolution—peaceful or violent, as the situation indicated—but also to build a state after the revolution had succeeded.

Ben-Gurion was an idealist who pursued the dream of Zion for eight decades. He was a realist who understood that a limit to Israel's geographical growth was imposed by the hostile forces that surrounded it and who was proudly confident of Israel's own capacity to make the best of what it already had. And he was a utopian in his belief that the Negev, Israel's southern desert, could someday flower into a home for Jews that would be neither wholly urban nor wholly rural in character.

Other Israeli leaders, then and since, have coveted more land. Not Ben-Gurion. He called himself a "crazy Negevist" and argued that Israel's mission was to reclaim the desert. Unimproved, he said, the desert was "a reproach to mankind" and "a criminal waste in a world that cannot feed its population." Improved, he insisted, it would provide all the space the Israelis needed. He spoke bitterly about the terrorists and other expansionists who wanted forcefully to enlarge Israel's territory; he argued that Israel had no reason to exist unless it was (a) a Jewish state and (b) a democratic state. The "extremists," he said, who advocated absorbing Arab lands, would deprive Israel of its mission: "If they succeed, Israel will be neither Jewish nor democratic. The Arabs will outnumber us, and undemocratic, repressive measures will be needed to keep them under control."

After the Six Day War of 1967, he surprised and offended many Israelis by suggesting that, except for East Jerusalem and the Golan Heights, the land captured from Egypt and Syria was "mere real estate" that should be returned to the Arabs. "The supreme test of Israel ... " he declared, "lies not in the struggle with hostile forces outside its frontiers but in its success in wresting fertility from the wasteland that constitutes sixty percent of its territory."

Ben-Gurion was Israel's Thomas Jefferson, George Washington, and Alexander Hamilton; his influence over Israel and Israeli life today is pervasive. He wrote the Israeli Declaration of Independence. He organized the first underground Jewish army and, acting both as Premier and Defense Minister after 1948, defended Israel against the Arabs on four fronts. After the bloody war of independence, he devised a defense strategy based on preemptive strikes that was designed to minimize Israeli casualties and that is still in force today. He approved the public trial of Nazi war criminal Adolf Eichmann, but also opened unofficial relations with West Germany and accepted war reparations from Konrad Adenauer, in spite of strong opposition among his countrymen. And his domestic policies were based on his egalitarian vision of a unified people working in common for one purpose: the development and defense of a modern Jewish state.

Unlike many others whose lives have been devoted to a single cause, Ben-Gurion was not parochial. I found him strong, articulate, and decisive in his observations, not only about Israeli-U.S. relations, but also about world affairs generally. He had a sense of proportion. After the Six Day War of 1967, de Gaulle had been openly critical of Israel and in the heat of the moment had made some mildly disparaging comments about the Jews. Golda Meir never forgave him. But Ben-Gurion later commented, "I think we have done de Gaulle a great injustice. The question is not whether he likes Jews. He saved France."

On a personal level he could be both gracious and patient. In 1959 he visited our home in Washington while he was in the United States on an official trip. Tricia was studying Judaism in the seventh grade at the Friends School, and she had an exam the next day. She plied him with questions. He gave her a half-hour dissertation on our common Judeo-Christian heritage while explaining to her such things as why the Jewish Sabbath falls on Saturday rather than Sunday and the meaning of the menorah. Tricia got an A on her exam and ever since has treasured an unforgettable experience.

David Ben-Gurion was a unique phenomenon, an elemental force of history. He had about him the fire, the faith, the certainty, of one whose stride carries him where none have gone before and who knows that his footsteps change the world. Some may argue that the creation of Israel was inevitable. But it often takes someone of extraordinary strength to make the inevitable happen.

The United States and Israel share one distinction that creates a powerful bond linking them together: They have been the two principal destinations for Jewish emigration from Europe and the principal havens for Jewish refugees. The intense spiritual and emotional attachment Jews everywhere feel toward Israel creates a special relationship between Israeli Prime Ministers and American Presidents. Many people assume that this relationship is merely a matter of politics. Politics enters into it, as do shared ideals and strategic considerations. But more fundamentally Israel has a unique importance to the United States because of its unique importance to so many Americans. Every President is aware of this and responds to it. To him Israel can never be just another country.

Nor, to me, could Golda Meir be just another leader. We both took office in 1969. We both resigned in 1974. She became Prime Minister just two months after my own inauguration, and she served until two months before my resignation. In effect, she was "my" Israeli Prime Minister; I was "her" American President.

For both countries those were difficult and, at times, searing years. The strains on our relationship were sometimes intense. She often wanted more than I was prepared to give. I sometimes took actions or pressed for conditions that she found it difficult or impossible to accept. We both knew that together we were playing for the highest stakes, that the balance between East and West, the lifelines of the industrial world, and Israel's existence all were at risk in the explosive conflicts of the Middle East. It was one of those situations in which each watches the other warily, knowing that a misstep by either can prove fatal for both. And because there were no entirely clear solutions, there were bound to be widely differing views about how the conflicts should be dealt with.

But going through crises together can also forge very strong bonds. Seeing the other leader tested gives a good view of what he or she is made of.

Georges Pompidou once described Golda Meir to me as *"une femme formidable."* She was that and more. She was one of the most powerful personalities, man or woman, that I have ever met in thirty-five years of public and private travel at home and abroad. If David Ben-Gurion was an elemental force of history, Golda Meir was an elemental force of nature.

Every good leader feels strongly protective toward his country. But her protective feeling toward Israel went beyond the usual. It was fierce, instinctive, as intense as a mother's toward her child. Israel to her was more than her country: It was a cause that transcended nationhood.

Some leaders are masters of intrigue, spinning webs of deception, planting suggestions that the unwary will take as promises, wheeling and dealing, constantly, even compulsively, plotting and maneuvering. For Lyndon Johnson this was second nature. FDR was a master at it. For many, scheming is the essence of statecraft, the most effective and sometimes the only way of navigating the threatening shoals of competing interests and getting things done. Not for Golda Meir. She was absolutely straightforward. There was nothing devious about her. The corollary is that she was implacably determined. There was never any question about where Golda Meir stood, or what she wanted, or why. She could be either the irresistible force or the immovable object, as the situation required. But as an object she was immovable; as a force she was irresistible.

Golda Meir had the look of a woman who had worked all her life. Her body showed signs of her years of backbreaking physical labor, and her face showed signs of mental and spiritual strain. But there was also a warmth in her face that photographs often failed to capture. Though a hard-headed negotiator, she could be openly and unabashedly sentimental. Brezhnev, too, could be sentimental, erupting with seeming spontaneity in a tearful outburst of goodwill. But with Brezhnev this was compartmented; a few hours later he would return for a snarling confrontation. With Golda Meir it was all of one piece. Her sentimentality and her determination flowed from the same source. She was stubborn in negotiations because she cared deeply about what she was negotiating to protect.

Her warmth came through spontaneously, in simple human ways. I remember well her first visit to the White House as Prime Minister, in 1969. It must have held a special meaning for her, having first come to this country at the age of eight as a poor immigrant from Russia, having been raised here, and having taught school in Milwaukee before moving to Palestine in 1921. At the state dinner we held for her, tears welled up in her eyes as the Marine band played the Israeli national anthem and then "The Star-Spangled Banner." For the entertainment after dinner, we had arranged for special performances by Isaac Stern and Leonard Bernstein. She sat between Mrs. Nixon and me, totally absorbed in the music, and when it was over she impulsively got to her feet and went over and embraced both musicians.

The episode that was most agonizing for her during her term of office was the 1973 Yom Kippur War. When Israel was threatened with defeat, I ordered that "everything that can fly" should be used for a massive emergency airlift of supplies. She wrote later that "the airlift was invaluable. It not only lifted our spirits, but also served to make the American position clear to the Soviet Union, and it undoubtedly served to make our victory possible. When I heard that the [cargo] planes had touched down in Lydda, I cried for the first time since the war had begun . . ." She told me later that she thought my actions, including the airlift and worldwide alert of U.S. forces when the Soviets threatened to send forces into the area, had saved Israel. The following January, when the Egyptian–Israeli troop disengagement agreement was announced, I called Mrs. Meir. The Watergate crisis was totally dominating the news in the U.S. at that time. At the end of the conversation I was deeply touched when she said, "Take care of yourself and get plenty of rest."

If toughness in a crisis was typical of Golda Meir, so, too, was that motherly admonition.

To the people of Israel she was known affectionately as *Golda Shelanu*—"Our Golda." She moved among her people with ease and informality. She was the Prime Minister who made soup and coffee for her cabinet while they gathered around her kitchen table, discussing affairs of state while shuttling back and forth from the stove.

Even in her seventies she drove herself unmercifully, working until the early morning and keeping her attention focused simultaneously on the biggest issues and the smallest details of government. She signed no letter, no matter how routine, without reading it first. She went to the airport to meet groups of immigrants, often breaking into tears of joy at the sight of them. She was shattered by letters she received during and after the Yom Kippur War from parents who blamed her government for the deaths of their children. Every soldier lost was a personal blow to her. When Nasser was waging his war of attrition in the Sinai, she left orders that she be notified immediately, at any time of the day or night, whenever an Israeli was killed. Her instructions were taken so seriously that once she was awakened with the news of the loss of twenty-five sheep.

Many leaders drive to the top by the force of personal ambition. They seek power because they want power. Not Golda Meir. All her life she simply set out to do a job, whatever that job might be, and poured into it every ounce of energy and dedication she could summon. When she emigrated to Israel in 1921, it was because she was committed to the Zionist dream. She wanted to help and to serve. She was seventy when she became Israel's fourth Prime Minister. Levi Eshkol had died suddenly of a heart attack, and the other leaders of the Labor party turned immediately to her as the only person who commanded the across-the-board respect to succeed him without touching off a divisive struggle. At first she protested. Then she accepted. Later she wrote, "I became Prime Minister because that was how it was, in the same way that my milkman became an officer in command of an outpost on Mount Hermon. Neither of us had any particular relish for the job, but we both did it as well as we could."

Mrs. Meir thought that too much attention was paid to the fact that she was a woman in high public office. To her, being female meant one thing: more work. Especially in her earlier, child-raising years, she had had to find time both for her public duties and for her family responsibilities. When my daughter Julie Eisenhower interviewed Mrs. Meir for her book, *Special People*, she asked how it had felt to be appointed the first woman Foreign Minister in 1956. Her reply was characteristic: "I don't know," she said with a smile. "I was never a man minister."

In 1971 I held a meeting in the Azores with French President Pompidou. At one point Secretary of State Rogers, in trying to make light conversation, observed that in the world's two major trouble spots, South Asia and the Mideast, women happened to be serving as Prime Ministers. "In India," he said, "we have Indira Gandhi, and in Israel Golda Meir—another woman." Pompidou, a faint smile on his lips, said, "Are you sure?"

Pompidou said this not disparagingly, but with a whimsical sort of admiration. And the point, of course, is that as Prime Minister, Golda Meir conducted herself in such a way that whether she happened to be a man or woman simply made no difference. Golda Meir and Indira Gandhi were alike in that each more than held her own in negotiating with a member of the opposite sex. Having dealt with both, however, I found that they were strikingly different in the way that they did it. While both were very feminine, Indira Ghandi used her femininity; Golda Meir did not. Mrs. Gandhi expected to be treated as a woman and acted with the ruthlessness of a man. Golda Meir expected to be treated like a man and acted like a man. She neither asked for any quarter nor gave any because she was a woman.

She dressed plainly, wore no makeup, and kept her hair pulled severely into a bun at the back of her head, though she admitted that the reason she kept her hair long was that her husband and her son had liked it that way. She was always very gracious in her conversations with Mrs. Nixon, and she showed an obviously sincere interest in our children and in personal matters. But generally her approach was to make short shrift of the "getting-to-know-you" sort of icebreaking comments at the beginning of a session and go directly to the serious issues at hand. The first time we met in the Oval Office, there was the usual idle chitchat while the photographers clicked away. But as soon as they had been ushered out, she crossed her legs, lit a cigarette, and got right down to business, running through a list of equipment she wanted for her armed forces.

Once wronged, Mrs. Meir was not one to forgive and forget. She carried a satchelful of grudges. She never forgave de Gaulle for his critical comments after the 1967 war. She never forgave the Germans, even their new postwar leadership, for the Holocaust. She never forgave Arab terrorists, and those Arab nations that supported terrorism, for the innocent blood they shed. She even bore a long grudge against Ben-Gurion after he split away from the ruling Labor party in the 1960s.

She particularly distrusted the Soviet Union. While she was a devout Socialist, she had no illusions whatsoever with regard to Soviet tyranny and the threat that it presented to Israel. One of her first conscious memories was of her father nailing planks across the door of their home in Kiev, hoping to protect his family from one of the periodic pogroms in which mobs with clubs and knives went hunting for Jews. She also told me of her horror when drunken policemen would knock on the door every Saturday night and beat up her father for being a Jew. Her memories of those early years in Russia were few, but they were mostly of cold, hunger, poverty, and fear—especially fear. To her the pogroms of czarist Russia continued, in different form, in Soviet Russia. She felt that Soviet support for Nasser, who was pledged to the destruction of Israel, was a further insult to Jews.

During one of her visits to Washington she expressed to me her strong disagreement with what she felt was the naive attitude of many European leaders with regard to détente with the Soviet Union, and she said that she was concerned about our own moves toward better relations with the Soviets. I responded by explaining how my approach to détente differed and told her that we had no illusions about Soviet motives. I said that, with regard to international relations, our Golden Rule was somewhat different from that of the New Testament—that it was "Do unto others as they do unto you."

At that point Henry Kissinger chimed in and added, "Plus ten percent."

Mrs. Meir smiled in agreement and said, "As long as you approach things that way, we have no fears."

There were moments when she could deal lightly even with what were, to her, the most serious issues. She repeatedly insisted to me that none of Israel's Arab neighbors could be trusted. As part of a broader drive toward peace in the Middle East, I was trying to build better relations between the United States and some of the key Arab countries. I pointed out to her that, from Israel's own standpoint, it was far better to have the United States be a friend of Israel's neighbors than to have that role filled by another nation hostile to Israel. She conceded the point, yet always insisted that in dealing with the Arab countries we should put trust not in agreements but only in deeds. At the conclusion of one such meeting I handed out to the participants small gift boxes containing gold-plated cuff links with the Presidential Seal. Each of them opened his box, and one of the boxes turned out to be empty. Mrs. Meir laughed and said, "Now you see what I mean about trust." She also showed her light touch when, after naming Henry Kissinger Secretary of State, I commented to her that now both of our countries had Jewish Foreign Ministers. Alluding to Kissinger's German accent, she replied, "Yes, but mine speaks English."

Internationally Golda Meir had the reputation of a statesman of great courage, skill, and tenacity. She was highly intelligent, honest, and tough. She had the ability to make it to the top in any major country, but it probably was only in Israel that she would have, because it was the drive of her singular passion for the country and the cause that carried her to the top. She did not seek power as a privilege. She exercised power as a duty—for Israel.

Americans rated her high on their lists of most admired women. Yet to the people of Israel she was a beloved grandmother-protector, the strong, solid, dependable woman who carried the weight of Israel on her shoulders but who also made time to serve soup to her aides at her kitchen table.

In my eulogy at the memorial service for President Eisenhower in 1969, I said that great statesmen are often loved at home and respected abroad, but that only a few, such as Eisenhower, are truly loved both at home and abroad. Golda Meir, too, was one of those few. And, as with

Eisenhower, it was not for what she did, but for what she so clearly was.

I saw her for the last time in June 1974, just twelve days after she had left office in the wake of controversy over Israel's preparedness at the time of the October 1973 war. We visited her in her modest apartment in Jerusalem, where she again thanked me for America's support in that war. I could see the pain on her face as she tried to get up from her chair to greet us. It was only later that I learned that she was suffering from phlebitis, as I was at that time, and also cancer of the lymph glands, which she had kept secret for years. Later, at a state dinner in the Knesset, I decided to break precedent and offer a special, additional toast before the traditional one to the head of state. I said that no leader I had ever met had demonstrated greater courage, intelligence, stamina, determination, or dedication to country than Golda Meir, and added, "I thought that I, having worked with her, having become her friend, and she has been my friend, that I might have the honor and the privilege to ask you to join me in a toast to the former Prime Minister. To Prime Minister Golda Meir. To Golda."

It was an emotional moment for her, and it also was for me. That toast was truly from the heart. I could have said "To Golda, with love," and I think that she would have known I meant it.

MODERN LEADERSHIP FOR OLD NATIONS: NASSER, SADAT, THE SHAH, FAISAL

Few places on earth match the Middle East as a focus of story and legend or as a strategic crossroads. Its history stretches back thousands of years. Not only dynasties but civilizations have risen and fallen there. Winds still carve the ageless desert as they did millennia ago, and bones still whiten in the sun.

But suddenly, in the brief period since World War II, these ancient lands have erupted in ferment. The creation of Israel was only one of the developments unsettling the old ways and bringing new conflicts.

When Iran was plunged suddenly back into medievalism, the West got a harsh lesson in how thin the veneer of modernity can be in this new world and how severe the strains when old and new collide. We were reminded that live and let live is not a traditional concept in the Middle East. Passions are more intense there, less disciplined, less restrained. Verdicts are harsher and vengeance is swifter. Traditions are older, and are clung to more fiercely by those determined to preserve them.

Yet change is coming, there as well as elsewhere.

What we have seen in the Middle East during these recent decades has been the political equivalent of those volcanic upheavals that created the great mountain ranges and shaped the continents and oceans. And although the particular issues and the form of the struggle are peculiar to the Middle East, they illustrate the challenges confronting the whole world when changes that once would have taken centuries are compressed into decades. One person today, in the space of his one lifetime, may have to adapt to what would, in an earlier period, have been many generations of evolutionary development. The process is unsettling, both for individuals and for nations, and it can be explosive.

We can see these processes dramatically in the lives of four leaders who took very different approaches but had what often were remarkably similar goals: Gamal Abdel Nasser and Anwar el-Sadat of Egypt, King Faisal of Saudi Arabia, and the Shah of Iran. Of the four, the Shah was overthrown and died in exile. Faisal and Sadat were cut down by assassins' bullets. Only Nasser died of natural causes while still a hero, and even his fate might have been different if his life had not been ended abruptly by a heart attack at age fifty-two.

All four were modernizers. Each sought to renew his people's pride. In doing so, Nasser, Sadat, and the Shah reached deliberately back across the millennia to the ancient roots of their countries' cultures in order to reclaim and burnish the symbols of national greatness. Nasser and Sadat reached back to the Pharaohs, the Shah to the Persian empire of Cyrus the Great. Faisal had no need to reach back. His was the land of Muhammad, the home of the holiest Muslim shrines. Muslims throughout the world bowed in the direction of Saudi Arabia each day as they said their prayers.

I first met Nasser in 1963, but I felt that I had known him long before that.

He was an obscure army officer when, with Anwar Sadat as one of his coconspirators, he planned and led the 1952 coup that ousted the corrupt regime of King Farouk. At first he used a well-known general, Mohammed Naguib, as front man. But after two years, in 1954, the fiery Nasser had Naguib arrested and made himself Premier; in 1956 he had himself elected President.

Nasser's leadership was pyrotechnic. He shot like a meteor across the sky of the Middle East, acting as leader not only of Egypt but of the Arab world. He meddled compulsively in the affairs of other Arab countries, staging coups, plotting assassinations, trying always to forge a pan-Arab unity with himself at its head. He made both firm friends and bitter enemies; few were neutral about him.

The constant din of his propaganda reached throughout the Arab world. When I visited the Middle East in 1957 I did not stop in Egypt, but wherever I went I heard his voice on the radio. In the markets and the streets of cities in Libya, the Sudan, Tunisia, and Morocco, I saw people, young and old, rich and poor, listening to his voice with looks of almost ecstasy. He used both radio and television with consummate skill, not only for his own exhortations, but to get his message across through the medium of entertainment. He mobilized the best entertainers in the Arab world, and they made songs such as "How We Build the High Dam at Aswan" popular hits.

One of Nasser's consuming dreams was construction of the Aswan High Dam. Through the centuries Egypt had looked to the waters of the Nile to give its desert life. Now Nasser would harness those waters to provide cheap electricity and also to create another million and a half acres of arable land. But even this dream got caught up in his foreign adventuring. When Nasser's flirtation with Moscow led him to sign an eastern-bloc arms agreement, the United States dropped the dam as an aid project. When he heard the news he was reported to have said, "Americans, may you choke on your fury!" He responded by nationalizing the Suez Canal. Israel, Britain, and France sent forces against Egypt. The United States faced down its allies and helped engineer a U.N. cease-fire that left Egypt in control of the canal.

A key reason for Eisenhower's intervention was that the Israeli-British-French action came just as Russian tanks were rumbling through the streets of Budapest, brutally suppressing a brave Hungarian bid for freedom. Having bitterly protested the Soviet use of force, it would have been difficult to acquiesce to its use by Israel, Britain, and France. But regardless of the reasons, Eisenhower's intervention saved Egypt from defeat—at great cost to the Atlantic alliance. It was a decision that, in retrospect, I think was wrong. Later Nasser privately expressed gratitude, but at the time he displayed only contempt. The upshot was that he put his country in hock to Moscow both for weapons and for help with the Aswan Dam. At the same time, as Sadat later wrote, Nasser became "preoccupied with the fable . . . that he was a hero who had defeated the armies of two great empires, the British and the French. Having completely disregarded the real part played by Eisenhower to that end, which turned military defeat into political victory, he became the first to believe that he had won."

Nasser was volatile, impatient, dictatorial, possessed by grandiose ambitions that forever got in the way of his people's more mundane needs. While most Egyptians subsisted in desperate poverty, he squandered the nation's scarce resources on foreign adventures. His implacable belligerence toward Israel bolstered his standing in the Arab world, but also brought his forces into a devastating defeat in the Six Day War of 1967. For five years he pressed a costly war in Yemen, trying to overthrow the Saudi-backed Imam and establish an Egyptian client state. Eventually he was defeated there as well. At home he did carry out a wide-ranging land reform, and he raised high the people's hopes for a new prosperity as well as a new freedom. But when death ended his rule, the people were as poor as before, and political prisoners filled the jails.

And yet, for all that, his sudden death in 1970 sparked one of the greatest outpourings of grief the world has ever seen. Five million people jammed the streets of Cairo for his funeral, hanging from trees and lamp posts, weeping hysterically, surging against the funeral cortege, tearing the flag from his coffin. Many Egyptians were so distraught that they committed suicide. In Beirut the French-language daily *Le Jour* declared that "one hundred million human beings—the Arabs—are orphans."

What Nasser did was to give his people back their soul, their spirit, and their pride. The son of a postal clerk, he grew up with a bitter hatred of British colonialism. It was a mark of the times that as a young man he was thought vulgar because his first language was Arabic rather than French. When he took power, he was eager to end not only the monarchy but the vestiges of the colonial past. As Britain and France withdrew from the Middle East, Nasser rushed to fill the vacuum with his voice; his brand of insistent pan-Arabism was at once pro-Nasser and anticolonial and frequently anti-West. In a sense what mattered most to the people of the Arab countries was not so much what he did on the international stage as that he did it. He stuck his finger in the eye of the West, and the people loved it. The more flamboyantly, the more outrageously, he did so, the better they liked it. He showed that he was somebody and, by extension, that they were somebodies. To those who have the least materially, this sort of spiritual lift can often be even more important than it is to the comfortable.

Though a fiery demagogue in public, Nasser could be both gracious and reasonable in private.

In 1963 Mrs. Nixon, our two daughters, and I made a private vacation trip to Europe and the Middle East. Nasser invited us to his home. He still lived in the same modest bungalow on the outskirts of Cairo that he had used as an army officer. A lean, handsome six-footer with an erect military bearing, he cut a striking figure. He was the essence of hospitality. He introduced his family and showed us a collection of books about Lincoln that he had in his library. He expressed great respect for Eisenhower and gratitude for what Eisenhower had done to save Egypt in 1956. He spoke softly, carried himself with great dignity, and demonstrated both high intelligence and common sense. He talked with deep feeling about his desire to bring a better life to the people of Egypt. He asked my assessment of the current attitudes and intentions of the Soviet leaders and listened intently. Though Egypt was by then heavily dependent on the Soviet Union, he clearly did not relish the idea of Soviet domination and expressed a desire for better relations with the United States. He was anxious for us to see the Aswan High Dam; in an expansive gesture of hospitality he insisted that we visit it in his private plane. We did, and on the way his pilot flew us low over the pyramids and the Valley of the Kings.

Our visit to the dam was an eerie experience. Because the daytime temperature was over 100 degrees, we went down into the dam excavation area at midnight. Nasser had told me that virtually all of the work on the dam was being done by Egyptians. But as we looked at the huge bulldozers digging away under floodlights, Mrs. Nixon astutely noted that none of the operators was an Egyptian. All of them were Russians.

During the 1960s Nasser continued to meddle on the international scene. He fomented revolutions in other Arab states and sank deeper and deeper into the morass of the Yemen civil war. At home his neglect of Egypt's economic problems and his political repressions continued. Despite his professed fear of Soviet domination his dependence on the Russians for economic and military aid increased rather than shrank.

Nasser was a revolutionary who dismissed the fact that the time for revolution had ended and the time to consolidate his gains had arrived. His pan-Arabic movement was useful rhetorically, and with it he created a new sense of commonality and pride among Arabs. However, its central tenets—hatred of Israel and distrust of the West—were destructive rather than productive. As a result, Nasser's policies led inevitably to an escalation of the hostilities between Israelis and Arabs and an unhealthy dependence on the enemy of the West, the Soviet Union.

In September 1970, I was on an aircraft carrier in the Mediterranean, observing maneuvers of the U.S. Sixth Fleet, when we received word that Nasser had unexpectedly died of a heart attack. I considered traveling to Cairo for the funeral, but decided that it would be unwise. At the time the Egyptian government still had close ties with the Soviets and was intensely hostile toward the United States. If Nasser's successors wished to improve Egyptian-American relations, I decided, the first step was up to them. I sent a delegation in my place.

At the time of Nasser's death Sadat had been waiting behind the scenes for almost two decades. He had been safe from Nasser's obsessive jealousy because he seemed to have no personal ambition. He willingly undertook whatever missions Nasser assigned him. Some called him "Nasser's poodle"; others said the mark on his forehead came not from touching his head to the floor five times a day in prayer, as all devout Muslims do, but from cabinet meetings in which Nasser smacked him in the face to make sure he was following the conversation.

For eighteen years Anwar Sadat watched and listened. Before the revolution, when the British were still in charge in Egypt, he had served time in prison, and he had learned the practice and the value of patience. He knew Nasser was fiercely jealous, so Sadat was careful not to appear to be seeking power for himself. Besides, Sadat was a man who could be counted upon to honor his friendships and keep his promises. But on his trips abroad for Nasser, he made other friends, including Crown Prince Faisal of Saudi Arabia. As President, he told Faisal privately that Nasser's Arab socialism and his dependence on the Soviet Union were failures.

When Sadat came to power in 1970 upon Nasser's death, many observers were sure that he would last only a few weeks. They said he had none of Nasser's charisma. They failed to recognize that there are different kinds of charisma and that only when one puts on the mantle of leadership is it possible to tell whether he has that elusive quality. Sadat did not attempt to fill Nasser's shoes. He made his own footprints on history. He began by deftly blocking all attempts by others to seize power and jailing his opponents. Soon his authority was unquestioned.

Sadat acted swiftly to break the fetters that bound Egypt to the Soviets. After Nasser's death he had sent representatives around the world with greetings. In Peking his envoy met with Zhou Enlai. During the conversation the Chinese Premier asked, "Do you know who killed Nasser at the age of fifty-two?" When the surprised envoy did not answer, Zhou said, "The Russians." Zhou was speaking figuratively, not literally. But Egypt's dependence on the Soviet Union, and its chilly relations with most of its Arab neighbors and the United States, were burdensome legacies. Nasser was a fiercely proud and independent man, and near the end of his life Egypt's isolation weighed heavily on him. Sadat believed that it caused both his spirits and his health to deteriorate.

Soon after Sadat took office, we began to pick up signals that Sadat wanted a thaw in relations between the U.S. and Egypt. The first in the series of dramatic initiatives that characterized his eleven years in power came in 1972, when he abruptly expelled sixteen thousand Soviet military advisers. He was motivated in part by his judgment that the Russians were unreliable, but also in part by an instinctive dislike of the Russians. When I visited Cairo in 1974, I told him that I thought one cause of the Sino-Soviet split was the Chinese feeling that they were more civilized than the Russians. Sadat smiled and answered, "You know, that's exactly the same way we feel: We Egyptians are more civilized than the Russians."

Nasser was a human dynamo. He involved himself in the details of government and often stayed in his office until the early hours of the morning to catch up on paperwork. Sadat was more withdrawn and contemplative. He often ignored his ministers, making his decisions by himself while walking along the Nile each afternoon after lunch. He rose comparatively late and did not work a long day. He abhorred detail. The day-to-day operation of his government was clumsy and inefficient, but the big decisions—those Sadat reserved for himself—were breathtaking and often transcendent. Some, such as the expulsion of the Soviets and his trip to Jerusalem in 1977, fundamentally changed the structure of Mideast politics. Seldom has one man rendered so much conventional wisdom about international relations suddenly obsolete.

Both Nasser and Sadat will be remembered by the world for their roles in foreign affairs. Both sought to repair the Arabs' injured pride; Sadat's Yom Kippur War in 1973 was undertaken in part to redress the psychological imbalance created by the Israeli victory in 1967. But Sadat went further. After Suez the hostility between Israelis and Arabs was as intense as ever. For Sadat the strong Arab showing in the Yom Kippur War was actually a step toward peace. He could make a grand gesture from a position of strength that he could not from a position of weakness.

Sadat was as practical as Nasser was flighty, as careful as Nasser was impulsive. His initiatives were carefully planned means to an end, undertaken with an eye to the full range of possible consequences. Sadat wanted to end Egypt's economic isolation. Peace with Israel meant new trade, new income from Suez oil, uninterrupted income from shipping through the Suez Canal. Nasser's foreign policy had few domestic payoffs; in one sense it had been a way to distract people from their problems at home. Sadat's was a step toward solving those problems.

Sadat succeeded where Nasser failed because he saw as his first responsibility the welfare of the Egyptian nation rather than the "Arab nation." He had a broader and better understanding than Nasser of the forces that move the world. But while he played an active role on the world scene, he carefully related what he did abroad to his goal of improving conditions at home.

The last time I saw Sadat was in August 1981, during his visit to the United States. He invited me to meet with him at the Egyptian mission in New York. Once again I was struck by his dark, distinguished features and the graceful way he carried himself. Sadat had suffered two heart attacks, and he carefully conserved his energy. But I also had the impression that he channeled physical energy into mental work. He made few unnecessary or flamboyant gestures and uttered few superfluous words. His sense of reserve and self-control was remarkable.

During this last meeting I found him optimistic about the Reagan administration; he said he was certain that Reagan would be forthright in his Mideast dealings and firm in his opposition to Soviet adventurism. On U.S.-Soviet relations he said that the Americans had lost a great deal of ground in the preceding four years and added, "The West must not give another inch." He said he expected a Soviet move in Poland, adding that the West should not respond directly but should use the Soviet intervention as a pretext for moving in some other area, such as Cuba, Angola, or Libya. "Fight them on the ground we choose rather than on the ground they choose," he said.

Two months earlier Israel had made a preemptive strike on a nuclear reactor in Iraq. I told Sadat that I felt Israeli Premier Menachem Begin had acted irresponsibly and erratically. He blurted out, "Yes, he is crazy." But then he added, "He is also probably crazy like a fox." I said that while I understood that Israel had to protect itself against its enemies, I thought it was unwise for Begin to embarrass his friends, such as Sadat and Reagan, in the process. Sadat agreed.

But when I added that more progress could have been made in the Mideast had Begin not been kept in power, Sadat demurred. "I prefer to deal with him," he said. "He is very tough and will be able to make a deal that others may not be able to make. Israel needs a deal, and I am confident that between Begin, Reagan, and myself, we will be able to make greater, more lasting progress than was made during the Carter administration."

At the end of our conversation Sadat invited me to visit him at his winter palace at Aswan sometime during the next few months. He said that he wanted to have a good, long talk then.

We never had that talk. I traveled to Egypt, but it was for his funeral. In October, while reviewing a military parade in Cairo, Sadat had been gunned down by a band of assassins. President Reagan asked the three former Presidents to serve as his representatives at the funeral. On the way to Cairo Presidents Ford and Carter and I exchanged reminiscences of Sadat. We agreed on his courage, his vision, his intelligence, and his shrewdness. But when we arrived in Egypt, the streets were almost empty, in stark contrast to the frenzy that erupted on Nasser's death eleven years before. Sadat's successor, Hosni Mubarak, told us that his people were probably still in a state of shock and not inclined to mourn in public.

I believe the explanation for the Egyptians' ambivalence toward Sadat runs deeper. Nasser had the common touch. Despite his absolute power, he never developed a taste for luxury. Compared to Nasser, Sadat lived elegantly. He maintained ten presidential residences. He had a sophisticated, articulate, impeccably groomed wife. He wore expensive suits and smoked imported pipe tobacco.

Though he never forgot his peasant beginnings, Sadat did not try to persuade the people that he was "one of them." In fact few really successful leaders are. Sadat had deep philosophical feeling for his people, but, like de Gaulle and his attitude toward the French, he did not have deep personal feeling for them. Still, they had much for which to thank Sadat. At the time of his death no Egyptian soldier was at war; though the economy was still shaky, Egyptians were more prosperous than they had been a decade before. Sadat had gone a long way toward dismantling Nasser's police state by reducing censorship, enhancing civil liberties, and curbing the secret police.

Nasser was an emotional leader. Sadat was a cerebral leader. Nasser had been able to see into the hearts of his people. Sadat was able to see over their heads. Because of his personal remoteness, he was more respected than loved. By the same token it was his solitary contemplations that helped him move the Mideast question to a new, higher plane, where problems seemed somehow less insuperable.

The lack of an extravagant emotional outpouring at Sadat's funeral should have been expected. There could be only one Nasser; the outpouring for him was because he was the first, the founder, the one and only. The people knew instinctively that someone like him would not come again. He could not be replaced. Though they identified these things with Nasser himself, what they loved was the spasm of history, the eruption of pride, the explosion of being that comes only once in a nation's lifetime.

Sadat was an antidote to Nasser. He built on his predecessor's accomplishments and, where necessary, corrected his mistakes. President Mubarak now has the opportunity to do the same with regard to Sadat. After the funeral I traveled to several other Mideast and North African capitals for private meetings with their leaders. They were all critical of Sadat because of the Camp David accords and what they felt was Sadat's inattention to the plight of the Palestinians. Many of them, subjected for so long to Nasser's meddling ways, had at first viewed Sadat as an ally, and they were bitterly disappointed by what they considered his separate peace with Israel. They resented his calling them "monkeys and hissing vipers" when they refused to go along with his peace strategy. I could understand their feelings, but I also understood that in Sadat, Egypt finally had a leader who put his own people first. More blood had been shed by Egyptians on behalf of the Palestinians and the Arab cause than by any other Mideast nation. Now, Sadat reasoned, it was time to try a new approach.

Sadat was a bold innovator. He took the greatest and bravest step toward peace in the Mideast; it is up to his successor to complete the process he began and at the same time mend Egypt's ties with its conservative Arab allies. In a sense Egypt was ready in 1981 to move to the next phase, just as it had been in 1969. This may under the circumstances seem ghoulish, but I believe it is a concept Sadat himself, with his mystical streak and his belief in preordination, would accept. Often a leader's greatest contribution comes after his death, when his successors build on the foundations he has laid.

Sadat was killed by forces of the old world that reached out into the new world to strike him down. Because he sought peace instead of holy war, his assassins said he had forsaken Islam. Egypt is in many ways a more modern, cosmopolitan country than many of its Mideast neighbors. Nasser, though a devout Muslim, was spreading his revolution through pop songs at a time when television was still banned in Saudi Arabia. Nevertheless Islam has its militant adherents in Egypt as well as in Saudi Arabia and Iran. Each step Sadat took toward peace was a step toward greater personal danger for himself, because many of his enemies had no interest in peace. Leaders in the Mideast run a great risk when they tread the frontier separating old ways from new; Sadat, like the Shah and Faisal, crossed that frontier and ultimately sacrificed his life in doing so.

Fourteen months before Sadat's death, I had walked with him in another funeral procession in Egypt, in honor of Mohammed Riza Pahlevi, the Shah of Iran. The Shah died of cancer, Sadat from assassins' bullets. But both were victims of the explosive tensions of the Mideast. The Shah died alone, an exile from his country, permitted to live out his final days in some measure of dignity only because Sadat, alone among leaders, had the courage to give him refuge, while others who had fawned over him when he was in power turned from him now that he had fallen.

When I arrived in Cairo and saw Sadat just before the funeral march began, he walked up to me with his hand outstretched and said, "How good of you to come." I told him how courageous he had been to give the Shah sanctuary after he had been turned away by the United States. He replied incredulously, "Courageous, sir? It does not take courage to stand up for a friend. I only did what was right." It was a measure of Sadat's quality as a man and a leader that his loyalty extended to those friends who were powerless as well as those who were powerful. He demonstrated this same quality when I visited him in his palace in Alexandria the day of the funeral. We discussed the upcoming American elections. He knew that I supported Reagan and that Carter's popularity was slipping away. But he never once made a disparaging remark about the man he affectionately referred to as "my friend, Jimmy Carter."

The Shah's dreams for the future were just as grand as Nasser's, his hopes for his people just as strong. Of the two the Shah was the better statesman, but Nasser was the better politician. I believe the Shah was one of the most able leaders in the Mideast. But because he underestimated the power of his enemies until it was too late, he was brought down by them. Because of the twentieth century's romantic preoccupation with revolution—and because most of his friends in the world, including the United States, treated the Shah as a pariah after the revolution—he was almost universally vilified.

Fundamentally the Iranian Revolution was a simple grasp for power by the religious elite, which had lost authority over Iran's political, cultural, and social spheres as a result of the Shah's liberal reforms. But the rebels, because they shouted the rhetoric of the left, were romanticized by the news media, particularly television, and the Ayatollah played the networks for patsies. The Shah soon lost his western support and eventually lost his country; Iran lost its freedom, its prosperity, and all the progress the Shah and his father had made. The Shah died a broken, bitter man—bitter not for himself, but for his people.

During the odyssey of his exile, while he was still living in Mexico in 1979, I went down to visit him. We had been friends for twenty-six years. I had first met him in 1953, when he was only thirty-four years old. I was impressed by his quiet dignity and his eagerness to learn. He was then reigning but not ruling; political power was in the hands of his enormously able Prime Minister, General Fazollah Zahedi, whose son, Ardeshir, was the Iranian Ambassador to the United States during my administration. But the Shah asked probing, astute questions, and I believed that he would be a gifted leader once he began to guide his country personally.

A quarter-century later the Shah had the same regal dignity, but his youthful eagerness was gone. In its place was an almost desperate frustration. His power had been wrenched from his hands by the leaders of a movement that was sworn to reverse all that he had done and plunge Iran back into medieval darkness. The Ayatollah's crimes against his people seemed to pain the Shah personally. He was a man who had been misjudged, misunderstood, and misused, and his knowledge of this was eating away at him as devastatingly as his physical illness. So, too, was knowledge of the fate that had befallen so many who had worked with him.

And yet, in spite of his spiritual and physical agony, he was a gracious host. I was deeply touched when he said proudly over lunch that his son, Crown Prince Riza, had made the salad himself. We talked not just of Iran but of a wide range of world issues; as usual he displayed an encyclopedic knowledge of the international scene.

Some leaders need power to give purpose to their lives. Others live for a purpose so compellingly strong that they crave power in order to advance that purpose.

The Shah lived for his country. He identified with it—not only modern Iran, but the ancient Persia of Xerxes and Darius and Cyrus the Great, an empire that once comprised much of the known world. Like these ancient emperors he lived luxuriously, with all the trappings of imperial splendor. But luxury was not why he clung to the Peacock Throne. He clung to it because, for him, it represented Iran and the hope of a better life for Iran's people. Building on foundations laid by his father, he had used his power to wrench his country out of the Middle Ages and into the modern world by teaching the illiterate to read, emancipating women, working an agricultural revolution, and building new industry.

Those who complained about the excesses of his secret police forgot how many enemies he had made in the process of remaking his country from the bottom up. He was despised by mullahs, traditional merchants, the landowning aristocracy, entrenched bureaucrats, blue-blooded socialites, and Communists. Ironically his bitterest enemies included young intellectuals, many of whom he had sent abroad for study. They came home wanting even more reform even faster than the Shah was willing to go. The women he had emancipated demonstrated against him. These impatient Iranians became, unwittingly, the fodder for the mullahs' coup d'etat. In rallying behind the Iranian revolution, they imagined they were moving the Shah's drive for modernization and liberalization into high gear, but instead they helped the ambitious clerics throw it into reverse.

The Shah could have avoided making enemies by doing nothing—by continuing to preside over an impoverished, backward Persia, living splendidly off the income of his royal estates, and establishing cozy, status quo relationships with the powerful at the expense of the powerless. But the Shah chose action over inaction. As he suggested to me when I saw him in Mexico, he may have tried to do too much. He had wanted to turn Iran into a major economic and military power with an educated populace and a landowning peasantry. Many in the West who have seen photographs of the Shah resplendent on his bejeweled throne may be surprised that most of his time was spent poring over paperwork in his relatively modest office, wearing a business suit, and that he greeted visitors by standing up and shaking their hands. He put little trust in advisers and refused to delegate much authority, preferring to work fifteen hours a day and do as much as he could himself.

He filled his mind with the most minute details of Iran's economic development. Under the Shah, Iran's GNP and per capita income rose dramatically. By the time of the revolution two-thirds of his people owned their own homes.

With the help of the United States, the Shah built a powerful military force and became a key American ally in the Mideast and a force for stability from the Mediterranean to Afghanistan. During the late 1970s, when his domestic difficulties escalated, the U.S. began to equivocate in its support for him. Many viewed his dependence on the U.S. as a fatal weakness. In fact these critics had it backward. In the modern era few smaller countries have managed to enter the international first rank without the support of major powers. The security agreement between the U.S. and Japan is an example of such an alliance. In the case of Iran the fatal weakness was America's. If the U.S. had wavered at the first sign of domestic unrest in Japan during the postwar years, the result could have been similarly catastrophic. In Iran we let a friend down when he needed us the most.

The instant verdict on a leader is often overturned by appeal to the higher court of history. Some shrink and some grow after they leave the scene. Allende in Chile, Nasser in Egypt, and Mao in China are examples of those who are canonized at death, but whose shortcomings become more apparent as time passes. The Shah died engulfed in controversy, but I am certain that he will be one of those who increase in stature as the years pass.

The modernizing monarch faces an unusually difficult balancing act. The traditional ways he is trying to change are also those that support his right to rule. To be successful he must carefully monitor the pulse of his people; his reforms must be steady but not too sudden. But if those who have the most to lose from reform and modernization do resist him, he must swiftly assert his full authority. Once he has chosen the path he intends to follow, he must be very cautious about making concessions to his critics. If he makes too many, he may never find his way again.

Contrary to popular myth, the Shah's fall came not because he was a heartless tyrant; quite the contrary. One reason was impatience; he may have tried to do too much, too quickly. But a second, also important reason was that he was not ruthless enough in quashing those who threatened his nation's stability. A well-timed crackdown on his enemies, rather than the ill-advised concessions he made to them as the crisis unfolded, would have been the best thing the Shah could have done to save Iran from the darkness that has now engulfed it. As we have seen so tragically since, the Shah's enemies were also the enemies of freedom and progress for the Iranian people.

Faisal Ibn Abdul-Aziz al Saud, the King of Saudi Arabia from 1964 to 1975, was, like the Shah, an absolute monarch who set out to reform a nation steeped in ancient values and practices. Faisal, however, did not fall into the trap of offending the powerful Muslim fundamentalists. He was so obviously devout himself, and he led such a simple life, that he was above personal reproach. His enforcement of Islamic law was just as rigid as his predecessors'. But at the same time, he went about reforming and modernizing his country. Faisal's life demonstrates the potential for a society in which the advantages of the modern world exist in harmony with devotion to the God of Islam. "Like it or not," said Faisal soon after he took the throne, "we must join the modern world and find an honorable place in it. . . . Revolutions can come from thrones as well as from conspirators' cellars." Like Yoshida in Japan, Faisal was a leader who encouraged helpful western influences but was careful to make sure they did not disrupt the traditional—in Faisal's case, Islamic—essence of his country.

I first met Faisal in the early 1960s at the Waldorf-Astoria Hotel in New York. He was then Crown Prince under his brother, King Saud, and he struck me as a sophisticated, far-above-average diplomat who felt completely at home in western surroundings. He spoke impeccable English. At that time Saudi Arabia was eager for American support against Nasser-backed rebels on its southern flank in Yemen. Though not the least bit obsequious, Faisal's manner was low-key and conciliatory.

Years later, in 1974, I visited Saudi Arabia as President. By then Faisal was King, and the international scene was strikingly different. Nasser was gone, Faisal's friend Sadat ruled in Egypt, and Saudi Arabia and its Mideast allies had just demonstrated the economic leverage their oil gave them over the West. He dealt with me in his own manner and on his own terms. He met me at the airport, wearing layers of traditional black-and-white robes in spite of temperatures in excess of 100 degrees. He was accompanied by a retinue of sheikhs and Bedouin guards, their long swords gleaming in the sun. His austere private office in Jidda contrasted sharply with the elegant hotel suite in which I had first met him.

During our 1974 talks Faisal never spoke English, and he exhibited a clear awareness of the enormous power he now wielded and a clear intention to use it to the hilt in pursuit of his objectives. He proved to be a skilled negotiator. He relayed requests from some of his Mideast and Muslim allies for American arms, and was diplomatically noncommittal in response to my urging that the oil producers should act to reverse the rapid rise in prices that had recently taken place. Nonetheless, I was honored at the departure ceremonies when he broke with both tradition and protocol to issue an indirect but unmistakable attack on my administration's domestic opponents.

Under Faisal and his successors, Saudi Arabia has been an important anchor in a tempestuous region. During my talks with him I found that in his otherwise impressive grasp of foreign policy he had one conspicuous shortcoming: a persistent, pervasive belief that communism and Zionism were fundamentally linked. At our meeting in 1974, his very first point was about the designs the Communists had on the Arabian peninsula and the connection he saw between these plots and the Zionist movement. It was impossible to disabuse him of this strange obsession. I assured him that, despite our firm support of Israel, the U.S. had no illusions about Soviet motives. Finally I was able to guide the conversation toward our hopes for encouraging the moderate, responsible governments in the Mideast. Faisal was one of our greatest hopes in this regard, and in this area he showed real statesmanship. He had helped turn his friend Sadat away from the Soviets and also was a quiet but firm supporter of our diplomatic efforts in the region. Except for his obsession about the linkage between Zionism and communism, Faisal had a well-balanced and nonparochial view of the international scene, and I came away from our 1974 talks convinced that he was one of the most impressive statesmen then in power in the world.

Faisal spoke evenly and quietly. He used words sparingly, both in his conversations with me and with his advisers. He was an attentive listener, however, who liked to say, "God gave man two ears and one tongue so we could listen twice as much as we talk." By speaking in Arabic and using a translator, Faisal, like de Gaulle, could hear each of my questions and comments twice and therefore take twice as long to form his responses.

Again like de Gaulle, Faisal was a soldier-statesman who took political power on his own terms. And he had a powerful vision of his nation and its mission in the world.

Ibn-Saud, Saudi Arabia's founding father, once said of his most able son, "I only wish I had three Faisals." Faisal was groomed for power almost from birth. At fourteen he was sent on his first diplomatic mission. He soon became a dashing and expert desert horseman, and his father made him commander of one of his armies. By 1932, with the help of his son, Ibn-Saud had welded a ragtag band of Bedouin tribes into a new nation.

When Ibn-Saud died, his oldest son, Sa'ud, succeeded him as King. Sa'ud's profligacy nearly bankrupted the kingdom. He spent extravagantly for his own pleasure and bestowed ill-planned public-works projects on his people as manna from on high. Legend has it that when Crown Prince Faisal took over the day-to-day operations of the government in 1958, he found less than a hundred dollars of ready cash in the treasury. Faisal cracked down hard on royal spending and started the kingdom on the road to a balanced budget. King Sa'ud's jealousy of his brother's administrative skill caused rising tensions that were capped by Sa'ud's ouster from power by the Saudi elders in 1964.

As King, Faisal initiated an education program for women, abolished slavery, and built roads, schools, and hospitals. He channeled his massive oil revenues into new industries and foreign investments designed to provide wealth in the future, when the oil is gone.

Faisal seldom smiled; when he did, as one observer remarked, it was as if he had bitten a lemon and found it sweet inside. His face was gaunt and wrinkled, his eyes tired-looking, his eyelids heavy. He worked sixteen hours a day, and his youthful aides said they had trouble keeping up with him. Like Italy's de Gasperi, he was often the one who turned off the lights in the government offices at the end of the day.

Faisal was troubled by ulcers and could eat only the blandest foods. At the state dinner he gave for us in 1974, his guests were served delicious roast lamb. He had only rice, peas, and beans, which he mashed with his fork and ate with a spoon. His busy schedule and his ascetic nature left little room for recreation. The leadership of nine million Saudis, and his spiritual responsibilities toward millions of other Muslims, sat heavy on his shoulders.

At a time when other conservative Arab states were establishing legislatures, Faisal's authority was absolute. He ruled through a network of several thousand princes spread throughout the kingdom. He surrounded himself with able advisers, listened to them carefully, and then did what he chose. Many Saudis who approved of the broad outlines of his program were still among his critics because of his refusal to delegate authority.

While rejecting democracy, Faisal remained close to the people he ruled. Soon after he took the throne, his wife showed him through his newly redecorated palace at al Ma'ather. When he saw the lavish royal bedchamber, he asked her, "Whose room is this? It's too grand for me." Instead he chose a tiny room down the hall and furnished it with a single bed. He disliked being kissed on the hand or called "Your Majesty"; he preferred "brother" or even "Faisal." The traditional Saudi majlis were an integral part of his government. During these weekly royal audiences he would listen patiently while his subjects complained about stolen livestock or property disputes.

The circumstances of Faisal's death were particularly ironic. In our talks in 1974 he had expressed deep concern about the loyalty of some of the junior officers in his air corps. They had been trained in the U.S. and he feared that they might have been infected by the revolutionary left-wing virus that was later to plague Iran. He did not realize that his fatal danger would come from the right rather than the left. One of his more controversial reforms was to allow television in his kingdom, though he saw to it that programming was strictly regulated. In 1965 a dissident Prince, believing television was an evil influence, led an unsuccessful raid on a broadcasting station in Riyadh. The Prince retreated to his palace, where he was killed by security forces. Ten years later Faisal was assassinated by the Prince's brother; many believe it was an act of revenge. In his talks with me Faisal had indicated that he considered television and the media generally to be, at best, necessary evils in the modern world. In the end he became probably the only leader to have lost his life because of television.

When Faisal was assassinated, one newsweekly said that the murder "demonstrated anew the instability of the Mideast oil states," even as power was being quietly and peacefully passed to Faisal's brother, Khalid, who became the fourth Saudi King since 1932. Similarly, when President Sadat was assassinated in the fall of 1981, many said the United States should not sell weapons to "unstable" Mideast governments, even as power passed quietly and peacefully to Sadat's handpicked successor, who became the third President of Egypt since 1956. In each case the transfer of power was no less orderly than that which followed the assassination of President Kennedy in 1963.

Many Mideast governments are indeed "unstable" when measured against American standards. While Egypt has constitutional provisions for an orderly succession, Saudi Arabia does not. Nonetheless comparatively few of the world's nations have dependable succession procedures. No Communist country does. Most who label the Saudi regime unstable are using code words to communicate their abhorrence of the idea of absolute monarchy. Their attitude is understandable in view of the long history of democracy in the West. But they overlook the realities of Saudi Arabia, which has no such history. Monarchy is a form of government that the Saudis are used to and are, for the moment, comfortable with. Jordan and Morocco also are monarchies, and under King Hussein and King Hassan respectively they are among the best-governed nations of the Arab world. In Tunisia, Habib Bourguiba had himself named President for life. While his benevolent authoritarian leadership has its critics, it is doubtful that western-style democracy would have produced the progress and stability he has provided for Tunisia.

Inevitably, as more Saudis are educated, they will clamor for western-style government. This development, however, will occur *as a result* of the reforms of the Saudi monarchy, not *in spite* of them. Though it may eventually be discarded in favor of a new form of government, the monarchy will have accomplished what Faisal intended it to accomplish: the carefully paced, peaceful transformation of Saudi Arabia into a modern nation.

Democracy would not necessarily be good for Saudi Arabia, just as monarchy has not necessarily been bad. King Fahd, who succeeded to the throne in June 1982, has said bluntly that his country is not ready for republican government. "We want to use the elite of our country," he said, "and we are convinced that elections would not put the elite into power until education is more widespread." As Faisal said, "The important thing about a regime is not what it is called, but how it acts. There are corrupt republican regimes and sound monarchies, and vice versa. . . . The quality of a regime should be judged by its deeds and the integrity of its rulers, not by its name."

Nasser and Sadat were revolutionaries; the Shah and Faisal were revolutionizing monarchs. As such the two Egyptians had a psychological edge over the other two men. The successful revolutionary leader has an innate attraction that cannot be matched by the monarch. The revolutionist is meteoric; he is the force in motion. The monarch is the force at rest. One is perceived as dynamic, the other as static. Even if the monarch has better ideas than the revolutionist, he must overcome terrific inertia to accomplish his goals.

To the revolutionary the traditions and practices of the past are no more than fuel for the engine of revolution. He may discard them or revise them at will. The monarch, however, depends on tradition for his power and authority. When tradition interferes with his plans for the future, he must either change his plans or integrate them with tradition in a way that will keep his culture and his authority intact. It is a difficult task, among the most difficult for a statesman.

Nasser came to power with a clean slate. When he deposed and exiled King Farouk in 1952, he was also expelling all of the bad memories of Egypt's recent and not-so-recent past: domination by the British, the Turks, the Romans, the Greeks, the Persians. For the first time in centuries he gave his people government by Egyptians, for Egyptians. At the same time he sought to unite Egypt with its Arab brothers. It was the perfect revolutionary idea—at once captivating and impractical.

Nasser's political power was absolute, but he ruled within the framework of an illusory republican government. He was known as "President" Nasser, not "the Egyptian strongman" or "Egypt's dictator." His regime was harshly authoritarian, but the harshness was eased because Nasser was a beloved revolutionary leader.

Nasser's goals were supranational; part of his appeal was that he gave his people a sense of a mission beyond their borders: Arab nationalism. The Shah's goals were primarily national but also geopolitical, as a bastion of the West against Communist aggression. He wanted Iran to be a major economic and military power and focused most of his attention on those functions that Nasser neglected. As a result the Shah's work lacked drama. He did not have a Suez Canal to nationalize; he did not hurl his armies against the Zionist hordes; he did not come to power riding a wave of anticolonial, revolutionary acclaim. He was, in fact, another in a series of Shahs—one of the few, in fact, to have died a natural death. Once, when he was asked why many did not trust him, he smiled and then answered frankly, "How many Shahs have deserved to be trusted?"

The Shah was talented and hardworking. His regime was no more authoritarian than Nasser's, and his domestic accomplishments were vastly greater. He produced progress with stability. Nasser produced instability without progress. But the Shah did not strike the emotional chord in his people that Nasser did.

The Shah, because he hesitated once his opponents began to challenge him, was overtaken and engulfed by the past. King Faisal, another absolute monarch, mastered the past.

He succeeded for both personal and institutional reasons. The Saudis have had five Kings. One, Ibn-Saud, created Saudi Arabia. The other four were his sons. Of the five, only King Sa'ud was corrupt, and even his corruption was benign rather than oppressive. King Sa'ud, in fact, began some of the reforms that Faisal brought to fruition.

Faisal was better equipped to be a modernizing monarch. His authority was both spiritual and temporal; it seemed to flow organically from the people. The King of Saudi Arabia is one of the few heads of state in the world who can be approached and engaged in conversation by any citizen. His nation is more homogeneous than the Shah's Iran was; also, it has not begun to experience the wrenching tensions produced by rapid industrialization and urbanization that helped bring down the Shah.

Faisal accomplished in Saudi Arabia much of what the Shah hoped to accomplish in Iran. He did not have to contend with an obstreperous clergy; Saudi Arabia has no separation of church and state. At the same time he was reforming, he was monitoring the impact the reforms were having on his country. He allowed only those influences that could be accommodated without tearing the cultural fabric of Saudi Arabia.

Saudi Arabia's vast oil riches alone will not buy it security or prosperity, as Iran has tragically demonstrated. Faisal's task was to set Saudi Arabia on the path toward modernization without destroying the essence of the God-fearing nation that he and his father had raised from the Arabian sands. In his eleven years in power he did precisely that.

BIG MEN ON SMALL STAGES: LEE, MENZIES

Of all the leaders I have met, two of the ablest have been Lee Kuan Yew, Prime Minister of the tiny city-state of Singapore, and the late Robert Menzies, Prime Minister of Australia. They shared the distinction of being big men on small stages, leaders who, in other times and other places, might have attained the world stature of a Churchill, a Disraeli, or a Gladstone.

Vastly different in character, the men were curiously alike in background and outlook. Both were leaders of former British colonies. Both were excellent lawyers who could have made a fortune at legal careers but who found the law to be both spiritually and intellectually confining. Both were vigorous, articulate, and talented men who, though restricted by accidents of history to the leadership of smaller countries, refused to view the world from a parochial or strictly regional perspective. Because of their sweeping and comprehensive views of the world, my conversations with them were among the most interesting I have ever had.

Also, though each had an essentially prowestern outlook, each realized, as MacArthur did, that the balance of power in the world was gradually but steadily shifting in favor of their part of the world. Both strived to ensure that their countries would be among the most prosperous, the most secure, and the most influential in the western Pacific area.

In more personal terms Lee and Menzies were quite different. Menzies seemed as big as all Australia in body as well as spirit and outlook. He was six feet two inches tall and weighed 250 pounds; he had an open, distinguished face; thick, curly hair; heavy John L. Lewis–type eyebrows; and amused eyes. His air of bemused superiority, though useful for dealing with annoying MPs and reporters, offended many of his colleagues in government and guaranteed that, like Churchill, though he was admired by his people, he would be little loved.

Lee is compact and muscular, like a champion prizefighter; he has a hard-edged glint in his eye that never softens. I found Menzies gregarious and witty; Lee is shrewd, opportunistic, calculating, and devious. Menzies enjoyed good conversation—enjoyed it, in fact, much more than parliamentary maneuvering, at which he excelled but which he never relished—and was a connoisseur of fine wine, good food, and well-mixed martinis. Lee considers most recreation a waste of time.

In my meetings with Menzies he usually spent the time smoking a fine cigar and regaling me with political advice, astute observations on foreign affairs, and sardonic comments about Australian politics. Our conversations were intense but buoyantly good-humored. In contrast, when I first met Lee in 1967, he paced the floor like a caged lion and talked in rapid bursts about matters far and wide. He acted as if he felt both physically and mentally confined to his modest office and wanted to break free and find more spacious surroundings. He did not engage in small talk.

Their greater similarity is in the goals they pursued. Neither was an ideologue. Menzies was a British-style parliamentary democrat whose deepest commitment was to the crown and the unity of the commonwealth in times of emergency. His economic conservatism found real expression only after his first term, when he viewed himself as an ally in the middle-class man's quest for comfort and security. Lee was above all a practical man, indifferent toward political theory and contemptuous of anything that did not contribute directly to his goal of strengthening and enriching Singapore. To both men nothing was more important than ensuring security and prosperity for their people.

Because of their nonideological outlooks, Lee and Menzies have been derided as materialists who were so interested in their people's physical needs that they ignored their spiritual ones. Each man's domestic accomplishments were principally economic; Menzies presided over the biggest burst of industrialization and economic growth in Australia's history, while Lee turned Singapore into a trading powerhouse. The people of both countries have become some of the richest in that part of the world.

The pursuit of affluence is much ridiculed by those who have never known the absence of it. Dozens of postwar leaders gave their people revolution, national pride, and independence, but left them poor and often hungry. We live in a time when leaders are often judged more by the stridency of their rhetoric and the coloration of their politics than by the success of their policies. Especially in the developing world, too many people have gone to bed at night with their ears full but their stomachs empty.

*   *   *

Lee was a revolutionist, but of a different kind. He never confused rhetoric with substance, and he never allowed ideology to overcome good sense. In 1959, when he came to power, Singapore was a tiny nation with no natural resources and a potentially volatile mix of Indians, Chinese, and Malayans. Anticolonial resentment against the British ran dangerously high. He realized that he could only forestall a Communist revolution by appearing to be much more radical than he really was, so he devised a political game plan that could best be described as talking left and walking right.

Before the election Lee's People's Action party was no more than a Communist front whose rhetoric mimicked Mao's. He played to the hilt the role of the anticolonial, antiwestern firebrand, campaigning in his shirt-sleeves and railing against the evils of the white man. But after he was elected, he jailed over one hundred of his former Communist colleagues and immediately set to work at placating Singapore's wealthy Chinese elite and assuring foreigners that any investments they might make in Singapore, and any business executives and workers they might send, would be safe. Today he presides in pinstripe suits over a prosperous nation some have called Singapore, Inc., whose livelihood is a healthy mix of Japanese, Western European, and U.S. investment.

Singapore's prosperity did not come easily. The city's only resource, besides its people, is a strategically important position as an international crossroads. Lee spoke contemptuously of those Third World nations that survived on the royalties paid for their mineral riches. "This place will survive only if it has got the will to make the grade," he said. "It's got nothing else but will and work." Since Lee took office, Singapore has increasingly had to fend for itself. The British military, for years a primary source of jobs for Singapore's workers, began to withdraw in the mid-1960s. A two-year-old federation between Malaysia and Singapore failed about the same time—the result, many said, of Lee's attempt to dominate it. Lee was so disappointed by the failure that he wept openly during his televised announcement of Singapore's withdrawal. But he was only momentarily daunted. "To sit on a stool is more comfortable than sitting on a shooting stick," he said, with his characteristic knack for colorful metaphor. "Now we have to sit on that shooting stick. It's all we've got. And don't forget this. The people of Singapore have a shooting stick made of steel."

Often it seemed that Lee expected his people themselves to be made of steel. He regulated the length of young men's hair and spoke out against drug abuse and sexual promiscuity. He cautioned against ostentatious displays of affluence, such as sports cars and marble floors. He has been criticized for being a harsh disciplinarian with a streak of Victorian moralism. But he believed that discipline and firm guidance were necessary to diminish the hostility among Singapore's three racial groups and to encourage them to work cooperatively. He urged his people to think of themselves as Singaporeans rather than as Chinese, Malays, and Indians. To a large extent he has succeeded, making Singapore the envy of many other multiracial societies.

Like Nehru, Lee was educated in England and returned home with strong Socialist impulses. Unlike Nehru, Lee was not dogmatic about socialism. He realized that a society must have a vigorous economy before it can afford rent subsidies, schools, housing, and clinics. Lee looked after the needs of his people, but first he looked after the needs of the economy that would pay the bill. He summed up his attitude about economics with the simple comment "We do not expect something for nothing."

Many of Lee's social reforms served a practical purpose. "It's the only hope," he said in the late 1950s. "If we don't try, Singapore will become Communist. If we try and fail, it will become Communist. The important thing is for us to try." Often he expected government agencies to pay their own way, which produced the unusual result of a national post office that turned a profit and a government printing office that accepted commercial work. Sloth and waste in government, so rampant in other developing nations, are cardinal sins in Singapore.

In spite of his intense concern for the welfare of his people, Lee rarely discussed domestic issues with me during our meetings. In some leaders a reluctance to address local problems indicates that they are either overwhelmed by them or, like Sukarno, unwilling to confront them at all. With Lee it was different. He did not have to discuss Singaporean issues because he had Singapore well under control. Early in my presidency I sent John Connally, my Secretary of the Treasury, on an around-the-world fact-finding trip. When he came to the White House to make his report, his opening comment about his stop in Singapore was brief and unequivocal. "Singapore," he told me, "is the best run country in the world."

Before I left on my Asia trip in 1953, Governor Thomas E. Dewey, who had visited the Far East after losing the presidential election of 1948, told me that the most impressive man he had met on his tour was Robert Menzies. When I met Menzies, I saw at once why Dewey had such a high opinion of him. He displayed an extraordinary grasp of issues affecting not only the Pacific region but the entire world.

The successful Australian Prime Minister must master a vast, sparsely populated nation that ranges in character from the English urbanity of Adelaide to the frontier primitiveness of the Great Victoria desert. Menzies, who served more consecutive years than any of his predecessors, had what it took to do so. Though he had all the reserve and dignity of a member of the British upper class, he also had a rough-and-ready willingness to tangle with opponents and the press and a knack for sharp, stinging repartee. The first time I met him he told me, "I am British to my boot heels, but I love America," and it always seemed to me that he combined the best qualities of British and American politicians.

There were actually two Robert Menzieses. I knew the second one, the confident, sophisticated politician who had mastered his time and who was overseeing the greatest economic boom in Australian history. I never met the first Menzies. He was Australia's young, intellectually arrogant leader during the first years of World War II, a man of good intentions who was finally overcome by events.

Menzies was Prime Minister of Australia twice: between 1939 and 1941 and again between 1949 and 1966. It was not until his second tour that he found a cause to champion: the forgotten man of the middle class who was being trammeled by the Socialist policies of the Labor party, which took over from him in 1941. As Prime Minister, he guarded the welfare of his people without hindering private enterprise, and, like Lee, encouraged new foreign investment. The result was a massive increase in productivity and prosperity. Between 1949 and 1961 Australia's GNP nearly tripled. At the same time Menzies developed a sensible, comprehensive outlook on foreign affairs that centered on Australia's growing role as a Far Eastern power.

During Menzies's out-of-power years it was clear that he would face enormous obstacles in any effort to regain power. After his resignation in 1941 and the victory of the Labor party, he was so thoroughly discredited that he was not even chosen to lead the Opposition in Parliament. In 1944 he formed the Liberal party. The experience of consolidating and retaining control over it—and then selling it to Australian voters—significantly honed his political skills.

Like so many other great leaders, Menzies was toughened by his years in the wilderness. When he took power again, he was much more confident of his abilities and sure of his goals. He was considered an excellent parliamentarian, a strong campaigner, and a dazzling speaker. He was accused of treating his Cabinet with contempt, but was in fact confident enough of his strength that he let his ministers talk all they wanted.

There was no question of who was in charge, however, and therefore no chance that Menzies's political house would be knocked down from inside as it had been during the war. In 1941, faced with dissension in his Cabinet, he meekly asked his ministers for suggestions about what he should do differently. After 1949 he handled his cabinet differently. One of Menzies's pet projects was sprucing up the capital city of Canberra, and one year he saw to it that a million pounds were included in the budget for the construction of an artificial lake for the capital. He then left for England. In his absence the Treasury Minister had the item deleted from the budget.

Upon his return Menzies said jovially to the cabinet, "Am I rightly informed that when I was away the Treasury struck out this item of one million for the initial work on the lake?" His ministers told him that he was. He responded, "Well, can I take it that by unanimous consent of ministers the item is now struck in?" The next morning, work on the lake was under way.

In *Great Contemporaries* Churchill wrote that "one mark of a great man is the power of making lasting impressions upon people he meets." Some do this through their physical presence, some through the strength of their intelligence. I also think it is no coincidence that virtually all of the major leaders I have known were exceptionally skilled in the vanishing art of face-to-face conversation. Leadership is persuasion, and the leader who fails as an interesting, impressive conversationalist is likely to fail as a persuader and therefore as a leader.

MacArthur's masterful monologues, de Gaulle's eloquent pronouncements, Yoshida's self-deprecating humor, Zhou Enlai's flashes of poetry, all were to today's run–of–the–talk-show chitchat as Rembrandt is to fingerpainting. Their conversation had both style and substance; it was at once lively and profound; it evoked in the listener an immense respect for the intelligence that inspired it, and this sort of impression is one of the ways in which a successful leader both establishes his power and exercises persuasion.

Whenever I was going to meet with one of these men, I looked forward to the occasion as I would to a performance by a great artist— which in fact it was. Yet if I were to rate one postwar leader even above the others in this category, it would not be one of the legendary European or American figures. It would be Robert Menzies.

His sense of humor was sharp but seldom cruel. He was an eloquent phrasemaker, and he loved the give and take of spirited dialogue. He was also a good listener. He was unusual in another respect: He was an excellent writer as well as a good talker. Often those who write well cannot speak well, and vice versa. A few—Churchill, Woodrow Wilson, and de Gaulle—could do both. But for one who wants to rise in the political world, being able to speak well, both in public and in private conversation, is more important than the ability to write well. It is virtually indispensable.

As a result of Menzies's skill with words, few were willing to tangle with him in public. Early in his career he learned, as Churchill did, that it was much more effective to turn aside a hostile question or comment with a snappy quip than a long-winded defense or explanation. At his first press conference as Prime Minister a leftist reporter jeered, "I suppose you will consult the powerful interests who control you before you choose your Cabinet." Menzies replied, "Naturally, but please, young man, keep my wife's name out of this."

The technique worked just as well in Parliament, which retained a dash of frontier vulgarity that Menzies sometimes found distasteful. Once he responded to a complaint from an MP that he had a superiority complex by saying, "Considering the company I keep in this place, that is hardly surprising." About another MP he said, "The conducted tour of the Honorable Member's mind would have been more instructive if it had not taken place in gathering darkness." The Labor party, stung once too often by such remarks, once actually advised its members not to cross Menzies unnecessarily.

Menzies's rejection by his party in 1941 had scarred him deeply. "It was the stroke of doom," he said later. "Everything was at an end." In fighting back from political obscurity during the 1940s, Menzies developed a crust of healthy cynicism toward his critics, especially those in the press. He was not afraid to cross swords boldly with them. After having to endure two hours of unmerciful roasting at one prestigious press gathering—the Australian counterpart of Washington's Gridiron Club dinner—he toasted the press as "the most overpaid unskilled labor in the Commonwealth." He once boasted to me that he treated the press with "marked contempt and remarkable success." Menzies also had contempt for his critics in the business world, particularly those who had deserted him during his long years in the wilderness. He told me, "These business types sit in armchairs and cut a politician down who loses." He said he knew how that felt when he had been struggling back after losing power to the Labor party. "They said I couldn't win," he said with a smile. In 1949 he proved them wrong.

Menzies often told me that politicians had to be thick-skinned, and he made some remarkably perceptive comments about one of our most thin-skinned Presidents, Lyndon Johnson. While he had great respect for Johnson's abilities—"a brilliant politician," he told me—even in the mid-1960s Menzies had detected in the Texan the obsession with public and press opinion that would cause him so much torment later in his presidency and after it. "Now, you and I know the press doesn't matter," Menzies said to me. "I often used to say to Lyndon, 'Don't be so sensitive about what these fellows write about you. They weren't elected to do anything—you were. They speak only for themselves—you speak for the people.' "

Appreciating and practicing as he did the art of conversation, Menzies pinpointed Johnson's other great weakness: his inability to sit still for even a few moments. "You never feel he is paying attention," Menzies said. "He's always grabbing for the telephone in the middle of a conversation."

Johnson had three television sets in the Oval Office so he could watch all three networks at once. In contrast Menzies's housekeeper told me that the Prime Minister never read about himself in the newspapers during controversies—"Though he once told me," she said, " 'When they quit abusing me, I'll know I'm finished.' "

Menzies was an astute observer of American politics. When I sent him a copy of my first book, *Six Crises*, which included a discussion of my televised debates with John F. Kennedy in 1960, he wrote back and said that he had always thought it was a mistake for me to agree to the debates. "I do not say this because I thought you lost . . . I saw two of them on television and I thought you won them. But I do think that when the campaign began you were well and favorably known to three times as many people as knew Kennedy, who, in any event, was best known on the East Coast. I thought at the time, and still think, that one of the great effects of going onto television with him with so vast a viewing public was to make him as well known as you were. I hope that you will not think me impertinent if I say that I think this was giving away a trump card."

At the time of his letter I had recently lost the 1962 California gubernatorial election. He wrote, "I cannot believe that we have, in the political world, heard the last of you." Characteristically he was unable to end without a quip: "Please give my affectionate greetings to your wife, who, like my wife, deserves a gold medal for putting up with a political husband."

Many who criticized the U.S. role in the Vietnam War did so from a neoisolationist perspective. They contended that, whether it was right or wrong to assist a free nation that was being attacked by Communists, South Vietnam was too far away to be of any real concern to the United States. No part of the new world is so far away that events there will not affect every other part of the world. Nonetheless, a quarter-century after he first coined the phrase, the "North Atlantic isolationism" that Douglas MacArthur fought against all his life was once again in vogue.

Lee and Menzies viewed the world differently. Each supported the American effort in Vietnam; Menzies, in fact, sent Australian troops to fight there beside Americans. Both leaders believed that North Vietnamese aggression presented a threat to the stability of the entire region. As Menzies put it, "To you Americans, it's the Far East. To us, it's the Near North."

Lee and Menzies were both staunch anti-Communists. As early as 1940 Menzies realized that after the end of World War II a Western European coalition including Germany, France, Great Britain, and Italy might have to be founded to contain the Soviet Union's westward thrust. Along with Lee he realized that his own country was on the front lines of the fight against communism in the Far East.

Lee's Singapore lay at the crossroads of free Asia, dependent on the continuation of trade between its neighbors. Lee believed that the spread of communism would have a deadening effect on productivity and commerce, like a heavy blanket of snow that freezes everything it covers in place. He told me as early as 1967 that a Communist Asia would experience economic and social Dark Ages. A decade later, true to his prediction, a dark age enveloped Indochina.

Lee was able to view the war in Vietnam from a global as well as a regional vantage point. "Above all," he told me, "a great nation like the United States must stand by the smaller nations who look to it for their security. If it fails to do so, the tide of Soviet expansionism and repression will sweep over the world.

"A national leader's first responsibility is survival for himself and his country," he continued. "If he loses trust in the U.S., he will have no other choice than to make the best accommodation he can with the Soviet Union."

Lee believed that only a strong America could guarantee the survival of the nations of free Asia. When he came to Washington in 1973, I told him during our private talks that the goal of my administration was to create a stable world order, including China and the Soviet Union, from which all nations would benefit, in terms both of enhanced security and of increased prosperity. That evening at the state dinner we held in his honor, he referred approvingly to my remarks and, in lighthearted but effective terms, described the discomfort a small nation could feel living among the unrestrainted, predatory Communist powers. "We are a very small country placed strategically at the southernmost tip of Asia," he said, "and when the elephants are on the rampage, if you are a mouse there and you don't know the habits of the elephants, it can be a very painful business."

Menzies also believed that it would be dangerous if the U.S. shirked its global responsibilities. He told me once that "if the Communists succeed in Vietnam, they will try elsewhere." When we talked about the war in 1965, he was visibly delighted that the U.S. had chosen to make a stand in the Far East. "Vietnam is a great new commitment in a new area," he said. When the subject of the antiwar movement came up, he just waved his hand in the air and barked, "Intellectuals!" In a way Menzies was paying back a debt with his active support of the United States in Vietnam. In World War II his country was saved from being attacked when the Americans stopped the Japanese a few hundred miles off the Australian coast in the Battle of the Coral Sea.

Menzies pursued an active foreign policy. He allied Australia with New Zealand and the United States in the ANZUS pact, an accomplishment he considered his finest; he joined SEATO; he began a politically unpopular but strategically sound rapprochement with the Japanese in the late 1950s that was capped by a state visit to Australia by Japanese Prime Minister Kishi. Under Menzies, Australia played such an active role in Asian affairs that positions in New Delhi and Djakarta were more coveted by foreign service officers than positions in Rome and Paris. "We can offer intelligent resistance to communism," he said. "There is certainly the possibility of Asian leadership before us. But we are not going to become leaders merely by proclaiming ourselves leaders."

Lee's maneuverability as a head of government was more limited than Menzies's because of Singapore's size. He was nonetheless an equally perceptive foreign policy analyst. As an ethnic Chinese whose family had lived in Singapore for several generations, Lee had a particularly intimate understanding of Asia's largest and oldest power. "Mao is painting on a mosaic," he told me in 1967. "When he dies the rains will come and wash what he has painted away, and China will remain. China always absorbs and eventually destroys foreign influences." Lee was speaking nine years before Mao's death, at a time when the Cultural Revolution was raging in China. Yet he proved to be right in predicting the decline of Mao's influence.

Lee employed similarly colorful terms as he divided the world into those nations that would make it and those that would not. "There are great trees, there are saplings, and there are creepers," he said. "The great trees are Russia, China, Western Europe, the U.S., and Japan. Of the other nations, some are saplings that have the potential of becoming great trees, but the great majority are creepers, which because of lack of resources or lack of leadership will never be great trees."

About one of Asia's "great trees," Lee said, "The Japanese inevitably will again play a major role in the world, and not just economically. They are a great people. They cannot and should not be satisfied with a world role that limits them to making better transistor radios and sewing machines, and teaching other Asians to grow rice." This had been my own belief since the early 1950s, when I first urged Japan to rearm and take its rightful place as a bastion of freedom in Asia. In Lee—who, both as a Singaporean and as an ethnic Chinese, had ample reason to resent Japan for its imperialism in the 1930s and 1940s—this attitude was the mark of a realistic and courageous leader.

Domestically Lee was one of the few postcolonial leaders in the Third World to overcome his wounded pride and channel his own and his people's energies into nation building rather than angry, destructive revolutionism. In his international thinking Lee showed a similar ability to rise above the resentments of the moment and of the past and think about the nature of the new world to come. This is a sign of true greatness, and the fact that a leader of Lee's breadth of vision was not able to act on a broader stage represents an incalculable loss to the world.

IN THE ARENA

Reflections on Leadership

"NOTHING GREAT IS done without great men," de Gaulle wrote, "and these are great because they willed it."

The successful leader has a strong will of his own, and he knows how to mobilize the will of others. The leaders in this book are ones who succeeded—some more than others—in imposing their will on history. They are men who have made a difference. Not because they *wished* it, but because they *willed* it. That distinction is vital in understanding power and those who exercise power. To wish is passive; to will is active. Followers wish. Leaders will.

Just as F. Scott Fitzgerald pointed out that the very rich are different, I have found that those who hold great power are different. It takes a particular kind of person to win the struggle for power. Having won, the power itself creates a further difference. Power is not for the nice guy down the street or for the man next door.

Of all the questions I used to be asked as President, some of the most perceptive related to the differences power makes. Some of the most irritating, on the other hand, were variations on the gushing query: "Isn't it fun to be President?"

John J. McCloy once told me of having talked with Henry L. Stimson, who had known nearly all the Presidents of the first half of this century, and asking Stimson who was the best President in terms of organizing and conducting the office. Stimson thought a moment and replied, surprisingly, that William Howard Taft was by far the most efficient and had the best-run office. But, he said, the problem with Taft was that he did not enjoy power. Who did enjoy power? McCloy asked. The two Roosevelts, Stimson replied.

Adenauer, Churchill, de Gaulle—they, too, immensely enjoyed power. But to speak of this as "fun" trivializes and demeans it. One who believes that his own judgment is best, even though fallible, and who chafes at seeing lesser men mishandle the reins of power yearns, even aches, to hold those reins himself. Watching another bungle and blunder can be almost physically painful. Once he has the reins, he relishes their use.

To enjoy power, he has to recognize that mistakes are inevitable and be able to live with them, hoping that he will make his mistakes on smaller things rather than on bigger things. Only if both elements are present—only if he enjoys power and is not afraid to risk mistakes—will he make the bold moves that great leadership requires.

Unless a leader cares so strongly about the issues he must deal with that things like "fun" become simply irrelevant, he ought not to be a leader and will probably be an unsuccessful, maybe even a dangerous, one. He should carve out time for recreation, and this can include "fun," however he defines it, but he must keep the separation between this and his work. He has to bring to his work a cold, impersonal calculation, and this applies to the ceremonial aspects as well as the substantive.

When people imagine that being President—or Prime Minister or King where a King has real power—is somehow fun, they may be thinking of the picture of a smiling leader in front of a cheering crowd, forgetting how much care went into assembling the crowd and ensuring that he smiled for the camera. Or they may be thinking of the superficial, ceremonial aspects—the panoply, the uniformed guards, the herald trumpets, the airplanes, the yachts, the motorcades, the flags. But these are not laid on for the President's pleasure. Like a judge's robes, they define the office and contribute to its functioning. A certain magisterial quality is needed, at times even a certain majesty. Foreign heads of state, especially those from smaller countries, need pictures showing themselves being welcomed with these visible totems of respect and esteem, not so much by the President personally as by the President on behalf of the nation. Anyone who thinks that standing at attention under a hot sun, having to remember names, trying to ensure that each detail of the ceremony comes off precisely as planned, is "fun" has never done it. It is part of the job.

I do not mean to suggest that I regarded the presidency as a "splendid agony" or in any of those other self-pitying terms sometimes applied to it. I wanted the presidency. I struggled to get it and I fought to keep it. I enjoyed it, most of the time—but, as with most leaders, not in the sense of fun.

History has had its share of despots who craved power for its own sake. But most leaders who rise to the top—certainly most of those whom we would call great leaders—want power for what they can do with it, believing that they can put it to better use than others can.

None of the leaders I have dealt with here was one-dimensional. None was pure. None was without mixed motives. But none wanted power solely for personal aggrandizement. Some, like Sukarno, were far too self-indulgent with regard to the demands of the flesh. Some, like Khrushchev or Mao, were far too callous about the suffering their policies inflicted. But all had a purpose beyond themselves. Each, rightly or wrongly, believed that he was serving a great cause. Each believed that he was leaving his mark on history for the better.

In speaking of leaders, we commonly use metaphors of height. We speak of them as climbing to the top, rising to the occasion, holding out a lofty vision. We routinely refer to meetings among heads of government as summits. Churchill, during his crisis over Gallipoli in World War I, once wrote an unsent letter in which he urged the foreign secretary not to fall "below the level of events."

Some leaders do, as individuals, tower over their contemporaries. But for all, the metaphors of height are peculiarly apt. They have to be able to see above the mundane and beyond the immediate. They need that view from the mountaintop.

Some people live in the present, oblivious of the past and blind to the future. Some dwell in the past. A very few have the knack of applying the past to the present in ways that show them the future. Great leaders have this knack. As Bruce Catton wrote of Lincoln, "once in a while, for this man, the sky failed to touch the horizon and he saw moving shapes, off beyond."

As military strategists, de Gaulle and MacArthur both stood above the clouds and saw into the distance. De Gaulle, protesting reliance on the Maginot Line, asked what would happen if the enemy refused to be drawn into the *compartiment de terraine*. MacArthur ignored the islands Japan had fortified and leapfrogged to those it had not.

In each case it was an example of thinking in terms of this war, this year's technology, while others thought in terms of the last war. Mobility was the key to the weakness of the Maginot Line and also to MacArthur's Pacific strategy. What seems obvious in retrospect is often not obvious at the time.

Great leaders are the ones who first see what in retrospect, but only in retrospect, is obvious, and who have both the force of will and the authority to move their countries with them. De Gaulle in the 1930s did not yet have that authority, but he demonstrated the qualities that would be crucial when he later got it. MacArthur in the 1940s had this authority. If de Gaulle had had the authority sooner, and if Churchill had had it in Britain, the history of Europe might have been different, and there might have been no World War II. De Gaulle and Churchill were, in the 1930s, ahead of their time—or, tragically, Europe had not yet learned the hard way that they were right.

Theorists like to treat power as if it were an abstraction. Leaders know better. Power anchors them to reality. Professors can go off on flights into the stratosphere of the absurd. Those with power have to keep an eye firmly on the results, the impact, the effects. Leaders deal with the concrete.

Hollywood dramatists, who have such influence through both screen and television on America's impressions of itself, are entranced by power but tend to sneer at executives, whether military, business, or political. The executive cannot tag along on giddy emotional roller-coaster rides through lands of illusion; and so he is seen as square, dull, brutish. He cannot operate as if he lived in a make-believe or ideal world. He has to cope with the imperfect world of the real. Therefore he is seen as callously indifferent to the suffering around him. In fact he is not indifferent to the ill; but he does have to concern himself with things that will actually work to help alleviate it, even if incrementally and therefore undramatically. Hollywood can posture. The executive has to perform.

In politics and statecraft, power means life or death, prosperity or poverty, happiness or tragedy, for thousands or even millions of people. No one who holds power can ever forget that, even though he must sometimes put it deliberately out of his mind while making a decision. Power is the opportunity to build, to create, to nudge history in a different direction. There are few satisfactions to match it for those who care about such things. But it is not happiness. Those who seek happiness will not acquire power and would not use it well if they did acquire it.

A whimsical observer once commented that those who love laws and sausages should not watch either being made.

By the same token, we honor leaders for what they achieve, but we often prefer to close our eyes to the way they achieve it. Schoolchildren are taught about George Washington and the cherry tree. Moralists praise the Wilsonian ideal of "open covenants, openly arrived at." Armchair pundits urge leaders to "stand up for principle," to refuse compromise, to be "a statesman rather than a politician."

In the real world, politics is compromise and democracy is politics. Anyone who would be a statesman has to be a successful politician first. Also, a leader has to deal with people and nations as they are, not as they should be. As a result, the qualities required for leadership are not necessarily those that we would want our children to emulate—unless we wanted them to be leaders.

In evaluating a leader, the key question about his behavioral traits is not whether they are attractive or unattractive, but whether they are useful. Guile, vanity, dissembling—in other circumstances these might be unattractive habits, but to the leader they can be essential. He needs guile in order to hold together the shifting coalitions of often bitterly opposed interest groups that governing requires. He needs a certain measure of vanity in order to create the right kind of public impression. He sometimes has to dissemble in order to prevail on crucial issues. Long before he acknowledged it publicly, de Gaulle confided privately that he believed independence was the only answer for Algeria. Roosevelt talked of keeping America out of war while maneuvering to bring it into war.

A leader can be out in front, ahead of public opinion, but not too far ahead. While trying to bring the public around, he often has to conceal a part of his hand, because to reveal it too soon could cost him the game. De Gaulle wrote that the statesman "must know when to dissemble, when to be frank . . . and only after a thousand intrigues and solemn undertakings will he find himself entrusted with full power." He also noted that "every man of action has a strong dose of egotism, pride, hardness, and cunning. But all those things will be forgiven him—indeed, they will be regarded as high qualities—if he can make of them the means to achieve great ends."

The less attractive aspects of leadership are not confined to politics. I have known leaders in business who were as ruthless as any politician, and church and academic leaders who schemed as deceptively and as manipulatively as any Washington bureaucrat. In fact, people who move from the academic world to government and back again often comment on how much more vicious and petty the competitive infighting is in the universities than it is in government. Academics are more sanctimonious, but hardly any more sanctified.

But whatever the field, the crucial moral questions are, in effect, those of the bottom line. Those who are wholly self-serving can be dismissed out of hand. And this applies whether their particular form of self-service involves riding roughshod over rivals or pious posturing. Those who wrap themselves in the robes of higher virtue and cause others to suffer so their own hands can remain clean—the moral robber barons—are fully as contemptible as business robber barons. Neither white collar, blue collar, nor clerical collar is any indicator of morality.

In politics the competitive aspects get more attention than they do in business, education, or the news media. But this is not because politics is more competitive. It simply is because the two fields in which competition is most public are sports and politics. In the other fields the competition is just as keen but better concealed. In my own admittedly biased view, the competition is nobler when the stakes are large questions of public policy or even the nation's survival, rather than when they are the market share for a particular brand of cereal or a couple of points in the network ratings war. Yet I find that time and again the same commentators who play the ratings game so ruthlessly turn pious when they pass judgment on the rest of us.

One of the most familiar arguments in the whole field of public philosophy is the one about whether the end justifies the means. This is sometimes addressed profoundly, but most of the discussion is superficial and fatuous.

It would be absurd to claim that a good end justifies any means; it is equally absurd to claim that when otherwise unacceptable means are necessary to a great goal, they are never justified. The human cost of defeating Axis aggression in World War II was staggering—tens of millions killed, maimed, or starved to death—but the goal justified it. Failing to fight Hitler or losing the war would have been worse.

The leader must always weigh consequences; this becomes second nature to him. He cannot be bound by rigid rules laid down arbitrarily, and in wholly different circumstances, by ones who bear no responsibility.

Neither means nor end, in isolation, can be used as the measure of a leader. Unless he has a great cause, he can never be in the front rank. Leadership must serve a purpose, and the higher that purpose the greater the potential stature of the leader. But purpose is not enough. He also has to perform. He has to produce results, and he has to do so in a way that serves that higher purpose. He must not use means that disgrace or undo the purpose. But if he does not produce results, he fails his cause and fails history.

We think of Abraham Lincoln as a supreme idealist, and he was. But he was also a cold pragmatist and a total politician. His pragmatism and his political skills were what enabled him to make his ideals prevail. As a politician, in terms of such nitty-gritty things as patronage, he played the game to the hilt. As a pragmatist, when he freed the slaves he did so only in the states of the Confederacy, not in those border states that remained within the Union. As an idealist, his one consuming passion during that time of supreme crisis was to preserve the Union. Toward that end he broke laws, he violated the Constitution, he usurped arbitrary power, he trampled individual liberties. His justification was necessity. Explaining his sweeping violation of constitutional limits, he wrote in a letter in 1864:

> My oath to preserve the Constitution imposed on me the duty of preserving by every indispensable means that government, that nation, of which the Constitution was the organic law. Was it possible to lose the nation and yet preserve the Constitution? By general law life and limb must be protected, yet often a limb must be amputated to save a life, but a life is never wisely given to save a limb. I felt that measures, otherwise unconstitutional, might become lawful by becoming indispensable to the preservation of the Constitution through the preservation of the nation. Right or wrong, I assumed this ground and now avow it.

More than forty years ago, Max Lerner wrote a brilliant introduction to an edition of Machiavelli's works. In it Lerner suggested that one reason we "still shudder slightly at Machiavelli's name" is our recognition that the realities he described *are* realities; that men, whether in politics, in business or in private life, do *not* act according to their professions of virtue ... Machiavelli today confronts us with the major dilemma of how to adapt our democratic techniques and concepts to the demands of a world in which as never before naked power politics dominates the foreign field and determined oligarchies struggle for power internally.

It is difficult to quarrel with Lerner's conclusion:

Let us be clear about one thing: ideals and ethics are important in politics as norms, but they are scarcely effective as techniques. The successful statesman is an artist, concerned with nuances of public mood, approximations of operative modes, guesswork as to the tactics of his opponents, back-breaking work in unifying his own side by compromise and concession. Religious reformers have often succeeded in bringing public morale closer to some ethical norm; they have never succeeded as statesmen.

It is often said that the key to success in any field, including politics, is to "be yourself." However, most of the great leaders I have known were accomplished actors, though only de Gaulle candidly admitted it. Like great stage performers, they played their public role so well that they virtually became the parts that they created.

Khrushchev was calculating in his use of bombast, de Gaulle equally calculating in his use of symbols of French grandeur. Each in a different way was compensating for his country's deficiencies. Khrushchev acted the bully, de Gaulle acted the haughty seigneur; each was playing at a sort of psychological gamesmanship. But although both were calculated, neither was phony. Khrushchev *was* a bully; de Gaulle *was* haughty; Khrushchev *was* crude; de Gaulle *was* a passionately patriotic Frenchman who believed in his country's grandeur. And this is important: To play the role successfully, the leader has to fit the role.

Adolf Hitler was the supreme demagogue of the twentieth century. With his voice, he could mesmerize the multitudes, and he whipped millions into frenzies of hate and fear as well as patriotism. Could de Gaulle have done the same if his goals had been those of Hitler? No. For de Gaulle's great strength, his appeal, lay to a crucial extent in his moral authority: One can no more imagine de Gaulle inciting a mob to murder than taking off his clothes in public. He succeeded because his character fit the role, and his role was one of marshaling the best of France.

Some great leaders take pains to conceal their humanity; some flaunt it, even exaggerate it. There is a vast difference of style between the lofty grandeur of a de Gaulle and the earthy exuberance of a flesh-pressing Lyndon Johnson. Yet each was effective in his own way, in part because each man was, in a very real sense, larger than life. The Johnson "treatment" was legendary, and it was physical as well as rhetorical. De Gaulle, like George Washington, remained always wrapped in a cocoon of almost regal reserve. The person Johnson was trying to persuade found himself wrapped in Lyndon Johnson.

No one becomes a major leader without a strong will, or without a strong ego. Lately it has become fashionable to try to conceal ego, to pretend that it does not exist, to present instead an outward modesty. But I have never known a major leader who was not an egotist. Some of these leaders affected a modest air, but none was a modest person. Modesty was a pose, a device, just as MacArthur's corncob pipe was a device and Churchill's strut was a pose. A person has to believe in himself if he is to win mastery over the forces leaders deal with. He has to believe in his cause if he is going to punish himself the way leaders must. Unless he believes in himself, he is not going to persuade others to believe in him.

In 1947 I was told by one French critic of de Gaulle that "in political matters he thinks that he has a direct telephone line with God and that in making decisions all he has to do is to get on the wire and get the word straight from God." Those leaders who succeed in imposing their own will on history are sometimes right, sometimes wrong, but seldom unsure. They listen to their own instincts. They assemble the advice of others, but follow their own judgment. The leaders I have dealt with in this book would sometimes make mistakes, but they were supremely confident that they would be more nearly right more of the time if they pursued their own vision and went by their own instincts. They had no doubt that they were at the top for a reason: because they were the best for the job. And, being the best, they were not going to defer to the second best.

That inner voice is something a leader's ear grows attuned to. The exercise of power trains it. As he grows accustomed to seeing large consequences flowing from his own decisions, the leader grows more comfortable making those decisions and more ready to risk the results of his own error rather than accept the consequences of someone else's error.

A leader may go through agony in deciding what to do. But few successful leaders spend much time fretting about decisions once they are past, wondering whether they were right. The hard decisions I had to make in trying to bring American involvement in Vietnam to an end were often close decisions. When advisers who participated in those decisions would privately express doubts afterward about whether they were right, I would often say, "Remember Lot's wife. Never look back." If the leader dwells too much on whether his decisions were right, he becomes paralyzed. The only way he can give adequate attention to the decisions he has to make tomorrow is to put those of yesterday firmly behind him.

This does not mean he does not learn from his mistakes. It does mean that his reflection on them should be analytical, not compulsive or guilt-ridden, and that it should basically be confined to those periods when he has time for reflection. De Gaulle in his "wilderness" years, Adenauer in prison and in the monastery, Churchill out of power, de Gasperi in the Vatican library—all had time to reflect, and all used it well. I found that some of my own most valuable years were those between the vice presidency and the presidency, when I was able to step back from the center of events and look in a more measured way at the past and the future.

All the great leaders I have known were, deep down, very emotional, which may be another way of saying they were very human. Some, like Churchill, displayed their emotions openly. Others, such as Khrushchev, used them shamelessly. De Gaulle, Adenauer, MacArthur, Zhou Enlai, and Yoshida were examples of the controlled, self-disciplined leader who presents to the public a front that conceals personal feelings. But anyone who knew them well would have found the deeply emotional core within the walls of an intense feeling of privacy.

One reason why it is frequently so difficult to sort out myth from reality in reading about political leaders is that part of political leadership is the creation of myths. Churchill was a master of this. He was constantly onstage. For de Gaulle mystery, honor, detachment, the applause of the multitude, were all instruments of statecraft, to be used to further the cause of France. The extraordinary emotional hold that hereditary monarchs have so often had on their subjects is less a matter of individual personality than it is of romantic myth. We wrap movie stars, rock stars, and now television celebrities, in the trappings of myth, and this is what makes the crowd swoon—and flock to buy tickets.

The politician, no less than the actor or the filmmaker, knows that to bore his audience is to lose his audience. Thus, few great political leaders are dull. They cannot afford to be. Political leadership has to appeal to the head, but it must also appeal to the heart. The wisest course is likely to fail unless the leader who advocates it is able to reach the people on an emotional level.

We cannot find the stuff of leadership in the dry pages of a history text. To find it, we have to look into the spirit of the man, to see what it is that sustains and drives him and enables him to drive or to persuade others. We see this in a MacArthur and a Churchill—proud, vain, paradoxical, posing always, yet brilliant, insightful, with their eyes on the long view of history; driven men, driving others, whose views of their own destinies coincided more often than not with their views of their countries' destinies. We also must look at the legends. Legends are often an artful intertwining of fact and myth, designed to beguile, to impress, to inspire, or sometimes simply to attract attention. But legend is an essential ingredient of leadership.

Some aspects of leadership are common to all fields—business, sports, the arts, the academic community. But some are peculiar to the political process or at least loom larger in the political process.

Prominence by itself is not leadership; nor is excellence. Excellence can be achieved in a solitary field without the need to exercise leadership. Writers or painters or musicians can practice their art without leading. Inventors or chemists or mathematicians can exercise their genius in solitude. But political leaders have to inspire followers. Great ideas can change history, but only if great leadership comes along that can give those ideas force.

By the same token the "great" leader is not necessarily good. Adolf Hitler electrified a nation. Joseph Stalin was brutally effective at wielding power. Ho Chi Minh became a folk hero to millions beyond the borders of Vietnam. The good and the bad alike can be equally driven, equally determined, equally skilled, equally persuasive. Leadership itself is morally neutral; it can be used for good or for ill.

Thus, virtue is not what lifts great leaders above others. Others are more virtuous but less successful. The maxim "Nice guys finish last" is far more applicable to politics than to sports. What lifts great leaders above the second-raters is that they are more forceful, more resourceful, and have a shrewdness of judgment that spares them the fatal error and enables them to identify the fleeting opportunity.

Neither is brilliance, in an intellectual sense, their defining characteristic. All the major leaders discussed here were highly intelligent. All had keen analytical capacities. All were deep thinkers. But they tended to think concretely rather than abstractly, to measure consequences rather than construct theories. The average professor sees the world through the prism of his own values and therefore exalts theory. To the leader theories can be a useful springboard for analysis. But they must never be a substitute for analysis.

One of the most obvious questions about leadership is also one of the most elusive: What is the most important characteristic a successful leader must have? There is of course no single answer. Different qualities are required in different circumstances. But certainly high intelligence, courage, hard work, tenacity, judgment, dedication to a great cause, and a certain measure of charm are all key ingredients. In political campaigns I used to say that what we had to do was "outwork, outthink, and outfight" the opposition. The great leader needs insight, foresight, and the willingness to take the bold but calculated risk. He also needs luck. Above all, he must be decisive. He must analyze his choices shrewdly and dispassionately, but then he must act. He must not become a Hamlet. He must not succumb to "paralysis by analysis." He also must want the job, and he must be willing to pay the price. There is a persistent myth that if only a person is well enough qualified, the office will—or should—somehow seek him. It will not, and it should not. This myth of the "reluctant candidate" was, for much of the intellectual world, a part of Adlai Stevenson's attraction. But show me a reluctant candidate and I will show you a losing candidate. A reluctant candidate will not give a campaign the intensity of effort it requires, nor will he accept the sacrifices leadership itself requires: the ruthless invasion of privacy, the grueling schedule, the sting of unfair and often vicious criticism, the cruel caricatures. Unless a person is prepared to accept this and still be ready to pursue the job with passion, he is not going to have the steel to stand it once he gets it.

One need, often overlooked, has tripped up many a brilliant prospective leader on the way to the top. Winston Churchill wrote of one of Britain's potentially great leaders of the nineteenth century that "he would not stoop; he did not conquer." In this country Thomas E. Dewey and Robert A. Taft lacked this quality, and the lack may well have cost them the presidency. At a political dinner in New York in 1952, I was sitting next to Dewey when a somewhat drunken guest slapped him on the back and greeted him with what Dewey considered a too-easy familiarity. Dewey brushed him aside and asked me, "Who was that fatuous ass?" It had been the owner of a chain of small but important Upstate New York newspapers. In the New Hampshire primary in 1952 a little girl asked Taft for an autograph. Taft refused, explaining stiffly that he would be glad to shake hands but that if he took time to grant all autograph requests he would never get his campaigning done. Unfortunately for Taft, the incident was captured on television and shown over and over again in the living rooms of America. However impeccable his logic, the effect was politically devastating.

Because the leader is busy, because he has a large ego, because he resents intrusions and distractions, because he considers himself superior, he may have little patience with those he perceives as his inferiors. The trouble with this inability to "tolerate fools" is threefold. First, the leader needs followers—and a lot of those he needs have ideas he would consider foolish. Second, the man he is tempted to dismiss as a fool may not be. Third, even if he is, the leader might learn from him. Leadership requires a sort of mystical bond between the leader and the people; if the leader appears to show disdain for the people, that bond is likely to snap. However, one must always remember that leaders *are* uncommon men. They should not try to appear to be common. If they do try, they will come across as unnatural—not only phony, but condescending.

People may like the boy next door, but that does not mean that they want him as their President, or even as their congressman. The successful leader does not talk down to people. He lifts them up. He must never be arrogant. He must be willing and able to "tolerate fools." He must show that he respects the people whose support he seeks. But he must also retain that quality of *difference* that allows them to look up to him. If he asks for their confidence, he must inspire their faith. This approach is not only honest—if he were common, he would not be a leader—but it also is necessary to creation of the leadership mystique in a democratic society.

The leader must learn not only how to talk, but also when—and equally important, when to stop talking. Carlyle once commented that "silence is the element in which great things fashion themselves." De Gaulle pointed out trenchantly that silence can be a powerful instrument for a leader. It also is when we are listening, not when we are talking, that we learn.

Time and again I have seen newcomers to Washington dazzle the media and even their colleagues with their seeming ability to speak articulately and at length on any subject. But soon the novelty wears off, and they find themselves judged not by how they speak but by what they say—and are dismissed as not being what the French call *hommes serieux*. Frequently the glibbest talker turns out to be the shallowest thinker. A good rule for the would-be leader, when he has a choice, is to exercise his tongue less and his brain more.

In his essay on Lord Rosebery, Churchill wrote: "Whatever one may think about democratic government, it is just as well to have practical experience of its rough and slatternly foundations. No part of the education of a politician is more indispensable than the fighting of elections."

Churchill knew what it was both to win and to lose, and to be roughed up in the political thicket. He was right about the educational value of waging a campaign. Elections are "rough and slatternly," but they are essential both to the democratic system and to the interaction between leader and led. Democratic government is an extremely complex process of give and take among a multitude of groups, forces, and interests. The cliché that a leader should be a statesman and not a politician is grossly condescending toward the democratic system and shows contempt for the voting public. The pundits who sit in their lofty towers dispensing disdain for the political process are really dictators at heart.

The leader should of course be out ahead of the people. He should have a clearer perception than they of where the country should be going, and why, and of what it takes to get there. But he has to carry the people with him. It makes no sense to blow the trumpet for the charge, then look back and find no one following. He has to persuade. He has to win the people's consent to the vision he holds out. In the process—in the wooing that precedes the winning—he can learn a great deal about their concerns, their reservations, their hopes and fears, all of which are things that, as a leader, he must deal with. In that same process he can also get a better idea of the kinds of compromises he is going to have to make.

The pundit who exalts "standing firm for principle" and condemns compromise demands, in effect, that the leader throw himself on the sword. Very few leaders are willing to do that. Nor should they. What the pundit fails to see is that the leader frequently has to compromise in order to live to fight another day. Knowing when to compromise is part of the process of choosing priorities. It is easy for the armchair strategist to conclude breathlessly that the leader must fight and win on this battle or that one without taking into account the other battles he must fight. There are times when the one who has responsibility will conclude that the cost of winning a particular battle is too great if he is going to succeed in winning the war. He must choose which battles he will fight and which he will not fight, so that he can husband his resources for more important battles to come.

If the successful leader has to know when to compromise, he also has to know when to go his own way. Too many politicians today ride toward destiny "at full Gallup." The candidate who slavishly follows the polls may get elected, but he will not be a great leader or even a good one. Polls can be useful in identifying those areas where particular persuasion is needed. But if he sets his course by them, he abdicates his role as a leader. The task of the leader is not to follow the polls but to make the polls follow him.

The successful leader must know when to fight and when to retreat, when to be rigid and when to compromise, when to speak out and when to be silent.

He must take the long view—he must have a clear strategy as well as a goal and a vision.

He must take the complete view—he must see the relation of one decision to others.

He must stay in front, but not so far in front that he loses his followers.

In the "rough and slatternly" process of electioneering, he has a chance to move his followers forward and also to measure how far ahead he can afford to get. If the Shah of Iran had had to campaign, he might not have lost his country.

A general needs troops but also a command structure. A political leader needs followers but also an organization.

One of the hardest things for many leaders to accept is the need for delegation. Eisenhower once put this in capsule form when he commented to me that the most difficult thing he had to overcome as an executive was learning to sign a bad letter: that is, to put his signature on one that had been written for him, even though he knew that he himself could have done it better.

A leader's most precious resource is his time. If he squanders it on the nonessentials, he will fail. Among his most important choices are those in which he selects what he will do himself and what he will leave to others—and also those in which he selects the people to whom he will delegate. The leader has to be able to get good people, and also to get rid of those who for whatever reason do not work out. Gladstone once commented that the first requisite for a Prime Minister is to be a good butcher. Firing people can be one of the most difficult tasks a leader faces but also one of the most essential. The easy cases are those where the subordinate is venal or disloyal. The tougher ones are those in which he is loyal, dedicated, but incompetent—or where there simply is someone else available who would be better. That is when the leader has to steel himself to put public responsibility ahead of personal feelings. But even this requires qualification. Loyalty is a two-way street, and he cannot retain a loyal staff if he operates a revolving door. So he has to strike a balance. But in striking it, he must resist the inertia that makes it easier not to make changes. He must be a butcher both to ensure that what he delegates is done well and to ensure that he feels free to delegate. He has only a limited time in which to exercise power. He has to make the most of the time that he has. If he cannot be a good butcher himself, he needs someone who can be. General Walter Bedell Smith once broke into tears as he told me, "I was just Ike's pratboy. Ike always had to have a pratboy." In my own administration Bob Haldeman got a reputation for ruthlessness. One reason was that he performed for me a lot of the butcher's tasks that I could not bring myself to perform directly.

Especially where a huge bureaucracy is involved, the butcher's function is vital for another reason. I have found that, generally, a few people in the bureaucracy are motivated by devotion to the leader, and some by devotion to the cause he represents. But most are motivated primarily by self-interest. Some want advancement—to move up the ladder competitively. Some want security—to keep the jobs that they have. The worst thing that an organization can do is to provide too much security. The people grow lax, and the organization grows ineffective. Positive incentives are needed to maintain morale. But an occasional firing, for evident good reason, will shake up the troops and provide a tonic that every organization needs.

In the final analysis, delegation can never be a substitute for the leader's thinking a problem through and making the key decisions on the major issues. He can and must delegate to others the responsibility for *doing* things. He cannot and should not delegate to others the responsibility for *deciding* what should be done. This is what he was selected to do. If he lets his staff do his thinking for him, he becomes a follower rather than a leader.

In assembling a staff, the conservative leader faces a greater problem than does the liberal. In general, liberals want more government and hunger to be the ones running it. Conservatives want less government and want no part of it. Liberals want to run other people's lives. Conservatives want to be left alone to run their own lives. Academics tend to be liberals; engineers tend to be conservatives. Liberals flock to government; conservatives have to be enticed and persuaded. With a smaller field to select from, the conservative leader often has to choose between those who are loyal but not bright and those who are bright but not loyal—in the sense not of personal integrity but of deep-rooted commitment to the leader's conservative principles.

Some things are relatively easy for a leader to delegate: those that others can clearly do better than he can. De Gaulle, Adenauer, and Yoshida were not first-rate economists themselves. Each had the good sense to put economic matters in the hands of people who were: Pompidou, Erhard, and Ikeda.

Eisenhower's bad-letter example points up the more difficult kind of choice: where the leader must delegate things he could do better, because he cannot or should not spare the time. This requires the ability to separate the essential from the important, as well as the self-restraint to let others handle the important. The tendency of many leaders is to get bogged down in small matters because they cannot bring themselves to "sign a bad letter." Lyndon Johnson's insistence on personally picking the bombing targets in Vietnam is a case in point.

In a sense it can be argued that everything that crosses a President's desk is important; otherwise it would never get that far. But he cannot attend to everything. The big man is hired for the big decisions, not to fritter away his time and attention on small ones. There will be times when urgent questions of social and economic policy require his attention; there will be times when he must concentrate on crucial questions of foreign policy; there will be times when he has to escape the urgencies and focus instead on transcendent questions of the long-term future. What he delegates today might not be what he would delegate tomorrow. He needs the flexibility to shift priorities with shifting needs. But he must have the ability to push away from his desk those decisions, however important individually, that would impair his ability to deal as he should with those that are his preeminent responsibility.

The situation has an analogy in baseball. Many good hitters hit for the averages, trying for singles in order to push their averages toward .300. But these are not the great hitters who make the headlines and draw thousands into the park. The great hitters, the Reggie Jacksons, are the ones who hit in the clutch, who go not for the averages but for the game-winning home runs. The leader must organize his life and concentrate his energies with one overriding goal in mind: to make the big plays. These are the ones by which he makes his mark on history. He can go for the averages and be average. If he tries too hard to do everything well, he will not do the really important things extraordinarily well. He will not rise above the pack. If he wants to be a great leader, he has to concentrate on the great decisions.

Before he became President, Woodrow Wilson delivered a speech in which he differentiated between men of thought and men of action. In politics it has been my observation that too often the man of thought cannot act and the man of action does not think. The ideal is one like Wilson himself, who was a great creative thinker and also, when he was still at his best, a decisive man of action. Generally the most effective leaders I have known have been among those few who were both men of thought and men of action. The French philosopher Henri Bergson once advised, "Act as men of thought. Think as men of action."

Those periods in which the right balance is maintained between thought and action are those in which leadership reaches its highest achievement. Certainly Churchill, de Gaulle, MacArthur, Yoshida, de Gasperi, Nehru, and Zhou Enlai were profoundly men of thought as well as decisive men of action. Superficial appraisals of Adenauer would conclude that he was an impressive man of action, but not in the others' league as a man of thought. In fact those who knew Adenauer would recognize the fallacy of such an appraisal. He did not wear his intellectual superiority on his sleeve. But those who failed to see it simply did not know the private man beneath the public facade.

Even the impulsive Khrushchev usually thought before he acted, though, like Brezhnev, he did not demonstrate great philosophical or intellectual depth. However, those who led the Communist Revolution in Russia—Lenin, Trotsky, and Stalin—were men of thought as well as men of action. Stalin does not have the reputation, but those who have studied his background have found that he was at least a voracious reader. Though the world would be better off without their achievements, those three rank high among the men who have left their mark on history.

Robert Menzies once told me that he regulated his day so that he could devote half an hour each weekday, and an hour each Saturday and Sunday, to reading for pleasure. This was not escapist reading: It was history, literature, philosophy. It lifted him out of the morass of reports, analyses, and other current reading that so consumes a leader's time and assails his mind. Though I regulated it less precisely, I also made a point of making time for such reading, even during periods of crisis. If the leader is to keep his long perspective, he must step back from the present. Sometimes the need for this is greatest when the crisis is most urgent, because that is when the long perspective is most needed. When young people whose goal is political leadership ask me how they should prepare themselves, I never advise them to study political science. Rather, I advise them to immerse themselves in history, philosophy, literature—to seek to stretch their minds and expand their horizons. The nuts and bolts, whether of politics or of government, are best learned by experience. But the habits of reading, the disciplines of thinking, the techniques of rigorous analysis, the framework of values, the philosophical foundation—these are things the would-be leader must absorb from the beginning of his educational process and must continue to absorb for the rest of his life.

Even at the age of ninety, my friend and mentor, the late Elmer Bobst, was still razor-sharp and had a phenomenal memory. I once asked him how he remembered so well. "I punish my memory," he replied. Rather than take notes, he forced himself to remember conversations, in all their detail, a day later. He also reminded me that the brain is like a great muscle. The more exercise it gets, the stronger it grows; unused, it withers away.

One common characteristic of virtually all the great leaders I have known is that they have been great readers. Reading not only enlarges and challenges the mind; it also engages and exercises the brain. Today's youth who sits mesmerized by a television screen is not going to be tomorrow's leader. Television watching is passive. Reading is active.

Another common characteristic is that all were hard workers, many of the sixteen-hour-a-day variety. One of the most dangerous traps for a leader to fall into is the trap of overly long hours. Some thrive on this. But most need to get away, to get a change of scene or a change of pace, so that they will be at their best when they need to be. Truman went to Key West, Eisenhower to Colorado and Georgia, Kennedy to Hyannis Port, Johnson to his Texas ranch; all were criticized for this, but none should have been. The important thing in a leader is not how many hours he spends at his desk, or where that desk is, but how well he makes the great decisions. If a game of golf is what it takes to put him in the right frame of mind, then he should push aside the paperwork and head for the golf course.

Of all the elements of luck that enter into a leader's success, perhaps the luck of timing is the most crucial.

Different cultures bring forth different kinds of leaders, and so do different ages. It would be difficult to imagine a Disraeli winning an election in the United States in the 1980s, or, for that matter, a Konrad Adenauer or a George Washington.

Sometimes a person comes along who would have been a superb leader, one of world stature, if only he had been born a few years earlier or a few years later. I am convinced that Senator Richard Russell of Georgia could have been one of the best Presidents America ever had if he had come along at a time when his southern origins did not disqualify him. As it was, he was an immensely influential power behind the scenes in the Senate, and a protégé whom he tutored and counseled, Lyndon Johnson, did make it to the White House. During my service as senator, Vice President, and President, I valued his judgment more highly than that of any other senator. Except on civil rights, we seldom disagreed. He was a moderate conservative on domestic issues and a tough-minded, farsighted pragmatist on defense and foreign policy issues.

Russell exemplified another phenomenon. He provided his guidance in the cloakrooms, in committee rooms, in private sessions. He seldom spoke even on the Senate floor, though when he did the entire Senate listened. What he wielded most spectacularly was not the power of actual decision, but influence; he had such influence that his influence became power. In his case the influence was rooted in the genuine respect that other senators, and Presidents, had for him. It was also rooted in his meticulous homework, his attention to detail, and his encyclopedic knowledge of the Senate and its members.

One of the defining characteristics of the new world is the increasingly rapid pace at which things change. A country that needs one kind of ruler for one phase of its development may need another kind for the next phase, and these phases may come in rapid succession. In terms of its impact on a leader's place in history, getting offstage at the right time can sometimes be as important as getting onstage at the right time.

If Nkrumah had turned over the reins to someone else after Ghana gained its independence, he would have exited a hero and remained a hero. Nasser's reputation is probably greater today than it would have been if death had not cut short his rule when it did. It may well be that one of de Gaulle's shrewdest moves was to exit when he did in 1946, so that he remained politically intact for the moment when the call came in 1958. George Washington knew when to quit. His refusal to run for a third term set a tradition that lasted until 1940, and that, once broken, was written into the Constitution. Lyndon Johnson stunned the nation when he announced in 1968 that he would not run for reelection. As the one who confronted the storms that swept the country during those next four years, I think that, however much he hated being in retirement, luck was with him in getting him off the stage at that time. He would have been savaged mercilessly if he had remained in office.

Different systems need different kinds of leaders, and different countries—with different cultural backgrounds and at different stages of development—need different systems.

One of the most persistent faults in America's dealings with the rest of the world has been our tendency to measure all governments by the standards of western democracy and all cultures by the standards of Western Europe. Western democracy took centuries to develop and take root, and its path was not straight or sure. Freedom advanced in Europe by fits and starts, moving ahead in one age only to be pushed back in another—as happened in parts of Western Europe in the 1930s and in Eastern Europe in more recent years.

Democracy is still the exception rather than the rule among the world's nations. As U.S. Ambassador to the U.N., Jeane J. Kirkpatrick has pointed out, "The truth is that most of the governments in the world are, by our standards, bad governments. [They] are not democratic [and] never have been. Democracy has been rare in the world. Most governments are, by our standards, corrupt." Among the majority of countries that are ruled by authoritarian or totalitarian methods, we must learn to be more discriminating. Every authoritarian ruler puts at least some of his opponents in jail, whether his aim is to exploit his people or to develop his country. But there are vital distinctions between those who arm for aggression and those who try to preserve the peace; between the murderous fanaticism of a Pol Pot and the progressive paternalism of a Shah. Some are good neighbors and some are bad neighbors. Some are benign and some are malign. These differences are real, and they are important.

We may not like authoritarian rule, but for many countries there simply is no practical alternative at their present stages. If democracy came tomorrow morning to Saudi Arabia or Egypt, the result would probably be disaster. They simply are not prepared to deal with it. We do less developed countries no service when we insist on imposing the same structures that have worked for us. And to insist on the forms of democracy, knowing that the substance is unlikely, is the worst form of self-righteous hypocrisy. We should learn to be less meddlesome.

Of all the changes taking place in the new world, one that will have a particularly dramatic impact on future leadership is the crumbling of those barriers that in the past have held women back. Few have made it to the top so far. Indira Gandhi, Golda Meir, and Margaret Thatcher have been the exception rather than the rule. But more and more women are moving into the ranks from which leaders are drawn. The woman candidate for a top executive office still has to overcome a residue of the old presumption that such positions are a male preserve. But as more move up, that presumption will fade.

If, in 1952, acceptance of the idea of women in high office had advanced as far as it has today, Clare Boothe Luce could well have been a strong candidate for Vice President. She had the brains, the drive, the political acumen, the judgment, and she was the first really interesting woman to make a major mark in American politics. She also had a well-honed ability to engage in the cut-and-thrust of political conflict and she was identified as a strongly committed anti-Communist—two of the specific qualities for which Eisenhower chose me. If he had chosen her instead, this book might never have been written. But she would have turned in a stellar performance.

In 1952 Clare Boothe Luce was ahead of her time. But I believe that before the end of the century we will probably elect a woman to the vice presidency and possibly to the presidency.

At first glance it may seem surprising that so many of the great leaders during this period were so old. And yet on reflection it is not surprising. Many had a "wilderness" period. The insights and wisdom they gained during that period, and the strength they developed in fighting back from it, were key elements in the greatness they demonstrated later. Churchill, de Gaulle, and Adenauer all made their greatest contributions when they were past what we think of as the normal retirement age. Churchill was already sixty-six when he began his wartime leadership of Britain, de Gaulle sixty-seven when he created the Fifth Republic, and Adenauer was seventy-three when he took the reins as Chancellor. De Gaulle was still President at seventy-eight, Churchill was still Prime Minister at eighty, and Adenauer was still Chancellor at eighty-seven.

The twentieth century has seen a medical revolution. We live longer and we stay healthier. But beyond this, the same drive and the same stamina that propel the great leader up often keep him going long after others have settled into placid retirement. Often we age because we allow ourselves to age. We grow old by giving up, or by sitting back, or by letting ourselves become inactive. Those who remember the long, drawn-out deathwatches over Churchill, Eisenhower, and MacArthur remember how stubbornly their bodies refused to give up, even long after they had sunk into unconsciousness. Great leaders make their own rules, and they are not the kind to surrender meekly to the calendar merely because that is the customary thing to do.

A leader must sometimes rally his people to follow a painful and difficult course, as Churchill so memorably did when he offered the people of Britain "blood, toil, tears, and sweat." More often, he has to win support for an unpopular idea, or prevail against strong tides of intellectual fashion. Philosopher-theologian Michael Novak has noted that today, "in a world of instantaneous, universal mass communications, the balance of power has now shifted. Ideas, always a part of reality, have today acquired power greater than that of reality. . . . The class of persons who earn their livelihood from the making of ideas and symbols seems both unusually bewitched by falsehoods and absurdities and uniquely empowered to impose them upon hapless individuals." Frequently the leader's toughest battles are not against the leaders of other political movements as such, but against those glib, superficial, and destructive ideas that so pervade the airwaves, entrance the "glitterati," and debase public discourse.

Television today has transformed the ways in which national leadership is exercised and has substantially changed the kind of person who can hope to be elected to a position of leadership. Abraham Lincoln, with his homely features and high-pitched voice, would never have made it on television. Nor would his speaking style, with its long, rambling anecdotes, have worked on the tube. The premium today is on snappy one-liners, not lengthy parables.

Television has drastically shortened the public's attention span. It also changes the way people see things and events. Like a mind-altering drug, which in a very real sense it is, it distorts their perception of reality. The neat little capsule dramas that we see on the screen—whether presented as entertainment, as "news," or as part of a magazine format designed as entertainment in the guise of investigation—are not mirrors of life. They are distorting mirrors. Real-life events seldom have so neat a beginning, middle, and end, nor are good guys and bad guys so clearly distinguished. Decisions that leaders sweat over for weeks are routinely dismissed in twenty seconds with the curl of a commentator's lip.

In the television age, celebrity has acquired a whole new dimension. A television actor is invited to advise a Senate committee on medical questions because he plays the part of a doctor on a popular weekly program. Another actor who portrays an editor is asked to lecture at journalism schools. The line between fact and fantasy is blurred into invisibility, and increasingly the public accepts this blurring.

Television is a home version of Hollywood. It is a fantasy land, and the more people get in the habit of viewing the world through the television screen, the more they will carry in their minds the image of a fantasy world.

Some argue that the worst thing about television is its pervasive left-wing bias. Others argue that the worst thing is its trivializing of events, its obsession with scandal or the appearance of scandal, its unwillingness or inability to present the dull or complex, or its milking of the emotional angle of every public issue. All of these, unfortunately, contribute to its distortion of public debate.

Whether democratic nations can survive against a determined totalitarian foe in a television age is perhaps still an open question. Television forces events into a soap-opera mold, and it does so with such emotional force and such an enormous audience that it all but eclipses rational debate. It especially does so in situations that lend themselves to dramatic, emotionally loaded footage of such scenes as a bleeding soldier or a hungry child. Hard choices often have to be made among different sets of painful consequences. By concentrating so powerfully on the pain from one of those sets of consequences, television badly skews the debate and, in effect, stuffs the ballot-box. Television cast the Iranian hostage crisis so exclusively in soap-opera terms that people eventually accepted a national display of yellow ribbons as a substitute for national policy. The kind of one-sided coverage television gave the war in Vietnam was probably the single most significant factor in so limiting our options there that the war was lengthened and ultimately lost.

Unless television steps up to its duty to reflect reality more accurately, whoever tries to lead responsibly in the years ahead is going to have a very difficult time.

Television does, however, provide the leader with one advantage that can be crucial, particularly in a crisis situation. It enables him to go directly to the people, to reach them in their own living rooms, and to make his case to them without the intervention of reporters and commentators. He can do it only occasionally. But when he does, for a few minutes, before the commentators again take over, he can explain the situation as he sees it, in his own terms, and try to persuade them of the course of action necessary. In the hands of a person skilled in its use, this can be an enormously powerful instrument. There is an inherent drama in a presidential appearance during a crisis, and this drama builds the audience and rivets its attention. He then has to get his message across to his viewers, and he has only a short time in which to do so: After twenty minutes or so, the audience for a speech usually stops paying attention. But he does have that one shot, once in a while.

As between the determinist and the "great man" approaches to the study of history, the truth probably is that each is partially right and neither is wholly right.

History does have its own momentum. When the "leaders" in power merely stick a moistened index finger into the air to see which way the popular wind is blowing, then history will go its own way despite them. But when leaders who do have a clear vision of the future and the power to sway nations are in command, they will change the course of history. That is when history becomes a series of tracks in the wilderness that show where one man went first and then persuaded others to follow.

Great leaders excite great controversies. They acquire strong friends and bitter enemies. It should be no surprise that different people see the same leader in different ways, or that judgments conflict, or that judgments change.

Always, the leader operates on multiple levels. There is the public persona and the private person, the face that millions see, and the face that the small group through which he governs sees. That group may see the private person or it may not; he often has to make every bit as much of an effort to be persuasive with the inside group as with the mass audience. Allies and adversaries may see different aspects of him, as may the representatives of the many different constituencies he has to reach. The parable of the three blind men and the elephant applies to the ways in which leaders are perceived. Each of the blind men encountered one part of the elephant and extrapolated from that. Similarly each critic, each commentator, each adversary, each ally, encounters one aspect of the leader and tends to extrapolate from that.

Sadat cited an Arab aphorism that says a ruler is naturally opposed by half of his subjects if he happens to be just. All leaders live with opposition. All hope to be vindicated by history. The reputations of some grow after they leave office. The reputations of others shrink. The judgment of history sometimes turns giants into pygmies. And sometimes the men earlier dismissed as pygmies are turned into giants. Harry Truman was scorned when he left the presidency in 1953, but he gets high marks as a leader today.

The final verdict of history is not rendered quickly. It takes not just years but decades or generations to be handed down. Few leaders live to hear the verdict. Herbert Hoover was an exception. No leader in American history was more viciously vilified. Deserted by his friends and maligned by his enemies, he finally triumphed over adversity. In the twilight of his life he stood tall above his detractors. His life illustrates the truth of de Gaulle's favorite line from Sophocles: "One must wait until the evening to see how splendid the day has been."

All of the leaders in this book had their successes and failures, their strengths and weaknesses, their virtues and vices. We can only guess how historians will evaluate their respective legacies a century from now. That will depend in part on who wins the world struggle and who writes the histories. But these leaders did not shrink from the battle. They entered the arena. And, as Theodore Roosevelt put it in a speech at the Sorbonne in 1910:

> It is not the critic who counts; not the man who points out how the strong man stumbles, or where the doer of deeds could have done them better. The credit belongs to the man who is actually in the arena, whose face is marred by dust and sweat and blood; who strives valiantly; who errs, and comes short again and again; because there is not effort without error and shortcoming; but who does actually strive to do the deeds; who knows the great enthusiasms, the great devotions; who spends himself in a worthy cause, who at the best knows in the end the triumphs of high achievement and who at the worst, if he fails, at least fails while daring greatly, so that his place shall never be with those cold and timid souls who know neither victory nor defeat.

AUTHOR'S NOTE

THIS BOOK IS a product of study and experience stretching over the better part of a lifetime. What I have learned about leaders and leadership has come from a combination of reading, observation, the advice of expert practitioners, and the experience of doing it.

When I was President, I found that preparing a major speech was a very effective discipline, not only for bringing policy decisions to a head, but also for refining my own thinking. The same was true of writing this book. In the course of delving more deeply into the lives of leaders I have known, I found that I acquired a much richer understanding of what they were up against and how they became what they were. I learned a great deal, some of it surprising, that helped explain to me why and how they sometimes acted as they did, and that taught me more about the nature of those who shaped the world in our time.

Like many political leaders, I have long been an avid reader of historical biographies. Even during the White House years, I made time for this. Since then, I have had more time for it. All of the leaders dealt with in this book are ones I knew personally, and my primary impressions of them are those based on my own observation and experience. But I have also learned much from their biographers. I consulted scores of books in the writing of this one. For those readers who want to pursue more fully the lives of these leaders, among the books I would recommend are the multivolume *Winston S. Churchill*, begun by Randolph S. Churchill and continued by Martin Gilbert; Lord Moran's *Churchill* and Violet Bonham Carter's *Winston Churchill*; *Churchill and de Gaulle* by Francois Kersaudy; Andre Malraux's *Felled Oaks*; *De Gaulle* by Brian Crozier and David Schoenbrun's *The Three Lives of Charles de Gaulle*; *American Caesar*, William Manchester's biography of Douglas Mac-Arthur; Terence Prittie's *Konrad Adenauer* and, by Paul Weymar, the authorized biography of Adenauer by the same title; Edward Crankshaw's *Khrushchev*; *Chou En-lai: China's Gray Eminence* by Kai-yu Hsu; *Mao* by Ross Terrill; and Brian Crozier's *The Man Who Lost China*.

Those who have contributed to my understanding of leadership include all the leaders profiled here, plus scores of others—particularly Dwight D. Eisenhower, under whom I served as Vice President for eight years. For all that they taught me, wittingly or unwittingly, I am grateful, as I also am to the many persons who contributed their ideas and recollections to this book. I owe a special debt to Dr. Taro Takemi, president of the Japan Medical Association, who served as a trusted adviser and confidant to Japan's Prime Minister Shigeru Yoshida. He answered many of my questions about Yoshida and provided a number of details that are not generally known in the West.

There are others for whose specific help with this book I am particularly grateful. I relied on Mrs. Nixon, with her keen eye, for help in picture selection, as well as for her memories of many of the events and people. My longtime associate Loie Gaunt was invaluable in searching the archives. Karen Maisa ably supervised the manuscript, together with Kathleen O'Connor and Susan Marone, as well as helped with research.

Two recent college graduates, John H. Taylor of the University of California at San Diego and Marin Strmecki of Harvard, worked long hours and provided immensely helpful research and editorial assistance.

Franklin R. Gannon, who had worked with Randolph Churchill before joining my White House staff, was very helpful with the Churchill chapter. Raymond Price, formerly chief of my White House speechwriting staff, served again, as he had for my previous book, *The Real War*, as my principal editorial consultant and coordinator.

—R.N.

Saddle River, New Jersey
June 21, 1982

INDEX

Academicians, 325, 331, 335
Acheson, Dean, 102–103, 122, 145
Adenauer, Emma, 154
Adenauer, Gussi Zinsser, 154
Adenauer, Konrad, 133–68, 253, 275, 338.
 See also Franco-German
 rapprochement.
 age, 36, 157, 161, 341
 Catholicism and Christian policies,
  147–48, 167, 257
 as Chancellor, 142–46
 and China, 94, 160
 cf. Churchill, 2, 144, 153, 166

 death of, 163
 and de Gaulle, 160–62
 cf. de Gaulle, 69, 162, 166
 and Dulles, 151–53, 162
 European unity, 134–35, 141, 148–49,
  152–53, 160, 164
 education and writings, 137, 153
 Erhard and, 78, 157–58, 163
 and family, 141, 154
 and German people, 110, 145–46, 150,
  156–57
 and German unification, 150–52,
  163–64, 167

Adenauer, Konrad (*continued*)
  and Kennedy/Nixon campaign, 159
  and Khrushchev, 154–56, 197–98
  last years, 133–34, 156–57, 160
  leadership style, 156–57, 321, 329,
    336–37
  and Nazis, 107, 140–41, 250
  Nixon friendship with, 136, 153
  Nixon meetings with, 153, 159–60,
    161–62
  personality and character, 135, 138–39,
    146, 152–53, 167–68
  physical appearance, 138, 146, 161
  political background before war,
    138–40
  use of press, 145, 159
  and Prussia, 149–50, 167
  quotes and comments:
    defense of Europe, 148
    de Gaulle, 60–61, 161–62
    Dulles, 150, 153
    Erhard, 139
    fence-sitting and neutrality, 152
    German people, 150, 156–57
    Gromyko/Nixon look-alike, 139
    Khrushchev, 156
    outsitting other politicians, 144
    patience, 151
    being right at the right time, 133–34
    Soviets, 162–63
    roses and Mrs. Nixon, 158–59
  and Soviets, 94, 134–35, 151–52,
    162–63
  and today's world, 165–66, 258
  and Vietnam War, 75, 162
  Washington visits: 1953, 146–147;
    between 1953 and 1961, 151
  and wine, 143–44
  cf. Yoshida, 111, 122
Adenauer, Libet, 154
Adenauer, Max, 141
Adenauer, Paul, 154, 163
Afghanistan, 165–66, 204
Africa, 37, 72, 170–71, 264–65
  and Nkrumah, 261–62

Aftermath, The (Churchill), 12
Age and leadership, 36
Albania, 232
Alexander the Great, 3, 45
Algeria, 49–50, 57, 75, 324
Allende, Salvador, 301–302
Allied Occupation of Germany, 143–46,
  149, 254
Allied Occupation of Japan, 81–82,
  108–11, 114–17, 122–23, 131–32,
  254
Allison, John, 115
American Dental Association, 194
American Legion, 194
American National Exhibition, Moscow
  (1959), 173, 175, 176–77, 181–82
Anglo-American relations, 9–10, 30–31,
  35
Angola, 204, 296
Anne, Queen of England, 215
Anne de Gaulle Foundation, 71
Antiballistic Missile Treaty (1972), 210
Antonov-Ovseyenko, Anton, 172
ANZUS pact, 318
Arab countries, 65–66, 165–66, 189. *See
  also* Egypt; Middle East; Saudi
  Arabia.
  Ben-Gurion and, 281–82
  Brezhnev/Nixon discussions during
    Yom Kippur War (1973), 207–209
  Golda Meir and, 287
  and Nasser, 290–91, 295, 307
  terrorists, 281, 287
Arden-Clarke, Charles, 260–61
Arms reduction, 210–11. *See also*
  Détente; Nuclear weapons.
Army of the Future, The (de Gaulle),
  46–47
Asakai, Koichiro, 126
Asia:
  Churchill and Communist aggression
    in, 9–10
  economic assistance to, 264
  MacArthur and, 93, 96, 99–103, 131
  Magsaysay and, 276

Menzies and Lee and, 317–19
  Nixon trip (1953), 9, 100
Aso, Kazuko, 113, 117, 125
Astor, Lady, 13
Aswan High Dam, 291, 293
Atlantic alliance. *See* Western alliance.
Atomic bomb. *See* Nuclear weapons.
Attlee, Clement, 34
  Churchill on, 13
Australia, 251
  under Menzies, 308–310, 310–18
Authoritarian government, 340
Ayatollah. *See* Khomeini.

Bakayaro, 104–105
Baldwin, Stanley, 26–27
Baltimore *Sun*, 159
Barres, Philippe, 46
Bataan, 86–87, 96, 102, 104, 278
Bay of Pigs, 92–93
Begin, Menachem, 296
Ben-Gurion, David, 251, 279–84
  on de Gaulle, 282
  Eisenhower on, 280
  on God and Bible, 280
  on Israel's territorial enlargement,
    281–82
  on reclaiming the desert, 280–81
Bennis, Warren G., 4
Bergson, Henri, 337
Beria, Lavrenti, 183–84
Berlin, Isaiah, 39
Berlin airlift (1959), 39, 100, 177
Berlin Wall (1961), 133, 150, 160–61, 164,
  170
Bernstein, Leonard, 284
Bevan, Aneurin, 13–14
Blake, Lord, 130
"Blenheim rat," 22
Bobst, Elmer, 338
Bohlen, Charles, 55, 61–62
  and de Gaulle, 42, 54, 66
  on "peaceful coexistence," 198
Bourguiba, Habib, 268, 306
Boxer Rebellion, 94

Bradley, General Omar, 130
Brandt, Willy, 150, 163–64
Brezhnev, Leonid, 201–10
  on Chinese, 210
  de Gaulle on, 77
  diplomacy, 187, 204–205
  emotions and sentimentality, 34,
    205–206, 284
  Khrushchev ouster, 200, 215
  cf. Khrushchev, 202, 207
  life-style of "new class," 203–204
  Nixon personal relationship with,
    210–11
  Nixon and summits:
    1972: 201–202, 205–206
    1973: 203, 206–207
    1974: 209
  philosophical depth, 337
  Western outlook, 199
  and women, 8, 203
  Yom Kippur War and joint force in
    Middle East, 208–209
British people, 21–22, 30, 150. *See also*
  Great Britain.
Brosio, Manlio, 4, 257
Bugovsky, Vladimir, 186
Bulganin, Nikolai, 156, 162
Bullitt, William, 17, 42, 113
Bureaucracy, 19, 51, 201–202, 273
  and butcher's function, 335

Caesar, Julius, 3, 45
Cambodia, 204
Campaigns and elections, 333–34
  Adenauer on, 142–43
Camp David summit (1973), 203, 206–207,
  210
Camp David Treaty, 298
Canada, 161
Captive Nations Resolution, 173–74, 191
Caracas incident, 190, 211
Caribbean area, 204
Carlson, Frank, 128
Carter, Jimmy, 175, 212, 296–99
Castro, Fidel, 170

Casualties (World War II), 275
Catholic Church (Italian), 255–57. *See also* Adenauer, Konrad; de Gaulle, Charles.
Catton, Bruce, 323
Central America, 204
Chamberlain, Neville, 15, 26, 29–30
Chambers, Whittaker, 102–103, 242
Charisma, 51
Charlemagne, 149, 161, 167
Cheka (Bolshevik police) joke, 181
Chiang Kai-shek, 217, 224, 240–46
  and Korea, 98
  Mao on, 241–42
  Nixon friendship, 218
  and Taiwan, 115, 224, 244–45
  Yoshida on, 125–26
  and Zhou, 220, 236
Chiang Kai-shek, Madame, 69, 113, 218
  cf. Jiang Qing, 242–43
  marriage, 243
Ch'in, Emperor of China, 217
China, 32, 79. *See also* Chinese-American rapprochement; Communist China; Republic of China (Taiwan); Sino-Soviet split.
  civil war, 220, 243, 245–46
  and Japan, 104
  Shah on, 271
  and Singapore, 310–11
  sense of superiority, 224–25, 305
  U.S. policy toward Asia, 99–100
  Zhou's background, 218–20, 226–28
Chinese-American rapprochement (1972)
  Adenauer on, 160
  de Gaulle on, 74
  Nixon meetings with Mao, 237–38, 241–42
  Nixon meetings with Zhou, 218, 220–21, 232–36
Chin Shih-huang, Emperor of China, 240
Christian Democratic Union (CDU), 134, 137, 143–44, 150, 161, 238
  and Erhard, 157

Christian Democratic party (Italy), 254–55, 258
Churchill, Lady Randolph (Jennie Jerome), 16–17
Churchill, Lord Randolph, 16
Churchill, Randolph (son of Winston), 21
Churchill, Winston, 6–39, 104, 123, 253, 309
  cf. Adenauer, 2
  and Anglo-American unity, 9–10, 30–31
  Isaiah Berlin on, 39
  and Boer War, 20
  and champagne, 11, 14
  and Chancellor of Exchequer, 26–27
  childhood and schooling, 16–17
  defeat, after war, 34–35, 59–60
  cf. de Gaulle, 43, 60
  and English language, 17–18
  and Gallipoli, 322
  and history, 3, 323
  Hitler and German rearmament, 15–16, 27–28, 250
  humor and invective, 13, 15, 181
  inactivity and depression, 24–26
  Iron Curtain speech, 31
  last years, 36–37, 239
  leadership, 27, 166, 321, 328–29, 337, 341–42
  life-style and comforts, 14–15
  and Lincoln Bedroom, 16
  marriage, 25
  newspaper war reports and articles, 18–19, 26
  Nixon first meeting (1954), 7–15
  Nixon last meeting (1958), 9, 36–37
  and painting, 14, 161
  party politics and Parliament, before war, 19–28
  Prime Minister (1940), 28–29
  Prime Minister (1951), 35
  and public speaking, 14, 20–21, 56, 314
  and Franklin Roosevelt, 32–33, 260–61
  and Stalin, 32

preparation of successor, 78, 157
use of tears, 34
temper and temperament, 24
and United Nations, 74
and West Germany and NATO, 149
world events today and, 37–38, 258
writings, 12, 20, 27, 153, 314
quotes and comments:
  Adenauer, 134
  Lady Astor, 13
  Attlee, 13
  Bevan, 13–14
  Château Lafite Rothschild, 15
  Cuba, 18
  de Gaulle, 41, 63
  difficulty of democracy, 261
  Dulles, 13
  elections and campaigns, 333
  his father, 16
  first speech as Prime Minister, 29
  Ghana's annexation of Guinea, 37
  great men and impressions, 314
  independence to former colonies, 9,
    260–61
  Indochina and U.S. policy, 9
  invasion of Europe, 10–11
  Robert E. Lee and Ulysses S. Grant,
    12
  lion's heart and lion's roar, 16
  losing of elections, 19–20, 25, 35
  MacArthur, 109
  McCarthy and communism, 13
  MacDonald, 13
  making history by writing it, 12
  ministers and popularity, 110
  nuclear war threat, 38
  his painting, 14
  Lord Plowden, 14
  power and youth, 36
  becoming Prime Minister in 1940,
    28–29
  retirement, 36
  Franklin Roosevelt's last month in
    office, 10

  meeting Franklin Roosevelt, 32
  George Bernard Shaw, 13
  Soviets as allies, 32
  Soviets and negotiations, 38
  socialism vs. liberalism, 23
  "stooping" to conquer, 330
  travel and seasickness, 12
  World War II most famous speech,
    34
  worms and glowworm, 7
  writing habits and dictation, 14
Civil War (U.S.), 12, 212
Clay, General Lucius, 136–37
Clemenceau, Georges, 19
Cold War, 33, 49, 150, 164
Cologne, Germany, 139–40, 142
Colombey-les-Deux-Églises, France, 41,
  59, 72
Colonies:
  and democracy, 261, 263
  and demagoguery, 269
  independence, 9, 30, 250, 259–61, 263,
    265
Commentators and reporters, 325,
  342–43. *See also* Press; Television.
Communism and Communists. *See also*
  Communist China; Marxism-
  Leninism; Soviet Union.
  and Adenauer, 139–40, 144
  Bohlen on "sincerity," 198
  and Chiang's land reform, 115
  Churchill on, 13
  drabness and colorlessness of,
    187
  expansion in Asia, 99–103
  in Indonesia and Sukarno, 265–66
  Nixon on, 181; U.S. policy toward,
    211–16
  in postwar Italy, 251–56, 275
  in postwar Japan, 103, 115, 117
  in Philippines, 275–76
  in Singapore, 310–12
  Soviet "new class," 203–204
  and Zionism linkage, 303–304

Communist China. *See also* Chinese-American rapprochement; Mao Zedong; Sino-Soviet split; Zhou Enlai.
  Adenauer on, 163
  agriculture and economy, 244
  American attitudes (1954), 224
  Brezhnev on aggressiveness of, 199, 210
  brutality of regime, 5, 172, 228–29, 240
  Churchill on, 10
  Cultural Revolution, 230, 237
  de Gaulle on, 73–74
  educational system, 17
  effects of Communist rule, 211, 228–29, 244
  and Japan, 119, 121, 126–27, 233
  and Korea, 93, 98, 126, 131
  Lee on, 318
  and MacArthur, 99–103
  Nehru on, 273
  Nixon visit (1971), 126–27
  revolution, 116, 220, 236, 243–46, 248
  and Soviet "new class," 203–204
  Soviet obsession with, 73, 210
  Yoshida on, 125–26
  Zhou and, 218–19, 229–33, 236–37, 246–48
Communist Vietminh, 10
Congo, 171
Congress, 10, 84, 173–74, 211. *See also* House of Representatives; Senate (U.S.).
Congressional Medal of Honor, 2, 87
Connally, John, 312
Conservative party (Great Britain), 22, 34–35
Conservative leaders, 335–36
Conversational excellence, 314
Corregidor, 86–87, 96, 102, 278
Crozier, Brian, 50
Cuba, 18, 93, 296
Cuban Missile Crisis, 170–71, 208, 258
Cultural Revolution, 230, 237
Czechoslovakia, 74, 77, 211

Dardanelles expedition, 24–25
Das Kapital (Marx), 178
de Gasperi, Alcide, 69, 251–58, 329
  character and personality, 252–54, 256
  and European unity, 257–58
  leadership style, 253–54, 275, 337
  postwar Italy and politics, 253–56
  work habits, 256, 304
de Gaulle, Anne, 70–72
de Gaulle, General Charles, 24, 34, 40–80, 238, 250. *See also* France; Franco-German rapprochement.
  and Adenauer, 161–62, 166
  Algerian crisis, 49–50
  analysis of American politics, 61–62
  dislike of Americans, 80
  and daughter, Anne, 71–72
  cf. Caesar, 54
  character and personality, 41–43, 52–53, 59, 67–68
  recognition of China, 126
  cf. Churchill, 43, 59–60
  Churchill on "Cross of Lorraine," 41
  conservatism, 129
  and Cuban Missile Crisis, 258
  death and funeral, 40–41, 79–80
  East/West tension and Europe, 73–74
  cf. Eisenhower, 43, 60
  eloquence and conversation, 314
  cf. Faisal, 304
  family life, 67–71
  Fifth Republic constitution, 50–51
  personification and spirit of France, 41, 44, 63–66, 79–80
  and French language, 56–57, 90
  and French people, 64, 80, 297
  French reverence for, 123
  and German reconciliation, 151, 164
  direct line to God, 328
  and Golda, 287
  and history, 323
  and Israel, 282
  Joan of Arc image, 63
  Kissinger on, 218

leadership style, 51–52, 166, 320–21,
    324, 327–29, 336–37, 341
cf. MacArthur, 43, 54–55
memoirs, 61
military strategy, 323
and 1960 U.S. presidential election, 54,
    60
Nixon evaluation of in 1964, 125
Nixon friendship with, 44, 60
Nixon meeting with (1960), 42–43,
    61–62
Nixon meeting with (1969), 58, 73–76
Nixon's last letter from, 78–79
and nuclear war, 73–74
against parliamentary system, 47–48
physical appearance, 43, 79, 253
as politician, 59–61
prescience, 46–47
public persona, "General de Gaulle"
    image, 41, 54–55, 57
public performance, 55, 59, 62–63,
    327–28
resignation in 1946, 48, 50, 339
resignation in 1969, 78
retirement period in Colombey, 59–60
and RPF, 48–49
Sophocles and, 345
Soviet threat to Poland and, 258
and successor, 78, 157
and war, 43, 47, 55, 58–59
and world events in 1960s, 64–66
writings, 43, 45–46, 61, 153, 314
cf. Yoshida, 111, 154
quotes and comments:
    Anne, 71, 72
    Arab/Israeli extremism, 66
    character and leadership, 56–57
    Chinese-American relations, 74
    death as the only winner, 74
    Europe's loss of war, 74
    family, 69
    failure of leaders, 63
    Fourth Republic, 49
    France, and Frenchmen, 63, 64
    France loss of battle, not of war, 47

making future policy, 46
grandeur and leadership, 62
great men and will, 320
leadership qualities, 45–46, 51–52,
    54, 57–58
MacArthur's dismissal, 99
modern warfare, 46
Nixon as "exile in his own country,"
    44
fall of Paris and French resistance,
    47
parliamentary government, 47
public personality, 54
public speaking, 56
resignation over minor issue, 78
solitude, 59
Soviet leaders (1969), 77
television delivery and performance,
    57
on United Nations, 74–75
Vietnam War, 76
de Gaulle, Elizabeth, 70
de Gaulle, Philippe, 70
de Gaulle, Yvonne, 68–72
Demagoguery, 269, 292
Démaret, Pierre, 54
Democracy, 269, 324–25, 340
    Churchill on difficulty of, 251
    and former colonies, 261, 263
    elections and campaigns, 333
    postwar Japan and MacArthur, 82–84,
        116–18, 131–32
    Japan and Meiji reformers, 104
    Nixon on, for Saudi and Tunisia, 306
    Saudi Arabia and, 306–307
Deng Xiaoping, 228
Deng Yingchao, 235, 243, 246
Depression (U.S. economic), 96, 101
Détente, 73, 161, 212, 215
Developing countries. *See* Third World.
Dewey, Thomas E., 42, 312, 331–32
Diefenbaker, John, 3
Disraeli, Benjamin, 30, 130, 251, 338
di Vittorio, Giuseppe, 252–53
Dobrynin, Anatoly, 206, 210

"Dugout Doug," 86, 129
Dulles, John Foster, 8, 11, 36, 139, 146
    and Adenauer's friendship, 145, 151,
        154, 159, 161–62
    Churchill on, 13
    on Communism, 193
    Eisenhower on, 280
    and Japan, 119, 126
    on Khrushchev, 172
    on "peaceful coexistence" policy, 198
    on Soviet "peace" overtures, 163
    Zhou and, 224, 232, 234–35
Dutch New Guinea, 265, 268–69

Eastern Europe, 9, 35, 164–65, 215, 250
    de Gaulle fear of destruction of, 73
    Nixon on communication with, 192
Eastern Front, The (Churchill), 12
East Germany, 74, 275
    Adenauer policy on unification,
        149–54, 155, 167
    Brandt and Ostpolitik, 163–64
    refugees from, 211
    western attitudes and, 164
East-West struggle, 250
    Churchill on, 37
    de Gaulle fears for Europe, 73–77
    and Middle East, 279, 283
    Sadat's advice, 296
Eden, Anthony, 15, 35–36, 78, 91
Edge of the Sword, The (de Gaulle), 45,
    51, 67
Edward VII, King of England, 16
Edward VIII, King of England, 15, 27
Egypt, 66, 306, 340
    and Israel, 207, 281–82
    under Nasser, 290–93
    Nasser cf. Sadat, 294–95, 297–98, 307
    under Sadat, 293–98
Eichmann, Adolf, 284
Eisenhower, Dwight D., 36, 43, 52, 100,
    121, 138, 338
    and Adenauer, 151, 159
    cf. Adenauer, 144

on Ben-Gurion and Dulles, 280
businessmen in Cabinet, 111
and Churchill, 33–34
death and funeral, 76, 78, 341
cf. de Gaulle, 43
on de Gaulle, 63–64
image during World War II, 130
and Khrushchev visit, 190–91, 193–96
leadership and delegation of authority,
    334, 336
love and respect for, 288
and MacArthur, 91–92
1954 Churchill visit, 8, 10–11
and politics, 60, 127–29
preparation of Nixon and succession,
    157–58
and Nixon presidential campaign
    (1960), 196
and Russians in Eastern Europe, 33
and General Walter Bedell Smith, 335
Suez Canal and, 291–92
and United Nations, 74–75
U-2 incident, 196–97
Eisenhower, Julie, 286
Eisenhower, Mamie, 11, 15, 78
Elections, 26, 58–59, 333
Elizabeth I, Queen of England, 215
Emancipation Proclamation, 221
Engels, Friedrich, 178
Engineers, 335
Erhard, Ludwig, 78, 121, 139, 148, 157,
    160
Eshkol, Levi, 286
Ethiopia, 204, 260
Europe. See also Eastern Europe;
        Western Europe.
    Adenauer's dream of unity, 141,
        148–49, 152–53
    and American generals, 96
    army, 149, 257
    Churchill fear of third world war, 10
    East-West conflict and, 38, 43–44
    historical impact of leaders, 323
    and U.S. foreign policy, 99–100

European alliance, 165–66
European Coal and Steel Community, 135
European Defense Community, 257
European Economic Community, 257

Fahd, King of Saudi Arabia, 306
Faisal Ibn Abdul-Aziz al Saud, King of Saudi Arabia, 251, 290, 294, 302–307
  assassination, 305–306
  and Communist link to Zionism, 303–304
  on integrity of rule, 306–307
  modernization and reforms, 302, 308
  Nixon 1960 and 1974 meetings with, 212–14
Farley, Jim, 94
Farouk, King of Egypt, 300, 307
Fascist Italy, 250, 254, 258
Federal Republic of Germany. *See* West Germany.
Fitzgerald, F. Scott, 320
Ford, Gerald, 297
Foreign service officers, 31, 42, 64, 111, 318
Foreign trade
  China and, 126–27
  Japan in 1890s, 104
  Soviets and West, 162, 214–15
Formosa. *See* Republic of China (Taiwan).
France, 76, 149, 165. *See also* de Gaulle, Charles.
  Algeria and, 49–50
  Communist China relations, 126
  de Gaulle as leader of, 47, 60, 166, 327, 329
  de Gaulle personification of, 42, 44, 63–65, 79–80
  defeat of European army concept, 149, 151
  Fifth Republic constitution, 60–61, 80, 167

Fourth Republic, 46, 48–49
  and German rearmament, 77, 135
  and Germany, 76–77, 149
  and Indochina, 9, 50, 265
  and Ivory Coast, 264
  parliamentary system, 47–48
  public attitudes toward Soviets, 161
  Suez crisis, 291–92
Franco-German rapprochement, 76, 80, 134, 142, 147, 149, 151, 162
  treaty (1963), 135, 149, 164
Franco, Francisco, 4
Franklin, Benjamin, 64
French people, 56, 64–65
French Revolution, 244
Freud, Sigmund, 17
Frondizi, Arturo, 3
Front de Liberation Nationale, 49
Fulbright, William, 89
Fuller, Lon, 147

Gandhi, Indira, 270, 273–74, 286
Gandhi, Mahatma, 270
"Gang of Four," 247
Gaullists, 50, 60
Geneva Conference on Berlin (1959), 139
Geneva Conference on Vietnam (1954), 224
German people, 152–53, 287
Germany. *See also* East Germany; West Germany; World War II.
  under Nazis, 27–28, 46–47, 140–41
  postwar, 30, 32–33, 139–40
  Russian fear of, 73
  and Ukrainian people, 183
Ghana, 259–65
Gladstone, William, 130, 251, 334
Goerdeler, Carl, 141
Goldwater, Barry, 93, 95
Grant, Ulysses S., 12
Great Britain, 15, 23, 26–27, 47, 76. *See also* British people; Churchill, Winston.
  Anglo-American relations, 9–10, 30–31

Great Britain (*continued*)
  Churchill's leadership, 29, 166
  East-West conflict and, 10, 73–74
  in Egypt, 292, 294
  and postwar European defense, 135,
    151
  and Ghana independence, 260
  and Hirohito, 109
  and India, 10, 270–71
  Suez crisis, 291–92
  at Versailles, 105
  influence on Yoshida, 106–107
Great Contemporaries (Churchill), 35
Greece, 170
Grew, Joseph, 107
Grew, Mrs. Joseph, 113
Gromyko, Andrei, 139, 177, 205–206
Grunwald, Henry, 35
Guinea, 262–64
Gulam Mohammed, 4

Haig, Alexander, 89
Haldeman, Bob, 335
Halifax, Lord, 28
Hamilton, Alexander, 282
Harriman, Averell, 97
Hassan, King of Morocco, 306
Heath, Edward, 238
Herter, Christian, 136
Herter, Mrs. Christian, 197
Herter committee trip to Europe (1947),
    136, 250, 259
Hinge of Fate, The (Churchill), 10
Hirohito, Emperor of Japan, 83, 109–10,
    126, 132
Hiroshima, 104
Hiss, Alger, 129
History, and great leaders, 1–6, 323, 344
  de Gaulle and, 44
  and Magsaysay's death, 274
  verdict of, 301, 344–45
Hitler, Adolf, 31, 46, 167, 179, 325, 327
  and Adenauer, 140, 156
  and Churchill, 15, 32

Hitler-Stalin pact, 183–84
Ho Chi Minh, 265
Hoffman, Paul, 272
Hokkaido, Japan, 117
Hollywood films, 323
Hoover, Herbert, 27, 31, 52
  history's verdict, 345
  and MacArthur, 91, 96, 98
  Nixon meeting with (1953), 90
  Nixon meeting with (1963), 94–95
Hoover, Herbert, Jr., 96
Hoover, J. Edgar, 197
Houphouet-Boigny, Felix, 264
House, Colonel Edward, 106
House of Commons, 20, 21, 35
House of Representatives (U.S.), 24, 53.
    See also Herter committee.
Hozier, Clementine, 25
Huenhlin, General Adolf, 46–47
Hukbalahaps, 275–77
Hungary, 74, 186, 211
  1956 revolt, 170, 291
Hussein, King of Jordan, 306

Ibn-Saud, King of Saudi Arabia, 302, 308
Ikeda, Hayato, 111, 121, 123
Inchon port, 97
India, 232, 248
  and British, 10, 27, 270–71
  and Indira Gandhi, 286
  and Nehru, 269–71, 274
  population, 271, 274
Indochina, 6–10, 50, 100, 104. *See also*
    Vietnam War.
Indonesia, 259, 265–69
Information leaks, 28
Iran, 299–300
  American hostage crisis, 299, 343
  and Islam, 298
  revolution and loss of freedom, 289,
    299, 305, 308
Iraq, 296
Iron Curtain speech, 31
Islam, 298, 302, 305

Isolationism, 15, 316
Israel, 251, 295–96
  and Ben-Gurion, 279–83
  de Gaulle on, 65–66
  Faisal and, 303
  and Golda Meir, 283–89
  Nasser hatred for, 293
  Nixon-Brezhnev confrontation, Yom
    Kippur War, 207–10
  Sadat's peace with, 295, 298
  and Suez crisis, 291, 295
  U.S. airlift and military alert (1973),
    207–209, 285
  U.S. special relationship with, 283
Italy, 30, 51, 251–58, 275
Ivory Coast, 263–64

Japan, 4, 102, 311, 318
  Allied Occupation period, 81–85,
    108–21, 253
  and communism, 117–18, 121
  and Communist China, 32, 127,
    232–33, 248
  constitution, 116
  democracy and, 82–85, 130–32
  economic growth, 83, 95, 100, 121–23
  and emperor, 109–10, 116
  Korean War and, 103, 119
  land reform, 115–17
  MacArthur's reforms, 95, 103–104,
    115–16, 118, 131
  Magsaysay on, 278
  prewar, 104–107
  rearmament issue, 119–21
  U.S. security alliance with, 120–21, 301
  World War II, 30, 32, 220, 275–76, 278
  Yoshida as Prime Minister, 110–123,
    129, 132
Jefferson, Thomas, 283
Jerome, Jennie. *See* Churchill, Lady
    Randolph.
Jews, 281–83, 287
Jiang Qing, 228, 242–43
Joan of Arc, 63

Johnson, Lyndon, 52, 68, 126, 338
  leadership style, 284, 328
  personality, 315–16
  physical contact, 204, 328
  refusal to run for reelection, 339–40
  and Vietnam War, 93, 336
Johnson, Samuel, 25
Joint Chiefs of Staff (U.S.), 96–98
Jordan, 306

Kaganovich, Lazar, 182–84
Kashmir, 269–70
Kausen, Herr, 137–38
Kendall, Donald, 185
Kennedy, John F., 52, 58, 161, 306, 338
  Adenauer on, 159
  Cuban Missile Crisis and de Gaulle,
    258
  MacArthur on, 94–95
  test-ban treaty, 94, 171
  presidential campaign (1960), 61, 149,
    197, 316
Kent, Dutchess of, 260
Khalid, King of Saudi Arabia, 306
"*Khitryi*" Khrushchev, 182
Khomeini, Ayatollah, 299–300
Khrushchev, Nikita, 5, 94, 169–201, 211,
    216, 267
  and Adenauer mission, 154–56, 164
  American presidential campaign (1960)
    and, 196–97
  background, 170–71, 184–86
  behavior, 171, 175–77, 225, 322, 327,
    329
  cf. Brezhnev, 202, 204–205, 206–207
  Captive Nations Resolution and,
    173–74, 191
  drunkenness, 172, 175
  Dulles on, 172
  failures, 171, 180
  foreign policy, 198–99
  humor and jokes, 181–82
  and Hungarian repression, 192
  inferiority complex, 195–96, 199

Khrushchev, Nikita (*continued*)
  intellectual depth, 337
  leadership, and strength, 172
  and Macmillan, 177
  and Marxist theory, 179
  Nixon visit to Soviet Union (1959),
    173–74, 176–77, 179, 181–82; dacha
    visit, 187–91; "kitchen" debate,
    184–86, 201
  Nixon attempt to see (1965), 201
  ouster by subordinates, 199–200
  personality, 180–82, 187
  quotes and comments:
    abstract art, 181
    Captive Nations Resolution and
      "horse shit," 174
    Caracas attack on Nixons, 190
    Chinese population, 163
    Communist uprisings, 190
    espionage, 197
    fable of humble man (Pinya), 169–70
    Kozlov, 178
    Marxist theory, 178
    Russians remaining Communist, 181
    Russia's telephones, 196
    shaking of fists, 178
    writers and revolution, 186
  and rivals, 215
  cf. Stalin, 171
  Stalin defrocking, 181, 186–87, 232
  successes, 170–71
  U.S. tour, 193–96
  and Zhou, 231–32
Khrushchev, Mrs. Nikita, 175, 188
King, Martin Luther, 261
Kipling, Rudyard, 19, 100–101
Kirkpatrick, Sir Ivone, 143
Kirkpatrick, Jeanne J., 340
Kishi, Nobusuke, 121, 318
Kissinger, Henry, 122, 206, 210, 287
  Chinese-American rapprochement
    talks, 233–35
  on de Gaulle, 218
  Golda on, 294
  and Mao's writings, 238

1972 summit meeting, 205
  Paris Peace with North Vietnam, 76
  and Yom Kippur War, 207–208
  on Zhou, 218, 221, 230
"Kitchen" debate, 184–85, 201
Kitchener, Lord (Horatio Herbert), 19
Kohler, Foy, 182
"Konrad Adenauer" rose, 158
Korean War, 119, 123, 126, 224
  Communist goals in, 103, 131
  MacArthur and, 81, 89, 97–99, 102–103
Kosygin, Aleksei, 75, 77, 163, 205
Kozlov, Frol, 153, 173, 178
Kubitschek, Juscelino, 3

Lafayette Marquis de, 222
Lafite Rothschild, Château, 15
Land reform programs:
  Japan, 115
  Philippines, 278–79
  Taiwan, 115–16, 244–45
Laos, 204
La Scala opera house, 255–56
Latin America, 47–49, 72, 264
Leaders. *See also* Leadership; names of
    leaders.
  age factor, 36
  and conversational excellence, 314
  followers and, 331–34
  friendships between, 135
  and goodness, 3
  history's verdict on, 301–302, 344–45
  and intrigue, 284, 328
  learning from the past, 6, 61, 250–51
  nation building vs. revolution, 319
  of newly independent countries,
    259–79
  and power, 38, 285–86, 300, 321–22
  revolutionary, 244, 265–95, 302, 307
  Theodore Roosevelt on, 345
  sacrifices, 67, 331
  of smaller countries, 2, 308–19
  speaking and writing ability, 314
  and grooming of successors, 121–22,
    127, 158

summit meetings and, 210
of superpowers, 215–16
and television, 342–44
toughness vs. gentleness, 43
in wartime, 2, 29–30, 34, 58–59
wilderness periods, 313
wives of, 242–43
Leadership, 7–13, 320–345
de Gaulle analysis of, 45–46, 51–52, 54, 57–58, 62, 320, 324–25
and demagoguery, 269
and foresight, 134
cf. management, 4–5
manners/strength correlation, 172
Lee, Harold, 224–25
Lee Kuan Yew, 251, 310–11, 317–19
cf. Menzies, 308–10
quotes and comments:
Japan, 318
Mao's decline, 318
nations as great trees, 318
Singapore and communism, 312
Singapore's survival and work, 311
sitting on a shooting stick, 311
U.S. and Soviet expansionism, 317
Lee, Robert E., 12
Le Jour (Beirut), 292
Lenin, Nikolai, 172, 178, 183, 219, 337
Leningrad, Siege of, 205
Lerner, Max, 326–27
le Trocquer, André, 50
Liberalism and socialism, 23
Liberal leaders, 335–36
Libya, 290, 296
Life magazine, 171
Lin Biao, 229–30
Lincoln, Abraham, 128, 222, 261, 292, 323
on violation of Constitution, 326
Lincoln Bedroom, 14–15
Lin Yutang, 230
"Little Folk" (Kipling), 19
Lleras Camargo, Alberto, 3
Lloyd George, David, 19, 24
Lodge, Henry Cabot, 195
Long March, 220, 222, 236, 240

Longworth, Alice Roosevelt, 42
Luce, Clare Boothe, 341
Luce, Henry R., 3
Lumumba, Patrice, 171
Lunik satellite, 173, 194

MacArthur, Arthur (son of Douglas MacArthur), 113–14
MacArthur, General Arthur (father of Douglas MacArthur), 87–88
MacArthur, General Douglas, 81–103, 113–19, 127–32
Asian outlook, 88, 93, 99–103, 130–31, 309
Churchill on, 33, 109
corncob pipe, 88, 328
courage, 87, 109
cf. de Gaulle, 43, 53, 73
disobedience and contempt for superiors, 95–96
"Dugout Doug," 86, 129
eccentricities of dress, 88–89
Eisenhower and, 91–92
eloquence, 53, 90, 153
and father, 87–88
as general, 86–87
Inchon landing, 97
Korean War and Truman, 81, 98–99, 102–103
and Japan, Allied Occupation, 4, 84–85, 103–104, 109–119, 130–32
last years and politics, 127–29
military background, 87–89
monologues, 11, 91, 314
mother and, 17, 88
Nixon conversations, friendship with, 90–94
Nixon's reinstatement resolution in Senate, 98–99
"North Atlantic isolationism" and, 101, 316
personality and character, 85–89, 329
and Philippines, 88, 101–102, 130–31, 275–76
and the Presidency, 128–29

MacArthur, General Douglas (*continued*)
  quotes and comments:
    Army defense budget in 1934, 101
    importance of Asia in U.S. policy, 101
    when dismissed without notice, 99
    Eisenhower, 91
    FDR, 96
    Inchon landing reinforcements, 97
    Kennedy, 92–93
    "Old soldiers never die" speech, 84
    prostitute's election in Japan, 116
    Nixon's gubernatorial campaign in
      California, 94
    soldiers pray for peace, 131
  relations with Presidents, 96, 101
  thought balanced with action, 337
  Truman on, 89, 96
  Wake Island meeting, 89, 99
  as West Point superintendent, 88–89,
    101, 131
  World War I, 86–88
  World War II, 86–87, 95, 101–102,
    108–109, 279
  Yoshida as partner, 81–85, 103–104,
    113–16, 131–32, 253
MacArthur, Mrs. Douglas, 91, 95
MacArthur, Pinky, 17, 88
"MacArthur seats," 86
McCarthy, Joseph, 13, 174
MacDonald, James Ramsey, 13
Machiavelli, 246
McCloy, John J., 138, 144–45, 149–50,
  161–62, 321
Macmillan, Harold, 177, 199, 215
Maginot Line, 46–47, 323
Magsaysay, Ramon, 251, 274–79
  quotes and comments:
    American values in Philippines, 279
    fight against communism, 277
    giving hope to youth, 277
Makino, Count, 105–106, 110, 125
Malayans, 310–11
Malaysia, 9
Malenkov, Georgi, 184

Malraux, André:
  and de Gaulle, 60, 74, 78–79
  on Mao, 237, 240
Managers vs. leaders, 4–5
Manchester, William, 115
Mao Zedong, 59, 116, 195, 199, 217–19,
    230–31, 236–41
  Brezhnev on, 210
  character, 238–40
  cf. Chiang, 241–42, 244
  conversational style, 235, 238
  Cultural Revolution and, 230, 237
  cf. de Gaulle, 58
  and Deng's memorial speech for Zhou,
    228
  history's verdict, 301–302
  illness, 237–39
  killing of countrymen and cruelty, 11,
    172, 228, 240, 322
  Lee's prediction, 318
  and Long March, 220, 222, 240
  Marxism-Leninism revised, 240
  Nixon meetings with (1972), 231,
    237–39, 241–42; (1976) 239
  poetry of, 233, 235, 247
  quotes and comments:
    Chiang, 242
    his changing of the world, 238–39
    his writings, 238
    Ping-Pong teams and improved
      relations, 223
    rightists, 238
    Zhou and foreign affairs, 231
  untidiness, 237, 244, 281
  and U.S. negotiations, 234, 237
  wife, 228, 242–43
  working habits, 239–40
  cf. Zhou, 218–19, 231, 238, 246–48
Mao (Terrill), 239
Maoism, 95
Maotai, 221–22
Marlborough (Churchill), 27
"Marseillaise, The," 80
Marshall, General George, 95–96

Marshall Plan, 99–100, 136, 145, 163
  for Third World, 264
Martin, Joe, 98–99
Marx, Karl, 178, 194, 219
Marxist-Leninist theory, 178–79, 229, 273
Media. *See* Television.
Meiji, Emperor of Japan, 104
Meiji reformers, 104–107, 109, 132
Meir, 251, 283–89, 341
  cf. Gandhi, 286
  grudges, 282, 287
  Nixon's last meeting with (1974), 288–89
  personality, 283–85
  Pompidou on, 283, 286
  quotes and comments:
    Arab neighbors, 288
    becoming Prime Minister, 286
    being a woman Foreign Minister, 286
    détente, 288
    Kissinger's accent, 288
  Yom Kippur War and, 207, 285
Memoirs (Yoshida), 84
Memoirs de Guerre (de Gaulle), 61
Menzies, Sir Robert, 251, 308–10, 312–18
  artificial lake incident and Cabinet, 313–14
  eloquence and repartee, 314–16
  cf. Lee, 308–310, 316–18
  quotes and comments:
    love for America, 312
    Australia's resistance to communism, 317–18
    businessmen, 315
    Churchill's speeches, 20–21
    Lyndon Johnson, 315–16
    Nixon-Kennedy debates, 316
    press "abuse," 316
    Sukarno, 265
    Vietnam, 317
  reading time allocation, 337
Merdeka, 266, 269

Middle East. *See also* names of leaders of Middle East.
  changes in, 279, 289–90
  de Gaulle on, 65–66
  Egypt and, 289–98
  Israel and, 279–88
  modernizing monarchs in, 299–307
  Nixon-Brezhnev talks (1973), 206–207
  transfer of power, 305
  Yom Kippur War and, 207–209
Mikoyan, Anastas, 177, 181, 188–89, 200
Missiles. *See* Antiballistic Missile Treaty; Nuclear weapons.
Mohammed Ayub Khan, 4
Mohammed Naguib, 290
Mohammed Riza Pahlevi. *See* Shah of Iran.
Molotov, Vyacheslav, 172, 184, 233
Molotov-Ribbentrop pact (1939), 156
Modernizing monarchies, 299–308
Monnet, Jean, 4, 149
Montgomery, Ruth, 159
Moran, Lord, 11, 34
Morgenthau Plan, 32, 163
Morocco, 300, 306
Moscow summit (1972), 75
Mozambique, 204
Mubarak, Hosni, 297
Muñoz Marin, Luis, 48
Muslims. *See* Islam.
Mussolini, 254
Myths, and leadership, 329–30

Nagasaki, 104
Napoleon, 3, 45, 51
  bathtub, 68
Napoleonic Code, 51
Nasser, Gamal Abdel, 251, 290–95
  and Aswan High Dam, 291, 293
  death and funeral, 292, 293, 297–98
  foreign adventures and Yemen, 262, 291, 293, 298, 303
  history's verdict, 301–302, 339
  and Israel, 65, 285, 287, 291, 293

Nasser, Gamal Abdel (*continued*)
  Nixon and, 290, 292–93
  personality and character, 291–92
  cf. Sadat, 294–95, 297, 307–308
  cf. Shah, 299, 307–308
Nation-building leaders, 269–89, 293–98,
  319
NATO alliance, 64–65, 134–35, 165–66
  and de Gasperi, 257
  and de Gaulle, 125
Nazis:
  and Adenauer, 107, 140–41, 153–54
  American image of Germans and, 146
  atrocities in Russia, 155–56
  Churchill on Soviet allies and, 32
  and Poland, 28, 165
  postwar German leaders and, 137
Negev Desert, 281
Nehru, Jawaharlal, 261, 269–74
  and democracy for India, 271–74
  Kashmir obsession, 269–70
  leadership style, 251, 259, 273–74, 337
  cf. Lee, 311
  "nonalignment policy," 272
  Pakistan threat, 272
  socialism and economic problems,
    273–74
Neutralism, 165
Newsweek, 171
New World (since World War II), 249–50,
  316, 319, 339
New York Times, 28, 152, 179
Nixon, Richard M. *See also* names of
  leaders.
  advice to political candidates, 22, 60,
    338
  airlift to Israel, military alert (1973),
    207–210, 285
  American bureaucracy and, 19
  on American financial aid to Third
    World, 264–65
  American relations with Germany,
    146–47
  Asia trip (1953), 9, 100
  on campaigning, 142

on China's future role, 248
Chinese-American relations and, 74,
  126–27, 218, 233–36
congressional investigation (1947), 211
on decision making, 53–54, 328–29
discussions with de Gaulle, 65–66,
  72–77
on détente, 161, 288
on Eastern European countries, 172
electoral defeats and, 26, 58–59, 61–62,
  124, 316, 329
and Ghana's independence, 259–61
resemblance to Gromyko, 139
Herter committee trip to Europe
  (1947), 136, 250, 259
and Japan's rearmament, 119–21
on leaders selected for inclusion, 3–4
reflections on leadership, 320–45
on Clare Boothe Luce, 341
and Moselle wine, 144
on nuclear freeze proposal, 213–14
on peace, 191, 239
reception in Poland, 192
on power, 31, 320–24
on presidency, 51, 321–22, 341; and de
  Gaulle's prediction, 61
presidential election (1960), 61, 92,
  196–97, 316
on press, 325
on psychobiography and "science,"
  16–17
reading time and, 337
on risks in politics, 21–22, 321, 329
on Soviet Union and American policy,
  211–16
on Suez crisis and Eisenhower's
  intervention, 291
on need for summit meetings, 210
on vice presidential nomination,
  341
and end of Vietnam War, 75–76, 329
on Western alliance, 258–59
Nixon, Mrs. Richard, 61, 100, 146, 175,
  203
  Adenauer and rosebushes, 158–59

and dinner for Adenauer, 153
and Caracas mob attack, 190, 211
on Churchill, 11
and de Gaulle, 68
on Yvonne de Gaulle, 71
foreign visits, 179, 260, 273, 280, 294–95
and Khrushchev, 188–89
and Yoshida, 113
Nixon, Tricia, 280, 282
"Nixon shock," 127
Nkrumah Kwame, 251, 259–65, 274
cf. Nehru and Sukarno, 265, 269
"Nonalignment" policy, 272
"North Atlantic isolationism," 101, 316
North Korea, 97, 120, 211
North-South economic development,
264–65
North Vietnam, 75–76, 211, 316
Novak, Michael, 342
Nuclear weapons:
and China, 210, 231
Churchill on "saturation," 10
de Gaulle on, 73–74
freeze proposal, 213–14
Germany and, 76–77
military superiority argument, 211–14
missile treaty (1972), 210
and nature of war, 250
nonproliferation treaty, 163
Soviet buildup under Khrushchev,
171
test-ban treaty, 160, 171

"Ode to a Plum Blossom" (Mao), 235
Okinawa, 121
One World (Willkie), 249
"One-Man Yoshida," 105, 111
Opinion polls, 334
Organization for African Unity, 262
Ostpolitik, 164–66

Pakistan, 270, 272–74
Palestinians, 298
Pan-Africanism, 261–62
Pan-Arabic movement, 292–93
Paris Peace Agreement, 76

Parliamentary system, 47–48
Parnell, Charles, 221
Patton, General George, 86
Paul VI, Pope, 4
Peace, 37–38, 120, 162, 239
"Peaceful coexistence" policy, 171, 178,
198
Pearl Harbor, 31, 104, 131
Pearson, Lester, 3
Peck, Gregory, 86
Peel, Sir Robert, 29
Pentagon, 95, 207–208
"Pentagon Junta," 96
Pentagon Papers, 28
People's Republic of China. See
Communist China.
Perry, Commodore Matthew, 104
Pershing, General John J., 95
Pétain, Marshal Henri Philippe, 46
Peter the Great, Czar of Russia, 3, 199
Philippines:
reverence for MacArthur, 109, 130–31
and Magsaysay government, 251,
274–79
politics, 278
World War II and, 86–88, 95, 100–102,
276
Ping-Pong team exchange, 223
Pius XII, Pope, 4, 154, 255–57
Plume, Christian, 55
Podgorny, Nikolai, 77, 205
Poland, 74, 183
and communism, 32, 211
1970s détente and Solidarity, 212
Nixon visit to (1959), 192–93
Soviets in 1959, 173
Soviets and, 1981–1982 crisis, 165–66,
258, 296
Political candidates, 21–22, 60, 331–32,
333–34, 338
Politics, 324–27
in Philippines, 278
Pol Pot, 340
Polk, James, 30
Pompidou, Georges, 55, 76, 78, 283, 286

Population:
  Indonesia, 266
  Singapore, 310–11
  of United Nations member nations,
    250
Potsdam Conference, 33–34
Power, political:
  effect on aging, 36
  Churchill exercise of, 38–39
  enjoyment of, 321
  happiness and, 324
  realist vs. theorists, 323
  and will, 320, 323, 328
Presidency, France, 50–51
Presidency, United States, 51, 321–22, 341
Presidential election of 1960, 61, 73,
    196–97, 316
Presidents (American):
  and direct contact with Soviet leaders,
    77, 210
  and Israel, 283
  and sense of privacy, 52
Press:
  Adenauer's use of, 159
  Krushchev's use of in 1960 U.S.
    election, 197
  and MacArthur, 82, 86
  and Menzies, 314–15
  on Nixon-Adenauer friendship, 159
  and Nixon speech on Japanese
    rearmament, 120
  Yoshida and, 113
Prince, The (Machiavelli), 326
Prittie, Terence, 151, 163
Prussians, 146, 149–50, 167
Public opinion, 215
  and Adenauer, 146
  Johnson obsession with, 315
  leaders and, 324
  and MacArthur, 98–99, 129–30

Queen's Bedroom, 14–15

Radford, Admiral Arthur, 9–10
Radio Free Europe, 192

Rally of the French People (RPF), 48–49, 59
Reagan, Ronald, 212, 296
Real War, The (Nixon), 211
Red Guards, 230
Reminiscences (MacArthur), 83
Renner, Heinz, 144–45
Republican governments, 306–307
Republican party (U.S.), 238
Republic of China (Taiwan), 99, 235
  Chiang and economy, 217–18, 244–45
Revolutions:
  American, 222, 244
  Faisal on, 302
  French, 244
  leaders of, 265–74, 289–93, 307
Rhineland, 149–50, 167
Riza, Crown Prince of Iran, 300
Robinson, Walter, 225
Rogers, William, 223–25, 286
Romania, 211
Romulo, Carlos, 278
Roosevelt, Eleanor, 31, 69
Roosevelt, Franklin Delano, 8
  and Churchill, 14–15, 32–33
  Churchill on last months of, 10
  and decolonialization, 30, 37, 260–61
  on de Gaulle, 63
  and Hoover, 29
  leadership style, 284, 321, 324
  and MacArthur, 86, 96, 101–102
  MacArthur on, 128
  and Stalin, 201, 215
  and Truman, 78, 158
Roosevelt, Theodore, 321, 345
Rosebery, Lord, 2, 333
Rousseau, Jean Jacques, 132
Ruiz Cortines, Adolfo, 3, 253
Russell, Richard, 339
Russia, Czarist, 287
Russian people, 176, 179, 199, 215

el-Sadat, Anwar, 261, 290, 293–99, 306
  assassination and funeral, 296–98
  and Carter, 299

cf. Faisal, 303
and peace with Israel, 295, 298
as leader, 251, 294–95, 307
cf. Nasser, 294–95, 297–98, 307
on Nasser's self-deception, 291
quotes and comments:
  Egyptians cf. Russians, 295
  just ruler and opposition, 344
  refuge for Shah, 299
  Soviet expansion, 296
and Yom Kippur War, 208–209, 295
Salisbury, Harrison, 179
Saragat, Giuseppe, 66
Sato, Eisaku, 121–23
Saud, King of Saudi Arabia, 302, 304, 308
Saudi Arabia, 300, 303–306
and democracy, 306–307, 340
kings, and modernization, 308
Nasser and Yemen, 291, 303
Scelba, Mario, 257
Schuman, Robert, 4, 148, 151
Scott, George C., 86
SEATO, 318
Sebald, William, 103, 111
Senate, United States, 98, 122, 126
Shah of Iran (Mohammed Riza Pahlevi),
  58, 334
on China and India, 271
as leader, 251, 290, 299, 307–308
modernization of Iran, 300–302
Nixon visit (1979), 271, 299
reasons for fall, 302
and Sadat's refuge, 298–99
Shakespeare, William, 38
Shanghai Communiqué of 1972, 218
Shaw, George Bernard, 13
Simpson, Wallis, 15, 27
Singapore, 251, 308–11, 317–19
Sino-Soviet split, 171, 231–32, 250, 294–95
Six Crises (Nixon), 316
Six Day War (1967), 282, 291
Smith, Walter Bedell, 234, 335
Snow, C.P., 24, 30
Snow, Edgar, 214, 230

Socialism, 23, 261, 270, 273–74
Soong, Ai-ling, 243
Soong, Charles, 243
Soong, Ch'ing-ling, 243
Soong, Mei-ling. See Chiang Kai-shek,
  Madame.
Sophocles, 345
South Korea, 89, 130
South Vietnam, 162, 204, 316
South Yemen, 204
Soviet Union, 17, 109, 150, 160, 177, 192,
  224, 248, 250, 318. See also
  Brezhnev, Leonid; Chinese-
  American rapprochement;
  Khrushchev, Nikita; Sino-Soviet
  split; Stalin, Joseph.
Adenauer and, 147–48, 154–56, 160,
  162–64
in Afghanistan (1979), 165
and China, 210, 248
Churchill on dealing with, 12–13
Churchill warnings, 31–33, 38
Churchill-Roosevelt disagreement over
  postwar policy, 31–33
de Gaulle on, 65–66, 73, 77
and détente, 73, 212, 215, 287
and developing countries into United
  Nations, 74–75
and Egypt, 291, 293–94
and postwar Europe, 32–33, 134–35,
  251–52
Europeanization of, 199
and possible war in Europe, 10,
  73–74
expansionism of, 31–32, 38, 75, 100,
  160, 204, 214, 296, 302, 317
Faisal and, 303–304
German unification and, 152–53,
  164–67
and Hungary, 291
Khrushchev ouster, 199–200
military buildup and defense
  spending, 77, 120, 189–190
"new class" of elite, 204

Soviet Union (*continued*)
  Poland in 1954, 32; in 1959, 173; 1981
    and 1982 crisis, 165, 258–59
  purges in 1930s, 182–83
  threat to postwar Japan, 117, 119, 121
  U.S. policy toward, 211–16
  and Vietnam War, 75
  wheat sales to, 161
  World War II casualties, 205
  Yom Kippur War (1973) and American
    military alert, 205–210, 285
Spaak, Paul-Henri, 4
Special People (Julie Eisenhower), 286
Stalin, Joseph, 12, 188, 219
  Churchill distrust of, 32–33
  death and struggle for succession,
    183–84
  denunciation of, 171, 186–87, 232
  geniality and charm, 187
  and history of Eastern Europe, 3
  and Italian Communists, 251
  cf. Khrushchev, 171–72
  killing of countrymen and purges, 172,
    182–83, 186, 200, 215
  nationalism of, 199
  quotes and comments:
    on changing facts to fit theory, 179
    on death being the winner, 74
  Roosevelt and, 201, 211
  working habits, 181, 239
  writings and reading, 178, 337
Stark, Admiral Harold, 63
Statesmanship and politics, 324–25
Stern, Isaac, 284
Stimson, Henry L., 321
Strauss, Franz-Josef, 159
Succession procedures, 306
Successors, and preparation of, 78,
  121–22, 157–58
Sudan, 290
Suez Canal, 291, 293, 295
Sukarno, Achmed, 261, 265–69, 311
  on Communists, 265–66
  leadership style, 251, 259, 265, 274
  on revolution, 266

sexual passions, 266, 268, 322
  on U.S. and Vietnam, 265
  and Yoshida, 112
Sulzberger, C.L., 152, 161
Summit meetings, 65–66, 190–91
  de Gaulle and, 77
  Nixon belief in annual, 210
  Nixon-Brezhnev meetings, 201,
    204–205, 206–207
Sun Yat-sen, 220, 243, 244
Superdoves and superhawks, 211–12
Switzerland of the East, 119, 121

Taft, Robert, 29, 90, 127, 331–32
Taft, William Howard, 321
Taiwan. *See* Republic of China (Taiwan).
Talleyrand, 25–26
Tanaka, Kakuei, 237
Tantau, Mathias, 158
Tanya's diary, 205–206
Target de Gaulle (Démaret, Plume), 55
Television, 338
  de Gaulle mastery of, 56–57
  effect on political leaders, 24, 342–44
  effect on public debate, 343
  Faisal's assassination and, 305
  Iranian hostage crisis and Ayatollah,
    299, 343
Templer, General Gerald, 9
Terrill, Ross, 239
Thatcher, Margaret, 38, 341
Third World countries, 74, 165
  and democracy, 340
  and Lee, 311, 319
  and Nehru, 372–73
  U.S. economic assistance and, 264–65
Thompson, Llewellyn, 174, 191
Time magazine, 171
Time of Stalin: Portrait of a Tyranny, The
  (Antonov-Ovseyenko), 172
Tito, Marshal, 4, 35, 177
Tojo, 107
Toure, Sekou, 262
Tournoux, Jean-Raymond, 71
Trotsky, 337

Troyanovsky, Oleg, 174
Truman, Harry, 29, 30, 52, 78, 119, 338
  Asian-European policies, 99–100, 127
  Churchill on, 10, 33
  and Korean War, 96–99
  and MacArthur, 81–82, 88, 95–99, 122,
    127
  on MacArthur, 89, 96
  not prepared for presidency, 10, 158
  and Stalin, 187
Truman Doctrine, 99
Tunisia, 300, 306
Turkey, 170

Ukraine, 182–83
"Uniformed politicians," 105–106
United Nations, 32
  Churchill and de Gaulle views of,
    74–75
  and joint American-Soviet force in
    Middle East, 208–209
  Khrushchev speech, 177
  Korean War and, 97–98
  membership, 74–75, 250
  Suez crisis, 291
United States, 150, 177, 248, 252, 258, 303,
    311. See also Allied Occupation of
    Japan; Chinese-American
    rapprochement; Congress; names
    of Presidents; Soviet Union.
  Asian policies, 99–100, 130–31, 317–18
  Churchill and, 10–11, 16, 29–32, 35
  Cuban Missile Crisis, 170
  defense spending, 120
  de Gaulle analysis of politics and
    policy, 61–62, 65, 73–77
  and Egypt under Nasser, 290–91, 293
  and Egypt under Sadat, 294–95
  as threat to Europe, 166
  foreign policy and democratic
    standard, 340
  foreign policy and Soviets, 211–16
  foreign policy decisions and secrecy,
    126–27
  relations with France (1960s), 64–65
  and India, 272–73
  and Israel, 282–83
  history of Japan and, 104, 106–108
  and Japan's rearmament, 119–21
  -Japanese Treaty, 122, 126
  Khrushchev ridicule of, 175–77, 179,
    181–82
  Khrushchev tour of, 193–96
  and military superiority, 177, 213–14
  and Philippines, 274–75, 278
  Revolutionary War, 222, 244
  and Shah, 299, 301
  and Third World countries, 264–65
  trade with Soviets, 161, 214–15
  U-2 incident, 196–97
  and Vietnam, 9–10, 75–76, 239, 265,
    316–18, 343
  and Western alliance, 166, 258–59, 291
  defense of Western Europe, 134–35,
    151
  Yom Kippur War (1973) airlift and
    military alert, 207–210, 285
Utley, Fred, 225

Van der Kemp, Gerald, 68
Vatican, 255–56
Versailles Treaty, 105–106, 125
Veterans of Foreign Wars, 99, 194
Vietnam War, 201, 209, 239, 265. See also
    Indochina.
  bombing of Hanoi, 75–76
  Brezhnev on, 205
  de Gaulle on, 75
  Lee and Menzies support, 316–18
  MacArthur on, 93
  and press, 28, 343
von Steuben, Baron Friedrich Wilhelm,
    147
Voroshilov, Kliment, 182

Wainwright, General Jonathan, 96
Wake Island meeting, 89, 99
Walters, Vernon, 44, 72, 78, 97, 119
Wang Yang-ming, 245
War, 46–47, 210, 250

Washington, George, 147, 282, 324, 328, 338, 339
Watergate crisis, 23, 285
Weinberger, Caspar, 89
West Berlin, 161, 167, 190–91. *See also* Berlin airlift; Berlin Wall.
Western alliance, 166, 258–59, 291. *See also* Western Europe.
  and Soviet containment, 317
Western Europe, 151, 259, 287, 311, 318
  Adenauer dream of unifying, 134–35, 141, 149–50, 152–53, 160, 164
  Churchill and, 3, 29
  colonial empires, 30, 250, 259, 263
  creation of Common Market, 148–49
  and democracy, 340
  Italy and, 257
  and possibility of war, 10, 73–74, 259
  rebuilding after war, 259
West Germany. *See also* German people; Germany.
  under Adenauer, 133–36, 145–68, 253, 256–57
  Berlin issue and Soviets, 100, 160–62, 164, 170, 177, 190–91
  Berlin Wall, 150, 160–61, 164, 170
  and East Germany, 149–50, 163–64
  economy and GNP, 148
  relations with Israel, 282
  in NATO, 149, 165–66
  in 1947, after war, 135–37, 275
  Nixon 1947 visit, 136
  Nixon 1963 and 1967 visits, 160–61
  "presidential crisis" of 1959, 157
  and Soviets, 155, 161–65, 190–91
West Irian. *See* Dutch New Guinea.
West Point, 88–89, 101
Weygand, General Maxime, 46
White, Theodore, 225–26
White House bedrooms, 14–15
Whitney, General Courtney, 90, 92
"Wilderness" period, 59, 62, 313, 341
Willkie, Wendell, 249
Wilson, Charles, 11
Wilson, Woodrow, 17, 105, 314, 324, 337

Women and leadership, 340–41
World War I, 12, 105–106
  casualties, 31
  Churchill and, 14, 24–25
  MacArthur and, 86–87, 95–96, 129
World War II:
  atrocities, 155–56
  and Australia, 318
  casualties, 31, 205, 325–26
  and Churchill, 10–11, 15–16, 29, 323
  consequences of, 30, 74, 134–35, 249–50
  and de Gaulle, 43, 63, 72, 80, 323
  Japan and, 110, 220, 268
  and MacArthur, 82, 86, 89, 95–96, 101–102, 108–109, 129–30
  and Philippines, 86–88, 95, 100–101, 276
  Roosevelt and Stalin, 201
  and Ukraine, 183

Yemen, 291, 293, 303
Yom Kippur War (1973), 207–209, 285, 295
Yoshida, Kenzo, 105
Yoshida, Shigeru:
  cf. Adenauer, 121–22, 145
  background, 105–107
  and campaigning, 142
  on China and Chiang, 125–27
  death (1967), 127
  and Emperor, 109–10
  cf. Faisal, 302
  humor, 112, 314
  and MacArthur's dismissal, 81–82, 103
  cf. MacArthur, 85
  MacArthur partnership, 103–104, 113–18, 122, 129, 132, 253
  Nixon 1953 meeting, 85, 112, 117, 119–20
  Nixon 1964 visit to, 105–106, 124–27
  no-confidence vote and loss of popularity, 122–23
  "One-Man Yoshida," 105, 111
  personality and character, 81–86, 110, 123

preparation of successor, 121, 157
as Prime Minister, 82–84, 104, 108,
   110–23, 132
quotes and comments:
  American attitudes toward
    Communists, 117
  friendliness of American troops,
    108
  Japan's modernization and enemy
    air raids, 111–12
  MacArthur's accomplishments, 82
  prison life, 107
  women, 113
  rearmament issue, 119–21, 125
  thought balanced with action, 337
Yoshida, Yukiko, 105, 113
Yugoslavia, 211

Zahedi, Ardeshir, 299
Zahedi, Fazollah, 299
Zhang Guotao, 227
Zhou Enlai, 36, 58–59, 217–48
  accomplishments and legacy, 218–19,
    231, 246, 248
  acting ability, 225–26
  background, 218–19, 226–27
  and Chiang, 220, 236, 242
  Chinese people and, 228
  and Cultural Revolution, 230, 237
  death, 246
  Dulles handshake incident, 224,
    234–36

and foreign affairs, 231
funeral, 228
"Gang of Four" and, 247
internationalism of, 199
Kissinger praise for, 218
last years, 247
leadership style, 229, 329, 337
and Mao, 3, 228, 236–38, 247
cf. Mao, 218–19, 238, 246–48
Nixon meetings with (1972), 220–25,
   233–36
personality, 218–24, 226
poetry, 235–36, 314
as Prime Minister, 229
quotes and comments:
  being "more Chinese than
    Communist," 226
  Dulles handshake snub, 234
  elderly Chinese leaders, 225
  false appearances, 225
  monolithic blocs, 235
  mother's grave, 227
  Nasser's death and Soviets, 294
  Nixon's handshake, 235
  Nixon's initiative, 236
  return visits and U.S. relations, 227
  wife of, 235, 243, 246
  ruthlessness of, 225–26, 228–30
  self-confidence and self-criticism,
    224–25
  Sino-Soviet split, 231–32
Zionism, 280–81, 286